NEW AGE SP ITUALITY

NEW AGE SPIRITUALITY
Rethinking Religion

Edited by
STEVEN J. SUTCLIFFE AND INGVILD SÆLID GILHUS

Routledge
Taylor & Francis Group

LONDON AND NEW YORK

To Jo for her kindness, from Steve
To Nils Erik for his support, from Ingvild

First published in 2013 by Acumen

Published 2014 by Routledge
2 Park Square, Milton Park, Abingdon, Oxon OX14 4RN
711 Third Avenue, New York, NY 10017, USA

Routledge is an imprint of the Taylor and Francis Group, an informa business

Editorial matter and selection © Steven J. Sutcliffe & Ingvild Sælid Gilhus, 2013
Individual chapters © individual contributors

Notices
Practitioners ... xperience
And knowledge in evaluating ... hods,
compounds ... experiments described herein. In using such information
or methods they should be mindful of their own safety ... e safety of
others, including ... sponsibility.

To the fulle... authors,
contributors ... d/or
damage to ... property ... products ... ,
negligence ... nethods,
products, instructions, or ideas contained in the material ... in.

ISBN: 978-1-84465-713-1 (hardcover)
ISBN: 978-1-84465-714-8 (paperback)

British Library Cataloguing-in-Publication Data
A catalogue record for this book is available from the British Library.

Typeset in Warnock Pro by JS Typesetting Ltd, Porthcawl, CF36 5BL

CONTENTS

INTRODUCTION: "ALL MIXED UP" – THINKING ABOUT RELIGION IN RELATION TO NEW AGE SPIRITUALITIES

Steven J. Sutcliffe and Ingvild Sælid Gilhus

THEORIES OF RELIGION AND NEW AGE SPIRITUALITIES

"New age" is among the most disputed of categories in the study of religion in terms of agreeing content and boundaries.[1] Because such disputes reproduce in miniature the debate about the cross-cultural stability of the category "religion", studying "new age spiritualities" tantalizingly reproduces issues central to defining and theorizing religion in general. It is the aim of this volume to bring two areas of research normally kept apart – empirical study of new age spiritualities and serious theories of religion – into close and productive interaction, with a view to opening up a new primary data set for general theories of religion.

The classical theories of religion – for instance by Edward Burnett Tylor, James Frazer, William Robertson Smith, F. Max Müller, Sigmund Freud and Émile Durkheim – were built on a varied pick and mix of religious phenomena. Some of these authors consulted ancient religions, as did Frazer and Robertson Smith; some looked to India as Müller did (without actually going there); while many were interested in so-called "primitive" cultures, as were both Tylor and Durkheim. None of these "armchair" masters did fieldwork, but relied on reports from missionaries, travellers and other reportage. And even if they tried to build their foundation on the data of pluralized formations, their ideas were mainly inspired by their concept of Christianity, as Evans-Pritchard persuasively argued in *Theories of Primitive Religion* (1965).

Notably these authors were not really interested in examining contemporary religious developments in their own societies, even less in using such developments in their own attempts to construct a comparative category of religion. For example, F. Max Müller writes in a letter about Theosophy: "Unfortunately, the only thing that the large public admires in India is the folly of Esoteric Buddhism and Theosophy, falsely so called. What a pity it is that such absurdities, nay, such frauds, should be tolerated!" (quoted in Van den Bosch 2002: 160–61). Somewhat exceptionally, Tylor was interested in the contemporary phenomena of Spiritualism, but he seems to have pulled back from using the term "spiritualism" instead of "animism" as the core concept in his definition of religion ("belief in Spiritual Beings") because he felt it would confuse his universal theory with the particularities of the Spiritualist movement. Frazer, meanwhile, was critically interested in the fate of contemporary Christianity, but he only treated this matter implicitly and on the basis of deductions from his history of comparative phenomena, which precluded Christian data. In sum, the pioneers of the study of religion largely ignored local phenomena in their own backyards and projected their theories onto "others", elsewhere.

Despite these blindspots, the academic study of religion from the beginning of its modern institutionalization around the end of the nineteenth century clearly wished to create a unified theory of religion (Thrower 1999; Pals 2006; Stausberg 2009). The first generation of scholars in "comparative religion" (Sharpe [1975] 1986) was driven by general theoretical questions like: What is religion? How did religion originate? What function/s does religion have? These questions have acquired fresh life in recent years as scholars have again started to present "grand theory" about the origin, function and meaning of religion. However, relatively few of these scholars build their theories on empirical studies, and even fewer on grassroots studies conducted from the ground up. For example, only three of seventeen contemporary theories in a recent collection have a basis in empirical research, and only one "has grown out of empirical work on a religious site" (Stausberg 2009: 11).[2] Significantly, none of these theories take their point of departure from the phenomena of new age spiritualities. One question to raise at the start, therefore, is how theories of religion can throw light on new age spiritualities. The corollary is whether new age spiritualities can provide primary sources for defining religion. If not, it might be because new age phenomena are seen as atypical. But to see new age as atypical could mean one is arguing in a circle: new age data become atypical simply because they are not included when the definitions and models of "religion" are first drawn up. This implies that unexamined preconceptions may be in play about what constitutes "proper" religion.

The presence of implicit models may explain why new age has frequently been seen as a "special case" among the phenomena of "religion", requiring a distinctive terminology. The development of the model of a "New Age Movement" as a special kind of new religious movement, or of "The New Age" as a falsifiable substantive milieu, are examples of this kind of thinking. This erstwhile solution to the problem of how to classify new age can be contrasted with the project of developing an inclusive taxonomy: one that covers all known specimens. The argument of this volume is that we need a model of religion that comprises new age phenomena, either as part of the old model of religion in such a way as to expand its parameters, or as part of a fresh prototype. The challenge, therefore, is to develop a general model of religion, with a terminology to match, which can cover all known religious phenomena in the present and in the past, including new age spiritualities.

DESCRIBING NEW AGE SPIRITUALITIES

But what are we talking about? The expression "new age" has been used in the academy since the mid-1980s to describe a sometimes bewildering variety of "holistic" or "mind body spirit" phenomena, including astrology, tarot and other kinds of divination; practices of possession, channelling and mediumship; magical ideas about multiple "bodies", and occult ideas about hidden anatomies; body practices like yoga, tai chi and ch'i kung; popular psychotherapies and counselling ideologies; and forms of healing positioned as either "alternative" or "complementary" to biomedical healthcare, from Reiki to homoeopathy. The ontological commitments range from weak transcendence to strong immanence: that is, from "a blend of pagan religions, Eastern philosophies, and occult-psychic phenomena" (York 1995: 34) to a "highly optimistic, celebratory, utopian and spiritual form of humanism" (Heelas 1996: 28).

The historical background to the term "new age" is both millennialistic and astrological (Sutcliffe 2003a; Campion 2012). In the 1930s, when a traceable modern tradition of use and interpretation of the term effectively began (Sutcliffe 2007), in large part through the dissemination of texts by the Christian-turned-Theosophist Alice A. Bailey (1880–1949), the trope signified an imminent global upheaval preparatory to a golden age of abundance, prosperity and peace. Popular prophecies in the 1950s and 1960s variously identify the nuclear arms race between the former USSR and the USA, UFO sightings, and environmental disasters as potential portents of this coming upheaval (Wojcik 1997). In these early expressions, the "new age" was an imminent historical phenomenon, poised to unfold through the agency of supernatural beings. Although cataclysms of various kinds would attend its "birth", the eventual outcome would be a new global order of stability, peace and mutual understanding.

Bailey's Christian millennialism also drew on astrological sources to broaden its appeal within the "cultic milieu" (C. Campbell 1972), in particular the core idea that the Earth was moving from the astrological "house" of Pisces, a "water sign" symbolized by the fish, into "Aquarius", an "air sign" symbolized by a waterbearer, and associated in primary sources with notions of the "Christ within" and the "cosmic Christ" (Campion 2012: 25). Titles for sources as diverse as Levi Dowling's *The Aquarian Gospel of Jesus the Christ* (1907) and George Trevelyan's *A Vision of the Aquarian Age* (1977) show that a variety of parties in modern cultural history have sought to position themselves in relation to this astrological trope. It signalled collective movement from the "old" era into the "new": as the chorus of the hippy musical *Hair* sang in 1968, "this is the dawning of the Age of Aquarius!"

The many references to discourses on both "aquarian" and "new age" among Theosophists, Spiritualists and non-aligned "occult" audiences from the early years of the twentieth century also show that new age spiritualities have definite historical roots, although as yet we know comparatively little about their extent and depth in this period. The historicity of the phenomenon extends beyond genealogies of discursive tropes like "new age" and "aquarian" to include beliefs and practices debated among Theosophists and Spiritualists, such as the invisible influence of karma and auras, and the power of mediumship and healing practices.

In recent years – especially from the 1980s – use and meaning of the term "new age" has become more subjective and idiosyncratic. From some two hundred primary sources discussed in three surveys of popular literature between the mid-1970s and early 1990s (Satin 1978; Bloom 1991; Hanegraaff 1996), only a handful of titles uses the phrase "new age", few authors self-identify as a "new ager" and none employs the collective term "new age movement" widely adopted by academics and critics. Structural indeterminacies compound uncertainties of identity and location: new age practices typically lack strong institutional parameters beyond local and/or temporary groups, and there are few umbrella organizations self-identifying as "new age" capable of, or interested in, co-ordinating and authorizing larger scale projects. It is perhaps little surprise that the North American activist, David Spangler (b. 1945), has written: "I have personal doubts that there really is something called the 'New Age movement'. The New Age *idea*, yes, but a *movement*, no" (Spangler & Thompson 1991: 64).

Following Hanegraaff (1996), a heuristic distinction can be made between new age in a strict and limited sense – *sensu stricto* – and new age in a more broad and diffuse sense – *sensu lato*. New age *sensu stricto* signifies an imminent new era inaugurated by "other-worldly" beings, particularly redolent of the earlier history of the field as defined by Alice Bailey's discourse, while new age *sensu lato* signifies a more this-worldly cluster of beliefs and practices with the "spiritual growth" of human beings at its centre, closely related to cultural consumption after the 1960s. New age *sensu lato* is strongly immanentistic and focused on life in the "here and now", and retains only weak traces of the original millennialistic goal, in the form of the transformative expectations attached by users to the many available beliefs and practices. After the 1980s these *sensu lato* expressions increasingly travelled under new names altogether, such as "holistic" or "mind body and spirit", or under revived subcultural rubrics such as "occult" or "esoteric". They tend to blur boundaries between expressions of "religion" and "culture" and they lack the strong structures and authorities of prototypical religious organizations. Hybrid forms such as "Jew Age" (Ruah-Midbar & Klin-Oron 2010) and analogue terms such as "Next Age" (Introvigne 2001) further foster the dissemination of key themes and practices into new cultural streams, especially under conditions of globalization (Rothstein 2001). In consequence the boundaries of new age *sensu lato* have become increasingly difficult to identify and the term "new age" itself has become largely redundant, except when a specifically millennialistic aim or object *sensu stricto* is brought into focus. These complex boundary issues have challenged researchers who approach the field with a more formative model of "religion", and have probably served to repel the interests of others. As a result new age beliefs and practices have remained analytically elusive despite their increased visibility in many societies.

Notwithstanding problems with identification and nomenclature, there is clearly an empirical field of activity still to be properly theorized. This field is lively and volatile and is constituted of a diffuse collectivity of individuals, networks and small groups crossing boundaries between alternative, popular and elite cultures, as well as the dichotomous separation of secular and religious domains. Their loose networks continue the values of new age *sensu lato* in their pursuit of "spiritual growth", healing and well-being. Such values have become increasingly detached from their original countercultural and subcultural locations and have percolated into mainstream institutions such as Christian churches and other religious institutions, schools and colleges, healthcare organizations, the entertainment industry, and corporate business sectors. By the 1980s this diffuse collectivity had become marked by an ethnically "white", lower-middle-class and/or middle-class profile, middle-aged (30–50 year olds), and superiorly educated, made up of professional, IT, arts and healthcare occupations, and strongly represented by women – typically in a 2:1 ratio to male exponents.[3] From the 1990s onwards "new age" came to denote a loose, hybrid, popular culture of "spirituality", to use a term increasingly employed by practitioners in preference to "religion". Similarly, "new age" is being replaced by signifiers like "mind body spirit" or "holistic" which relinquish the other-worldly, millennialistic associations of the root emblem in favour of the kind of this-worldly, well-being disposition described in Heelas and Woodhead's (2005) ethnographic study of participants in the "holistic milieu" in the English town of Kendal. In some areas, practitioners may simply describe what they do as "spirituality" without feeling the need to qualify this term. However, due to the multiplication and differentiation of discourses about the meaning and value of "spirituality", scholars are increasingly faced with a complex empirical field composed of multiple varieties of "spirituality" that in turn interact both with other religious formations, and with ostensibly secular institutions such as healthcare and education.[4]

The task of circumscribing the parameters of new age spiritualities is further complicated by the co-existence of so-called "esoteric" and "paranormal" formations. For example, Wouter Hanegraaff (1996) has argued for the historical influence on new age spiritualities of "esotericism", simply defined as hidden knowledge with gnostic potential. The potential inclusivity of the "esoteric" category is analogous to the breadth of content shown by new age *sensu lato*, as is demonstrated by the material presented in the collection *Contemporary Esotericism* (Asprem & Granholm 2013) which ranges from Scientology and Chaos Magick to occulture and entheogens. The scope of "paranomal" beliefs and practices appears to be no less broad. For example, the textual survey in Jeffrey Kripal's *Authors of the Impossible* (2010) includes Fredrick Myers in the Society for Psychical Research, Charles Fort's catalogues of weird and anomalous data known as "forteana", and Jacques Vallee's UFO writings, while Annette Hill's *Paranormal Media* (2011) focuses on contemporary popular audiences for paranormal magazines, television shows and ghost hunts.

Despite areas of overlap both empirical and theoretical, the focus of the present volume is to describe and theorize the "spirituality" discourses and practices that have emerged from the historical background of new age *sensu stricto* and *sensu lato*. The wider purpose is further to differentiate the historiographical and ethnographical coverage so that new age spiritualities can be seen to be as variegated and nuanced as any other field of religion.

NEW AGE STUDIES: FIRST, SECOND AND THIRD "WAVES"

As with the general category "religion", the evidence of modern scholarship suggests dissent rather than consensus about the boundaries and content of new age spiritualities. This situation has generated some rich and lively exchanges. But more than a quarter of a century since the publication of probably the first peer-reviewed paper about "new age" phenomena (Sebald 1984), and twenty years since the pioneering collection *Perspectives on the New Age* (Lewis & Melton 1992) opened up the field for the study of religion, the sub-field of "new age studies" has not yet produced a clearly defined and cumulative set of research questions. The most common question remains the basic problem of demarcating "new age" phenomena within wider cultural formations. Certainly this remains a pertinent and to some degree a productive issue, not least as a basic problem in how to demarcate a set of data within a taxonomy of "religions" which inherently residualizes them, as we discuss below. But this question is really a preliminary matter which is better examined within an explicit research programme. By way of giving a shape to the academic development of "new age studies", Sutcliffe (2003b) has argued that the scholarly study of new age has devolved from a "first wave" of macro-level analyses of the content and boundaries of the so-called "new age movement" (Steyn 1994; York 1995; Heelas 1996), towards a "second wave" of more variegated and contextualized studies of particular beliefs and practices. This second wave has produced rich micro-level ethnographies and histories: for example, Courtney Bender (2007) on American reincarnation narratives, Judith Macpherson (2008) on Reiki healing in Scotland and Ingvild Gilhus (2012a) on the reception of angels in Norway. It has also fostered mid-range or meso-level analyses of local and regional dynamics: for example, Adam Possamai (2005) on the circuits of detraditionalized spiritual "seekers" in Melbourne, Australia; Matthew Wood (2007) on the social class dynamics of small groups in the English East Midlands experimenting with practical adaptations of occult and esoteric knowledge; and Peter Mulholland (2011) on the psychologically "compensatory" function of new age beliefs in the uncertain economy of post-"Celtic Tiger" Ireland.

This "second wave" admirably takes its lead from fine-grained empirical data which it unpacks within specific contexts. As a result we now know more about the interaction between particular "new age" beliefs and practices and the dominant culture in specific locations and circumstances, especially in northern Europe, the Nordic countries, North America and Australasia, but increasingly also in central and eastern Europe, and in east Asian countries like Taiwan and Japan. These lines of enquiry are likely to blossom as more scholars outside the study of religion turn their attention to practices and beliefs previously considered marginal or eccentric in the human sciences, but now freed up for enquiry by the pluralizing and differentiating forces of postmodernity. For example, Andrew Ross (1991) pioneered attention to new age healthcare in cultural studies in North America by discussing the subjective attractions of "softer" new age science and technology. In Australia, Guy Redden (2002, 2011) has explored aspects of the ideology of radical consumer agency and "spiritual" self-empowerment in everyday life, while Ruth Barcan (2011) has investigated reasons behind the uptake of "complementary" healing in a technologically advanced consumer society.

The risk with the "second wave" of new age studies is that the disconnect with general theories of religion which we have already noted may become even wider as the question of what constitutes "religion" is deemed a commonsense or otherwise settled matter, especially when the research is being pursued beyond departments for the study of religion. In response to this risk of the "second wave" studies, we can identify a few new avenues of interlinked enquiry which seek to draw out the full theoretical potential of new age for general studies of "religion", and thereby constitute a "third wave" in new age studies.

First, there is room for new macro-theoretical approaches in which new age is tackled not in relation to the morphology of "new religious movements", as characterized by the first wave, but in relation to specified general theories of religion. For example, there is room to develop spatial as well as cognitive studies of the mechanisms driving the appeal and dissemination of new age ideas and practices; to further analyse new age practices within a comparative study of "theologically incorrect" (yet no less widespread) folk and popular religiosity, often within Christian churches, but potentially within other supposedly "correct" religious formations as defined and prescribed by their elites; and to theorize new age data as Durkheimian "elementary forms" of religion collected in the homes, businesses and leisure industries of modern Western societies.

Second, the relationship between new age *sensu lato* in the 1970s and 1980s and contemporary discourses on "spirituality" in various contemporary spaces and disciplines – theological, healthcare, well-being, leisure, psychotherapy, social work – merits sustained analysis. In very simple terms, the popular language of "spirituality" emerged as a *lingua franca* around the time of the decline of new age *sensu stricto*, but empirically we know surprisingly little about the details of this evolution.

Third, more nuanced attention is required to the cultural capital provided by new age beliefs and practices for certain social groups within modern risk societies, especially middle and lower-middle classes. The data unanimously suggest that new age spiritualities are neither a working-class or manual labour preference, not the preserve of social elites, but have "elective affinity" with the middle social classes jostling for status and position in modern risk societies. In particular, the economic and political commitments of particular new age and holistic formations require to be teased out: for example, the analyses of "new age capitalism" and "capitalist spirituality" by Kimberly Lau (2000) and by Jeremy Carrette and Richard King (2005) respectively raise germane issues about the cultural impact of neo-liberal economics, but suffer from rather polarized and polemicized arguments on their precise effects, as Paul Heelas (2008) among others has shown.

These brief examples of the kinds of contribution a "third wave" of new age studies could make contain diverse emphases. But they share a commitment to producing a theoretical big picture of the data in the context of creating a general model of religion in which new age phenomena play a full role. Taking up the challenges of this "third wave" agenda in new age studies returns scholars to the kind of macro-level analysis preferred by first wave scholarship, but now benefitting from subtleties of representation and an awareness of multi-causal factors gleaned from the second wave microstudies. It is our hope that this combination of insights from micro- and macro- levels of analysis will help to steer new age spiritualities towards the centre of theoretical attention in the modern study of religion, and the present volume is offered in this light.

NEW AGE SPIRITUALITIES: FROM FUNCTION SYSTEM TO UNSTABLE ELEMENT

Despite the manifold theoretical promise evident within each of these three "waves" of studies, new age spiritualities have usually been considered a marginal phenomenon in the general study of religion. There are probably several reasons for this. One reason is that, as pointed out by scholars such as Fitzgerald (2000) and Masuzawa (2005), the "world religions" paradigm remains a powerful force in the study of religion, reinforced by Christianity as the prototypical religion (Saler [1993] 2000). The "world religion" paradigm models religion as a complex differentiated institution, typically possessing a long history and clearly defined authorities. New age spiritualities do not fit easily into this paradigm, partly because new age presents as a "new" phenomenon against the joint backdrop of secular culture and familiar religious formations, and partly because it is populated by multiple sources of authority which tend to relativize and hence to undermine each other (Wood 2007), in the process creating formations of varying depth and longevity whose busy, mobile profile can disorient the researcher. Although these relativizing forces also operate at certain levels within "world religions", nevertheless in general, and certainly relative to the dominant organizational paradigm, new age spiritualities can be characterized as de-institutionalized religion.

In *Religions in Global Society* Peter Beyer discusses what he calls "the global religious system" (Beyer 2006). In line with the ideas of Niklas Luhmann, Beyer sees religion as one of several differentiated function systems in the contemporary world (*ibid*.: 3). Beyer agrees with Roland Robertson (1992) that a major characteristic of globalization is the thematization of society itself as a globalized phenomenon (Beyer 2006: 14), including the construction of religion as a global category. Beyer's allocation of religion to a separate function system gives it a sharp social profile and also an awareness of what does not count as religion within the terms of the system, which leads him to raise an inevitable question about new age: "Is it religion and is it a religion?" (*ibid*.: 281). He anticipates the answer in his introduction where, commenting on the use of the term "spirituality", he writes: "Designating a variety of activity or orientation as spirituality is a way of seeking exemption from certain of the characteristics of what has come to be regarded as religion, but not others. It is a way, as it were, to 'look like a duck and quack like a duck', but avoid identification as a duck" (*ibid*.: 8). Beyer thus points to the role of strategic positioning among new age practitioners who want to have their cake and eat it in so far as they claim the (serious) purpose of "religion" but avoid the baggage that is increasingly perceived to accompany this label. But the strategy comes at a price, for as Beyer points out, "the self-identification and its effects on New Age communication … is relatively weak when compared to the more clearly institutionalized and formed religion" (*ibid*.: 279).

Beyer in many ways draws an accurate picture of the contemporary religious situation. His model of differentiated, functional systems captures how "world religions" and "new age spiritualities" are publicly conceived and what happens (or does not happen) in their interactions. However, new age spiritualities are structurally disadvantaged by the inherent logic of this model whose point of departure lies in sharply differentiated societal sectors.

Beyer's model is also arguably restricted by its avowedly contemporary focus. If, instead of seeing new age spiritualities always in relation to religion in the *modern* or in the *contemporary* world, we bring in a comparative historical perspective, how will it look? One could argue that there has been no such comparable global pluralized culture, but if we are generous, we could point to the Roman Empire as in some ways similar and sharing some of the characteristics of contemporary religious globalization (Gilhus 2008). The Roman Empire was conceived as one single place, had a common field of communication and transportation and common cultural, political, economic and religious institutions. Some general traits of religious development were connected to the global situation: for instance, plurality of religions, the coming on stream of new religious identities and universalized religious techniques and concepts (*ibid.*: 135–40).

From a similar angle, Jörg Rüpke's research programme "Lived Ancient Religion: Questioning 'Cults' and 'Polis Religion'" offers a new perspective on the religious history of Mediterranean antiquity (Rüpke 2012). Traditionally, two main types of religious formation have been seen as formative: polis religion, as the religion of the political unit of the city-state; and cults, as local formations with more intensive social interactions and soteriological benefits. In particular Rüpke criticizes the traditional view of ancient Mediterranean religion that sees it as the sum of the religions of political units like city-states, and which assumes that all members of a society are equally "religious" and take part in the same rituals. Furthermore he criticizes the view that religion is "thought to be particularly well suited to develop 'collective identities' and to act as instruments for the justification of power" (*ibid.*). According to Rüpke, the "paradigms of 'cults' and 'polis religion' leave a major gap" (*ibid.*). His research project starts from the perspective of "the individual and 'lived' religion instead of cities or peoples" (*ibid.*). Rüpke focuses on experience rather than symbols and on embodiment rather than rituals, and on culture in interaction rather than on culture as text. The shortcomings that he detects in the traditional study of ancient religion from using the crude filter of polis religion and cults are similar to the way in which new age is constructed as an oddball category when seen through the lens of the world religion paradigm.

The salient theoretical point is that modelling "religion" only in terms of strongly institutionalized forms, whether conceptualized as "world" or "polis", is only one approach to category formation and carries inbuilt normative commitments. In fact modern institutional religions are in themselves complex organizations in which beliefs and practices related to super-empirical beings are only one dimension, as Hugh Urban points out in relation to that most emblematic of new religious formations, the Church of Scientology, which he sees as "an extremely complex multi-faceted transnational organization" (Urban 2011: 131).[5]

One point of departure for Jörg Rüpke's critique of polis and cult in the ancient world is Meredith McGuire's term "lived religion" (McGuire 2008).

Originally developed for use in the study of contemporary religion, McGuire's term describes a more basic and vital aspect of religion as the articulation and expression of beliefs and practices in everyday life and as such is a point of reference for the present volume. Particularly relevant is that McGuire uses her term to invite wider structural rethinking: "Rather than conceptualize individuals' religions as little versions of some institutional model, let us rethink the notions we have of the institutional model of religions" (*ibid.*: 185).

The coining of the term "lived religion" implies that what is usually meant by the term "religion" is not primarily "alive" in the sense of indexing the beliefs and practices of embodied individuals and groups. Both the world religion paradigm and the polis model promote a view of religion as an entextualized system. What happens on or closer to the ground, particularly among small groups and reflexive individuals, has been given relatively little weight in contrast to events towards the other end of the spectrum, which is where strong institutions, firm authorities and sharply defined systems cluster, and from where they exert hegemony over the total formation. To integrate the study of new age spiritualities into the comparative study of religion requires a model of religion capable of accounting for the praxis of diverse individuals and groups, rather than pre-selecting the perspectives of hierarchically constituted authorities in temples and churches. This entails taking "theologically incorrect" data into account: that is, beliefs based in the kind of "folk" or "popular" representations generated in real time, online cognitive processing (Barrett 1999; Slone 2004), and which tends to be expressed through pragmatic and non-systematic responses in everyday life settings (Stringer 2008a: 108).

Developing a new approach might seem to suggest we reverse the order of things. This follows the superficially attractive logic that the traditional models, be they the world religion paradigm or the polis model, are structured according to a "top down" perspective, while the significance of new age data or "lived ancient religion" (Rüpke 2012) appears to lie in the "bottom up" approach they invite by virtue of their pragmatic and non-elite disposition. But although simple inversion seems clearer and more decisive, we may end up with an equally tendentious interpretation in so far as our aim is to represent phenomenological complexity rather than to recreate a polarizing effect. A more productive analogy might be to effect a lateral top-slicing of culture in order to expose the different sedimentary layers of beliefs and practices constituting the whole. Rather than squeezing a complex problem of representation into another false dichotomy, this time between a "top down" and a "bottom up" approach, a series of lateral incisions may be a better analogy for the purposes of sampling the fullest data.

Another reason why new age spiritualities have been regarded as marginal lies in one of the seemingly ineradicable presuppositions associated with the category "religion", which is usually reinforced by traditional authorities. The presupposition is that religion is something *sui generis*, something of its own kind, something that has an essence or at the very least a delimitable and impermeable boundary. This presupposition has several roots. One is the phenomenological sensation of the presence of "holiness" or "the sacred" associated with the models of Otto and Eliade. According to these writers, these sensations are by definition circumscribed and temporary, implying that religion is most "genuine" when these qualities are present. Another presupposition, theoretically more substantial, has its root in the question of the modern relationship between "religious" and "secular" orders. The modern concept "religion" is dependent on coexistence and even co-creation with the category "secular", which means that religion tends to be regarded as an oppositional and pure category (Douglas 1966), and further, to be regarded as more "authentic" precisely to the extent that it is not mixed with other things. In strong contrast, even in opposition, to this ideal and purified category of religion, new age spiritualities are inherently composite and amalgamated: they are all mixed up with ideas and practices relating to health, well-being, leisure, relaxation, self-help, training, reading and entertainment. But since the object of the study of religion has traditionally been configured as religion in a pure, unmixed and/or *sui generis* form, the inherently mixed composition of new age spiritualities is difficult to handle and perhaps even disagreeable to scientific taste.

In regard to this mixed quality, religion is similar to the element magnesium. Magnesium is the eighth most abundant element in the crust of the Earth, but the free element is highly reactive and is not found in nature. It is, however, possible to produce pure magnesium; this was first achieved in 1808, but it is an inherently artifical procedure. In a similar way, religion does not exist in a pure form in cultural processes. Historical and ideological processes have managed to separate "religious" from "secular" at significant sites in the modern world, but this separation is artificial and remains unstable. Religion is not a *sui generis* entity, although for strategic pedagogical reasons, the secular study of religion tries to isolate it, meaning that (ironically) "religion" only appears in a pure state in the textbooks of the study of religion. The empirical data for religion are impure and reactive and potentially mix with everything else, just like magnesium. New age spiritualities encapsulate this wider condition of "religion": they are all mixed up with other cultural elements.

NEW AGE SPIRITUALITIES: A CORE PHENOMENON

If instead of regarding new age as a marginal phenomenon or a "special case" we argue that it is part of the core phenomena in the general category "religion", what arguments and consequences follow?

Our point of departure is to see religion, like culture in general, as something mixed and fluid. This mixed presentation appears at both the social and collective level, and at the individual level. The data for religion in Western societies are entangled in processes of different kinds: for example, globalization, pluralization, individualization, secularization, re-sacralization and, of course, capitalism and mediatization. This means that the data for "religion" are inherently dynamic and in a continual process of change. New age spiritualities encapsulate that change.

On this model, data for "religion" are not only produced in the designated Beyerian religious sector, but in non-religious sectors as well. Courtney Bender argues that when secularization comes into theoretical focus within a particular argument or debate, religious activity taking place outside its assigned function system is usually ascribed to the acts of individuals:

> The secularization and restriction of religion into the sphere of the religious – a central narrative in the story of sociology – suggests that any religious activity, action, or purpose that is located "outside" of the religious institutional field is the work of "individuals" rather than produced within the discourse, practices, or structures of nonreligious fields.   (Bender 2010: 45)

She continues: "Rethinking the ways that the religious (or what we have herein been calling the spiritual) is not only *lived* but *produced* within non-religious sectors may suggest numerous settings that actively contribute to the complicated stories of … religious history" (*ibid.*: 46). Bender's focus is specifically the US, but the putative "private" nature of new age spiritualities has increasingly been questioned beyond the supposedly "exceptional" circumstances of North America. Dick Houtman *et al.* (2011: 34) claim that "this sociological orthodoxy is not much more than an institutional intellectual misconstruction" and they call for "a radical sociologization of research into New Age and spirituality" in order to "document how precisely spirituality is socially constructed, transmitted and reinforced" (*ibid.*: 53). This complements Matthew Wood's call, in his study of local English new age networks, for closer examination of "how authority and organization are constructed and maintained between people in relatively informal groups and relationships" (Wood 2007: 9).

We have argued that the institutional model of religion has been the normal way of conceptualizing religion, and that the study of religion as an academic enterprise has largely been conceived as a task of comparing organizational types within a functionally differentiated system. Approached in relation to that model, what McGuire calls "lived religion" appears inevitably to be something "other" or "in addition": it is religion with "qualifications". Instead, we claim that "lived religion" is in fact a normal and even typical state of religion, perhaps a minimum version or elementary form: in short, what should simply be called "religion". From this perspective, new age spiritualities are core phenomena, similar to other "lived" varieties, and giving particular insights into the production and distribution of religious representations in modern societies, especially in non-religious sectors. It is the sharply differentiated institutional forms such as "world" and "polis" formations that are really "other" or "peculiar".

OUTLINE OF THE BOOK

The book consists of fifteen illustrative chapters sampled from new age geographies largely in northern Europe, but also from the US and East Asia, driven by the comparative theoretical concerns outlined above. It is divided into three parts. In the first part, "Rethinking New Age Spiritualities", we bring macro level theories into focus.

The first chapter, by Steven Sutcliffe, argues that the perceived problem in defining what is (not) "new age" is closely connected to shortcomings in the general taxonomy of religious forms. The definitional problem is better understood as a conceptual distortion wrought by the "world religions" paradigm. One possible solution is to use new age data to grow and restructure Durkheim's model of "elementary forms".

In the second chapter, Ingvild Sælid Gilhus discusses the terminology of new age phenomena in relation to her expanded version of Jonathan Z. Smith's spatial model of religion. Gilhus's case study is the religious situation in Norway. According to this chapter, new age phenomena should be contextualized in the general spatial field of religion to make a more integrated and dynamic model.

Liselotte Frisk in the third chapter engages critically with the general theory of religion by Rodney Stark and William Bainbridge. She relates their theories to her mapping project of contemporary religion in Dalarna, Sweden. Frisk explores fresh interpretations of this material in the spirit of Benson Saler's prototype theory and argues that new age data could be used as the basis of a new prototype of religion.

In the fourth chapter, Paul Heelas presents two theoretical positions derived from Durkheim: that the secular is insufficient due to its imperfections, and that the "sacred" can be redefined as the "perfect". His "transgressive" thesis maintains that the limitations and failures of the secular stimulate movement beyond itself; to flesh out this process he draws attention to vitalistic currents within "life" that produce yearnings for perfection.

Ann Taves and Michael Kinsella concentrate in the fifth chapter on the organizational forms of "unorganized" religion in modern historical perspective. They clarify the organizational forms adopted by several supposedly "unorganized" groups – especially Spiritualism, Theosophy and Metaphysical Healing – and they scrutinize the largely unacknowledged capacity of "unorganized" groups to have a formative influence on individuals and groups.

The second part of the book, "Comparing New Age Beliefs and Practices", consists of five comparative studies which relate new age spiritualities to a particular broader context of religion.

The sixth chapter, by Norichika Horie, re-examines the concept of "new age" within comparative religious studies, and in connection to the discussion of global/local relationships. He makes a distinction between different types of new age expression and he relates the interest in new age spiritualities in Japan with the revival of indigenous and folk religiosity, making comparison to similar material from the US and the UK.

In Chapter 7, Mikael Rothstein concentrates on human–animal relationships as a generative factor in the production of religious ideas and behaviours. By comparing the new age focus on anthropomorphized whales and dolphins with concepts of anthropomorphism in two Brazilian societies, Rothstein shows how animals, through human identification and representation, serve as mediators in the collective endeavour to reach the spirits or gods.

In Chapter 8, Trude Fonneland and Siv Ellen Kraft use Sami shamanism in northern Norway as a case study to examine the interplay between secular and religious dynamics. They seek to develop "indigenous spirituality" as an analytical category and to illuminate its relationship with new age spiritualities. They stress the hybrid character of these types of spiritualities and explore their general cultural influence in light of global communications.

Dorota Hall points in Chapter 9 to similarities and differences between traditional "folk" religiosity and the "holistic milieu". Their subtle relationship is discussed within the context of relations of power governing the social field, using examples from Poland and the position of the Catholic Church. Hall concludes that in Catholic Poland, traditional collective values have restricted the development of the kind of modern individualism necessary for the growth of a separate "holistic milieu".

Lisbeth Mikaelsson takes her starting point in Chapter 10 in the discussion about religion and consumer society. Her chapter identifies particular cognitive modes, concepts and values in new age spiritualities as central to its development into a commercial market. In particular Mikaelsson shows how the new age concept of "energy" has become a common ideological currency, displaying multifaceted layers of physical, magical and cosmic meanings.

The third part of the volume, "Putting New Spiritual Practices to Work", focuses on more micro level and localized accounts of how new age spiritualities operate and circulate in modern societies.

In the eleventh chapter, Stef Aupers and Dick Houtman argue that new age spirituality is much less individualistic, and more socially and publicly significant, than the sociological consensus has tended to acknowledge. Through their discussion of the use made of the "doctrine" of "self-spirituality" within a Dutch business firm, they call for sociologically theorized explanations of how new age spiritualities are learnt and enacted in modern societies.

In Chapter 12, Frans Jespers describes the modern historical development of different forms of alternative religiosity in the Netherlands beyond the new age *sensu stricto*, including a general process of re-enchantment, a gradual "spiritualization" and especially a popularization of religious beliefs and practices. Jespers distinguishes between religious and secular forms of spirituality and presents a new typology to make sense of these extensive "secular sacralizations".

Olav Hammer draws in Chapter 13 on Harvey Whitehouse's theory of two different modes of religion: the imagistic and the doctrinal. Hammer argues that new age practices generally, and healing in particular, provide examples of "cognitively optimal" religion. He suggests that a theory of cognitive optimality provides a necessary addition to Whitehouse's two modes theory and helps to explain the ubiquity of new age representations in the wider population.

In Chapter 14, Shu-Chuan Chen employs a social constructionist approach to examine two new age healing practices operating in Taiwan. These courses teach participants to express their feelings appropriately and to negotiate positive outcomes in their emotional interactions. The author shows how these types of new age practices serve as a form of emotional labour by means of which practitioners can operate more efficiently in an advanced technological society.

Finally, in Chapter 15 Terhi Utriainen asks what kinds of agents are constructed within new age practices, especially angel culture. She works with constructivist and pragmatist theories and understands "religion" to be about "making things happen" in everyday life settings. She argues that, through their angel work, practitioners seek to balance individual agency with "intimate alterities" in order to create achievable destinies.

NOTES

1. We have worked with a "mixed economy" of descriptive terminology in the titles and content of chapters in the present volume. Once past our singularizing title, "New Age Spirituality", which serves strategically to demarcate the field, readers will meet a plurality of descriptors used by contributors to suit local configurations and differing theoretical emphases: especially "New Age", "new age" and "new age spiritualities", sometimes in quotation marks (for constructionist emphasis or reflexive nuance in a particular context) and sometimes without (when such emphasis or nuance is formally redundant). This non-standardization of terminology reflects the historical exigencies of the field. For a systematic discussion of issues in terminology, see pp. 3–6.
2. This exception is Tweed (2006), who studies a diaspora Cuban Catholic community.
3. For a UK data study, see Rose (1998); for an international overview, see Frisk (2007).
4. See, for example, the work on popular spirituality by Knoblauch (2008, 2009, 2010) in a German context and by Jespers (2009b, 2010, forthcoming) in a Dutch context.
5. In this respect not unlike the Catholic or Anglican churches, to use more familiar and less "othered" examples.

1. NEW AGE, WORLD RELIGIONS AND ELEMENTARY FORMS

Steven J. Sutcliffe

NEW AGE: AN UNRULY OBJECT?

This chapter argues that recurring uncertainties in demarcating "new age" phenomena are in important respects an effect of conceptual constraints upon our thinking about "religion" in general. These constraints are imposed by the existing taxonomy of religious formations, which is derived from the prototype of a "world religion". The apparent broadening of this taxonomy from the early 1970s on, through the use of adjunct terms like "new religion" and "new religious movement", while appearing to differentiate and pluralize representations of religious formations, in fact left the basic prototype undisturbed and even strengthened. Under its terms, the popular practices and beliefs which circulate under the name "new age" (and related modern rubrics such as "holistic") can only register on the conceptual radar of religion as an anomalous or residual category. The often-remarked problem of defining new age is therefore better understood not as an empirical question – we now know a fair amount about the varieties of beliefs and practices in circulation – but as a fresh and pressing example of how our concepts (continue to) construct our data. The world religions paradigm is a recognized conceptual problem in the study of South Asian traditions, especially in relation to "Hinduism" (Fitzgerald 1990; Geaves 2005). "New Age" phenomena raise similar questions, but now in relation to the construction of religion in a "Western" context.[1]

Read against the grain of the world religions paradigm, new age phenomena show continuities with a level of popular beliefs and practices expressed within and across a range of different religious traditions. Sorting new age data according to different criteria – for example, portraying them as "local" (introducing the dimension of geography) and "popular" (introducing the dimension of social strata and power) – can help to steer new age studies away from constructing marginalia and exotica, and towards the recovery of a hitherto camouflaged data set located as much "within" as "outside" traditional formations, and which also straddles the religious–secular divide. Reading the data in this way frees the study of new age from captivity within a self-reinforcing model of the sociology of "new religions", and instead contributes to a larger comparative project of reconstructing what Durkheim one hundred years ago called the "elemental" or "elementary" forms of religion (Durkheim [1912] 2008).

I will therefore argue that the widespread perception that there is a "problem" in how to classify new age beliefs and practices, in that they appear to constitute a major "unruly object" in the study of religion, has emerged at least in part as a discursive effect of the world religions taxonomy. In contrast I wish to model new age data as a practical and everyday level of beliefs, practices and modes of thought which cuts across the religious field as a whole, and is particularly clearly illustrated in the phenomena currently being studied under the rubric of "popular spirituality" (Knoblauch 2008, 2010).

My argument is programmatic but also evidence-based, and it moves between the levels of the empirical study of new age and related phenomena, and their conceptualization within academic discourses. Let me first briefly state the overall shape and direction. The prevailing taxonomy of "religion entities" – the array of corporate objects instinctively imagined as "religion" by members of modern Western societies – is derived from a "world religion" prototype. This is not only confessional in origin, but impresses a crude reified framework upon a class of phenomena that is typically distributed through a series of cultural practices, rather than contained in a set of ideological boxes.[2] Under the terms of this system of classification the category "new age" has come to signify what is left over after "world" religions, "new" religions, and other declensions have taken their share of the cake. New age data are effectively the crumbs left over from the division of self-evident religious forms. At the same time, their core empirical elements – including phenomena like animism, healing, divination, mediumistic and prophetic practices – continue to exist as identifiable components at different levels within the self-same "world" and "new" religions. The effects of the taxonomy thus put researchers of new age data in a quandary: their data become either a residual heap of colourful anomalies – the "crumbs" of the cake – or they are swallowed up and obscured within the powerful internal structures and discourses of the ideal "religion entities" promoted by the world religions taxonomy.

Although this seems to imply a bleak prognosis for continuing to study new age formations, their raw data (healing, mediumship, divination and prophecy, among other forms) are worth recovering and comparing precisely because they offer elements of a very different model or prototype of "religion". To do this we must first extract this raw data from within the reified representations fostered by the world religions paradigm, and use it to construct a morphology of elementary forms which is empirically truer to religion as a distributed phenomenon in human brains, bodies and behaviours. The aim is to recover and to retheorize the data "from below", based on levels or layers of practice closer to the ground, rather than continuing to assimilate expressions to a conceptual scheme like the world religions paradigm which is rolled out "from above" and which largely serves to legitimate the self-representations and vested interests of various social elites. In a chemical analogy, we must break up the amalgams of world religions to isolate their constituent "elementary forms" (Durkheim [1912] 2008).[3]

As early as his 1899 paper "Concerning the Definition of Religious Phenomena", Durkheim proposed that "religion" should be understood as a synthetic noun incorporating a number of semi-autonomous constituent elements distributed within the wider culture:

> [R]eligion is a totality of religious phenomena, and the whole can only be defined in terms of the parts. Moreover, there are innumerable religious manifestations which do not belong to any properly recognised religion. In every society, there are scattered beliefs and practices, be they individual or local, which are not integrated into a definite system. (Durkheim [1899] 1975: 74)

This description of "religion" as a totality consisting of the sum of various parts which also have a life of their own, as it were, is a useful reminder of the aggregated nature of its component elements. Furthermore, alongside "religion" as a complete and systematic phenomenon, Durkheim appears to impute sociological significance to the "innumerable" unintegrated beliefs and practices existing at "individual" and "local" level, although it is not part of his project to develop this analysis. As we shall see, this is a realistic and theoretically productive description of the scattered or distributed nature of new age beliefs and practices.

Durkheim develops this discussion of "elemental" constituents in the opening pages of his introduction to *The Elementary Forms of the Religious Life* (Durkheim [1912] 2008). Readers primarily interested in Durkheim's case study of aboriginal totemism in relation to his famous definition of religion tend to skip these preliminaries, but they repay attention in teasing out the theoretical implications of Durkheim's distributed morphology. As he puts it: "At the basis of all systems of belief and all cults there must be a certain number of fundamental representations and ritual practices that, despite the diversity of forms they assume in the various religions, have the same objective meanings and fulfil the same functions" (*ibid.*: 6). Durkheim is keen to stress that such a comparative theory must be grounded in "a concrete reality that historical and ethnographical observation alone can reveal" (*ibid.*: 5). To isolate these "fundamental representations" empirically, Durkheim recommends we "begin by returning to [their] simplest and most primitive form" (*ibid.*: 5). The methodological advantage of studying simple forms is that "the primary material can ... be observed with little effort" since the "inessential, the secondary, the extraneous have not yet concealed the main line of development" (*ibid.*: 8). Durkheim argues that simple examples reveal "what is indispensable" and establish "the minimal requirements" (*ibid.*), thereby reducing religion to a level of practice which "the popular or priestly imagination has had neither the time nor the means to refine and transform" (*ibid.*: 7–8). Despite the contemporary social evolutionist and colonialist resonance in selecting the "simplest and most primitive form", Durkheim at the same time distances himself from a crude historical quest for origins: "There is no crucial moment when religion began to exist, and the point is not to find a way to transport ourselves there by thought" (*ibid.*: 9). Instead, in a formulation vital for the present argument, Durkheim proposes that we "find a way of discovering the *ever-present causes* that generate *the most essential forms* of religious thought and practice" (*ibid.*: 10; emphasis added).

Through adopting a modified Durkheimian approach to recovering "elementary forms", new age data can be seen to be neither anomalous nor residual, but broadly central to re-thinking the production and arrangement of forms within the religious field as a whole. Like shaking a kaleidoscope, inverting and disaggregating the "religion entities" releases a fractionated pattern of mosaic fragments.

Taking this step will help to bring the study of new age to fresh maturity, although it will likely be at the cost of a continuing academic sub-discipline of "new age studies" since it implies that there is nothing inherently special or peculiar, after all, about new age data.[4] Theoretical renewal of a research programme in comparative elementary forms entails the longer term qualification of a separate field of "new age studies", in the same way as treating "religion" as a constructed category called into question a methodologically *sui generis* "Religious Studies" (McCutcheon 1997).

NEW AGE AND THE POLITICS OF CLASSIFICATION

The received wisdom that classifying new age beliefs and practices is a "problem" has in part been generated by the features of novelty, fluidity and ephemerality regularly ascribed to the data against the backdrop of standard representations of Western religion. These features have almost certainly been exaggerated and, again, are in part a discursive effect of the dominant paradigm. In contrast, the history of alternative religion suggests that constructs such as "new age spirituality" and the "holistic milieu" can profitably be understood as phenomena rooted in complex interactions of modern "traditions".[5] Religious studies as an academic field, especially in anglophone contexts, has tended to neglect historical methods in preference for sociological approaches. But while crucial for investigating the fundamental sociality of religion, sociological methods alone are inadequate. I would go further and argue that, in so far as they have steered explanations of new age data into a kind of ahistorical presentism, the sociology of new age has in some respects stymied enquiry, constructing new age as a phenomenon without a past.

Some problems with a purely sociological approach to new age can be seen in the ingenious efforts made in the pioneering monographs to adapt new age data to the sociology of "new religious movements" (NRMs), which became a burgeoning academic sub-field in the 1970s and 1980s. Seminal studies such as Michael York's *The Emerging Network* (1995) and Paul Heelas's *The New Age Movement* (1996), while laudably opening up the very possibility of studying new age in the academy, treat the data almost entirely in this way. Both York and Heelas portrayed new age as a special kind of NRM which they call the "New Age Movement" (NAM); although the term was already in popular use, their monographs lent it analytical credibility. Variations on this perceived solution to classifying the "unruly object" include Kemp's (2001) composite model of new age as a "new socio-religious movement" (NSRM) and Shimazono's (1999) hybrid term "new spirituality movements and culture" (NSMC), conceived on the basis of Japanese data. Despite different emphases, these and related approaches found common cause in NRM studies by adopting "movement" as a theoretically salient classification.[6]

But the term "movement" is morphologically difficult to apply in respect of new age data and representations of a "New Age Movement" tend to defy empirical falsification. For example, Paul Heelas includes individuals as diverse as Helena Blavatsky, Carl Jung and Georg Gurdjieff alongside Carl Rogers, Prince Charles (of the British royal family) and Paul Tillich within the bounds of his portrayal; he also includes organizations like Transcendental Meditation, Soka Gakkai and the Church of Satan (Heelas 1996). The sheer diffusion of these examples is striking. A similar charge of hyper-inclusivity could be made in respect of Michael York's elastic description of an "emergent network" which includes "New Age, Neo-paganism, the ecology movement, feminism, the Goddess movement, the human potential movement, Eastern mysticism groups, liberal/liberation politics, the Aquarian conspiracy, etc." (York 1995: 330). A positive interpretation of these models' boundlessness (encoded in York's final "etc.") is that they signal the penetration of new age representations into the surrounding culture, and hence de-reify rather than hypostatize. This is certainly helpful, but the problem remains that it is difficult to identify consistent grounds to exclude phenomena on the basis of the examples given. Models of new age as a NRM, NAM, NSRM or NSMC suffer from a "falsifiability deficit" in which the intuitiveness of the criteria of selection makes it difficult, if not impossible, to say what is not part of the "New Age Movement". The resulting uncertainty is an unfortunate effect of good intentions to make an apparently unruly research object viable within the terms of a fundamentally unsympathetic taxonomy.

A more radical response in the struggle to classify new age has been to deconstruct it (Frisk 2005; Klippenstein 2005). Wood (2007, 2010) argues that the long-running preoccupation with questions of definition and demarcation obscures rich opportunities to explore how power and authority are being negotiated by practitioners in more fluid and less determinate regions of the religious field. Wood emphasizes the impact of social relationships on practitioners' uptake of new age practices in order to contextualize idealistic representations of self-authorized "self-spirituality" (Heelas 1996: 18–21). Wood presents a model of authority operating on a spectrum between "formative" and "nonformative" poles. Formative authority is characterized by a capacity to reproduce and propagate its forms and structures as effective traditions. Nonformative authority is characterized by weakness of reproduction resulting from relatively ineffective mechanisms of legitimation, and this tends to generate incomplete and fragmentary outcomes and effects. Wood's approach helps to explain the relative weakness (rather than the absence) of new age authorities. The outcome is a subtle and transposable analysis of new age as a dynamic social field, but it struggles to make a mark within a taxonomy predicated upon complete and self-contained "religion entities".

The real challenge of new age data is therefore not a substantive matter, as if one day we will finally be able to confirm the content of this unusual species of "religion entity". Rather, the difficulties in developing a cumulative research programme in respect of new age derive in good measure from constraints on our powers of representation produced by a classification system which authorizes the reproduction of only a limited set of approved religion entities. Membership in this set is controlled by the terms of the world religions taxonomy. Furthermore it is not limited to formations conforming more or less strictly to the prototype but has been extended in the form of various sub-types which, although appearing to challenge the taxonomy, remain bound by its classificatory logic. The result is that, despite genealogical and historiographical critiques, the "world religions" paradigm is embedded in the basic fabric of our thinking about religion and continues to steer research and teaching either directly or by proxy. But theoretical repositioning of new age beliefs and practices can challenge the paradigm at its roots.

NEW AGE AND THE "LEAGUE TABLE" OF RELIGION ENTITIES

Despite some honourable theoretical exceptions, anglophone religious studies since the 1960s has played a leading role in expediting the incorporation of the world religions taxonomy into the academic study of religion (for example, in the design of degree programmes, course syllabi and textbooks) as well as within primary and secondary schools.[7] The taxonomy is further reinforced by its recognition and approval on the part of many religious organizations, which can derive practical advantage in the form of enhanced social capital and related benefits in so far as they are able to position their own traditions in "world" terms.

As remarked earlier, the idea of a "world religion" has been in circulation since at least Tiele's 1884 entry in the *Encyclopædia Britannica*. However, the category does not seem to have attracted sustained critical attention until the early 1990s (Fitzgerald 1990; Young 1992) although the seeds of critique were present in the early 1960s in the well-known argument to reject the category "religion" by Wilfred Cantwell Smith ([1962] 1991). It is certainly possible to argue that representations of "religion" as a pluralized set of historical formations were an important advance upon traditional understandings of the category as synonymous with Christian theological truth, and as such signalled a significant cultural shift within the study of religion. However, what appeared in the context of late 1960s multiculturalism to represent a positive and liberal curriculum development looks, under the spotlight of discourse analysis, like a more ambiguous transposition of meaning by means of which, to put it bluntly, "European universalism was preserved in the language of pluralism", to cite the subtitle of Tomoko Masuzawa's *The Invention of World Religions* (2005).

A salutary case study in the taxonomy's staying power can be found in J. Z. Smith's retrospective self-examination of the editorial process governing the *HarperCollins Dictionary of Religion*, published in 1995, on which Smith served as general editor. Smith describes how he solicited contributions on the basis of the joint operation of two classification systems: a sevenfold world religion taxonomy of fairly standard issue consisting in Buddhism, Chinese religions, Christianity, Hinduism, Islam, Japanese religions and Judaism; and a supplementary threefold schema of his own devising, comprising "religions of antiquity, new religions and religions of traditional peoples" (J. Z. Smith 2004: 166–7).

Smith goes on to suggest that admittance to the rank of "world religion" has historically been rooted in what he calls "a sort of pluralistic etiquette":

> If Christianity and Islam count as "world" religions, it would be rude to exclude Judaism … Likewise, if Buddhism, then Hinduism. And again, if Buddhism, then Chinese religions and Japanese religions. The *unprincipled nature* of this list is made plain by the fact that some scholars list only five, omitting Judaism and Japanese religions, while no typology includes Manicheism, perhaps the first, self-conscious "world" religion.
>
> (*Ibid.*: 169; emphasis added)[8]

The effect of Smith's reflection is a sobering realization that his approach has been little different from the political "etiquette" practised by his forebears. That such a "relentlessly self-conscious" scholar – to cite the key methodological requirement in his seminal text, *Imagining Religion* (J. Z. Smith 1982: xi)[9] – should have recourse to an "unprincipled" taxonomy as the mechanism of selection within an important contemporary dictionary signals its formidable staying-power.

The next stage of my analysis is to expose the paradoxical consolidation of the authority of the "world religion" prototype through the internal diversification of the wider taxonomy. This consolidation has gradually occurred over the last forty years or so through the introduction of adjunct taxons such as "new religions", "indigenous religions" and "Western esotericism". Ostensibly these supplementary categories foster plurality and heterogeneity, but they can be more critically understood as expressions of the continuing discursive effects of the prototype. The overall grip of the taxonomy is ironically entrenched rather than eroded through their accretion.

In the 1970s the taxons "new religion" (NR; Needleman 1972) and "new religious movement" (NRM; Barker 1982) came into use to represent formations which, because they were described by the term "movement" and qualified by the adjective "new", inevitably implied an unfinished and immature formation against the backdrop of the world religion prototype. Although they seemed not to qualify for "world religion" status, they still warranted scholarly attention. In consequence an implicit ranking of an expanded variety of "religion entities" began to develop from the 1970s on. To use a sporting analogy (football works well), a system emerged which has come to resemble a three-tier "league table". As befits their size, wealth and status as corporate organizations, world religions inhabit the "premier league", NRMs/NRs inhabit the "championship", and the "others" or "the rest" are squeezed into a semi-professional "first division" of residual forms such as indigenous, folk, popular, esoteric – and new age.

These tiers or leagues of religion entities are not static. They allow for "relegation" of world religions which, as a result of complex cultural, educational and political developments, lose status (at least within the "Western" academy): for example, Confucianism and Zoroastrianism. The league table also allows "promotion" in the case of ambitious NRs like Mormons and Bahá'ís,[10] or in the parallel case made by earlier scholars for the sub-saharan "indigenous" amalgam, "African Traditional Religion", to be counted as a world religion.[11] A status hierarchy is inscribed in league competition which promises the players access to strengthened social and cultural capital: for example, in terms of enhanced public profile or recruitment opportunities.

The classification "world" offers maximum exposure and legitimation in an era defined in terms of the economic and cultural conditions of globalization.[12] In the next league down, to be identified as a NR may be preferable to NRM on grounds of parsimony and impending "coming of age": that is, the

succinct compound "new religion" suggests a rounded and near-mature formation, and a potential future candidate for promotion to the "world" tier,[13]
whereas the word "movement" suggests continuing volatility and immatu-
rity. Both terms, however, are more advantageous than their predecessors
"cult" and "sect" due to the fact that "cult" now popularly connotes charismatic manipulation and brainwashing while "sect" suggests a segregated
community with a "narrow" outlook.[14]

As previously mentioned, the taxonomy is further entrenched through
its recognition and approbation by practitioners seeking enhanced social
capital. It rewards structural rationalization by encouraging religious formations to self-represent as corporate organizations consisting in internally differentiated "departments", roles and procedures. In this way "a religion" has
increasingly come to denote a functionally differentiated institution analogous to a multinational firm. This in turn has fostered the modern academic
study of religion as the identification and representation of a set of rationalized "religion entities". Religious education in schools, and public discourses
about religion, abet this normalization. "World religion" implicitly becomes
the prototype "religion entity", and ostensibly reforming initiatives become
recuperated as sub-types through its hegemonic logic. The self-evidence of
the prototype means that it becomes increasingly harder to conceptualize a
different paradigm of classification of the data for "religion".

However, significant kinds of formation that do not fit this corporate
model are structurally disadvantaged, particularly those which are local,
small-scale, diffuse, informal, situational, hybrid and syncretic (to which
many if not most "live" religious formations conform). In 2000 Gerrie ter
Haar gave a paper entitled "World Religions and Community Religions:
Where Does Africa Fit In?" (ter Haar 2000). This is an appropriate question in that it extends the problem of the effects of the prototype beyond its
European matrix. However, the issue of making anomalous formations "fit
in" is not only a problem for data in colonial/post-colonial Africa or South
Asia, which have been subject to acknowledged processes of projection
and "othering".[15] One could ask the question in respect of new age beliefs
and practices in North America and northern/western Europe. Here the
evidence suggests that "spirituality" (Knoblauch 2010) is increasingly well
represented among sociodemographic groups with a high profile in contemporary debates in education, healthcare and gender equality, for example,
and that "spirituality" is often practised simultaneously with a continuing participation in more formative traditions.[16] But like "community" and
"indigenous" formations in Africa and South Asia, new age spiritualities in
modern Western and post-industrial societies have been considered a special case. This is because in both locations scholars are working with a faulty
prototype.

HOW TO RE-MODEL NEW AGE: TWO PRACTICAL RESPONSES

Thus far I have argued that the world religion taxonomy substitutes implicit pluralistic "etiquette" (J. Z. Smith 2004: 169) for an adequate theory of classification, and that this has serious consequences for the study of new age phenomena. Two responses to this position are possible from the perspective of developing a more robust research programme.

First, we could consider mobilizing the category "new age" as an act of "strategic essentialism" to gain visibility for our data. In her essay "Subaltern Studies: Deconstructing Historiography", Gayatri Chakravorty Spivak defends what she calls "strategic use of positivist essentialism in a scrupulously visible political interest" (1987: 205). What Spivak means is that using an essentialized category generated according to the logic of a hegemonic dicourse, but applied against the grain or larger intention of that discourse, can be justified if such strategic usage obtains enhanced representation or similar status benefit. Spivak is writing in the context of postcolonial historiographical debates dominated by complex questions about the relationship between colonizers and colonized, and this specific geopolitical context must be kept in mind when adapting her approach. At the same time, we have seen that real questions of epistemic power and legitimation arise in the struggle to represent new age practices against the backdrop of the world religions paradigm "at home"; thus "new age" could reasonably be considered to possess "subaltern" potential within a taxonomy generated by and on behalf of social elites "here" as well as "there". A Spivakian approach would require us to over-emphasize the formative elements in new age data – for example, exaggerating the strength of new age collective identity and boundaries – in order to register more positively against the taxonomy's criteria, thus enhancing researchers' access to academic capital and resources, and also granting greater legitimacy to new age practitioners themselves. Like using the term "indigenous" to re-affirm marginalized and colonized formations previously labelled "tribal" or "primal" (Harvey 2000; J. Cox 2007), or like the institutionalization of a research programme in "Western esotericism" to legitimize the academic study of "occult" and "hidden" knowledge (Hanegraaff 2012), the logic of strategic essentialism within the academy is that strengthening the taxon "New Age" might register sufficient substance and difference to be taken seriously as a theoretical object.

A viable "strategically essentialist" articulation needs to register positively and unambiguously within an asymmetrical taxonomy. An immediate syntactic problem is that the difference between a strategic and a naive utterance of the term "new age" is not self-evident. This is a subtle result of the long-standing confusion between emic and etic uses of the term (see Sutcliffe 2003a: chs 2–5). In short, because use of the same term can be heuristic, naïve or even pejorative as much as epistemically or politically strategic, listeners must infer the intention of the utterance in ambiguous use contexts. But now the empirical question kicks in: how can a phenomenon with such disputed content, porous boundaries and uncertain "membership" be faithfully represented in terms of the kind of essentialized formation required by a strategic approach – without fundamentally misrepresenting its structure and morphology?[17] The phenomenological "nonformativeness" (Wood 2007) of new age beliefs and practices cannot be easily reconciled with the singular or "formative" authority required for meaningful classification as a New Religious Movement, for example.[18] The frustration for all parties seeking to stipulate the boundaries of the posited new age or holistic "movement" – practitioners, activists and scholars alike – is clearly illustrated by the relative paucity of self-identified "new agers" and by practitioners' repeated disavowals of labels and identities of all kinds. Such evidence strikingly illustrates the "falsifiability deficit" outlined earlier.

The larger theoretical problem raised by essentialist uses of the new age taxon – whether strategic or naïve – is simply to reinscribe the legitimacy of the prototype which generated the wider taxonomy. Each iteration, no matter its intention, is inevitably received as a reiteration. Strategically essentialist use of "new age" might be justified if it clarified boundaries, or enhanced theorization, or brought new age beliefs and practices into sharper focus against the wider religious field. In fact the possibility of meaningful demarcation and comparison becomes incrementally more difficult each time "new age" is used with a slightly different qualification, or as it oscillates in use with surrogate terms like "alternative" and "holistic", or – as is increasingly the case – it dissolves into popular "spirituality" discourses. That some histories and ethnographies offer strikingly different "big pictures" of the field suggests the continuing challenge in agreeing its basic co-ordinates. For example, Hanegraaff's (1996) representation of new age as a form of "secularized esotericism" which is best understood against a history of ideas backdrop in eighteenth and nineteenth century print culture contrasts squarely with Sutcliffe's (2003a) cultural history of new age beliefs and practices as a form of popular millennialism firmly located in the early to mid-twentieth century. In sociology and ethnography, Kemp's (2001, 2003) study of the vanguard ideological role of "Christaquarians" (his name for people employing a hybrid Christian–new age identity) offers a very different sociodemography to Wood's (2007) study of a local arena of activities and identities largely constituted by people engaging "occult" and "spiritual" resources to address their ambiguous social class positioning. Taking his lead from an oral comment by a conference panel chair who "questioned whether Wood's research covered New Age *spirituality* or rather a continuation of lower-social class based *Spiritualism*", Kemp suggests that "if Wood's informants were ambiguous about the term New Age, perhaps this was because he was not studying the New Age movement" (Kemp 2003: 34). The implicit judgment is, of course, that Wood's ethnography, unlike Kemp's, does not represent the "real" phenomenon.

In sum, the cumulative evidence suggests that the larger taxonomy will be neither infiltrated nor subverted by further positive deployment of the term new age, however strategic the intention. This is also in part due to the reactive nature of Spivakian strategizing: as Spivak herself cautions, "a strategy suits a situation; a strategy is not a theory" (cited in Morton 2002: 75).

The second response to the situation is to deconstruct and re-assign the data for new age. This entails freeing clusters of "elementary forms" of beliefs and practices from a conceptual procrustean bed based on a model of rationalized organizations. Working afresh with freed forms could contribute to the construction of a new model of "religion", based on a common stock of elementary representations extracted from a spectrum of formations straddling the religious–secular divide. This common stock would be populated not just from formations marginalized within the taxonomy, such as indigenous, Pagan and indeed new age formations, but from data sourced from within the dominant "religion entities" themselves, particularly in the form of vernacular and "theologically incorrect" testimonies expressed by different social groups at different levels of practice beneath their broad canopies. That all formations within the "league table" are capable of yielding elementary forms protects against reproducing the old polarization between the "world religions" and "the rest". "New Age" data would therefore not occupy a privileged position within the new model or prototype, and would contribute just another data stream.

I will make a few general observations on the likely shape of these "elementary forms" before sketching two brief case studies to indicate the direction in which such comparative research might develop. A preliminary catalogue of the "elementary forms" which are strongly represented in new age might include the vitalistic and animistic concepts of "energy" and "spirit"; an expanded pantheon of superhuman agents including gods (small and large), intermediaries (spirits and angels) and deified humans (Masters and Gurus); the normalization of an ethos of search or "seekership"; the instrumentalization of practice through a renewed emphasis on divinatory, oracular and prophetic practices and techniques; "moveable feasts" in the form of ritualized small group gatherings and colonies; and an expanded and intensified material culture. These elementary forms are already discernable as components of the environments described in Judith Macpherson's ethnography of women Reiki practitioners in Scotland (2008) or in Courtney Bender's (2010) narrative of the "new metaphysicals" in Cambridge, Massachusetts, for example.

Creating a different sort of taxonomy of religious representations to model an alternative prototype of "religion" is, of course, not a new proposal. Around the same time as Tiele (1884) began to cement the idea of "world religions", other Victorian scholars were identifying what we can in retrospect think of as variations upon a theme of "elementary forms". As is well known, Robertson Smith argued for the centrality of practices (the sacrificial meal); Tylor proposed a core institution of animism; Marett argued for the place of affect and expressivity (religion "not so much thought out as danced out"); and Durkheim focused on totemic ritual. With the exception of Durkheim, these early proto-taxonomies of distributed religious elements have tended to be relegated to the history of the field (although Tylor has gained new admirers in the cognitive science of religion). Because they typically drew on non-Western data, these models suffered in a period of decolonization through their perceived colonial mindsets, including use of terms like "primitive" and "savage". At a theoretical level their anthropological focus on distributed elements became sidelined by the "Protestant" prototype of the "world religion" (Masuzawa 2005). But these early attempts at a model of distributed religion, shorn of vestiges of cultural evolutionism, are worth revisiting and reconsidering in light of the collective cataloguing project suggested here. Moreover we are increasingly in a position to supplement them with "Western" data, including new age spiritualities, in order to expand the comparative data base. The incorporation of beliefs and practices from quintessentially modern, post-industrial, "Western" societies can help to break up the association of a concept like "elementary forms" with a neo-colonialist project conducted in and upon "other cultures".

Example I: Christian animists

I want briefly to illustrate the idea of recovering a set of "elementary forms" by switching to the examination of a European data track parallel to new age. In *Western Ethnography and the Definition of Religion*, Martin Stringer presents data from a number of ethnographies of contemporary "folk" Christian cultures in England. Stringer is interested in the practical, situated practices of laypeople, often women, observed at local and everyday levels, rather than in the discourses of professional clergy and theologians. His evidence is derived from interviews about astrology and Spiritualism in mother and toddler groups and about graveyard visiting practices, among other sources (Stringer 2008a). Stringer argues forcefully that, despite dominating the discourse on religion, the "major world religions" are in practice "aberrations", forms of religion "generally accepted only by a small minority" – even when, he adds, "they form the basis of the dominant religious discourse in society" (*ibid.*: 114). On the evidence of these European Christian ethnographies, he argues that most people are not interested in "sophisticated systematic theologies … transcendent gods and … salvific aims". These interests are "exceptions rather than the rule" (*ibid.*). Despite what we are led to expect by the terms of the dominant discourse, we are more likely to find ordinary practitioners, especially women, discussing interpretations of "star signs" (*ibid.*: 68–74) or "chatting to gran at her grave" (Stringer 2008b).

Generalizing from English practitioners he describes arrestingly as "Christian animists", Stringer argues that the form of "religion" practised by most people, most places, most times (certainly by non-elites) is characterized by three elements:

- "situational, unsystematic" belief
- "intimate association with the non-empirical"
- a response to "pragmatic questions concerned with daily life and coping with everyday problems" (Stringer 2008a: 108).

From Stringer's perspective these three elements represent a "base layer of the religious structure". As such, they "can in some way be understood as the most "elementary" or "elemental" form of religion, the ground on which all other forms are built" and as such express "the form of religion to which human beings revert when all other forms collapse" (*ibid.*: 100, 101). Drawing on E. B. Tylor in particular, Stringer identifies this form as an "animistic layer of religious practice" (*ibid.*: 111).

As in my proposed approach to disaggregating and redistributing new age data, Stringer is inverting "top down" vectors of representation and their legitimating discourses in order to lay bare a widespread practice base located – in this example – in vernacular English Christianity. He calls this "base layer" the "elementary, 'animistic' form of religion" and he claims that it "remains constant in its 'form', in how it fundamentally works" while simultaneously "adapt[ing] constantly to the dominant discourses around it" (*ibid.*: 113).

Example II: new age seekers

Forming a complementary example of an elementary form, this time of a disposition to search, I now describe new age seekership. In a benchmark paper Campbell defined the "seeker" as a person who has "adopted a problem-solving perspective while defining conventional religious institutions and beliefs as inadequate" (C. Campbell 1972: 123). The disposition to seek or search is well represented in new age networks in both cognitive and behavioural aspects. For example, *The Seeker's Handbook: The Complete Guide to Spiritual Pathfinding* is a compendium of essays by an American author, who addresses his readers like this:

> Like you, I am a seeker. My quest began with dreams in early childhood, followed in my teens by some disturbing inner experiences ... Quite soon I was led to worldwide travels and ... spontaneous mystical experiences, followed up by years of esoteric studies and various disciplines of self-work. It is a quest that still continues.   (Lash 1990: xi)

The combination of a "problem-solving perspective" with the "inadequacy" of any one source of authority recurs as a common plot device in new age biographies. Tropes of "journey", "search" and "adventure" are prominent in the titles of testimonies such as Judith Boice's *At One With All Life: A Personal Journey in Gaian Communities* (1990), David Spangler's *Pilgrim in Aquarius* (1996b) and Timothy Todd Tattersall's *Journey: An Adventure of Love and Healing* (1996). It is no accident that these examples have strong connections to the new age colony at Findhorn in North East Scotland, since the biographies of the founders of the colony, both before and after its settlement in 1962, also demonstrate Campbell's model of seekership.

In these and other primary sources, the identity of "seeker" and practices of "seeking" capture the skill set required to negotiate a stimulating yet also potentially disorienting environment of multiple traditions. Seeking may be enacted at a concrete level as a search for practices and techniques; it may also be represented at a more abstract level as an investigation of sources of meaning and truth. The register is restless and pragmatic. *Pilgrim in Aquarius* advises its readers to "do some sampling of ideas and images" (Spangler 1996b: 181); William Bloom urges Findhornians to "do something, anything, to deepen your relationship with the sacred" (Bloom 1993: 18). Sometimes disillusion sets in, suggesting a perilous side to the "adventure", as when former English hippie C. J. Stone remarks: "I was always looking, but I never found what I was looking for" (Stone 1996: 196).

In *Creation of the Sacred*, Walter Burkert argues that a biological dimension underpins basic narrative structures. Burkert argues that a confluence of "natural" and "cultural" forces can explain more compellingly how and why "the tale is the form through which complex experience becomes communicable" (Burkert 1996: 56). In a chapter entitled "The Core of a Tale" based on Vladimir Propp's formalist method, Burkert explores evidence for the existence of a "quest" structure, one of the earliest narrative devices, citing examples from Greek and Sumerian mythology. Concluding that "the sequence of the quest is surprisingly persistent and nearly ubiquitous through more than four millenia" (*ibid.*: 63), Burkert turns to ethology to explain the longevity of this "tale-telling program" (*ibid.*: 63). By analogy to the search for food among animals, Burkert argues that "practically the whole of the Propp [quest] sequence is prefigured in [a] series of biological necessities" (*ibid.*: 63). In other words, "The biological equivalent of the quest is the search for food, which includes the struggle against others who are in quest for the same resources, and the possibility of tricks, fight and flight" (*ibid.*: 64). According to Burkert, the basic quest sequence can be reduced even further: to verbal language forms. He points out that "actions are represented by verbs, and the verbal root ... in most languages ... is the imperative". On this line of analysis, he concludes that "the deepest deep structure of a tale would, then, be a series of imperatives: "get", that is "go out, ask, find out, fight for it, take and run" (*ibid.*: 64).

Adapting Propp, therefore, Burkert argues not only that "the quest is established as the means for problem-solving" (*ibid.*: 65) but, crucially, that "the soul of the plot" operates "at the level of biology". If we expand Burkert's definition of "resources" and "imperatives" to include the search for less tangible cultural goods such as sociality and meaning, we have a rough working model with which to connect a (cultural) emplotment such as Campbell's role of seekership to (natural) biological drives to "get". From this perspective, new age seekership is no longer the superficial and whimsical "dabbling" represented by Lofland and Stark (1965: 869) in which the seeker is seen to be "floundering about among religions", but a proportionate response to a cultural environment characterized by enhanced stimulation and even informational overload. Following Burkert and Propp, we can consider the new age disposition to "seek" within an environment populated by multiple traditions to be an adaptation of an elementary form of behaviour rooted in psychological and biological drives. The biological search for food becomes transposed into a register of meaning and security. The search is crystallized in a particularly raw form in the new age context due to the relative paucity in this sector of the religious field of more complex institutions that may elsewhere camouflage its operation. But the search is not unique to new age; as Burkert plausibly argues, the quest narrative is "nearly ubiquitous through more than four millenia" (Burkert 1996: 63). This only strengthens the argument to include raw search, derived from the example of new age seekership, among the items for a new catalogue of the elementary forms of religion alongside the animistic sensibility induced by Stringer.

"NO PROBLEM": NEW AGE AND ELEMENTARY FORMS IN COMPARATIVE PERSPECTIVE

Bowker and Star (1999) have demonstrated the political and ideological interests expressed in schemes of classification operating in very different social practices from those considered here, from the international classification of diseases to apartheid racial classification. As J. Z. Smith rightly advises: "the rejection of classificatory interest is ... a rejection of thought" (J. Z. Smith 2000: 43). Classification (like politics) is everywhere and unavoidable. The question is therefore not whether to classify new age data, but how to do it – and do it better. Stringer's work on Christian animists in England in conjunction with my excavation of raw search from within new age seekership suggests that a tension between demotic practices and the "theologically correct" (Barrett 1999) discourse of elites runs as a faultline through modern European societies as much as on the colonial frontiers which so fascinated Victorian scholars. The collective evidence broadly supports the recent case made within cognitive studies of religion that under conditions of immediate "online" cognitive processing, "theological *in*correctness" (Slone 2004; my emphasis) is more prevalent among all parties than either theologians or social scientists, as systematicians, allow. Although induced from Christian practices, the three elements of Stringer's prototype of "religion" – unsystematic belief, intimate association, pragmatic coping – make good comparative sense of the new age *habitus*. His ethnographies of the "intimate" intentions, "situational" ideas, and "coping" practices of local English people he describes as "Christian animists" reward juxtaposition with biographies and ethnographies within the "holistic milieu" (Heelas & Woodhead 2005).

A model or prototype of religion based on "elementary forms" rather than on rationalized religion entities predicts horizontal similarities and interfusion across formations in general. I have argued that theorizing "elementary forms of religion" on the comparative evidence of vernacular Christian animism and new age search undermines the authority of the world religions taxonomy from a fresh and productive direction. It has become a postcolonial commonplace that this taxonomy routinely distorts data outside Europe. Comparative analysis of elementary forms, such as that begun here, challenges the viability of the taxonomy within Europe itself. The "animistic layer" discerned by Stringer in England, for example, is not new. But as he observes, thus far "we have not sought it, and have therefore never seen it" (Stringer 2008a: 110). What happens when we renew the systematic study of elementary forms?

NOTES

1. For critical discussions of themes and issues in "new age studies" between 1984 and 2007, see Iwersen (1999), Sutcliffe (2003b) and Chryssides (2007).
2. Following J. Z. Smith (1998), I treat Tiele (1884) as the principal modern source of the "world" prototype (which Tiele also calls "universal"), but genealogical connections with Weber's concept of *Weltreligionen*, for example in "Die Wirtschaftsethik der Weltreligionen" (1915–19, English translation: "The Social Psychology of the World Religions", Weber 1970), and the earlier German concept of *Weltgeschichte* ("world history"), merit investigation. For a more extensive enquiry into the effects of the trope, see Masuzawa (2005).
3. Martin Stringer similarly invokes the idea of "elementary forms of religious life" in the final chapter of his monograph *Contemporary Western Ethnography and the Definition of Religion* (Stringer 2008a) to help explain the behaviour of "Christian animists" in England: see my discussion later in the chapter.
4. See the critiques of "new age studies" as a *sui generis* enterprise in Sutcliffe (2003a: 21–5) and especially in Wood (2007: ch. 2) and Wood (2010).
5. For some suggestions in this respect, see Sutcliffe (2007, 2011).
6. The extreme flexibility of "movement" classification is shown by Melton's (1988: 35–6) assertion that new age can be considered "a genuine *movement*" (emphasis in original) on grounds of *lacking* organizational features. As Sutcliffe (2003a: 21) comments: "ironically the absence of just those empirical variables appropriate to a … NRM – leaders, headquarters, prescribed texts, boundaries, public policy, common goal – is seen as confirmation".
7. At university and secondary or high school level there appears to be a continuous demand for textbooks such as Markham's *A World Religions Reader* (1996), Ridgeon's *Major World Religions* (2003) and Urubshurow's *Introducing World Religions* (2008),

to name just a few recent examples; see review essays on this genre by MacWilliams *et al.* (2005) and Olson (2008), and cogent critiques by Geaves (1998) and Owen (2011). At school level in the UK, for example, the Shap Working Party on World Religions in Education (est. 1969: www.shapworkingparty.org.uk, accessed August 2013) has been influential.

8. Counting the world religions has fluctuated considerably since Tiele's original "big three" (Christianity, Islam, Buddhism) and is itself an index of the contested nature of the enterprise "offstage": compare the "ten great religions" in Clarke (1888) with the five "major world religions" in Ridgeon (2003) or the twelve "traditions" presented in Urubshurow (2008).

9. "The student of religion ... must be relentlessly self-conscious. Indeed, this self-consciousness constitutes his primary expertise, his foremost object of study" ("Introduction", J. Z. Smith 1982: xi).

10. On the Church of Jesus Christ of Latter-Day Saints as a new world religion, see the early framing by Stark (1984); on Bahá'ís, see Fazel (1994).

11. See Parrinder (1954) and Idowu (1973).

12. Compare the function of the "world music" category in creating an international arena for the circulation of local "folk" and "indigenous" musics. In a rough parallel to the legitimating effect of the Parliament of the World's Religions, first held in 1893 and last held in Melbourne in 2009 (see www.parliamentofreligions.org), Connell and Gibson (2004: 358) describe the annual World Music Expo, established in 1994, as "a crucial site for determining which musicians get signed, promoted and distributed": see www.womex.com.

13. See, for example, York's (2003) argument for conceptualizing Paganism as a world religion.

14. In a similar vein Morris has remarked on the "not-fully-acknowledged liberal Christian perspective" operating within Smartian phenomenology of religion, which delivered "a sort of evaluation of world religions, with historical Judaism only getting 4/10, but liberal Judaism receiving 8/10; fundamentalist Christianity only gets 2/10, along with traditional Islam, while modernist Islam gets an 8/10 and liberal Christianity full marks with 10/10" (Morris 2010: 328; thanks to Carole Cusack for bringing this source to my attention).

15. See Chidester (1996) and Bloch *et al.* (2010) on problems in using the category "religion" in South Africa and South Asia.

16. For an overview of new age sociodemography in light of these and related cultural politics, see Rose (1998), Heelas and Woodhead (2005), Houtman and Aupers (2007) and Frisk (2007).

17. That this is a practitioner (emic) headache as much as a theoretical (etic) problem is shown by the recent attempt by the Foundation for Holistic Spirituality, a project headed by the long-standing English activist, William Bloom (b. 1948), compiler of *The Holistic Revolution: The Essential New Age Reader* (Bloom 2000), to create a reflexive movement around the perceived core value of "holism". The Foundation's most recent project was to campaign for respondents to enter "holistic" to the question "what is your religion?" in the 2011 UK census: see www.f4hs.org (accessed April 2013). As the Foundation explains: "When asked your religion on official forms, you might find it appropriate to say "holistic", or "I take a holistic approach". Modern culture is full of spiritual diversity and *none of us wants to start another religion or faith community*. Nevertheless it would be good and helpful if this modern and inclusive approach were given official recognition" (www.whyholistic.org, accessed April 2013; emphasis added).

18. For a more sustained argument, see Sutcliffe (2003a: 21–5, 197–9).

2. "ALL OVER THE PLACE": THE CONTRIBUTION OF NEW AGE TO A SPATIAL MODEL OF RELIGION

Ingvild Sælid Gilhus

"New Age" phenomena are frequently seen as atypical forms of religion, and a specific terminology is created to describe them. This terminology includes, for instance, terms like "New Age" itself, "New Religious Movements", "new religiosity", "neo-spirituality", "spirituality", "alternative religiosity", "alternative spirituality", and "holistic". Terms and theories establish the research object, which also means that terms highlight some aspects of a phenomenon and leave other aspects in twilight or darkness. Do the terms mentioned above point at the most characteristic aspects of the phenomena they describe – and if not, what terms could be used instead? In this chapter I will discuss the terminology of New Age phenomena in relation to a specific model for the study of religion and argue that to develop a fruitful terminology, it is necessary to develop a more complete and dynamic picture of contemporary religion. Religion in both the historical Roman Empire and in contemporary Norway is used as an example, and my broader argument is that a historical approach can provide important comparative insight into a phenomenon usually considered *ur*-contemporary.

TERMINOLOGICAL PROBLEMS

The terms mentioned above are problematic for several reasons. *One problem* is that they imply a polarized approach. Most of the terms situate their objects as secondary in relation to established religious institutions and religious power, for instance by using the prefix "new/neo" or the term "alternative". The dominance of the "world religion" category implies that "New Age" phenomena in the Western world are seen in relation to Christianity and to established churches. Taking into consideration that the category "world religion" is heavily influenced by Christianity and that Christianity dominates the Western world, the terminology implies that "New Age" phenomena are doubly measured against Christianity, both because of the terminology and because of the religio-political situation. Peter Beyer has constructed a sociological theory about religion in contemporary global societies (Beyer 2006). Influenced by Niklas Luhmann, his point of departure is that religion is one of several differentiated function systems in the world today. In addition to religion these systems cover for instance science, law, economy, entertainment and health. The function system of religion does not include everything religious, but has, all the same, brought about a new global model of religion (Beyer 2006: 3). In many ways the so-called "world-religions", and especially Christianity, are the prototypes of religion in this system (*ibid.*: 15–16). One of the things that Beyer discusses is what is accepted or rejected as religion in the global model of religion. However, New Age/spirituality does not fit very well with this system (*ibid.*: 279–82; cf. the Introduction to this book). The challenge in a study of New Age is to look for alternative theoretical approaches and models that are broad enough to include it without making it into something odd and unique.

All of the terminology referred to above is part of a polemical discourse of inclusion and exclusion, of identity marking and making and, as such, is itself, of course, also part of the global discourse on religion. This means that the terms that are used refer to the contemporary situation and that they are comparative. Comparative approaches to the study of religion are in principle to be welcomed, but perhaps they are not comparative in a way that is optimal? Use of these various terms signals that believers, critics and scholars alike seek to maintain clear water between religion and "New Age" phenomena. When, for instance, the believers use "spirituality" as a preferred term in relation to religion, it includes a criticism of religion as being on a lower level than spirituality. "Alternative" used by the believers, signals something that is better than or superior to religion, while when it is used by the critics and scholars the term signals that "New Age" phenomena are secondary and inferior.

A second problem is that the use of the terms mentioned at the beginning implies that emic terms are translated into etic terms without their intellectual baggage being fully identified (Sutcliffe 2006). Some of these terms started out as emic terms, and are still used as both emic and etic terms: for instance "spirituality", "the alternative movement" and "holism". "New Age" was originally an emic term but is now mainly used as an etic term. It has not been sufficiently questioned what the mutual transfer of values and meanings between emic and etic terms in these cases implies.

A third problem is that two of the most commonly used terms – "New Age" and "spirituality" – one-sidedly stress religious ideas. By this I mean that the concept "New Age" is based on the idea of the coming of a new world age, the age of the Aquarius, while "spirituality" refers to the idea of an immaterial reality – the spirit. A variety of everyday practices are in fact included in the "New Age" phenomena such as communication with angels, meditation, yoga, magic and divination. When the descriptive terms refer in the main to the narrative or mythic dimension of religion,[1] they are reductionistic in a way that is not especially fruitful in relation to the multi-layered formation which they aim to describe.

A fourth problem is that the implicit dualistic terminology used for "New Age" phenomena both under-communicates the more complex interface between Christianity and New Age/spirituality within the field of religion and at the same time makes light of the interplay between New Age and broader social and cultural phenomena belonging to non-religious fields (cf. Knoblauch 2008).[2] In the words of Jonathan Z. Smith, "Given the triumphalist associations of the term 'world religions', the maps and diagrams fail to display the ecological complexity of religions cohabiting contiguous space." (J. Z. Smith 1996: 398). The terminology tends to freeze a religious situation and to describe it as an opposition between two different types of religion instead of trying to grasp the dynamic interaction in the religious field itself where so-called "new age" practices are increasingly found in the repertoire of "traditional" religious practitioners in different formations, especially in Christian denominations. Timothy Fitzgerald has correctly pointed out that categories like religion have no fixed meaning – they are "fundamentally rhetorical and strategic" (Fitzgerald 2007: 23; Stuckrad 2010). This is, of course, also the case with terms that are used for "New Age" phenomena. They try to give fixity to fluidity, but refer to something that is by nature continually in the making.

A fifth problem is that the terminology attempts to make a huge diversity into one unity (cf. Sutcliffe 2003a). Terms like "New Age", "New religious movements" and "spirituality" signal that they cover the same phenomena more globally, but do they really? These are high-level abstractions that are used for complex and subtle phenomena whose expression may differ from country to country. In the same way as it is now common to speak about "Christianities", the designations used for "New Age" phenomena should allow for plurality as well. Different patterns of "New Age" phenomena probably exist. Similar processes are at work in Western countries which change the religious landscape, but the details of the landscape that is changed varies from country to country.[3]

DEFINITIONS AND MODELS

How are phenomena that are described as "New Age" usually studied? The question is closely connected to another question: How is *religion* best studied in late modern societies? These questions are intimately connected with the use of terminology, and use of terminology is dependent on how we conceptualize what counts as religion.

Conceptualizations of religion have in common that religion is set apart from the other fields of society. Researchers usually work with a two-field approach in which a basic division is made between religion and the scientific study of religion, whether this is actual or rhetorical. In this approach the study of religion is ideally freed from religious elements and is generally seen as of a different functionality to religion and sometimes also as superior to religion. The opposition between religion and the study of religion can be considered as part of a larger picture of differentiated functional systems or fields in modern societies in line with the ideas of Peter Beyer.

JONATHAN Z. SMITH'S MODEL OF RELIGION IN ANCIENT SOCIETY

How can we represent religion to get a more comprehensive picture, not only of "New Age" phenomena, but of religion in general, including mediatized religion (see discussion below) and "New Age" phenomena in contemporary Western societies? One fruitful approach for mapping religion is the spatial model constructed by Jonathan Z. Smith for the study of religion in the late ancient world (J. Z. Smith 2003). This model is general and can be applied to areas other than the former Roman Empire as well.

Smith's model deals with *where* religion is situated in society and *how* people practise religion.[4] According to his model religion is found "here", "there" and "anywhere". Thus the natural habitat of religion includes three "spaces", as follows:

- *Religion there* is civic, national and imperial religion, largely based in temple constructions, characterized by urbanism, sacred kingships, temples, hereditary priesthoods, sacrifice and writing (*ibid*.: 27–30). This type of religion has to do with relations to power. A central ritual is the civic sacrifice of one or more animals in the presence of civic authorities, priests and common people, ending with a public meal.
- *Religion here* is domestic religion, located primarily in homes and burial sites. Religion *here* belongs to the family, to former generations and generations to come. It is about the continuation of the family as a biological and social unity (*ibid*.: 24–7). Rituals in this space focus on familial meals as well as on meals on graves.
- *Religion anywhere* is the rich diversity of religious formations that occupy an interstitial space between the other two loci. Entrepreneurs, associations, magic and astrology are found in this locus that also combines elements from here and there (*ibid*.: 30–36).[5] Wandering religious specialists who offer their services, for instance selling magical formulas, casting horoscopes or holding out better prospects for the afterlife of potential buyers, are in this category as well as members of religious associations who meet at certain dates for festive meals.

I suggest that a fourth space is added to Smith's model, which is religion "everywhere":[6]

- *Religion everywhere*: While religion in the three loci mentioned so far (here, there and anywhere) consists of communication with super-human beings like gods, ghosts and souls, the religious field includes in addition communication *about* religion. In antiquity, for instance, which is the period that Smith's model is based on, images, inscriptions and architecture became important media of public communication (Rüpke 2010: 204).[7] This dimension was public and everyone was exposed to it.

Today in contemporary Western societies churches, chapels and graveyards are traditional examples of *religion everywhere* that publically communicate about religion. What I have called *religion everywhere* is particularly strong and takes to a high degree the form of what has been called the "mediatization of religion", which describes a general and pervasive cultural process. Examples of the contemporary mediatization of religion are advertisements for oracles and magicians in the newspapers and programmes about ghosts and other supernatural phenomena on television – frequently staged interactively, because people are invited to call in and tell about their own experiences.

A professor in Film and Media Studies, Stig Hjarvard, defines the mediatization of society as "the process whereby society to an increasing degree is submitted to, or become dependent on, the media and their logic" (Hjarvard 2008a: 113). According to Hjarvard the mediatization of society is not a universal process, but "primarily a development that has accelerated particularly in the *last years of the twentieth century* in *modern, highly industrialized, and chiefly western societies*, i.e., Europe, USA, Japan, Australia and so forth" (*ibid*.: 113; emphasis in original). Mediatization implies both that media have become independent institutions and that they "provide the means by which other social institutions and actors communicate" (*ibid*.: 115). In contemporary society media do not primarily mediate between religious institutions and people, for instance by broadcasting a Christian service (although they continue to do this in many European societies), but media have their own agenda, for instance by transforming religious ideas that have been considered marginal or "superstitious" or religious ideas that have become disconnected from their former institutional belonging and making them part of general cultural knowledge and concern (cf. Hjarvard 2008b). This implies that media act as agents of religious change. As a result in Europe, and especially in northern Europe, "religion is formatted according to the *genres of popular culture*" (*ibid*.: 12).

Institutionalized religion is no longer the prime source of mediatization. Instead religious issues

> are produced and edited by the media and delivered through genres like news, documentaries, drama, comedy, entertainment

> and so on. Through these genres, the media provide a constant
> fare of religious representations that mixes institutionalized reli-
> gion and other spiritual elements in new ways.   (*Ibid.*)

Hjarvard calls these religious representations "banal religion" and see them
as sources of re-enchantment. "Banal" implies that the representations are
"primary and fundamental in the production of religious thoughts and feelings, and that they are also banal in the sense that their religious meanings
may travel unnoticed and can be evoked independently of larger religious
texts and institutions" (*ibid.*: 15).

One common type of definition within religious studies is that religion is
communication with hypothetical superhuman beings. If we instead experiment with a broader definition and define religion as "communication with
and also about hypothetical superhuman beings" (cf. Gilhus & Mikaelsson
2001: 29), the more comprehensive definition includes religion as a major
topic of discussion in Western societies as well as its strong mediatization.
Knut Lundby has recently stressed the last point in his use of a communication perspective on religion (Lundby 2010: 113). If one does not want the
scholarly communication about religion to be part of the field, one could
mention this point explicitly: religion is communication with hypothetical
superhuman beings and non-scientific communication about them. The
definition is well suited to include the fourth "space", *religion everywhere*,
which is mediatized religion.

How does the quadripartite model – religion *here, there, anywhere* and
everywhere – respond to the five terminological problems that were presented above, that is, how does it help to create a terminology that avoids
a polarized approach to New Age phenomena; embeds New Age phenomena in contemporary cultural and social processes; avoids unintended inter-
ference from emic terms; includes religious practice in the definition; and
opens up to diversity within the "new age" category itself?

CASE STUDY: RELIGION IN NORWAY

In order to relate terminology to a concrete example, I will apply the quadripartite model to the religious situation in Norway. Norway is in many
ways a typical European country, but in relation to many other countries it
has a small population and is still very homogenous. The country is not a
member of the European Union and is a welfare state with stress on social
equality and an economy based on export of raw materials such as oil and
fish. Norway is both an example from which it is possible to generalize at
the same time as its religious situation shows some peculiar traits. Like the
other Scandinavian countries it is often described as one of the least religious countries in the world (Zuckerman 2008), but at the same time it has

a dominant church. About five million people live in Norway and around 77 per cent of the population belong to the Church of Norway (*Den norske kirke*). At the beginning of 2012, roughly 10 per cent of the Norwegian population were members in religious and life stance communities[8] outside the Church of Norway; more than half were members of Christian communities, the Roman Catholic church, for instance, including 102,286 members. The biggest non-Christian community is Islam with 112,236 members. There is also a large Humanistic movement with 83,100 members (discussed briefly below).

Religion there

The Constitution of Norway from 1814 stated that "The Evangelical-Lutheran religion shall remain the official religion of the State. The inhabitants professing it are bound to bring up their children in the same" (§2; cf. E. Smith 2010). This paragraph was changed in May 2012 and is now: "The values shall remain our Christian and Humanistic heritage. This Constitution shall ensure Democracy, Rule of Law and Human Rights".[9] The change reflects that Norway has become a secular society and to a higher degree than before a multi-confessional and multi-cultural society.[10] However, the Constitution also says that the Church shall still have a special position and be supported by the state.[11] According to these recent changes in the Constitution, the king is no longer the head of the church (§3 and §16), although "The King shall at all times profess the Evangelical-Lutheran religion" (§4). The state still has employer's liability for bishops and priests and the church is supported by means of taxes.

Church taxes are collected alongside other taxes and not specified, and everybody pays unless they make a personal effort to contract out of the system. Relatively few do. The Church has served and still serves in the building of the nation and is seen as an important part of what is now frequently called "the Norwegian cultural heritage" (Selberg 2008). It contributes to creating a Christian Norwegian identity and is the religious dimension of national identity (Beyer 2006: 69). Lutheranism is integrated with the life of the state and part of the national policy.[12] Inger Furseth sums up the situation when she says that in "many ways, the Church of Norway is conceived of as a public good" (Furseth 2006: 21).

People who both believe in a personal god and recognize Jesus Christ as their saviour consist of approximately 20 per cent of the population (Botvar 2006: 2) and 68 per cent say they believe in God or a higher power. Only a small percentage (around 2–3 per cent), goes to church regularly at Sunday services. In spite of poor attendance at Sunday services, the majority takes part in all or some of the rites of passage of the Church: in 2011, for example, 66.4 per cent of the newborn were baptized in the church, 39.2 per cent of couples were married there and 91.6 per cent had church burials (Botvar & Urstad 2012).

In short, Grace Davie has aptly labelled this type of religion "vicarious religion" and characterized it as "belonging without believing" (Davie 2007).

Religion here

There is not much recent research on domestic religion in Norway, except on death and rituals in the graveyards. Some families are saying grace and are having evening prayers with their children on a daily basis. There is also an interaction between church and families in the religious education of children although educational studies in Norway have mainly focused on religion in schools (Høeg 2010). Around 20 per cent of Norwegians say that they have prayed during the week. From 1991 to 2008 the number of those who said that they had lit candles on graves during the year had increased from 40 per cent to 60 per cent. This tradition has been developed independently of the church and mainly in peaceful co-existence with the church (Aagedal 1994).

Religion anywhere

Religion anywhere is characterized by small-scale entrepreneurs and by client- and audience cults. Approximately 15 per cent of the Norwegian population say that they believe in ideas like astrology, reincarnation, Karma, fortune telling and Spiritism (cf. Botvar 2006). There is a conglomeration of activities related to, for instance, healing treatments, UFOs, channelling, shamanism, fortune telling and crystals. In addition to a great diversity of independent initiatives there are in Norway relatively strong initiatives to create umbrella organizations and a common ideology. Two organizations are especially important: *Alternativt nettverk* and *Holistisk forbund.*

The organization *Alternativt nettverk* ("Alternative network") was established in 1992. It publishes a magazine, *Visjon* ("Vision") for spirituality, alternative medicine and alternative ways of living,[13] and arranges alternative fairs (*Alternativmesser*) in several cities once a year.[14] According to Georg Rønnevig, "*Alternativt Nettverk* succeeded in co-ordinating many alternative practitioners and activities and giving a strong voice to what was increasingly referred to as 'the alternative movement' (*alternativbevegelsen*) in the 1990s … Through its network and contacts, its magazine and fairs, *Alternativt Nettverk* reached a mass audience during the 1990s" (Rønnevig 2009–11: 8).

Holistisk Forbund ("The Holistic Federation of Norway") was founded in 2002. It aims to promote healthcare, support sustainable commerce and economics, nourish ecological and global awareness and stress the importance of knowledge and insight. The organization attempts to develop a comprehensive view of life and a well-defined alternative to traditional religions.[15] The English version of the homepage says: "The Holistic Federation of Norway differentiates between spirituality and religion and represents a non-dogmatic approach to spirituality". The concept of "holism" probably also signals a wish to reach out to a larger audience, but so far *Holistisk*

Forbund has few adherents. The connotations of the concept further imply a move against fragmentation, hint at ancient roots and signal a therapeutic outlook. When different practices and groups that have usually been labelled "New Age" are collected and presented as one ideology by its adherents, we seem to be witnessing an attempt at "religionification" (cf. also *ibid.*).

Another indication of the process of "religionification" is that the Holistic Federation has started to offer rites of passage for its members,[16] and thus tries to match what is one of the most important elements in church religion in Norway. Similar to the Humanistic Association (*Human-Etisk Forbund*), which offers alternatives to the Christian rites of passage, the Holistic Federation has asked for and been given status as a "life stance" community ("livssynssamfunn") rather than a religious community. The organization takes part in a process of "religionification" by building umbrella organizations and creating life phase rituals, but at the same time it dissociates itself from traditional religion/church religion and thus attempts to break loose from the function system of religion as modelled by Beyer (2006).

Religion everywhere

Religion appears in the media in the main when it clashes with secular and liberal values and as part of the entertainment industry. The main clashes with secular and liberal values are related to secularism, national belonging, social equality, sex and gender. This is in accordance with Beckford and Richardson who say that media "express the values of the dominant culture in coverage of religion" (Beckford & Richardson 2007: 408). When, for instance, in the summer 2010 the press came to know that the Minister for regional affairs had consulted a Zen-coacher, she was heavily criticized. In several interviews the minister countered the criticism by repeating the same well-rehearsed sentence: "I am well anchored in the Christian cultural heritage, and there is no danger that I will ever convert to Buddhism."

Another example of media criticism, based on a clash with secular values, happened in 2007 when the daughter of the Norwegian king and her companion Elisabeth Samnøy initiated a so-called School of Angels (*Astarte Education*). The initiative was followed by a vehement discussion in the newspapers about superstitions, beliefs and science. Experts in several fields, representatives for the church as well as journalists, were in the main critical of the princess. However letters to the newspaper editors as well as Gallup polls supported her (Kraft 2008; Gilhus 2012a).

In contrast, the Church of Norway and Lutheran Protestantism are seldom in the news so long as they are conducting "business as usual". When a Norwegian theologian, Olav Fykse Tveit, was, in 2009, elected general secretary of the World Council of Churches, a symbol of Christian unity and a consultative organ with half a billion Christians, which includes many of the Protestant and some of the Orthodox churches, the election was barely mentioned in the Norwegian newspapers.

The other main aspect of mediatization of religion in Norway is the spread of popular religious culture in the form of entertainment. Television is a main source for this aspect of mediatization. Interestingly the national channels broadcast programmes about Christianity and other world religions, while it is left to two of the commercial channels (TV Norge and Kanal FEM) to offer a range of programmes about alternative religion/spirituality (Kalvig 2009). The broadcasting of the Easter services in 2009 on the state channel was viewed by 57,000 to 83,000, which is about 1.1 to 1.6 per cent of the population, while some of the alternative programmes on the commercial channels had about half a million viewers, which is about 10 per cent of the population (*ibid.*). Examples of "alternative programmes" are "Åndenes makt" ("The power of spirits"), "Fra sjel til sjel" ("From soul to soul"), "Den andre siden" ("The other side") and "Jakten på den sjette sans" ("The hunt for the sixth sense") (Kalvig 2009).

Strong religious influence in Norway today comes from people who combine alleged superhuman powers with writing books and appearances in the media. The main examples are Margit Sandemo, princess Märtha Louise, Elisabeth Nordeng (formerly Samnøy) and Joralf Gjerstad (Gilhus 2012b). Margit Sandemo writes novels in which supernatural helpers frequently appear. Sandemo has in countless interviews during the last forty years told about her wide experiences with superhuman beings and miraculous occurrences in her own life. Märtha Louise and Elisabeth Nordeng run Astarte Education ("the School of Angels") and have written two books about therapy, meditation and angels. Joralf Gjerstad, a bell-ringer in the local church, popularly called "Snåsamannen" – "the man from Snåsa" (a small place in North Western Norway) is famous for his alleged powers to heal (Kraft 2010a). All three have obtained huge national fame. One could add that the English medium Lisa Williams, now based in USA, and her talking with the dead frequently appear on Norwegian commercial channels (cf. Kalvig 2012: 140).

To conclude this part of the chapter: *Religion there* – the Church – is intertwined with the monarchy, cultural heritage and national identity and has a leading role in staging life phase rituals. The private religion of the family – *religion here* – has not been much studied. *Religion anywhere* has two sides: it is on the one hand a conglomeration of practices, but on the other hand also includes attempts at creating ideological and organizational unities, which can be characterized as network-building as well as an incipient process of "religionification". *Religion everywhere* especially includes mediatized religion. This aspect is strong and ideas about superhuman beings and supernatural experiences like angels, ghosts and miracles are effectively spread by means of the media.

The Church of Norway – *religion there* – is challenged by what takes place in the spaces of *religion anywhere* and *religion everywhere*. These two last mentioned spaces strengthen each other while not completely excluding *religion there.*[17] For example, Margit Sandemo, Joralf Gjerstad and the princess Märtha Louise and Elisabeth Nordeng combine the spaces of *religion anywhere* and *everywhere*, at the same time as Gjerstad (strongly) and the princess (more modestly) signal that they belong to the Church.

THE QUESTION OF TERMINOLOGY AGAIN

Which terms are most apt to describe the distribution of religion in Norway and the religious development in this country? How is the dynamic religious situation best grasped? What we try to grasp is how religion in the different spaces speaks to contemporary concerns, in particular the fluid field of New Age spiritualities, and the terminology should be helpful in making us do exactly that. At the same time the terminology should also be helpful in describing what is taking place in that which has here been defined as four "spaces" of religion; and, finally, the terminology should be part of a systematic and comparative study of religion.

Ulrike Popp-Baier has recently pointed out that spirituality "appears as a mega-trend in the mass media marketing commodities and in the publications of social scientists trying to attract a broader audience" (Popp-Baier 2010: 34). She wants to introduce instead the concept of "self-controlled religiosity" (*ibid.* : 59). By this term she means that people select and combine elements from different belief systems, practices and organizations to meet their own specific needs and interests (*ibid.*: 60). Self-controlled religiosity is "a combination of (or oscillation between) critique, consumption, accommodation and sometimes even commitment with regard to religion" (*ibid.*: 59). According to her, religion offers resources for different things, some of which are even profane (*ibid.*: 59–60).

Hubert Knoblauch focuses on experience and makes a similar point to Popp-Baier when he says, "this kind of spirituality is communicated by the market and the media in such way that it overlaps the boundaries between religious institutions and popular culture, thereby becoming a 'popular religion' that overcomes the boundaries between 'privatized' and 'public' religion" (Knoblauch 2008: 142). Knoblauch also points out that "the model of religion as a binary distinction between the sacred and the profane is changing into a non-binary model" (*ibid.*: 149). Since the boundaries of religious and non-religious communication tend to dissolve as well as the boundaries between private and public, this basic transformation of religion demands, according to Knoblauch, "a reconceptualization in terms of transcendence instead of the binary code of sacred/profane" (*ibid.*: 140). The idea of transcendence is dependent on the phenomenological approaches of Schütz, Berger and Luckmann. Knoblauch includes non-religious forms of transcendence in the concept and sees religion as a special form of the domestication of transcendence (*ibid.*: 142).

It is well worth listening to the analysis that Popp-Baier and Knoblauch have made of the contemporary religious situation. The traditional terminology presents dichotomous and polarizing views of how the religious field is linked together – traditional religion versus new religion, religion versus science, and religion versus non-religion. The last dichotomy in particular is dependent on the traditional and stark polarity that has been constructed between sacred and profane. The polarity is focused on (as it is in part derived from) church religion – religion *there* – as the pre-eminent locus of the sacred and not so much on religion *here*, *anywhere* and *everywhere*, which is one reason that it is dubious if it catches the contemporary situation in an adequate way since the latter spaces encompass the majority of religious life.

Too little has further been made out of the common basic building blocks involved in constructing all types of religion – church religion as well as "New Age" religion – in what have sometimes and with reference to Émile Dukheim been called "the elementary forms of religious life" (Stringer 2008a).[18] These elementary forms include communication with and about superhuman beings and belief in and communication about superhuman experiences. The religious building blocks are common in all four spaces. While religious systems and institutions have combined the building blocks – the elementary forms of religious life – into comprehensive religious systems, contemporary processes of mediatization (*religion everywhere*) as well as religious entrepreneurs (*religion anywhere*) make these systems unstable and produce fragmentation, new narratives and changed contexts for religious elements. Not least do these processes promote religion that is thinly spread (Gilhus & Mikaelsson 2000).

I will suggest that the answer to the terminological conundrum could be to stick to terms that are universal and comparative. Peter Beyer has remarked about New Age that it tends "to 'look like a duck and quack like a duck', but avoid identification as a duck" (Beyer 2006: 8).[19] This is, of course, a perfectly legitimate strategy on the part of the adherents, but not equally legitimate for researchers to imitate. It is a considerable theoretical advantage to be able to use a terminology that speaks to the common subject of religion and which does not make the contemporary situation into something unique by means of a specialized terminology. The same terminology should be used to describe contemporary Western religion and contemporary non-Western versions as well as ancient religions. I therefore tend to disagree with, for instance, Hubert Knoblauch who sees "the need for the concept of 'religion' to be complemented by a more basic and less biased notion such as 'transcendence'" (Knoblauch 2008: 142).

Another option to creating a specialized terminology, cut loose from the term religion, is to prefix an adjective to it. Hence Stig Hjarvard, for instance, talks about "banal religion" (which is not a very elegant term). Mikael Rothstein has mentioned a series of similar terms for phenomena which in the present chapter have been described as *religion anywhere* and *everywhere*. These terms include, according to Rothstein, "implicit religion", "invisible religion", "absorbed religion", "assimilated religion", "incorporated religion", "co-opted religion", "hybrid religion" and "popular religion".[20] To use religion with an adjective prefixed is a better approach than skipping the term altogether. But even better, I think, is to link these metaphorical concepts (i.e. invisible, absorbed, assimilated etc.) to an explicit and comprehensive model of religion.

CONCLUSION: NEW AGE "ALL OVER THE PLACE"

"New Age" phenomena are frequently seen as a peculiar type of religion. This impression is misleading. These phenomena include astrology, divination, healing, magic, communication with superhuman beings and a lot of other practices that have much in common with the oldest and most durable forms of religion that we know. They are basic forms of religion, and not something that is strange and anomalous. Not least because of mediatization and the market, these phenomena are now "all over the place". In this chapter the mediatized version of New Age is included in a spatial model and described as *religion everywhere*.

If the study of what we usually call New Age shall contribute to generalizing theories of religion, the study should be contextualized and comparative. This requires us, first, to contextualize New Age phenomena in their contemporary general field of religion within Western culture, which I have tried to do by using Norway as an example. It also requires us to compare the contemporary field of religion with another general field of religion, which I have done by means of an expanded version of Jonathan Z. Smith's spatial model of religion that originally refers to the religious field in the Roman Empire. In accordance with this model I suggest that religion is analysed and described in relation to its different spaces and that New Age spiritualities are recognized as a vital component of a total spatial analysis.

It is important to note that there is no hierarchy between the spaces – they are equally valuable. In Norway and other European countries belief, theology and dogma are, because of the dominance of Christianity and especially Protestant Christian traditions, more in focus than rituals, even when, as in Norway, church rites of passage still have strong roots in the population. The terminology that is typically used for *religion anywhere* and *religion everywhere*, for instance "New religious movements", "New Age", "spirituality", "Alternative Movement" and "Holism" – in the main expresses the ideological side of religion and is thus ironically directly dependent on Church religion/traditional religion because the terms construct "New Age" phenomena as something that is alternative and new. Jonathan Z. Smith's model also highlights, in my opinion, that when we use the category religion, the category fits much better *religion there* than it fits the other spaces. Especially *religion anywhere* and *religion everywhere* may easily appear as somehow anomalous – not only in relation to "New Age" phenomena, but also more generally. I will further draw attention to the fact that because of the stress on the "new" and the "alternative", too little has been made out of the complementary nature of what has here been described as the four spaces of the religion and the interaction between them.[21]

NOTES

1. According to Ninian Smart's model of religion, religion has seven dimensions. The mythic or narrative is one of these dimensions (Smart 1992: 10–21).

2. According to James Beckford, "one of the virtues of framing studies of religion in terms that make connections with broader social and cultural phenomena is that religion can be shown to dramatise these phenomena and throw them into sharper relief" (Beckford 2003: 186).

3. As Christoph Bochinger argues for Germany (Bochinger 1994), Liselotte Frisk and Peter Åkerbäck for Sweden (Frisk & Åkerbäck 2013) and Dorota Hall for Poland (in this volume).

4. Jonathan Z. Smith applies a definition inspired by Melton Spiro: religion is the "manifold techniques, both communal and individual, by which men and women sought to gain access to, or avoidance of, culturally imagined powers by universally patterned means." (J. Z. Smith 2003: 9).

5. According to Smith there is a significant difference between ancient/classical and late antique forms of Mediterranean religion in that the third locus expands and becomes prominent – sometimes at the expense of the two other loci. In parallel, a new geography (more travelling), a new cosmography (from a two-story to a three-story cosmos), and a new polity were developed (J. Z. Smith 2003).

6. Smith seems not to include this space, when he points out that it is important to his topography that "'anywhere' is not read as 'everywhere'" (J. Z. Smith 2003: 22, note 6).

7. The ancient discursive field of religion consisted further of philosophical, apologetic and critical conversation about, for instance, *religio*, *hairesis/secta* and *superstitio* – a conversation that continues to infiltrate many scientific debates today.

8. The term "life stance community" ("livssynssamfunn") was coined by Harry Stopes-Roe and is used by the British Humanist Association and the International Humanist and Ethical Union with the original intention that the term includes both religious and secular views of life. In Norway "life stance community" is often used as a contrast to religious worldviews.

9. My translation. ("Værdigrundlaget forbliver vor kristne og humanistiske Arv. Denne Grundlov skal sikre Demokratiet, Retsstaten og Menneskerettighederne.")

10. *Religion there* also includes mosques, and churches from other Christian denominations, for instance Roman Catholic.

11. §16: "Den norske Kirke, en evangelisk-luthersk kirke, forbliver Norges Folkekirke og understøttes som saadan af Staten".

12. This is in consonance with the early modern shift in Europe that Craig Martin recently characterized as "a shift from one Christian discursive regime to a different Christian regime, in which Christian norms and ideology continued to operate as authoritative for the state." (C. Martin 2009: 145). José Casanova says that the two wars of religion in Europe and especially the thirty years war (1618–48) did not,

or at least not immediately, bring forth the secular state, but the confessional state (Casanova 2009: 8 ff.).

13. Originally the magazine was called *Nettverksnytt* ("News of the network"), then *Alternativt nettverk* and, from 2006, *Visjon* ("Vision"). It includes articles on, for instance, aromatherapy, homeopathy, zone therapy, regression therapy, holistic massage, Reiki massage, yoga, Osho body therapies, astrology, healing, chakra balancing, aura interpretation, tarot and acupuncture. It also includes articles about international alternative spiritual thinkers and regularly presents new books and offers a separate section with advertisements for alternative therapists ("Therapists in network").

14. The *alternativmesser* include self-presentations by religious organizations, therapists who offer their services, sales booths for New Age objects and courses in alternative thinking. These fairs were visited by around 100,000 people in 2012.

15. At present Holistisk Forbund is building up local branches and has established an alternative to the confirmation ceremonies offered respectively by the Church of Norway and Humanistisk Forbund. The federation has its root in the alternative movement and especially in the milieu connected to Alternativt Nettverk.

16. The Norwegian Humanist Association (founded in 1956), probably the largest humanist organization in the world in relation to the population, includes roughly 1.7 per cent of the population in 2012. Religious and life stance communities are entitled to State funding.

17. According to Stig Hjarvard, "some strands of faith were previously considered to be superstition and denounced as low culture. The increased presence of such forms of faith on international and national television has increased the legitimacy of 'superstition' and challenged the cultural prestige of the institutionalized church" (Hjarvard 2008b: 11).

18. "Instead of accepting the institutionalized religious texts as the most valid and true sources of religion and belief and consequently considering folk religion or 'superstition' as incomplete, undeveloped or marginally religious phenomena, it is both theoretically and analytically far more illuminating to consider the banal religious elements as constitutive for religious imagination, and the institutionalized religious texts and symbols as secondary features, in a sense as rationalizations after the fact" (Hjarvard 2008b: 15).

19. According to Beyer, "spirituality is a term which seeks escape from the perceived limitations of religion constructed as one of the function systems" (Beyer 2006: 281). But he also says: "As long as we do not insist that all religion has to look like those religions which stress other-worldliness, the character of New Age as religion can appear as only too evident" (*ibid.*: 281–2).

20. Mikael Rothstein, symposium at Solstrand, Norway, November 2010.

21. There are attempts to see distinctions as well as connections and likeness between the different varieties of religion, for instance in Paul Heelas and Linda Woodhead, *The Spiritual Revolution: Why Religion is Giving Way to Spirituality* (2005), where the "holistic milieu" and the "congregational milieu" exist in a kind of mimetic rapport. Inspired by this book Pål Ketil Botvar distinguishes on the basis of empirical studies between three forms of religiousness in Norway (Botvar 2009: 180). One form of religiousness is connected to the Church, the other two are characterized by Botvar as "alternative religousness" ("alternativreligiøsitet"). He labels them "the New Age type" ("New Age-retningen") and "the Spirituality type" ("Spirituality-retningen"). The New Age type is characterized by a positive interest in astrology, divination, reincarnation, holistic medicine and supernatural phenomena in magazines. The Sprituality type is characterized by people interested in a richer spiritual life, the deeper meaning of life, values, strong emotional experiences and life stance questions. Botvar relates these religious types to different social groups and political views.

3. TOWARDS A NEW PARADIGM OF CONSTRUCTING "RELIGION": NEW AGE DATA AND UNBOUNDED CATEGORIES

Liselotte Frisk

In this chapter, I will use the general theory of religion by Rodney Stark and William Sims Bainbridge from the 1980s as a starting point to discuss some challenges of constructing religion. Stark and Bainbridge presented their general theory of religion in several books and articles, the main ones being *A Theory of Religion* from 1987 (paperback edition 1996) and *The Future of Religion* (1985). The theory highlights some important issues concerning religion generally, but in particular focuses on new religious movements and the more unorganized environment popularly called "New Age".[1] The issues it deals with are still very much up-to-date, and attempts to solve them have been classical in religious studies for decades. Triggered by some results in my research in the contemporary New Age environment, and in relation to more recent discussions about how to understand and deal with the problematic concept of religion, I would like to discuss their theory anew.

The aim of this chapter is thus to discuss selected parts of the Stark and Bainbridge theory of religion in relation to contemporary empirical studies and some recent theoretical discussions about "religion", including the prototype theory of Benson Saler ([1993] 2000). In particular, I will use material from a local mapping project of religion and worldview that I have conducted in Dalarna since 2008.[2] A questionnaire distributed by one of my students to participants in a yoga class in Dalarna is also used as a base to discuss parts of the theory of Stark and Bainbridge, as one of the aims of this questionnaire was to operationalize some of their postulations (Andersson 2010).[3]

In particular, three special issues, addressed by Stark and Bainbridge and crucial to their theory, are discussed and problematized in this chapter. These issues are: degree of organization; degree of tension to society (the surrounding sociocultural environment); and the secular/religious dichotomy. The last issue is given particular attention. The chapter will conclude by presenting some ideas which may be valuable for fruitful approaches to the concept of religion, oriented towards a new paradigm for the study of religion.

THE STARK AND BAINBRIDGE THEORY OF RELIGION

The theory of Stark and Bainbridge as a whole is quite complex. I will below explain and discuss only the parts most relevant in the context of New Age phenomena and to the purpose of this chapter.

Rewards and compensators

The starting point of the theory is the postulate that humans seek what they perceive to be *rewards* and avoid what they perceive to be costs. Through the quest for rewards, people are forced into exchange relationships, where everyone seeks high exchange ratios. Power is defined as degree of control over one's exchange ratio, and Stark and Bainbridge observe that individual and social attributes which determine power are unequally distributed among persons and groups in any society (Stark & Bainbridge 1996: 27–34).

In the absence of a desired reward, Stark and Bainbridge claim that explanations will often be accepted which posit attainment of the reward in the distant future or in some other non-verifiable context. In this context, they introduce the concept of *compensators,* which they define as postulations of rewards according to explanations that cannot be immediately evaluated. Compensators are a promise of a reward in the future. If the promise turns out true, the compensator becomes a reward. If not, it remains a compensator, a substitute for the desired reward. Compensators could be *specific,* that is they could substitute for single, specific rewards like the curing of a disease; or *general,* that is for a cluster of many rewards or for rewards of great scope and value. The most general compensators offer explanations for questions of ultimate meaning, such as questions like "Does life have a purpose?", "Is death the end?", or "Why do we suffer?". Some of these questions require, according to Stark and Bainbridge, a supernatural answer, as "purpose" implies a conscious agent beyond the natural world. Other general compensators could encompass untestable and extremely general explanations like "God created heaven and earth", or philosophies of life or theologies, or the promise of eternal life (*ibid.*: 27–39). Compensators fall along a continuum from the specific to the general, so there is really no clear boundary between them (Stark & Bainbridge 1985: 7).

Religion, magic and science

As clarified above, the most general compensators can be supported only by supernatural explanations. "Supernatural" refers, according to Stark and Bainbridge, to forces beyond or outside nature which can suspend, alter or ignore physical forces. Stark and Bainbridge define *religion* as referring to systems of general compensators based on supernatural assumptions. *Magic* is, in contrast, limited to compensators for fairly specific rewards. Religion may, for example, promise eternal life, while magic would be limited to recovery from a particular illness or to a charm against contracting the illness.

As magic deals in specific compensators, it may become subject to empirical verification. Therefore only magic, not religion, is vulnerable to scientific test. While religion is always based on supernatural assumptions, magic is not necessarily, but could be. Another difference between religion and magic is that religion may create stable organizations because the most general compensators do require long-term, stable patterns of exchange. Magicians, however, serve individual clients, not lead organizations (Stark & Bainbridge 1985: 31–3).

Stark and Bainbridge distinguish magic and *science* on the basis of the results of empirical testing (*ibid.*: 31). Magic consists of beliefs that are assumed true in the presence of disconfirming evidence (Stark & Bainbridge 1996: 105). In short, science works; magic does not.

Church, sect and cult

Stark and Bainbridge differ between *church*, which is a conventional religious organization, *sect* which is a deviant religious organization with traditional beliefs and practices, and *cult* which is a deviant religious organization with novel beliefs and practices.[4] Sects come into being through schisms with existing organizations in their religious tradition. Cults represent either cultural innovation or cultural importation. Another way to describe religious deviance is, according to Stark and Bainbridge, that both sects and cults are in tension with the surrounding sociocultural environment. A church is a religious group that accepts the social environment in which it exists. A sect is a religious group that rejects the social environment in which it exists. There is, however, a continuum running from high to low tension with society (Stark & Bainbridge 1996: 124–7). Cults could differ in their degree of tension to society, depending on their degree of organization.

Stark and Bainbridge further classify cults into three categories, depending on degree of organization. The least organized category they call *audience cult*. An audience cult has no formal organization, and the participants could rather be seen as consumers (of lectures, magazines or books) than members. *Client cults* are more organized, and offer specific compensators, which means that they deal with magic. Client cults are also characterized by a relationship between therapist and patient or between consultant and client. Considerable organization may be found among those offering the cult service, but the clients themselves remain little organized and may often retain an active commitment to another religious movement or institution. Only *cult movements*, the third category, offer the most general compensators, the kind we have defined as available from religions. Cult movements basically explain the meaning of the universe and how to gain everlasting life. Thus, only cult movements are fully developed religious movements, aiming at satisfying all religious needs of converts. There is no dual membership with another faith (Stark & Bainbridge 1985: 26–30).

Cults can enjoy relatively low tension with their environment as long as they do not organize into religious movements. Audience cults often stay in low tension with their environment. Client cults, too, do not provoke great hostility in the surrounding sociocultural environment. It is when cults become religious movements that their environment heats up, since according to the model the more total the movement, the more total the opposition (*ibid.*: 36).

SOME RESULTS FROM THE MAPPING PROJECT IN DALARNA

New Age activities mapped in Dalarna

Having sketched the salient features of Stark and Bainbridge's ambitious theory of religion, I turn now to my empirical findings on New Age in Sweden. Dalarna is a predominantly rural and small industrial area in Sweden with about 270,000 inhabitants, including some smaller towns, two with a population of 40,000–50,000 inhabitants. The project aimed at mapping all groups with religious social activities, or meetings with some kind of religious connotation in a broad sense (with two or more participants present), with special focus on activities outside traditional Christianity. The reflections below are based on the preliminary results of this study, in combination with a basic knowledge of the New Age field in Sweden studied since the beginning of the 1990s.

From an organizational perspective using Stark and Bainbridge's terminology, both audience cults and client cults were found to be abundant in Dalarna. We found, for example, several annual or biannual fairs taking place all over Dalarna, with a predominantly New Age content attracting a relatively large attendance taking the form of audience cults. They would offer no long-term commitment, but opportunities to try, for example, short séances, tarot readings or energy massage, as well as an opportunity to buy books with New Age content, or crystals or other items with New Age implications. In several of these fairs, however, we found that the New Age activities were often presented side by side with mainstream activities like, for instance, physiological massage, foot care, handicrafts or local chocolate goods. The fair was often called "health fair" or "harmony fair", not signaling any specific spiritual content, although the "spiritual" would be the dominant generic content.

We also found some small holistic centres where different New Age practitioners worked together and shared premises offering treatments like yoga, mindfulness, healing, acupuncture or different kinds of massage. According to Stark and Bainbridge, these would be client cults. Interestingly enough, there were also sometimes mainstream health activities in the same premises, for example mainstream physiotherapists, health advisers, or even doctors and psychologists. Sometimes the same persons conducted both mainstream health activities and New Age-related activities, as in the case of one producer who had stress management, weight management and stop smoking advice on the programme, but also personal spiritual development.

Also classifiable as client cults were the seven retreat centres situated in the relatively small area of Dalarna. They all have different orientations, but several mix different kinds of activities and sources of inspiration. Examples, both situated close to the town Rättvik, are the Baravara retreat centre with a post-Osho inspired orientation, and Berget, a predominantly Christian retreat centre where different body practices like Zen meditation or yoga are also practised.

There seems, however, to be less engagement in what Stark and Bainbridge call cult movements and sects. Few of these were found in Dalarna, and when found they attracted relatively few members. Our tentative conclusion is that, compared to twenty years ago, there seems to be an increasing engagement in activities with less degree of organization, that is, audience cults and client cults. It also seems that the borders with "mainstream activities" are weakening.

From the perspective of content, the market of health and healing seems to be quite dominant in Dalarna. There were several different kinds of healing techniques, like Reiki healing, reconnective healing, diksha, or acupuncture, and body practices like yoga. But there were also several health activities closer to mainstream sociocultural interests, like spa procedures or advisers for diet and exercise.

There seemed also to be a certain emphasis on psychological orientations and the personal development sector, often with some roots in the human potential movement from the 1960s (see Anderson 1993). This would include, for example, reincarnation therapy and personal development. Recently the "life coaching" phenomenon has grown, very much based on the concept of inner potential and personal development. Much of this development is also part of the dominant sociocultural environment, with societal institutions like schools, universities, hospitals and even churches offering courses and sessions with this content. We found several personal life coaches in Dalarna, who included what they themselves called spiritual dimensions, some working in mainstream areas like the employment office, or as "existential advisors" at a health centre otherwise inclined towards mainstream treatment.

Finally, we found many Eastern-inspired body, breathing and awareness practices like yoga and mindfulness. Yoga boomed in all parts of Sweden at the turn of the twenty-first century. National surveys show that around 20 per cent of the Swedish population have practised yoga[5] and courses in all kinds of yoga are abundant in Dalarna. Also these courses are sometimes offered in established societal institutions, such as in hospitals for pregnant women, or in the Christian retreat centre. Neither the amount of yoga on offer, nor its mainstream orientation, was the case twenty years ago.

The questionnaire distributed to fifteen yoga practitioners in Dalarna

In spring 2010, as part of a student assignment at Högskolan Dalarna, one of my students constructed a questionnaire which was distributed to fifteen participants in yoga classes in Dalarna. One of the purposes of this question-naire was to operationalize the Stark and Bainbridge concepts *rewards* and *specific and general compensators*, and to discuss those concepts in relation to a small empirical study. The number of respondents was quite small and the respondents were not chosen according to any particular method, so the study should be considered as a pilot case study rather than being repre-sentative of any larger group of yoga practitioners. The method and results are discussed in an unpublished thesis (Andersson 2010).

There were several questions in the questionnaire, but only two items are discussed in this chapter. First, "What is yoga?" Here, the respondents were instructed to mark statements they thought corresponded to their under-standing of yoga. Several statements could be marked by each person. The options were devised to correspond to Stark and Bainbridge's definitions of specific and general compensators. Below the number of marks for each statement is indicated:

Yoga may help with physical problems like back pain and headache	14
Yoga is good for the spiritual dimension of the human being	8
Yoga can diminish depression	13
Yoga can give enlightenment	9
Yoga can diminish stress and give relaxation	15
Yoga can make you come closer to god	2
Yoga can improve your karma	6

As we see, almost everyone marked the statements intended to correspond to specific compensators (physical problems, depression, stress). But around half of the respondents also marked alternatives intended to correspond to general compensators, statements which included a spiritual dimension, enlightenment or improving of karma. Further, two respondents marked the alternative that yoga can make you come closer to god.

The second question was open-ended and the answers subject to inter-pretation: "Why did you begin to practise yoga and what did you at that time think that the practice of yoga would give you? Have you found what you wanted?"

The answers could be classified in more than one category. Fourteen of the fifteen respondents gave answers that related to physical or mental health, like physical training, balance, increased mobility, pain relief or inner peace. One replied that she searched for help to meditate. All except two said that they had found what they wanted from yoga.

In summary, the motivations to start to practise yoga seemed to be more oriented towards specific rather than general compensators. However, most of the respondents claimed to have received what they were looking for from yoga. In Stark and Bainbridge's terminology, this would move the motivations from compensators to rewards. This matter will be further discussed below.

DISCUSSION: CAN STARK AND BAINBRIDGE'S THEORY OF RELIGION EXPLAIN NEW AGE?

Degree of organization

Classification is a problematic subject. One problem is that reality often does not seem to fit into the boxes that a classification system constructs; there are often cases in between. Second, the basic criteria for a classification system have to be chosen with care. To be meaningful, the criteria should be chosen so that the subjects sorted into one and the same category share more features than the one criterion that the category is based on (see the discussion in Hammer 2004b). Stark and Bainbridge's criterion of *degree of organization* seems to fill this basic demand. Degree of organization appears to reveal something characteristic about the group which may also predict other features with some certainty. Although a relation is not always the case, a high degree of organization, a high level of participation and an expected participation in one unique organization are often related features (cult movements). Likewise, a low degree of organization, a low level of participation and simultaneous participation in several phenomena also often belong together (audience cults).

The preliminary results of the mapping project in Dalarna seem to indicate that there is an inclination towards participating in audience and client cults rather than towards membership in sects and cult movements in contemporary Sweden. This tendency is connected to the increasing individualism in Nordic and northern European societies. People are expected to select and choose for themselves in all areas, and also to be responsible for their choices.

In the religious sphere there seems to be a trend towards not belonging to an organization, but choosing one's own life style and combining and composing belief elements with inspiration from different sources. The unwillingness to engage in organizations may be illustrated by some statistics from the Swedish Lutheran Church, where membership figures fell from 95.2 per cent in 1972 to 89.0 per cent in 1990 and to 71.3 per cent in 2009, while confirmation figures fell from 76.3 per cent in 1972 to 63.4 per cent in 1990 and as low as 32.0 per cent in 2009.[6]

Not only religions but also political parties and welfare organizations have problems engaging people in contemporary Sweden. Ronald Inglehart connects this trend to the increasing growth of the post-industrial society in Western culture, where there is a shift from survival values to self-expression values or individualism, which brings increasing emancipation away from traditional sources of authority (Inglehart & Welzel 2005: 1–5).

The structure of audience and client cults fits into this pattern of individualism and choice, and the observation that these categories are well represented in the religious sector is therefore quite expected.

Degree of tension to society (the surrounding sociocultural environment)

Degree of tension to society is another criterion that Stark and Bainbridge use to categorize religious groups. Like their other criteria, the degree of tension is postulated as a spectrum from low to high degree, and it is also related to other features in religious groups like degree of internal organization. It is a criterion often used in classical typologies concerning religious organizations, starting with Troeltsch's typology of church and sect (Troeltsch 1981).

However, there are some problems with the conceptualization of tension to the "surrounding sociocultural environment". One implicit postulation is that there is a kind of "mainstream" sociocultural environment, and that there are phenomena which are not part of this mainstream. Exactly in what ways sect and cult differ from the postulated surrounding sociocultural environment is, however, not made clear.[7]

Based on the empirical material from Dalarna, I make the observation that the borders between mainstream and New Age activities seem to be weakening. Not having yet identified what is meant by "mainstream", this statement may be seen as problematic. I do not intend to discuss this problem thoroughly here but will below make some hints as to in which directions solutions could be attempted. By "mainstream phenomena" I first include state-funded institutions like hospitals, schools, universities and the employment office. Second, such healthcare activities that are paid by the state insurance system, like physiotherapists, acupuncture for pain relief, or psychotherapy. Third, private healthcare and related activities that might seem very peripheral to "religious" or worldview questions (but see the discussion below about the secular/religious dichotomy). These activities could include foot care or classical physiological massage. Fourth, maybe traditional Christianity, represented particularly by the Swedish Church, should be counted as mainstream. This matter could, however, be discussed from different angles, since church and state were divorced in Sweden in 2000 and Christian orientations are weakening in the Swedish population. When I point to a weakening of borders between New Age and mainstream activities, therefore, I intend to denote activities where phenomena with "more" of a religious or worldview orientation, but with some distance to traditional Christianity, are either incorporated in or funded by state institutions, or become mixed with mainstream secular activities in such a way that the borders and boundaries in the individual perception may become vague or even disappear.

During the fieldwork in Dalarna, it became obvious that "traditional" and "non-traditional" phenomena are now mixed together in the same premises. Established institutions arrange courses in yoga or mindfulness, and traditional foot care (chiropody) mixes with acupuncture and healing. My impression is that, due to the continually stronger individualism in our culture, traditional boundaries have broken down and are today continually crossed over, creating new cultural phenomena. Thus the criterion of degree of tension to the sociocultural environment suggested by Stark and Bainbridge is still interesting as an analytical instrument: however, in the empirical field, such differences tend to be more and more vague.

The secular/religious dichotomy

The definition, boundaries and understanding of religion has been a heated debate in religious studies for many years (for a recent contribution, see Vásquez 2011). One of the areas where this question becomes important is in the New Age context. The New Age environment demonstrates a strong orientation towards different kinds of physical and psychological therapies, which seem to exist on the very borders of what might be considered religious.

Stark and Bainbridge try to solve the problem of differentiating between religious and non-religious (secular) by defining religion as "systems of general compensators based on supernatural assumptions". The first element in their definition, as discussed, is the distinction between rewards and compensators in which a reward is something you get, and a compensator is something you hope to get in the future. One problem with this differentiation is that it is sometimes a subjective interpretation as to whether you get what you wish or not. Stark and Bainbridge exemplify a specific compensator with a cure of warts, which may be quite easy to judge if it works or not. There are, however, also problems of a more vague and subjective character, like for example "pain", "depression" or "disharmony". These problems may also be graded: you can have "more" or "less" pain or disharmony, and they could thus also be cured "more" or "less".

Most respondents to the yoga questionnaire replied that they had hoped to get either physical or mental rewards from yoga, like physical training, balance, increased mobility, pain relief or inner peace – specific compensators, in other words. But at the same time almost everyone also responded that they had received what they hoped for. This means that in their own interpretation they received rewards, not compensators.

The concept of compensator builds on the notion that "magic" does not work.[8] But although many therapies in the New Age environment may not "work" in a scientific way (in the sense that the warts disappear by a process which could be scientifically explained and replicated), the *experience* that they work or not is subjective. The process of therapy may change the individual's attitude to and perception of the problem and thereby the experience of the situation. In these cases, it seems that the outcome has to be considered a reward, not a compensator. Which might move these activities, in the terminology of Stark and Bainbridge, from magic to science – which is certainly not what they intended.

The same problem holds for what Stark and Bainbridge call general compensators. Even general compensators do not necessarily postulate future rewards. I am, for example, thinking of an "enlightenment movement" with retreat centres in Dalarna and with influences from the Indian advaita philosophy. Here, "enlightenment" should, as far as I can see, be categorized as a general compensator – but nevertheless there are several people in Sweden claiming to have received the "reward", to be "enlightened".[9] In the subjective experience, enlightenment may not be something hoped for in the future, but something already here and experienced. In this case it must be conceived of as a reward, not a compensator.

Furthermore, what is the exact difference between specific and general compensators? Stark and Bainbridge elaborate surprisingly little on this matter. At one end, the compensators are more "specific" – like the curing of warts – and at the other end the compensators are more "general", like a cluster of different compensators, or compensators of great value. At one end of the spectrum there is magic and at the other end there is religion.

Evidently the constructed difference between rewards and compensators has many problems, and is based on the faulty presumption that it can be objectively determined what works or not. Concerning specific and general compensators, this categorizing seems to fill the basic need that the approach says something interesting about the topic and that the basic criteria coexist with other important characteristics. However, the only way of using the concepts of specific and general compensators constructively, as far I can see, would be to use a graded terminology like "more or less of an orientation towards the specific spectrum", and "more or less of an orientation towards the general spectrum". These categories should be seen as open and not bounded, and could then be used as one perspective among others to increase our thinking and understanding about the borders of religious and secular phenomena.

The natural and the supernatural

Another problem with the application of Stark and Bainbridge's theory to New Age phenomena is the "supernatural" criterion which refers to forces beyond or outside nature which can suspend, alter or ignore physical forces.

Just as it is difficult to differ between general and specific compensators, it is difficult to differ between what should be considered natural or supernatural. Like specific and general compensators, these are analytical constructions. As seen from the questionnaire, the individual may practice yoga with the aim of getting increased body mobility, pain relief or inner peace, but may just as well connect yoga to realizing enlightenment or getting

59

closer to god. However, whether any of these aims are perceived of as connected to "forces beyond or outside nature" is very much subject to individual understanding and interpretation. The postulation of a differentiation between forces "inside" and "outside" nature may also have the basic fault of being culturally biased. In fact, from my fieldwork in New Age environments, I would suggest that a difference between natural and supernatural is not one that many people make or which appears important to them. "Enlightenment" or "inner peace" may well be seen as a condition immanent in nature, if it is even thought of in these terms at all. Often, the intentions, motivations and explanations of individuals active in this environment seem to be very much connected with emotions, experiences and identity, with no emphasis on consistent and intellectually oriented world interpretations where a differentiation between "natural" and "supernatural" would make sense. Individuals form their own religious expressions and symbols, mixed with secular elements. This postulation by Stark and Bainbridge may therefore not be possible or advisable to apply in a New Age environment.

STARK AND BAINBRIDGE'S THEORY OF RELIGION IN A WIDER PERSPECTIVE

Theories of religion, like all theories, are historically and culturally situated. The theory of Stark and Bainbridge was created in the mid 1980s. Since then, post-industrial society has been through some changes. A few decades ago, Christianity was still the dominant religious tradition in many Western societies and it could at that time make sense to model the concepts of sect and cult against this influence, as Stark and Bainbridge did in their theory. Today, however, this approach could well be questioned, as the innovative and imported characteristics have intermingled over time with the traditional elements, creating new traditions, however none of them "dominant". With increased globalization and religious pluralism it has become more problematic to determine what is meant by "the surrounding sociocultural environment". Which particular sociocultural environment are we measuring against in a pluralistic society?

The theory of religion of Stark and Bainbridge also shares some premises with earlier theories of religion in that the concept of "religion" has a Western and Christian background, and the understanding of the concept has been deeply coloured by the characteristics of Christianity (McGuire 2008: 19–44). The secular/religious dichotomy makes perfect sense from a Christian perspective as Christianity historically has been a sector quite distinct from the secular world, but is less evident in many other forms of religion. In the same way, the dichotomy natural/supernatural makes more sense in a Christian context than in many other cultures. Christianity may thus be an example of a quite special and unusual religion in comparison to other religions, yet it has strongly coloured academic understanding of what religion is. To study other religious approaches, like contemporary New Age spirituality, some new thinking is necessary.

TOWARDS A NEW PARADIGM OF CONSTRUCTING RELIGION

Based on my research in the New Age environment, I would now like to present some thoughts about fruitful approaches to contemporary religion. Basically, I start by perceiving "religion" as a cultural phenomenon, with no clear boundaries towards other cultural phenomena. In the context of New Age, there are certainly no clear cut borders between what should be considered religious and what should be considered secular. "Enlightenment" or "self realization" may, for example, be interpreted by the individual practitioner as either psychological or religious, but most probably the individual is not even thinking in those terms. In a global and historical context, it may even be the case that clear borders as to what should be considered religious or not is an exception, and that unclear borders, and blending of different kind of phenomena, is the normal state.

How then to solve the problem of defining religion? Do we need definitions at all? Yes, certainly we need definitions in different contexts. For example, as researchers with the task of studying religion, we need to know what phenomena should be included and excluded in our studies. My point is, however, that the definitions we use are always artificial constructions and should be treated as such. From this it follows that there is no universal "best" definition, but that several different definitions could and should be postulated and worked with, depending on their usefulness in different contexts. A multidimensional approach should be encouraged.

In *Conceptualising Religion* (2000), the anthropologist Benson Saler presents one interesting approach in which he suggests approaching religion as an unbounded and graded category, with "centrality" and "more or less" as important concepts. Saler uses a blend of Wittgenstein's discussion of family resemblances combined with selected insights derived from prototype theory in the contemporary cognitive sciences. For analytical purposes, Saler suggests that religion could be conceptualized in terms of a pool of elements that often cluster together but may do so in greater or lesser degrees. The various examples of the category popularly called "religion" need not, however, all share one feature, or some specific conjunction of features. We should deal with religion in terms of a pool of elements without supposing that any one element should be necessary.

Prototype theory works with central tendencies and peripheries rather than necessities and borders. The clearest or best examples should, according to Saler, be treated as the prototypes of their categories. As the category religion is a relatively recent Euro-American creation Saler claims that we should acknowledge that for most Western scholars the clearest examples of the category religion, the most prototypical exemplars, are the families of religions that we call Judaism, Christianity and Islam. Those families of religion are connected in complex ways to the development of religion as a Western category, and ideas about them continue to influence how Westerners and persons educated in the West use the term religion. Because of that, Saler suggests that the Western monotheisms might be used as markers that map a productive starting place. Saler argues that some amount of ethnocentrism is probably unavoidable as a cognitive starting point in the search for transcultural understandings. By recognizing such bias, Saler means that we are in a better position to correct for it.

Saler, however, also recommends that anthropologists selectively borrow non-Western categories and experiment with them for describing the cultures of people who do not employ them, just as they use religion as a category for describing the cultures of people who have no word and category for religion. Concepts from native categories could be experimented with as transcultural tools in an attempt to go beyond a Western framework to produce a multicultural anthropology. Saler suggests the concept of "dharma" as one example.

Saler emphasizes that the categories used should rest on central tendencies. Centrality, however, is a concept that implies distance and periphery, and Saler notes that peripheral cases are in fact extremely interesting. With this approach, there will be some clear cases of what we mean by religion, and then candidates that are increasingly less clear and more problematic. As our typicality features diminish, there are fewer reasons to term peripheral candidates religions. Saler recommends deciding by reasoned arguments whether or not to include under the rubric religion candidates that strike us as representing lesser degrees of prototypicality. Ideally, our reasoned arguments will include some statement of what we hope to accomplish by designating phenomena "religions" or "religious".

In the approach that Saler recommends, there are no clear boundaries drawn about religion. Rather, elements that we may perceive as religious are found in phenomena that many people may not be prepared to call religions. But if our ultimate purpose as scholars is to say interesting things about human beings rather than about religions and religion, appreciation of the pervasiveness of religious elements in human life is far more important than "bounding" religion (Saler 2000). By systematically exploring elements that we associate with religion among less clear exemplars of religiosity, we expand our opportunity to study "religious" elements in a rich diversity of cultural settings. Saler says that we may hope to transcend "religion" as such while coming to understand more about the religious dimension in human life (Saler 2009: 180).

CONCLUSION: NEW AGE AND UNBOUNDED CATEGORIES

Definitions of concepts and classification systems are definitely necessary to clarify our thoughts, conceive of patterns and reflect about new insights in how cultures, societies and human beings work. However, definitions and classification systems are all constructions, some being useful in some contexts, and others in other contexts. As this is the case, multiperspectives in these matters should be encouraged.

Stark and Bainbridge's theory of religion discusses many important features relevant to New Age. Their three interrelated criteria of degree of organization, degree of tension to the sociocultural environment, and the secular/religious dichotomy all relate to classical discussions about different kinds of religious organizations. Based on empirical research in the New Age environment, their theoretical assumptions can, however, be problematized. Some of their postulations seem to be culturally biased and do not fit into how contemporary individuals engage in this environment. One suggestion is that their postulated categories should rather be understood as unbounded than bounded, and also that more subjective and experience-related approaches to religion have to be considered.

An example of an approach to the New Age environment, based on unbounded categories and central tendencies, is a study I conducted in the mid 1990s. My approach was not as elaborate as the approach of Saler, and only dealt with New Age, not with religion as a wider category. Unwilling to construct any borders around the concept of New Age, I investigated which concepts were central in this environment, and which were gradually more peripheral. I found that the concept of "healing" was the most central concept in this kind of spirituality, and that also "energy" was quite central. Very central were also different kinds of practices, like meditation, crystals, massage and Reiki, which indicated a practical orientation rather than a belief orientation. "Body" also got high scores, which indicated corporeal body-centredness and this-worldliness. Also "reincarnation" scored quite high. Some concepts, however, were quite peripheral, for instance, "god" or even the notion of "New Age" (Frisk 1997).

One disadvantage with adapting Saler's approach may be the risk that non-Christian religions would still be constructed as marginal and atypical, since Saler recommends using Western monotheism as a starting place. Personally, I believe it is important to try out other possibilities. Instead of focusing on the constructed New Age category, the concept of "healing" could be used as the prototype, as it was found to be central in my own investigations from the 1990s. This attempt would break the boundaries of the constructed category of New Age, and also include as central, for example, charismatic healing currents and different kinds of traditional healing. Some other features, which are traditionally included in the New Age category, such as certain kinds of divination, may be found to be peripheral in this approach. In this way, cultural expressions may be categorized in new ways, which may bring some new insights as to how human beings deal with the world.

Another disadvantage with Saler's approach is his emphasis on intellectual elements as central in religion. I would like to add that religion, for the individual, is also deeply connected to other dimensions of the human being, such as emotions, attitudes, experiences, social exchange, and identity creation and confirmation (how people position themselves and navigate in life). These aspects of religion may be more difficult to pinpoint and analyse, which is one reason why they are under-researched in religious studies (Riis & Woodhead 2010: 1–3).

Theories are always historically and culturally situated. Today, in comparison with the time when the Stark and Bainbridge theory was launched, individualism is a stronger cultural tendency. In contemporary Dalarna, there is a tendency towards individual experiences and less organized religious engagement. Further, the effects of globalization and increasing pluralism challenge all kinds of traditionally conceived borders. Religious features mix, especially on an individual basis but also organizationally. In an increasingly pluralistic society, it becomes problematic to conceive of a mainstream sociocultural environment set over against a separate New Age environment.

Many theoretical approaches to religion reflect a historical and cultural base in Christianity, and it is clear that we need new ways to think about religion. The New Age environment as such especially actualizes problems with the constructed secular–religious border and thus with the concept of religion itself. In this context, I would welcome experimentation in the spirit of Saler, who suggests working with prototypes and unbounded categories. It is important, however, that we do not stay within the borders of the families of Christianity, Judaism and Islam, but that we also take into account other religions and popular cultural expressions, as well as the increasingly more important subjective dimensions of religiosity. In this connection New Age data offer rich possibilities for constructing a new prototype of "religion".

NOTES

1. No discussion about the definition of New Age is conducted here, but see for instance Frisk (1997) for one discussion about what kind of phenomena could be included.
2. Together with Peter Åkerbäck of Stockholm University, with funding support from The Swedish Research Council (Vetenskapsrådet).
3. Thank you to my student Mariella Andersson for permission to use this material.
4. This classification of religious organizations differs from most other sociologists of religion. See, for instance, McGuire (2002). Stark and Bainbridge have particularly developed the concept of "cult" to cover not only loosely organized religious orientations but also more strict religious organizations, making the main criteria not the looseness of organization but novel beliefs and practices.

5. See, for example, the survey by the newspaper *Dagen* reported in various articles in 2008. Divided by age, the survey showed that among young people (younger than age 29), about 40 per cent had practised yoga.
6. See www.svenskakyrkan.se/default.aspx?id=645562 (accessed October 2010).
7. For a discussion about different understandings of society and sociocultural environment, see Frisk (1993).
8. The concept "magic", as Stark and Bainbridge use it, is of course highly negatively loaded. "Magic" means something that does not work. I would, in the New Age context, prefer to use the concept of "therapy". As this is also the emic concept used in this environment, it may, of course, also be questioned. It seems to me, however, to be more neutral than the concept of magic, However therapy may have mainstream healthcare connotations which are not really valid.
9. See for instance Shanti Kristian, www.uniomystica.se/shanti.html (accessed August 2013).

4. ON TRANSGRESSING THE SECULAR: SPIRITUALITIES OF LIFE, IDEALISM, VITALISM

Paul Heelas

The context of this chapter is set by two major schools of thought. On the one hand, it is argued that the secularization of Christianity ends with the secular, a condition that is *self-sufficient*. Émile Durkheim ([1912] 1971), Steve Bruce (2002) and David Voas (2009) are among those who argue the case. On the other, there is the argument that the secular is *insufficient*. Insufficiencies generate transgressions of the secular condition; movement into the non-secular. A hegemonic secular age is but a pipe dream. Among others, Georg Simmel (1997), Peter Berger (1999) and Charles Taylor (2007) argue along these lines.

The incontestable marginalization of Christianity means that it is now possible to test the idea that the outcome of the decline of Christianity is a self-sufficient secular age; and the opposite idea that insufficiencies of the secular generate sufficient transgression to prevent the advent of a secular age; and to promote "alternative" spiritualities.

Rather than providing a review of all the evidence that counts for and against the two arguments, the aim of this chapter is to strike at the very heart of the idea of self-sufficiency. In face of the evidence supporting the self-sufficiency argument – most noticeably the collapse of Christianity and corresponding movement into the secular – the aim is pursued by arguing that secular sources of motivation are currently in operation. The *transgressive thesis* maintains that the secular – the very state of affairs that scholars like Durkheim and Bruce hold to be self-sufficient – is frequently believed to be insufficient. The secular is not enough; not able to cope on its own. Accordingly, it generates transgression; movement out of itself to the beyond: quite often towards, or into, "New Age" inner-life spirituality.[1]

Temporal and geographical contexts
The temporal context lies with what is taking place today; or in the recent past. The best way of criticizing the self-sufficiency argument is to find evidence of transgression at a time when – according to the self-sufficiency

argument – it should not be taking place: that is, when certain countries are allegedly entering, or have already entered, a secular age. Geographically speaking, attention is limited to northern quarters of the European Union (EU): an area running from the Baltic to the Atlantic.

THE SELF-SUFFICIENCY ARGUMENT

Around a hundred years ago, Émile Durkheim observed that "The old ideals and divine figures that embodied them are in the process of dying". Durkheim continues with an exemplary formulation of the self-sufficiency argument:

> [T]here is one idea that it is necessary for us to get used to: it is that humanity is deserted on this earth, left to its capacities alone and able to rely upon itself to direct its fate. As one moves forward through history, this idea only gains ground; I doubt, therefore, that it will lose any in the future. At first glance, the idea can upset the man who is accustomed to depicting as extra-human the powers that he leans on. But if he comes to accept that humanity by itself can provide him with the support that he needs, is there not in this perspective something highly reas-suring, since the resources that he is calling for are found thus placed on his doorstep and, as it were, right at hand?
>
> (Quoted in Christiano 2007: 50)

As Christianity – the "old ideals and divine figures" – fades away, "human-ity" takes over; and is set for the future.

Today, the argument runs, that great hope of the secular wing of the Enlight-enment – that the secular is self-sufficient – has more or less come to pass. The secular is on the brink of becoming hegemonic. The argument is that the secular is self-sufficient, self-sustaining, self-containing, self-limiting – able to roll on into the future within its own frame of endeavour. Slogans come to mind: "The Triumph of the Secular"; "The Defeat of the Transgressive"; "The Collapse of Transgression"; "The Death of Secularization", to emphasize the point that secularization ends when more or less everything is secular.

Charles Taylor (2007: 514) refers to the "shattering" decline of Christen-dom. Many scholars have inferred that this decline entails that the most potent form of transgression has become history. The secular is far enough along the road of undermining all that transgresses it – the major trans-gressor of the past, Christianity, the more recent upstart, "New Age spirit-uality" – for it to be clear that religion and/or spirituality are not required. The fact that the secular does not generate sources of motivation orientated towards the beyond is held to demonstrate that there is no longer any need for religion. Sacralization – movement towards the sacred – also belongs to the past. The secular, itself, is quite up to the job of handling its own insufficiencies, with no apparent loss for social processes and personal well-being. The long-standing argument, advanced by propagators or defenders of faith – that social and personal life will collapse into the anarchical, antinomian, anomic, the alienated, the "demoralized", the "moral blindness" of a recent volume by that arch-pessimist, Zygmunt Bauman (Bauman & Donsiks 2013) – is false. Strongly secularized countries, like Sweden, attest to the flourishing of social and personal life – beyond the sacred. It is perfectly possible to live a worthwhile, fulfilling life without Christianity, or any other form of religion or spirituality. People appreciate that they are far better off without the compensatory illusions, delusions, irrationality or non-rationality of religion/spirituality. Nothing should stand in the way of secular potential. The cultivation of the valued life is grounded in the secular itself. The route to human flourishing lies with the human of the secular order. The secular is the end point for all that lies ahead. "Faith in the secular" is the cry for the future.

Richard Dawkins's *Unweaving the Rainbow* (2006) is a paean for secular humanism; for science as poetry, the ground of purpose in life, meaning and beauty. Although the following is from an interview with an apostate living in North America, it is included here because it serves as such an excellent formulation of "the spirit of Dawkins":

> I must tell you when I let go of religion, one thing I felt was relief. I feel a profound sense of relief. I don't have any more unanswered questions. I know there's science to explain it and everything makes sense to me now. I can just live my life knowing I have control of my life. There is no afterlife. This is it, make the most of it and that's why I feel a great sense of relief.
>
> (Zuckerman 2012: 13)

The faithful secularist, we might say.

THE INSUFFICIENCY THESIS

The insufficiency thesis maintains that the secular condition is not up to the task of serving as a self-contained home for humans. With the fading of Christianity in northern Europe, ever more people realize that the secular is not enough. The greater the extent to which "the human condition" is framed in terms of the secular life-world, the greater the likelihood of the magnification of the insufficiencies of the secular: prompting transgression. Rather than the outcome of the collapse of Christianity in northern Europe (and elsewhere, in countries like Australia) taking the form of an enduring condition of secularity, people have experiences, apprehensions, comprehensions or outlooks that transgress the secular condition itself. And having lost faith with Christianity, transgressions tend to take a non-Christian direction.

Georg Simmel illustrates the thesis:

> The Enlightenment would be utter blindness if it were to assume that with a few centuries of criticism of the content of religion, it could destroy the yearning that has dominated humanity from the first stirrings of its history. ... Yet this very point illustrates the whole predicament in which an enormous proportion of civilized humanity finds itself today: it is beset once more with powerful needs, although it sees the historical and the sole existing means of fulfilling these needs as mere fantasy. (Simmel 1997: 9)

Like Durkheim, Simmel draws attention to the collapse of Christian tradition. Unlike Durkheim, he argues that the secularization of Christianity does not eradicate "powerful needs". "Yearning" demonstrates that the secular, alone, is not enough. "Yearning" prompts transgression: to that which lies beyond failed Christian orthodoxy, to that which would now be called "New Age" spirituality (*ibid.*: 18–19).

More recently, two highly influential figures – Charles Taylor (2007) and Peter Berger – are among those who have provided powerful statements of the insufficiency argument. In the words of the latter:

> The religious impulse, the quest for meaning that transcends the restricted space of empirical existence in this world, has been a perennial feature of humanity. This is not a theological statement but an anthropological one – an agnostic or even an atheist philosopher may well agree with it. It would take something close to a mutation of the species to extinguish this impulse for good.
> (Berger 1999: 13)

All in all, secular motivations, the secular transgressing itself, the secular acting to defeat itself, entail that the very idea of a secular age is an illusion. Slogans run, "The Limits of Secularization"; "The Failure of Secular Enclosure".

ON TESTING THE TRANSGRESSIVE THESIS: PRELIMINARY CONSIDERATIONS

Bruce's thought experiment

With customary agility of mind, Steve Bruce (2002) has conjured up the idea of a *tabula rasa*, a human condition absolutely devoid of religion and/or spirituality. Bruce's prediction is that people would stay "blank". My conjecture is that people would start to move beyond. Since the condition they move out of is devoid of religion and/or spirituality – and so of all non-secular sources of motivation – movement can only be generated by the secular. Using a term with a long history in anthropology and developmental psychology, something akin to "independent invention" takes place (see Segal 1999 on uses of this term).

The Holy Grail is to implement the thought experiment of the *tabula rasa* in the everyday world. As with all quests for the Holy Grail, though, the ideal is unattainable. In the everyday world, the *tabula rasa* does not exist. In some form or another, to some extent or another, religion and/or spirituality is present in every culture: not just among believers, but also among those secularists who have heard of "heaven" (and who hasn't?), who see religion/spirituality on the news, or who remember past events.

Nevertheless, it is worth pursuing a research route that is as close as possible to the Holy Grail. The realistic aim is to seek out the best approximation to the thought experiment, a context where motivation to the non-secular is most likely to be generated by the secular itself; where non-secular motivations are as minimal as possible.

Conditions for testing the transgressive thesis

Charles Taylor (2007: 530) argues that "the longing for and response to a more-than-immanent perspective … remains a strong *independent* source of motivation in modernity" (emphasis added). In context, it is clear that "independent" refers to the idea that sources of motivation lie with the "immanent" of the secular itself (including the "wearing out" of utopian secularity, with the attendant sense of "there is something more"; *ibid.*: 533): not with motivations supplied by faith in the sacred, expressed *via* religion and/or spirituality.

What is involved in testing the idea that "independent" (that is secular) sources of motivation are at work today? All that has to be done to test the transgressive thesis is to ascertain whether or not significant numbers of thorough-bred secularists move out of, away from, the secular to the non secular. A straightforward enough matter, it might be thought. What makes it more complicated, though, is demonstrating that transgressions are due to the secular *alone*: *without* any non-secular motivations; that is, without motivations that are not due to the secular world.

Minimal "lures" To minimize the possibility of transgression being due to non-secular motivations, the aim is to find a culture where the "lure effect" is least likely to be in evidence. The lure effect takes place when people are prompted to move out of the secular by what faith formulations, such as literature espousing cosmic consciousness or the spirituality of nature, have to offer or promise. Secular motivations might well play a role in movement of this kind: for example, generating existential disquiet to encourage transgression. But the allures of non-secular cultural "learning models" (as social psychologists call them) do not serve as secular motivations, alone.

Thinking of non-secular lures that are secular for the secularist, consider those ideas – like "some sort of spirit or life force that pervades all that lives" – which might be non-secular for those who believe in them, but which are secular for those who (needless to say) do not believe in them. On the one hand, lures have a non-secular component. They contain promises pertaining to "the beyond". On the other hand, promises of lures (say "eternal life") are understood in secular mode ("would that I could live forever"): which means that lures serve as secular motivations. To play it safe, the transgressive thesis is best tested when lures, of whatever kind, are least likely to be operative: thereby minimizing the difficulty (or impossibility) of disentangling motivations that are at one and same time secular and non-secular. This means finding a context (country, culture, etc.) where there is the least possible faith in religion and/or spirituality; where it is is most likely that people are indifferent to, and/or ignorant of, religion and/or spirituality; where religion and/or spirituality are unpopular (perhaps treated as a cultural failure); where aversion of any variety is in evidence.

Christianity   Given the ubiquitous presence of Christianity in northern Europe, what role does it play as a non-secular source of transgression? Christianity is certainly transgressive. As a transgressive faith formation, which transcends the secular, Christianity appears to support the insufficiency argument. By and large, though, Christianity does not provide the kind of evidence required to support the transgressive thesis. Since secular sources of motivation, to Christianity, are of little significance today, the tradition does not strike at the very heart of the self-sufficiency argument.

Whatever the role that transgression from the secular might have played in the past, currently very few become Christian by virtue of secular impulses alone; and, for that matter, very few are lured. "Transgression" is bound up with faith socialization. Rather than providing evidence of secular motivation, non-secular motivations are at work. People "become" Christians by being socialized with/in faith. Motivations are primarily *intra-religious*: that is, they come from within Christianity. People are "made" in faith for reasons of faith (Crockett & Voas 2006: 577–8).

This said, it is true that insufficiencies of the secular enter the picture. Faith socialization teaches the value of staying transgressed in face of the insufficiencies of the secular, thereby sustaining the transgressive value of Christianity. Or consider movement from those wings of Christianity, where the sacrality of human life is to the fore, to "New Age" spirituality: *intra-spiritual* movement which, too, is partly sustained by negative evaluations of the secular; an aversion to giving up the sacred for sake of the secular alone. In both cases, the insufficiency argument is supported; but not the transgressive thesis.

Overall, the way in which Christianity functions, today, simplifies the task of testing the transgressive thesis. To a large extent, Christianity does not enter the picture.

TESTING THE TRANSGRESSIVE/INSUFFICIENCY THESIS

Within the confines of the EU, testing is best implemented where there is as "blank" a sheet as is possible, prior, that is, to any transgression that might take place. We have to look for the nation with the most "blank" population: people who might know about religion/spirituality but who are not attracted; people who treat religion/spirituality as secular; people with minimal religion/spirituality at home or school; a culture with minimal religion/spirituality. The "blankest" population is most likely to be found in the most secular nation.

From a thought experiment to cultural engineering: Estonia

Of all the current EU nations, Estonia best fits the bill. The closest approximation to a *tabula rasa* occurred during the years leading up to 1991. In that year, Estonia obtained independence from the Soviet Union. This marked the close of an exercise in social engineering. The independent variable lay with Soviet atheism; the dependent variable with religious tradition in Estonia. To all intents and purposes, the cultural "experiment" worked. In the words of Estonian academic Lea Altnurme (2011: 77), during the period of Soviet occupation (1940–91) "Estonia became strongly secularized, judging by the loss of influence of the traditional churches, both in society in general and in the lives of individuals".

1991 provides an excellent base line for determining whether or not secular sources of transgressive motivation would make a mark; and with minimal possibility of being embroiled by lure factors – even the lures of what people take to be secular religion and/or spirituality in the culture. So what has happened since that date? Writing of the "great changes" that have taken place in the country, Alturme refers to "a noticeable tendency toward church-free spirituality" (*ibid.*: 80); to the fact that "in the circumstances of religious freedom that followed the restoration of Estonia independence (in 1991) the number of people professing individual spirituality increased significantly" (*ibid.*: 85); and to the fact that "fundamental changes are [have been] taking place in Estonia. A new monistic/holistic paradigm has taken its place alongside the monotheistic/dualistic paradigm that has dominated for centuries as the foundation of Christianity" (*ibid.*: 92).

By 2005, Eurobarometer could report that 54 per cent of Estonians "believe there is some sort of spirit or life force", with just 16 per cent maintaining that they "believe there is a God" (Altnurme 2011; Eurobarometer 2005; Heelas forthcoming a). The former is the highest percentage in the EU; the latter the lowest.[2]

Those born between 1960 and 1980, respectively aged between 31 and 11 in 1991, provide the closest approximation to a blank sheet. And these people are precisely those whom Altnurme reports to be most New Age inclined at the time of her research (around 2000). The unintended consequence of the cultural engineering of the Soviet colonialists is to have triggered transgression. Out of something very close to a *tabula rasa*, many of the younger of the Soviet era, it seems, have moved on to adopt New Age "mythic patterns" (Altnurme 2011: 77).[3]

Elsewhere in northern Europe

Elsewhere in the EU countries of northern Europe, there is a greater chance that transgressions are (partly) due to spiritual–religious presence in the culture. This said, Sweden provides the next best opportunity for looking for evidence of the secular transgressing itself.[4]

Sweden's reputation as a secular nation can be traced back to at least the 1970s. During that decade, "church attendance and popularity were at a low ebb" (Scott 1988: 575); and it is virtually certain that "New Age" spirituality was only beginning to develop in the country. By 1990, though, RAMP (the Religious and Moral Pluralism survey) found that 36 per cent of Swedes selected a questionnaire option stating, "I believe that God is something within each person, rather than something out there": the third highest percentage of the eleven European countries surveyed by RAMP; the second highest in northern Europe, after Great Britain. (Unfortunately, Estonia was not included in the RAMP study.) Comparing the percentages of "God within" respondents with those selecting the questionnaire option "I believe in a God with whom I can have a personal relationship", Sweden comes top of the rankings: with "God within" at 36 per cent and "personal God" at 16 per cent, the "God within" percentage is 18 per cent higher than that for "personal God". Eurobarometer (2005), it can be added, reports that 53 per cent of Swedes agree with a "I believe there is some sort of spirit or life force" option: compared with the 23 per cent who select "I believe there is a God". It is also noteworthy that the percentage of Swedes participating in holistic, "New Age" mind–body–spirit practices is almost certainly higher than in countries like Britain (Heelas forthcoming a; and see Heelas & Houtman 2009 for discussion).

It looks as though up to 36 per cent of Swedes have transgressed in favour of "God within"; and/or up to 53 per cent in favour of "some sort of spirit or life force". And with "God within" formulations being relatively rare in the national culture, it very much looks as though transgressions of the kind under consideration are largely due to "independent invention". Unfortunately, there is not any longitudinal data on "God within"; and I have not been able to track down longitudinal data for "spirit or life force". In all likelihood, however, the greater the number of Swedes who have lost faith in the sacred of Christianity, the greater the scale of the transgressive.

Beyond Sweden and Estonia, evidence of secular transgression can be teased out from the kind of material drawn upon above, together with data on Complementary and Alternative Medicine (CAM), "spiritual but not religious" research, and the study of spiritual/religious experiences (see Heelas forthcoming a). From a comparative perspective, Dick Houtman and Stef Aupers (2007: 305) draw on World Values Survey longitudinal data, from fourteen countries (nine in northern Europe), to explore the statistical connection between the "weakening of the grip of tradition" (not least religious) and "a spiritual turn to the deeper layers of the self". Their main finding – that "the sacred becomes more and more conceived of as immanent and residing in the deeper layers of the self" (*ibid.:* 315) – supports the transgressive thesis. From a qualitative perspective, Abby Day's (2012) excellent essay illustrates the kind of approach which is most likely to elicit evidence of transgression. She sets the scene by citing a major transgressive theorist, Max Weber:

> ... the metaphysical needs of the human mind as it is driven to reflect on ethical and religious questions, driven not by material need but by an *inner compulsion* to understand the world as a meaningful cosmos and to take up a position toward it.
>
> (Weber 1922: 117; emphasis added)

Referring to her own research, Day writes that she "designed questions to begin discussion about what may or may not be an "inner compulsion" (Day 2012: 444). So long as discussions with people are carried out on a relatively systematic basis (female and male, from rich to poor, from conservative to liberal, etc.), Day is surely pointing the way to more sophisticated qualitative-cum-representational inquiry of the transgressive (or not).

As things stand, a great deal of material is available for the theorist of transgression. It is found in virtually every source one can think of: academic literature, popular magazines, newspapers, novels, music, and so forth. My own favourite is the autobiography. And the material covers everything, from the most tentative of transgressions (perhaps indicating the authoritative, or demanding, nature of the "hold" of the secular) to the most arresting. To illustrate the former, by drawing on Phil Zuckerman's discussion with Morten, a Danish man aged 55 from Aarhus, about belief in God:

> Uh-h-h ... I don't know. I don't know if ... well ... I haven't had ... I don't think I have experienced God, especially. But at the other hand, I have also ... if everything is just a matter of – if everything is just by chance, well, then, there may be something. But I don't know what it is and I haven't any idea of what it would be.
>
> (Zuckerman 2012: 15)

And to illustrate the latter, little could be more arresting than Bertrand Russell's autobiographical account of what he encountered when he finally moved beyond the world of his secularity: "In the union of love I have seen, in a mystic miniature, the prefiguring vision of the heaven that saints and poets have imagined. This is what I sought, and though it might seem too good for human life this is what – at last – I have found" (Russell 1975: 9).

There is a wealth of wonderful material. If only there were ethnographic studies of a kind that provided *representative* portrayals of the cultural, let alone addressed the easier task of systematically exploring more particular modes of life (among the retired, for example).

THE MEANING OF TRANSGRESSION

What does it mean to transgress the secular? This simple question raises immensely complicated issues; issues which remain unresolved. What is the secular? What is it to refer to "beyond" the secular?

Discussing the ideal of "a perfect society", and arguing that "it is towards the realization of this that all religions strive", one of the most significant passages of the "Conclusion" of Durkheim's *The Elementary Forms of the Religious Life* continues:

> But that society is not an empirical fact, definite and observable; it is a fancy, a dream with which men have lightened their sufferings, *but in which they have never really lived.* It is merely an idea which comes to express our more or less obscure aspirations towards the good, the beautiful and the ideal.
> (Durkheim [1912] 1971: 420; emphasis added)

The perfect society, that is the utopia of the sacred, has never existed in this world; and never will. The world in which all humans have to live is too imperfect.

In Durkheim's sense, in the "Conclusion" of *The Elementary Forms*, the sacred is the perfect. And the secular is the imperfect. Without going into all the evidence which supports this distinction, it seems to be safe to equate movement from the secular to the sacred with movement from the imperfect to the perfect. However, it would be silly to assume that every movement from the secular to the non-secular is towards or "into" the sacred. Consider the following extract from an interview with a Dane:

> I don't really think so much about it [God]. So I wouldn't know right now how to define it. But I believe in something. ... Well ... there's *more between heaven and earth* ... you know? And there's

75

more than I can understand, but I don't think it's a big father sitting up in the sky watching us and helping us, or whatever. But there's something … maybe … I don't know.

(Zuckerman 2012: 15; emphasis added)

It is virtually inconceivable that this interviewee is searching for *the* perfect. Yet to a degree, transgression is in evidence. So what is it to? As the interviewee observes, it is to a "more"; a term, it can be noted, favoured by William James ([1902] 1974).

The "more", "something there", "something more": terms that are frequently encountered among those who – to varying degrees – transgress the secular. And it is reasonable to suppose that terms like "the more" often refer to the less-than-perfect. (Think of the interviewee's *"between heaven and earth"*.) When transgression is to the less than perfect – to the imperfect beyond the imperfect of the secular – a tricky issue emerges: distinguishing between the imperfect of the secular and the less than perfect of the beyond. Suffice it to say, for present purposes, that those who favour terms like "the more" clearly have a distinction in mind: between everyday life (the secular) and that which lies beyond. It could well be said, at this point, that participant understanding trumps attempts at analytical clarity and simplicity of the secular–sacred/imperfect–perfect contrast. Whatever, distinctions there are: which justifies the notion of transgression.[5]

ON EXPLAINING TRANSGRESSION

What is it about the secular condition that can generate transgression? Of all the explanations which could be offered, one lies with the simple idea that ideals, in the context of the imperfect of the secular, play the pivotal role. Durkheim's idealism, in the sense of prioritizing the significance of ideals for sociocultural life, inspires his thesis. For Durkheim ([1912] 1971: 421), the process of "idealization" explains the shift from the "world" of the imperfect of the secular to the "world" of the perfect of the sacred. Belonging to the secular, ideals are imperfect. The fulfilment of secular ideals takes place through the ritual process. Ideals come true. Hence the sense of the sacred (*ibid.*: 420–27).

Applying Durkheim's approach to the generation of transgression in northern Europe today, the key lies with the transgressive power of ideals. In the secular world of the imperfect, ideals stand out as beacons of hope and promise. To be seriously engaged with secular ideals *is* to believe in, and pursue, the very best that the secular has to offer. Those engaged look to the future and the past. At one and the same time, their ideals promise and fail. People look forward to promises coming true. However, since secular ideals are imperfect, they are never "truly" fulfilled. Movement towards the realization of "wholeness" of being, "true" love, the perfect car, or "ultimate" satisfaction, is assailed by the accidents, contingencies, disruptions, distractions, flaws of everyday life. And given failure to fulfil, those engaged with pursuing any particular ideal look to the past: to reflect on their progress in achieving their ideals, what has held them back, what needs to be done to get *on* in the world. The sense of "the promised to come" is enhanced by the very failure of ideals. In face of failure, it becomes even more important to overcome adversity by following ideals "through" until they are achieved. And ideals throw the imperfections of the secular into relief. Relative to ideals, deprivation is cast in the spotlight. Relative to failure, the prospect of living with the imperfections of the secular becomes yet more fraught. Motivation to fulfil ideals is enhanced.

Since secular ideals cannot be fulfilled within the secular condition, one solution is to move "beyond". Secular ideals "point" out the beyond (in both senses of the word). Secular ideals prompt thoughts like "well, there must be something more to the ideal", a something that will bring about completion. The point is brought out by the secular-inclined "spiritual" humanist, Julian Huxley, in his ill-neglected *Religion Without Revelation* (1941: 25), where he writes of "the *infinity* of the ideal", as opposed to "the finite actuality of existence" (emphasis added). Secular ideals – like "true" love – are limitless. And so they can serve as "avenues" to the beyond (Taylor 2007: 533); to the "even better" ideal, perhaps the perfect of utopia itself. And why not? After all, secular ideals frequently proclaim, imply or image the perfect; contemporary "ideal-ogies" of human flourishing, including those embedded in consumptive and productive capitalism, and the culture of romance, call for completion. Progressivist personal culture constantly draws attention to the "something more to life"; to what Taylor (*ibid.*: 509) calls "the 'Peggy Lee' response" to the "inadequacy" of the secular (see also *ibid.*: 533). The "more": so "where is it?; how can I find it?; how can I experience it? I long for it, yearn for it" (see Heelas 2012a for further discussion).

On the embedded operation of ideals

The Romantic influenced Sapir-Whorf hypothesis – in its strongest form, the idea that language determines thought – remains too controversial to take fully on board. (See J. B. Carroll 1956 on the hypothesis itself.) Nevertheless, it is reasonable to suppose that the "graded" language use, so essential for the functioning of everyday – secular – life, plays an important role in guiding movement towards the beyond; and encourages it. Continua, like "impoverished, poor, getting by, reasonably well-off, wealthy, mega-wealthy", are embedded in language. Calibrated for life in the secular, language gradations point to their termini: not "mega-wealthy"; rather "infinitely wealthy". Ideals belong to, are constitutive of, gradations. And the imagination follows the dynamic "logic" of gradation. "Grades" stir the imagination: the finite exists; so something must be infinite, for instance. Guided by language use, the imagination is transported to the beyond; to what is pointed to by secular ideals. And since grades are composed of "motivational formations", they are bound up with desire, longing, yearning. Grades encapsulate hierarchies of cultural value: from the negatively evaluated of the imperfect to the most positive of the perfect. Each grade (like "wealthy") directs feeling-attention to the one above it ("fabulously wealthy"). The momentum of continua, the desire to pursue "higher grades" readily flows over into the beyond: sometimes as a pipe dream; in "New Age" prosperity spirituality, for example, as the experienced/actual reality of "infinite" wealth.

Recalling Bruce's *tabula rasa*, it is virtually inconceivable that people do not "think beyond"; minimally, in their cognitive imagination. It is virtually inconceivable that people are unaware of "the finite" (in some sense or another), without this promoting them to think of "the infinite" (in some sense or another). The die-hard atheist included, virtually everyone is transgressive in this sense. For some – atheists, the indifferent, "casual" agnostics – "thinking beyond" is of little or no value. To various degrees, and in various ways, though, it is highly likely that the majority of people are more attentive to, more feeling-full about, where language grades could lead.

On some trajectories of ideals

To really *feel* the ideal, to really *sense* that the secular cannot provide fulfilment: it is not surprising that so many "follow" their ideals into the beyond. Accordingly, more needs to be said about ideals at work; how ideals link up with various kinds of transgression. Unless I am very much mistaken, though, the sociology of ideals is not exactly flourishing. In northern Europe, there is little systematic evidence of the connections between particular secular circumstances and particular *beacons of promise*, as secular ideals can be called. Neither is there much systematic evidence bearing on the possibility of recurrent links between relatively specific ideals and ways of signally moving beyond the imperfect secular: for example, between particular ideals and expression of "God within and not without".

Nevertheless, it is possible to illustrate trajectories in action. Consider *health*. The secular context is concern about health. The language gradation runs through illness, somewhat better, normal health, better than normal, top of the world, to perfect health. The beacon is the cessation of illness, the best possible health, becoming as healthy as absolutely possible, experiencing health incarnate. Movement beyond is most likely to be to spiritual CAM. Or consider the *"only connect"* of humanist E. M. Forster. The secular context is provided by a sense of division or separation: the gulf between the "ego" of the "I" and everything else (a theme vividly conveyed by Sam Harris 2005); all that is implied by notions like "atomized", differentiated, "fragmented", "alienated", "homelessness", "anomie". The gradation runs from the divided, the divisive, through to engaging as much as possible, being "truly" engaged; or through to "utterly" absorbed; to the perfect relationality of "true" love. Resonating with the Neo-Platonic, the beacon shines with "unity", "union", "harmony", "balance", "integration". Movement could well be to spiritual yoga or akin. To give one more illustration, consider *the full*. The secular context is provided by feeling empty, feeling nothing, feeling "unfinished", as portrayed by Theodore Roszak in his *Unfinished Animal* (1975). The beacon signals "completion", "the complete", "whole", "finished", "the finish", "being all that one can be", "the ideal man" as Schiller put it. Movement is probably to those numerous practices which promise (Nietzschian) expansion of "life"; or to apprehensions-cum-comprehensions of the holistic, or cosmic, variety.

Further considerations on motivations of transgression

Three especially significant issues are raised by the "ideals approach". The first is explaining why by no means all secularists come to transgress. An obvious answer is that those who do not transgress are those "held" by the secular to a greater extent than, or in different ways to, those who "move on". People could be held back by being deeply absorbed in the secular, most obviously by consumer culture; or by strong faith in critical reason. The second is the closely related task of explaining why the significance of movement beyond varies so much. Relatively few follow their ideals right through to where they come true: as sacred. Why is this? Why are many more transgressors content with relatively minor "infringements"? An answer which addresses both these questions is that many are content with minor transgressions *until* their sense of the worthwhile is undermined. People remain content with the transgressive that belongs to a kind of a "waiting room": until, that is, they are aroused to go "further"; are aroused by the intrusion of circumstances that undermine the prospect of fulfilling ideals of the worthwhile within the secular. To illustrate: the ideal of vibrant family life; the emptying of the home (offspring going to university; divorce); then the mother or father, already "spiritual" in a subdued, "in the waiting" sense, taking up mind–body–spirit practices (see Heelas 2012a on the notion of the waiting room; and see also Heelas 2012b, 2012c.)

Vitalism The third issue raised by the ideals approach concerns its relationship with endogenous explanations. On first sight, endogenous theorizing – seeking to explain sources of transgression by reference to natural causes belonging to the human itself – is by no means the same as attributing sources of transgression to ideals, where transgression is "natural" in that it is motivated by ideals that belong to the very nature of the sociocultural itself. However, it is perfectly possible to combine the two: the endogenous of the intrinsic vitality of life (the primal sense of being alive) plus the exogenous of sociocultural ideals (required for *human* being).

In an illuminating discussion of endogenous approaches, Malcolm Hamilton (2012: 523) writes, "If man is an animal religiosum this suggests that religion is rooted in evolved *cognitive and emotional* structures of the human brain and mind" (emphasis added). Although cognitive processes might play a role in stimulating, or guiding, transgression, my very strong hunch is that the generative thrust of the endogenous primarily lies with the sense of inner vitality: with passions of the heart, energized feeling, Byronic sensation, emotionality, potency, impulse, pulse, the pulsating, the surge, Spinozan affective force; in the language of psychology, the physiological arousal of the somatic, the Freudian inchoate, transgressive id. Schleiermacher locates "individual" life within the dynamics of the whole, Feuerbach argues for the "projection" of human animation, Nietzsche stresses the life force of the ever expansive "will", Simmel grounds life spirituality in the "emotional reality" of "life itself", Simmel and his student/friend Buber attribute the sense of the "beyond-within" to the charged "I-Thou" relationship: all emphasize the raw vitality of life itself; the animus of life in the sense of the animating spirit or "intention". Or one can think of others aligned with the Romantic trajectory of modernity, including novelists like Nietzschian D. H. Lawrence on the natural instincts released as raptures of intimacy, or the "blood consciousness" of "The Plumed Serpent"; Diaghilev's ballet, *Le Sacre du printemps,* that climactic expression of the "pagan" torrent of raw earth; film-maker Leni Riefenstahl's *Triumph of the Will,* which, in one way or another, cannot but stir the elemental pulse of the viewer; Riefenstahl's astonishingly evocative photographs of the Nuba; Van Gogh's genius in divining the flow of the sacred within nature; the "sensational" (in both senses of the term) of Bacon's "raw life" (Deleuze 2005).

Without going too far down the path leading to the elusive vitalism of the Nietzschian or Bergsonian legacies, it is surely plausible to argue that the impact of being alive can inspire transgression of the secular.[6] Not given to hyperbole, a conservative not Romantic vitalist, sociologist Edward Shils (1967: 42) nevertheless writes, "The idea of sacredness is generated by the primordial experience of being alive, of experiencing the elemental sensation of vitality and of fearing extinction". Applying this account to secularistic northern Europe, the vital impulse, from within, serves as the source of force, the ground of the existential significance, that can prompt transgression. Beyond northern Europe, if vitalist theorizing of the kind put forward by Shils is valid, human nature itself is not a *tabula rasa.* Vitalistic springs of transgression are universal, and do not require the sociocultural – most especially ideals – for the transgressive impulse.

The vitalist approach is probably more effective, though, when it is combined with sociocultural factors. The argument is that the intensity of the sense of primal "agency" of the within naturally varies in accord with sociocultural circumstances. When the person is *absorbed* by "life-as" identity formations of secular or religious tradition, when the person is *devoted to* "outer-directed" progress laid out by the orthodox order of things, it is unlikely that the focus lies with what life *itself* has to offer. Life largely dwells with all that lies beyond the person. Conversely, the greater the extent to which values proclaim personal "life", the greater the likelihood of the vital impulse being experienced with intensity.

Cultural ideals enter the picture. Weber's "inner compulsion", better, "inner expression", flourishes with the contemporary "experience economy"; flourishes, that is, when life is idealized as the summation of "inner" experiences; the more arresting the better. When the person is valued as experiential, expressive, creative, autonomous, authorial or sovereign, the "raw" energy of life itself readily comes into play: to serve as an inner-dynamo, vitalizing agency (Heelas 2006). For those who do not treat this life as a preparation for the next, what matters is making the most of life in the here-and-now. Life is the most valuable *presence* of all. Hence the encapsulation of the force of experiential/existential life in popular notions like "universal life force", "something more to life", or "God-within". And hence the popularity of spiritual CAM in secularistic northern Europe. The sheer value of life instils thoughts like "life cannot go away", "life deserves the ultimate, the eternal" (see Taylor 2007: 720 on that "love" that seems "to demand eternity"; that is too valuable to die). The ideals of CAM are in tune with this value: cultivating and expressing life, vitalizing body and mind, perpetuating life, ideally for ever. By enabling participants to contact their "energy" (*the* key theme of CAM), life itself is put to work to fulfil ideals as "well" as absolutely possible. Expression of "energy" is guided by ideals; "energy" serves to fuel their transgressive thrust. Vitalism in action, with ideals helping ensure that action is not simply a matter of taking "the lid off the id".

Vitalism and the countercultural   If participants (including myself as a participant observer) are believed, the countercultural "sixties" was a time when "the vital" came to the fore: in the sense of a flourishing of selfhood, relationality and humanity as a whole; in the sense of tapping into the throb of life itself. With the rejection of, or alienation from, mainstream institutions – secular and religious – the vitality of "life" was not incorporated by the mainstream. Instead, untrammelled "inner potency" stood "revealed". In experience, naked *life* fuelled transgression. And the oppositional ideals of the counterculture affirmed the foundational value of inner life – wherever it might be experienced – as the source of the sense of being as alive as possible. Values like equality, freedom, expression, creativity, the sanctity of life or humankindness were celebrated – as affect-charged expressions of "life-in-all" (and see Tipton 1992). The powerful current flowing within, the power of ideals to arouse and direct elemental desires: hence the "sixties" as one of the great "ages" of the "yearn". Hence the pervasiveness of searching away from the secular, to truly experience the force of love, the sentiment of humankindness, for example.

With an eye on advancing the study of "New Age" spiritualities of life, cross-cultural inquiry (historical and contemporary) should illuminate ways in which ideals, with countercultural leanings, and the vital/ity of "life", can inter-fuse to generate, or sustain, the transgressive: most especially in the mode of spiritualities of the inner-life. Unless I am very much mistaken, social scientific inquiry – rather than theological or metaphysical argumentation – will add more and more substance to the idea that there is a perennial connection between spiritualities of life and the more countercultural. Suffice it to say, for the present, that it is hardly a coincidence that the signature tune of the rebellious Romanticism of the later eighteenth century, through to today, is the expression of vitality from within, in the context of oppositional ideals. It is not a coincidence that the Dionysian spirit of life flourishes among those who transgress the secular while also rebelling against soul-destroying conformity to religious tradition. It is not a coincidence that younger Estonians tend to transgress by affirming their own spirit of life, in terms of ideals opposing conformity to overarching systems.

Neither is it a coincidence that the nexus of countercultural values and a passionate inner life have flourished elsewhere in the world: the early flowering of de-traditionalized Sufism in Damascus; or, in contemporary Pakistan, the immensely popular Sufi, Bulleh Shah: a man who rejected mainstream Islam and promises of the secular; a counterculturalist who sought the ideal of "true love" by "going within"; a man who sought a "blank sheet" beyond the agitations, the irrelevant vitality, of the homelessness of the imperfect world of the secular – to be consumed by the sheer passion of the "Beloved" of the perfect life itself:

> I do not know how to swim. I have no oars and my boat is too old to be used.
> The whirlpools are furious, and I have no place to rest and stay.
> By crying my palms are hurt.
>
> I am consumed by the fire of separation and the longing for my Beloved.
> Crazy in Love I am standing and whisking away crows.
> (Ahmad 2003: 25)

In effect: the vitalization of the ideal of love; the idealization of vitalization; potent transgression.[7]

CONCLUSION

It is easy to argue the case for the self-sufficiency of the secular – and to do so apparently without bias. It is not so easy to argue the case for insufficiency. I trust that on the basis of exploratory examination of approximations to societal *tabulae rasae*, I have provided a reasonable argument in favour of the transgressive thesis: that imperfections, insufficiencies, limitations, failures of the secular can generate movement: beyond itself. Obviously, there is a great deal more to say about the strengths and weaknesses of the self-sufficiency and insufficiency arguments – and how, with modifications, the two can be combined in a variety of cultural settings.

Equally obviously, there is a great deal more to say about the human condition, taken to incorporate the sense of being alive and those ideals required for human life within the sociocultural, specifically the countercultural: to fuel transgression, of a spiritualities of life orientation, around the globe.

NOTES

1. For readers interested in a more sustained discussion of the evidence that underpins many of the points made in this essay, see Heelas (forthcoming a).
2. Similar percentages for Estonia are reported by a Eurobarometer poll of 2010. Thinking of church attendance, Eurobarometer finds that just 4 per cent of Estonians attended church services on a weekly basis in 2004, the lowest percentage of the ten countries which joined the EU in spring 2004 (Manchin 2004). Olaf Muller (2009: 73) reports that "in Estonia … church attendance rates have more or less remained as low as at the beginning of the 1990s".
3. Several essays in *Religion and Society in Central and Eastern Europe* provide more information on Estonia and serve to place the country in broader comparative context: see, for example, Olaf Muller (2011), Miklos Tomka (2010) and David Voas and Stefanie Doebler (2011). Broadly speaking, the argument advanced in the present essay is supported.
4. Within Europe as a whole, the Czech Republic is almost certainly the next best site for exploring the transgressive thesis. Further afield, Russia is one of the countries that could usefully be considered: see Heelas (forthcoming a).
5. Gordon Lynch (2012) is among those who attempt to dissolve the secular–sacred distinction, thereby ignoring what really matters: that the great majority of people distinguish between modes of meaningful reality; and that the secular is transgressed.
6. Daniel Heller-Roazen's *The Inner Touch: Archaeology of a Sensation* (2009) is a brilliant comparison of senses of being sentient; of what it can mean to feel that one is alive. For ways of connecting the vitalistic, as "affect", with the transgressive, in general, see Melissa Gregg and Gregory Seigworth (2010).
7. See Heelas (forthcoming b) for Sufi transgression in Pakistan that accords with the kind of inner-life, vitalistic perennialism under consideration.

5. HIDING IN PLAIN SIGHT: THE ORGANIZATIONAL FORMS OF "UNORGANIZED RELIGION"

Ann Taves and Michael Kinsella

There has been much debate over whether New Age spirituality (NAS) is a useful category and, if so, how best to characterize the phenomena clustered under that heading. Historically minded scholars generally agree, however, on the value of distinguishing between narrower and broader uses of the term "new age". In the narrower sense, it refers above all to ideas in the writings of post-Theosophist Alice Bailey (1880–1949), which were picked up by the new age networks of the 1950s, many of them UFO related, and transformed into a more activist form by 1960s utopian communities, most notably Findhorn. The movement, narrowly conceived, was British-based and relied upon occultist traditions that had long been influential there (Melton 1995; Sutcliffe 2003a; Albanese 2007; Hanegraaff 2009: 345). In a more general sense, scholars have used "new age" as a catch-all term for the much more extensive and complex "cultic milieu" of the 1980s and beyond, which was dominated "by the so-called metaphysical and New Thought traditions typical of American alternative culture" (Hanegraaff 2009: 344–5). Sutcliffe depicts this as "a popular hermeneutical shift in the meaning of 'New Age' … [such that] at the turn of the 1970s, … 'New Age' as apocalyptic emblem of the near future gave way to 'New Age' as humanistic idiom of self-realisation in the here-and-now" (Sutcliffe 2003a: 5). Although many people self-identified as new age in the general sense in the 1980s, the number of self-identified "new agers" declined in the 1990s with most becoming just "spiritual" as the movement moved "from its traditional status as a counterculture" and into the mainstream (Hanegraaff 2009: 345; Albanese 2007: 496–516; MacKian 2012).

In this more general sense, scholars tend to characterize new age spirituality in terms of:

1. individualism
2. shopping, spiritual supermarket
3. seeking, and

4. in-built resistance to organization (Hanegraaff 2009: 351) or at least to vertical (hierarchical) organization, as opposed to lateral-networked organization (Sutcliffe 2003a: 224–5).

For Hanegraaff, the central feature of NAS broadly defined is "a basic mythology that narrates the growth and development of the individual soul through many incarnations and existences in the direction of ever-increasing knowledge and spiritual insight" (2009: 352). Attention to one's own "inner voice" is not only central to the myth, as Hanegraaff depicts it, but the means by which the individuals navigate their way through the spiritual marketplace. As researchers, we should acknowledge, however, that practitioners do not characterize themselves as consumers (Heelas 2008: 81–96). In so far as our goal in drawing upon the marketplace metaphor is to illuminate new lines of inquiry and not just to disparage practitioners, the single-minded scholarly focus on practitioners as consumers is unduly limiting. Markets are not simply made up of consumers, but also of producers, who create businesses, manufacture and promote products, and compete for the loyalty of their customers.

When Matthew Wood argues that much of what is commonly referred to as new age spirituality should not be viewed as a distinct area of belief and practice, he does so on the grounds that these beliefs and practices are "non-formative" (2007: 9). In making his case, Wood again highlights the NAS resistance to organization but he does so, at least tacitly, from the point of view of producers and promoters. Because people are free to pick and choose based on their own individual tastes, "authorities [are unable, he argues] … to shape people's and organizations' subjective identities and habitus" in any definitive way (Wood 2009: 243). Theoretically, he suggests, authorities could do so in three ways:

1. by structuring legitimation by "providing common standards for practice, belief, dialogue and contestation"
2. by managing experience, "especially through what may be called control over the means of possession", and
3. establishing careers of participation "that enabled those involved to be classified, assessed and treated in appropriate ways" (*ibid.*: 243).

The ability of authorities to shape subjective identities and habitus in these ways thus presupposes structures that legitimate standards, authenticate experience, and authorize specialized roles.

Wood characterizes channelling, which he views as central to NAS, as non-formative based on his attendance at two one-day channelling workshops conducted in Nottinghamshire by pseudonymous American channellers (*ibid.*: 101–19). Anthropologist Adam Klin-Oron (2011) reported similarly superficial effects of a one-day channelling workshop in Israel.

Klin-Oron, however, followed up on the one-day workshop by participating in a ten-week training class. In contrast to the one-day workshop, the ten-week training class was designed and did in fact train people to become (professional) channellers and, in doing so, it managed experience, formed practitioners, and established careers of participation. It was, in short, formative in terms of all the criteria that Wood sets out. This suggests that simply referring to NAS as non-formative is too simplistic.

Sutcliffe, as already noted, takes a more nuanced position on the organizational question, highlighting the presence of

> a large amorphous collectivity, insufficiently institutionalized or internally cohesive to develop singular goals or a falsifiable boundary, [that] remains to be accounted for. Its typical fora are lectures, workshops, small groups and societies, and calendrical and ad hoc gatherings; a few dedicated buildings, including the administrative centers of groups and societies, as well as libraries, bookshops, and other commercial premises; and the open-ended networks of association – that loosely articulate these relatively simple, but immensely flexible and resilient, cultural institutions.   (Sutcliffe 2004: 479)

Sutcliffe is right that we have not accounted for this amorphous collectivity well-enough. If formation (or formativeness) is linked to authority and structure, we need to look more carefully at how this "amorphous collectivity" is organized in order to assess the extent to which it has the capacity to form individuals or groups.

Research on new age, metaphysical and occult traditions (e.g. Hanegraaff 1996; Albanese 2007; Hammer 2001), however, has emphasized the history of ideas and largely overlooked the history of organizational forms. Sociologists of religion still tend to discuss "organized religion" in light of variations on the church–sect–cult/NRM typology, although they have shifted in recent decades to the marketplace analogy (Roof 1999) and, most recently, to the idea of networked religion (York 1995; Sutcliffe 2004; H. Campbell 2012). As Wood (2007: 4) points out, these phenomena can be studied in either of two complementary ways: by focusing on networked interconnections between individuals, groups and events as a whole, or on the different groups and events, each with their "own histories, social organizational and authority structures, beliefs and practices". While the former is particularly suited to ethnographic methods, the latter requires an investigation of routes of dissemination across time and space. As the contrast between Wood's and Klin-Oron's research on channellers suggests, the formativeness of channelling practices cannot necessarily be decided based on what is available in a single location. Following Sutcliffe's lead (2003a), we will learn more if we look at the actual organizational forms adopted by the traditions that fed into NAS whether narrowly or broadly conceived. Doing so, will not only allow us to return to the question of formativeness with a more nuanced eye, but will also allow us to reassess the way that narrow conceptions of what constitutes "organized religion" have blinded us to the historical range of "religious organizations".

The groups that fed into what has been called "new age spirituality" tended to draw on organizational forms that historically coexisted alongside and interpenetrated rather than competed with "official" religious organizations. While attitudes toward "organized religions" varied among these groups and among the individuals within them, most of the organizations were esoteric and/or universalist in their theology and, thus, generally viewed their organizations as compatible with membership in "organized religions". They, thus, constituted an organizational "third way" that with some exceptions did not adopt a formal "church" structure, did not view themselves as "organized religions", and for the most part were not viewed that way by others. Characterizing themselves variously as nonsectarian, spiritual, metaphysical or occult, they viewed themselves neither as "[organized] religions" (the first way) nor completely non-religious (the second way). Preoccupation with the church–sect–cult typology has hidden them from sociological view, obscuring the extent to which organizations of this sort not only provide the deep structure of the amorphous collectivity we call "new age spirituality" but also prefigure many of the features of the "networked religion" of the Internet era (H. Campbell 2012). As scholars, we have been unduly captivated by these traditions' rhetorical critique of "organized religion" and have failed to recognize the various alternative forms of organization they adopted in order to distinguish themselves from it. The argument unfolds in three parts in which we consider the organizational forms adopted by several ostensibly "unorganized" groups, first, in relationship to the "organized religion" of their era, then in relation to extant concepts in the sociology of religion, and finally in relation to their capacity to form individuals or groups.

PART I: ORGANIZATIONAL FORMS

There are many places we could begin with an analysis of this sort, but since the need is for greater historical and contextual specificity, we will focus on three movements – Spiritualism, Theosophy, and Metaphysical Healing – that had their proximate origins in the United States and are widely recognized as contributing to what we call NAS, and then consider the organizational form developed by Alcoholics Anonymous in the twentieth century. Alcoholics Anonymous and the twelve step movements derived from it are not usually linked with new age spirituality but definitely adopted a "third way" form of organization and, thus, provide an illuminating comparison when considering the formative potential of these practices.

Spiritualism

The rappings produced by the Fox sisters in 1848 in upstate New York are generally recognized as launching the modern spiritualist movement. The characteristic form of the movement, however, took several years to emerge and resulted through "the fusion of *ideas* about spirits of the dead and the *practices* of animal magnetism" (Taves 1999: 166–73). The practices associated with animal magnetism or mesmerism, in which practitioners demonstrated the effects of an unseen force (whether magnetic, mental, cosmic, etc.) of one person on another, took three basic forms: public lectures and demonstrations, small groups (circles or séances), and therapeutic dyads. In the 1840s and 50s in both England and the US, peripatetic lecturers publicly demonstrated the power of mesmerism and related phenomena, such as phrenology and clairvoyance. Lectures were typically held at literary, scientific, or "mechanics" institutes, lyceums, and guildhalls, rather than at churches. They often precipitated the formation of small groups intent on investigating the phenomena for themselves as well as dyadic consultations between a practitioner and a client (Winter 1998: 109–24, 137–62; Oppenheim 1985: 216–19). All the practices, which ranged from diagnosis and healing of disease to displays of information regarding individual lives or unseen objects, were viewed as experimental, investigatory and demonstrative. Modern spiritualism, as a movement, built on these practices, placing small group meetings (referred to as circles or séances) at the centre of spiritualist practice (*ibid.*: 217–27; B. Carroll 1997: chs 6–7) and utilizing lectures, often held in lyceums, as a means of publicity and recruitment. Like their mesmeric predecessors, Spiritualist lectures were generally held in non-church venues, while circles met in domestic spaces. Spiritualist circles enabled different levels of involvement. Investigators could attend intermittently out of curiosity. Others could attend regularly to establish and maintain contact with spirits through the mediums in the group. Still others could discover mediumistic abilities, cultivate them within the context of the group and launch into a mediumistic career giving public lectures, founding new groups and/or advertising their services in spiritualist periodicals (Braude 1989: 82–98, Taves 1999: 177–80).

Spiritualists held varying attitudes toward the churches. Most were critical of "organized religion", criticizing religious organization as "inherently tyrannical and antirepublican" (B. Carroll 1997: 39). They were particularly critical of the perceived "formalism" of religious institutions, as well as their reliance on professional clergy. Like many present-day groups their rhetoric was individualistic and anti-organizational. Despite a great deal of anti-ecclesial rhetoric, Spiritualists' attitudes towards "organized religion" were not monolithic and did not necessarily preclude membership in the organizations they criticized (*ibid.*: 39–44). Some severed ties with their congregations and denominations, while others did not. The more liberal denominations, such as Unitarians, Universalists and Quakers, were generally more open (Braude 1989: 43–9, B. Carroll 1997: 45–7) and many Spiritualists remained within their denominations in order to promote a spiritualist interpretation of Christianity (Taves 1999: 181–90). The spiritualist interpretation of Christianity was universalistic, which was one of the reasons, along with its populist membership, that spiritualism made greater inroads into Universalism than other liberal churches (Braude 1989: 47). But many Spiritualists went beyond Christian Universalism to view Spiritualism as a universal form of religion and the spirits as a universal doorway to the other world and the common denominator of all religions. In doing so, Spiritualists promoted a new understanding of universality as persuasive testimony to truth rather than as a degrading lack of uniqueness, thus, modelling a universalistic stance that other third way organizations would adopt as well (Taves 1999: 190–200, 348–51).

Spiritualists in the UK and the US were slow to organize beyond the state and local level. Ann Braude analyses the heated debates over whether to create a national organization at the first national convention in 1864 (Braude 1989: 162–73). Some Spiritualists in Britain and the United States eventually began to form churches, some of which affiliated with national organizations such as the National Federation of Spiritualists, founded in the UK in 1891, and the National Spiritual Association of Churches (NSAC), founded in the US in 1893. NSAC, which incorporated as a nonprofit religious organization, touts its status as "a legitimate religious organization" and now limits membership to persons who are "not a member of any other Spiritualist Church, or Spiritualist organization which grants certificates, or a member of another denomination".[1] NSAC, in other words, has become an "organized religion".

Theosophy

The Theosophical Society, founded in 1875 by Helena Blavatsky and Henry Olcott, followed a different pattern, choosing to adopt the lodge structure of the fraternal organizations (e.g. Freemasons, Oddfellows, Knights of Pythias, the Grange) and build on the esoteric ritual foundations already developed by the Freemasons. The fraternal lodges that flowered in the eighteenth and nineteenth centuries were derived from the medieval craft guilds of the stonemasons, whose lodges provided housing while working away from home (B. F. Campbell 1980; Greer 1998: 1–22; Mazet 1995: 253–62). The lodge structure was subsequently adopted by a number of esoteric groups with connections to Theosophy and Freemasonry, such as the Hermetic Order of the Golden Dawn, some forms of Martinism and the Anthroposophical Society.

Other esoteric groups that draw from Theosophy have adopted an educational format (B. F. Campbell 1980). Heindel's Rosicrucian Fellowship (founded in 1909) organizes its students in centres and study groups. Steiner reorganized the Anthroposophical Society in 1923 around the newly founded School for Spiritual Science. Alice Bailey set up the Lucis Trust as an educational charity in 1922 and founded the Arcane School, which uses a correspondence school format, as a subsidiary in 1923.

These organizations are universalistic in their theology. Guild structure presupposed a training model that proceeded in stages beginning with apprenticeship, fellowship and then mastery. The educational model was also structured around levels, such as classes and grades. Both the guild and educational models were easily recast as spiritual training programmes. The combination of universalistic theology and spiritual training within a "non-religious" organizational format allowed them to create a recognizable legal entity, differentiate themselves from "religions" and "sects", and conceptualize dual membership. Mazet (1995: 248) illustrates a typical conceptual pattern when he states: "Freemasonry is definitely not a religion, but its members must be religious men. They may belong to different religions, and they must be tolerant of others' opinions. It is forbidden to discuss religious matters during masonic work". At the same time, he continues: "They [Masons] must all believe in God, the Great Architect of the Universe, and in the immortality of the soul. They must also believe that God reveals himself to humanity in the volume of the sacred law, which is for each of them the sacred book of his own faith, on which he takes the oath that bind him to the order". In parallel fashion, the Constitution and Rules of the Theosophical Society (1891) stated that the Society was "absolutely unsectarian, and no assent to any formula of belief, faith or creed shall be required as a qualification of membership; but every applicant and member must lie in sympathy with the effort to create the nucleus of an Universal Brotherhood of Humanity" (Olcott 1891). The Anthroposophical Society and the Arcane School both describe themselves as nonsectarian and offer membership regardless of religious affiliation.[2]

Metaphysical healing

We can identify another basic organizational form – the dyadic relationship of healer and patient – which, like Spiritualism, also built on mesmeric practice, but focused more on the healing powers associated with the unseen (mesmeric) forces than on contacting spirits. Phineas P. Quimby (1802–66), who described himself initially as a mesmerist, then a mental healer, who used the power of mind alone to heal, is often cited as the father of the metaphysical healing tradition that encompassed both Christian Science and New Thought and deeply infused NAS broadly conceived. As an independent practitioner, Quimby taught Mary Baker Eddy, founder of Christian Science, as well as Warren Felt Evans, whose writings, which drew from Christianity and Theosophy, informed the New Thought movement. Eddy's renegade students, Ursula Gestefeld and Emma Curtis Hopkins, in turn taught others. Hopkins, who blended Eddy with Evans, was particularly important, training scores of students, who in turn founded New Thought schools, churches, associations and periodicals (Satter 1999; Albanese 2007: 283–329).

The metaphysical healing tradition centred on teacher-healers who positioned themselves in relation to various recognizable professional roles – author-publishers, teachers, medical healers, and clergy – and, given their orientation, created books and periodicals, fee-for-service healing practices, schools, associations and/or churches. While church-like organizations founded by metaphysical healers, including Mary Baker Eddy's Church of Christ, Scientist and New Thought denominations, such as the Unity School of Christianity, the Church of Divine Science and the Church of Religious Science, are typically treated as organized religions, scholars have had difficulty categorizing metaphysical healers who adopted other organizational models. As Paul Johnson (1998: 1–3) has noted, independent practitioners, such as Edgar Cayce (1877–1945), whose influence on modern religious history was arguably as great as many founders of religious movements, have posed a particular challenge.

With the rise of the holistic healing movement in the twentieth century, some metaphysical healers have adopted medical models of professional organization and training. The National Center for Complementary and Alternative Medicine distinguishes between five healing modalities many of which involve some sort of spiritual component. Those classified as "energy medicine" draw from the metaphysical healing tradition and are often discussed under the "new age" heading.[3] Therapeutic Touch and Healing Touch illustrate the new organizational possibilities available to metaphysical healers who align themselves with the holistic health movement. Therapeutic Touch, co-developed in the 1970s by Dr Dolores Krieger, who has a doctorate in nursing, and Dora Kunz, a "natural healer" and Theosophist, has a membership organization, the Therapeutic Touch International Association, with a board of trustees that oversees a credential process for TT Practitioners and TT Teachers (Albanese 2007: 508–9).[4] Janet Mentgen, who began developing healing touch in the 1980s, established a certificate programme, certified by the American Holistic Nurses Association in 1993. She founded Healing Touch International as a non-profit educational and membership organization in 1996 and the Healing Touch Worldwide Foundation, a non-profit charitable organization in 1997. Healing Touch sponsors classes, certifies practitioners and instructors, and holds annual regional and worldwide conferences. HT courses are open to "all nurses, massage therapists, body therapists, counselors, psychotherapists, physicians, other allied healthcare professionals as well as individuals who desire an in-depth understanding and practice of healing work using energy based concepts and principles".[5]

Alcoholics Anonymous

In the 1930s, the founders of Alcoholics Anonymous Bill Wilson and Dr Bob Smith created a distinctive organizational structure built around small groups, initially modelled on the evangelical Protestant Oxford Group, adapting the Oxford Group's "Six Principles" to create AA's "Twelve Steps". In editing the "Big Book" and the Twelve Steps outlined within it, participants in the movement explicitly debated how they wanted to position the book. According to Bill Wilson, who produced the initial draft,

> Fitz wanted a powerfully religious document; Henry and Jimmy would have none of it. They wanted a psychological book which would lure the reader in … As we worked feverishly on this project Fitz made trip after trip to New York from his Maryland home to insist on raising the spiritual pitch of the AA Book. Out of this debate came the spiritual form and substance of this document, notably the expression, "God *as we understand Him*," which proved to be a ten-strike. As umpire of these disputes, I was obliged to go pretty much down the middle, writing in spiritual rather than religious or entirely psychological terms.
>
> (Anon. 1957: 17)

With the publication of the Big Book in 1939, AA positioned itself as spiritual rather than religious (Fuller 2001: 112–15) and, with the substitution of "awakening" for "experience" in the second printing, the Twelve Steps were expressly conceived as a path to a "spiritual awakening" (Step Twelve).

The most distinctive innovations in organization form, however, came in the 1940s with the formulation of the Twelve Traditions (Anon. [1952] 1981). Developed through a process of trial and error (and a desperation born of addiction), they place the "common welfare" of the group as a whole above that of the individual (Tradition One). As AA commentary explains, however, AA explicitly rejected a top down hierarchical structure governed by a central authority as a means of maintaining the unity of the group, instead locating authority in "a loving God as He may express Himself in our group conscience", that is, in the "conscience" of the local AA group (Tradition Two). Group membership was open to all who wanted "to stop drinking" (Tradition Three), regardless of "race, creed, politics, and language" (*ibid*.: 141). Tradition Nine proclaimed that "AA, as such, ought never be organized; but we may create service boards or committees directly responsible to those they serve". The commentary on the ninth tradition declares AA an exception to the general rule that "power to direct or govern is the essence of organization everywhere" (*ibid*.: 172–3), arguing that those elected to serve at the local, intergroup or worldwide level were caretakers and expediters who could at most make suggestions. While AA's claim that it is "a society without organization" (*ibid*.: 175) seems unwarranted, characterizing itself as "without organization" served to position it among the third way organizations.

Whether these organizations are considered "new age" or not (and AA and other twelve step programmes generally are not), they all involve some sort of spiritual or esoteric practice, accept members regardless of religious affiliation and, with a few exceptions such as NSAC, position themselves in contrast to "organized religions". They vary, however, in the emphasis that they place on local groups, therapeutic dyads and public education. While Healing Touch practitioners meet with other HT practitioners in the context of training groups, conferences and continuing education workshops, their practice is primarily dyadic. HT stands in marked contrast to AA and the other twelve step programmes, where local groups constitute the heart of the movement. Although AA produces a great deal of literature and periodically holds conventions, "working the programme" means going to meetings. Nineteenth-century spiritualist circles and fraternal orders were also small group oriented. Theosophists and the more occult groups varied. Although many were founded on the lodge model, many adopted an education model instead or as well and, depending on the nature of the school and its role in the organization, placed more or less emphasis on small groups.

As we have seen, the third way type organizations generally viewed themselves as "nonsectarian" due to their esoteric and/or universalist presuppositions about spirituality and/or religion. Their organizational structure, membership requirements and relationship with "organized religions" were congruent with their inclusivist theological outlook. The attitudes of "organized religions" towards these groups in turn varied depending on their theology. The Roman Catholic Church prohibited involvement in the Masonic and other non-Catholic "secret societies" (Gruber 1910) and encouraged the formation of specifically Catholic fraternal orders. The Second Plenary Council in Baltimore (1866) discouraged Catholics from attending spiritualist seances and the Vatican condemned "spiritistic practices" in 1898 (Pace 1912). The Catholic hierarchy did not prohibit Catholics from joining AA, however, due to AA's careful solicitation of input from Catholic leaders and their successful effort to position the fellowship as "spiritual but not religious".

Protestant attitudes toward these groups varied much more widely. During the early nineteenth century (post-1826), there was considerable anti-masonic sentiment among American Protestants, especially those in more conservative denominations with Calvinist roots (Goodman 1988: 60). Anti-masonic Protestants were hostile towards dual membership and "attempted to force people to choose" (*ibid.*: 61). Still most men who joined fraternal orders were Protestant church members. Later in the nineteenth century, many Protestants not only joined fraternal orders, they also attended spiritualist seances, read New Thought periodicals and, of course, beginning in the 1930s, joined AA.

PART II: THIRD WAY ORGANIZATIONAL FORMS
AND THE SOCIOLOGY OF RELIGION

In light of this survey of a few examples of third way forms of organization, we can return to the traditional church–sect–cult typology that still structures much of the sociological discussion of organizational form. Although there have been numerous efforts to refine the church–sect–cult typology (for an overview, see Roberts & Yamane 2012: 175–85), we focus on Stark and Bainbridge's distinctions between audience cults, client cults and cult movements, since their distinctions are embedded in a larger theory of religion and are often used to characterize new age spirituality.

Audience cults

Stark and Bainbridge (1985) characterize audience cults as:

> the most diffuse and least organized kind of cult … Sometimes some members of this audience actually may gather to hear a lecture. But there are virtually no aspects of formal organization to these activities, and membership remains at most a consumer activity. Indeed, cult audiences often do not gather physically but consume cult doctrines entirely through magazines, books, newspapers, radio and television. (Stark & Bainbridge 1985: 126)

None of the groups just discussed could be characterized simply as "audience cults", although all disseminated literature and most held public lectures or workshops that would have allowed some to participate at an audience level. From the point of those promoting these traditions, lectures, workshops and texts can be seen as means of recruiting new members to their organizations and/or initiating a process of initiation or training. Stark and Bainbridge do not discuss those who give the lectures, write the books or run the workshops. As producers, they might be deeply involved in an organization, regularly attending meetings, assuming leadership roles, and/or legitimated, credentialed or certified through various organizationally-recognized means.

Client cults and client movements

Stark and Bainbridge's distinction between client cults and client movements is even more problematic, due in large part to their faith in Durkheim's assertion that "there is no church of magic" (Stark & Bainbridge 1985: 214). Initially, however, they seem to characterize the client cult simply in terms of a dyadic relationship, such that "the relationship between those promulgating cult doctrine and those partaking of it most closely resembles the relationship between therapist and patient, or between consultant and client. Considerable organization may be found among those offering the cult service, but clients remain little organized" (*ibid.*: 26). So far this definition fits the format of independent metaphysical healers and Therapeutic and Healing Touch practitioners pretty well.

Because Stark and Bainbridge define these client services as "magical" and assume that there is "no church of magic", they do not distinguish between dyads and small groups. Small group participants are defined as "clients" rather than "members" as long as they "retain their participation in an organized religious group" (*ibid.*: 29). A cult movement is not born, according to Stark and Bainbridge, until a cult leader "is able to get his or her clients to ... sever their ties with other religious organizations" (*ibid.*: 29). This formulation hides non-exclusive groups from view and overlooks the subjective views of participants, many of whom would undoubtedly identify themselves as group members and feel a sense of group identity. In defining membership in terms of exclusivity, Stark and Bainbridge adopt criteria that the groups themselves do not. In doing so, they obscure the less familiar but potentially stable, intentional forms of organization we have been considering here. Although Stark and Bainbridge's elaboration of the church–sect–cult typology is only one of many efforts at refinement, the entire effort seems mired in problematic presuppositions of the sort just illustrated.

Dyads and small groups

If we jettison distinctions between sects and cults and between religion and magic and simply distinguish between dyadic relationships and small groups, we can recognize the role that dyadic relationships play and have played in many of these organizations. Thus, Spiritualist mediums advertised their services (as diagnosticians, healers and channellers of spirits), as did other more esoteric practitioners and metaphysical healers. The twelve step programmes encourage newcomers to find a sponsor, thus establishing a dyadic relationship with someone who can help them work the programme. This should not detract, however, from observing the constitutive role that non-exclusive small groups – Spiritualist circles, Theosophist lodges or AA meetings – play in many of these organizations. Nor, of course, should it detract from examining how those who maintain multiple memberships characterize themselves, for example, as Christian Spiritualists or Buddhist Twelve Steppers.

Movements and networks

Whether and/or at what point something should be called a movement is also fraught with controversy. Given that movements are often defined in terms of networks and that both new age spirituality and religion in the Internet age are often characterized in terms of networks, we focus here on networks rather than movements. We see similarities between the way people have moved back and forth between third way and "organized religion" and the way people shift between religion online and offline.

H. Campbell (2012) identifies five key traits of the "networked religion" that emerge as people move on and offline – networked community, storied identities, shifting authority, convergent practice and multisite reality. In contrasting today's "religious social networks" with "traditional religious rituals and institutions" (*ibid.*: 66), Campbell's modern-traditional dichotomy obscures the obvious continuities between online religion and third way organizational forms. In both cases, the emergence of new sites of activity that do not prohibit multiple membership allows for:

1. the creation of loose social networks with varying levels of religious affiliation and commitment;
2. fluid, potentially hybrid, multiple and/or shifting, rather than static, identities;
3. challenges to and levelling of authority;
4. beliefs and practices that draw from multiple sources and lead to the emergence of new hybrid forms; and
5. multisite realities, such that practices in different contexts are simultaneously connected and mediated.

Taking inspiration from research on Internet religion, we can bring the questions scholars are raising about the relationship between online and offline religion to the study of "organized religion" and the ostensibly "unorganized" third way sector, asking how people relate them, how they understand themselves, how authority is shifted and pluralized, and so on. In light of even this preliminary analysis of third way forms of religious organization, we can ask how new these ostensibly new Internet related developments actually are. Campbell highlights the distinctive features of the Internet as "flattening of traditional hierarchies, encouraging instantaneous communication and response, and widening access to sacred or once-private information" (*ibid.* 68). To what degree were these features already present in some third way organizations long before the Internet? To what extent were features built into the structure of the Internet prefigured by the third way organizations' theological commitment to universalism and "nonsectarian" membership policies? Campbell suggests that the rise of online religion poses challenges to "conventional forms of connection, hierarchy, and identity management" (*ibid.*: 68). Are these not precisely the features that have left scholars struggling to understand "new age religion" and led Wood to characterize NAS as "non-formative"?

PART III: FORMATIVENESS REVISITED

This analysis suggests that, while characterizing NAS or simply contemporary spirituality as "non-formative" is far too simplistic, third way organizational forms, like online forms of religiosity, do raise important questions regarding both the formative capacity of organizations and the formative process itself. In considering these questions, we should resist caricaturing the formative capacity of "organized religion" and, following the lead of the Internet researchers, compare the capacities of so-called organized and third way groups. In practice, the formative capacities of the more traditional "organized religions" are also limited by various contextual factors. Thus, for example, the Catholic Church has the most power to form its members when membership is mandatory, the process begins in childhood, and the family is supportive and itself properly "formed" in the eyes of the institution. In the absence of these supporting factors, the Catholic Church also has difficulties forming its members.

Religious orders offer a more precise comparison. Both offer in-depth spiritual formation intended primarily for adults. Both allow for varying levels of affiliation and commitment. Catholics and non-Catholics can read books on Benedictine or Jesuit spirituality, attend retreats or workshops on these spiritual paths, and Catholics, if they are sufficiently motivated, can become lay affiliates or enter into the intensive formation process required of full-fledged members of the various orders. In doing so, they take on dual membership in their order and in the Catholic Church. Consideration of the difficulties that even the most traditional religious institutions face in forming their membership should alert us to the many factors that effect formation. Most crucially, just as charismatic leadership depends as much on followers' willingness to follow as leaders' ability to lead, so too the ability to form depends as much on people's willingness and interest in being formed as it does in the formative capacities of authorities. In so far as an individual or a group can formulate a coherent formative path (or at least give that appearance), the ability and capacity to form depends largely on the willingness of others to enter into the process under their guidance or direction.

We can return in light of these general observations to Wood's claim that channellers, who in his view epitomize NAS, are unable to form either individuals or groups due to their inability to structure legitimation by:

1. providing common standards
2. managing experience, and
3. establishing careers of participation (Wood 2009: 243).

Channellers, however, do not need to establish common standards for channelling any more than Buddhist teachers need to establish common standards for authenticating enlightenment experiences. Buddhist enlightenment is transmitted through lineages, passed down from teacher to student; lineages may hold to different standards and do not necessarily recognize the authenticity of the transmission through other lineages. Nor would we expect experience to be managed or careers established via one-day workshops on Buddhist or Christian practice. Although opportunities for in-depth formation as a channeller may not be available in the locations that Wood studied, they clearly are available in Israel, as Klin-Oron's (2011) research attests. Indeed, he found the training offered in the ten-week class he attended so formative that midway through he, as a skeptical, secular anthropologist, felt compelled to choose whether he was going to continue with his dissertation (and formation as an anthropologist) or throw himself completely into the training in order to become a professional channeller. Of his class of trainees, he was the only one who chose not to launch a professional practice!

In sum, we should not let participants' antipathies towards "organized religion" nor well-worn sociological typologies blind us to the organizational forms that NAS practitioners and their historical precursors have hidden in plain sight. To assess the formativeness of these groups and practices, we need a better understanding of formative processes based on nuanced comparisons across traditions, between types of groups and practices, and in both online and offline contexts. To do justice to the organizational question, we must supplement ethnographic network modelling with historical developmental analysis.

NOTES

1. See www.nsac.org/nsac.php (accessed August 2012).
2. See http://en.wikipedia.org/wiki/Anthroposophical_Society#Principles (accessed August 2012) and www.lucistrust.org/en/arcane_school (accessed August 2012)
3. See www.ahna.org (accessed August 2012).
4. See http://therapeutic-touch.org.
5. www.healingtouchprogram.com (accessed August 2013).

6. NARROW NEW AGE AND BROAD SPIRITUALITY: A COMPREHENSIVE SCHEMA AND A COMPARATIVE ANALYSIS

Norichika Horie

In this chapter, I will compare the interest in New Age spirituality in Japan, the US and the UK, and I will clarify the relationship of the two concepts of New Age and spirituality, before proceeding to make a classification of four types of spirituality.

HOW TO UNDERSTAND "OLD AGE" SPIRITUALITY

Shintō, Animism and spirituality

I am researching individualistic or non-religious "spirituality" in Japan. This is called *seishin sekai* (精神世界), which would be translated as the "Spiritual World" or "Inner Space" in English (Shimazono 2004). In addition, since 2000, the word "spiritual" has been used frequently as a noun, *supirichuaru* (スピリチュアル), in Japanese without being translated (Horie 2012). The Japanese "spiritual" is affected by the best-selling New Age books published in English-speaking countries. For example, *Out on a Limb* (MacLaine 1984, Japanese translation in 1986), *Many Lives, Many Masters* (Weiss 1988, Japanese translation in 1991), *The Celestine Prophecy* (J. Redfield 1993, Japanese translation in 1994) and *Spontaneous Healing* (Weil 1995, Japanese translation in 1995) are well known among Japanese "spiritual" people, too. These books use various English jargon words, for example channelling, ascension, healing and transpersonal, which are carried over to the Japanese texts without being translated.

However, the Japanese "spiritual" is not a mere imported culture. People who are interested in the spiritual also represent an aspect of revivalism. For example, they re-evaluate Shintō. The animistic worship of nature in Shintō is thought to be an effective idea in solving global environmental issues:

> Many polytheistic religions all over the world, including Shintō, believe that nature is a living being of which humanity is but

one element, and that humans should strive to coexist, to live in harmony with nature. These religions are today looked upon positively as belief systems that are less destructive to the environment. In this climate, theories that characterize Shintō as a form of animism have once more become common.

(Matsumura 2007)

This description quotes the *Encyclopedia of Shinto*, which Kokugakuin University provides online. Kokugakuin is considered the centre of the academic study of Shintō. In this way, it is common to understand Shintō positively in terms of animism. This understanding is shared not only among the researchers of Shintō but also among "spiritual" people. *Gaia Symphony No. 7*, the newest in a series of documentary films, inserts Shintō ceremonies between interviews with prominent activists and authors who have "very insightful messages for the future of the Earth in the 21st century".[1] The films have been supported by many spiritual people in Japan since the 1980s. This suggests that Shintō is a symbol of symbiosis with nature for spiritual people who are interested in the issue of the global environment.

Zen Buddhism is popular in New Age bookshops in Europe and America, but it is classified as a traditional religion in Japan. It does not attract as much interest as Shintō among "spiritual" people. The famous Shintō shrines do well as "power spots" filled with *ki* (the spiritual atmosphere filling and circulating in nature) and energy. "Power spot" is a Japanese–English phrase. The word "spot" is the one that is often used to refer to an interesting place in the context of tourism. "Power" has no political connotation and is often used to mean an invisible spiritual force (Okamoto 2012). Many women in their thirties and forties gather there. The pattern of genders and ages is similar to that of those who come to other spiritual events. In contrast, people coming to temples for Zen practices are relatively older, and the majority are men.

Though Shintō is classified as a local ethnic religion, it is considered to have the same status and quality as the globally circulating New Age spirituality, mainly from the US.[2] These findings excite one's interest in the relationship between the global and the local, and in this light I conducted firsthand research into the Anglophone New Age spirituality that affects the Japanese understanding of "spiritual".[3]

Neo-paganism and folk Christianity

In the British New Age scene, I realized, neo-paganism is important. New Age shops relevant to neo-paganism form a line around the High Street in Glastonbury, Somerset. They sell products associated with Wicca, Druid or the goddess (Bowman 2000; Prince & Riches 2001; Ivakhiv 2001). The seasonal pagan festivals tend to attract a large number of people. The

Beltane Fire Festival at Calton Hill in Edinburgh resembles a rock festival and requires a ticket to enter. More than 30,000 people gather around Stonehenge to celebrate the summer solstice.[4]

In contrast, neo-pagan phenomena have hardly appeared in Japan. Japanese "spiritual" people like various types of angel cards, some of which feature pagan figures such as non-Christian angels, fairies, goddesses or spirits (Virtue 2002). However, the Japanese do not have a passion for reviving the ancient Celtic paganism; they only give a romantic glance at the exotic pagan figures. On the other hand, Shintō, which occupies an important position in Japan, is little known in the UK (except in scholarly books). Both Shintō and neo-paganism are similar in that they are popular only on the local level: the former only in Japan, the latter only in a Western European context.

In the US, Christianity is still deep-rooted and the "New Age" was not as prominent as I had expected. However, I noticed that many liberal Christians were interested in a variety of spirituality. For example, while I stayed in Berkeley, California, from 2009 to 2010, the Unitarian Universalist Church of Berkeley[5] and Northbrae Community Church[6] (a multi-denominational community church) offered lectures and study groups concerning the spirituality of Eastern religions.

From a different point of view, some of the Christian denominations in the US refuse to accept New Age ideas: for example, the Pentecostals and Charismatics might already have satisfied their desire to experience a heightened state of "spirituality" through seeking an altered state of consciousness at their enthusiastic meetings (H. Cox 2001). I hypothesized that the adherents of such denominations might not need the New Age. These denominations could be classified as "folk Christianity" in that they hold grassroots ritual practices and experiences that may be seen as unusual from the formal Christian viewpoint but are supported by ordinary people. Although folk Christianity would reject New Age teachings, it could be understood as an effort to experience spirituality from within. The Pentecostals are moved by the Holy Spirit to speak in tongues in a kind of altered state of consciousness. Even though the evangelical Christians are seen to be far from inner experiential spirituality due to their literalistic form of faith, Luhrmann (2012) pointed out that many of them regarded God as an intimate loving person who responded to their prayers like a therapist. The history of religion in the United States shows that there have been wavelike upsurges of revival (McLoughlin 1978). Personal rediscovery of inner spirituality has formed a spiritual tradition in the US, which started from religious ideals and has sought modernization and urbanization. In addition, recent works by scholars of spirituality have suggested a historical view that there has been a metaphysical tradition that has nurtured American spirituality in a broader sense before and after New Age in the strict sense (Albanese 2007; Bender 2010).

Thus, in each country, there is personal rediscovery and reinterpretation of the local folk and traditional religions, in parallel to the globally received New Age in a narrow sense. These phenomena should be called rediscovered "*old* age" spirituality rather than "New Age" spirituality. This "old" spirituality has a deep relationship with religion or tradition before "world religion", and is difficult to categorize as New Age which is supposed to be opposed to religion. (Conceptions of religion differ from country to country. Here, the word "religion" is used as a social construction woven into each cultural context.)

Actually, the frequency of use of the word "spirituality" and the term "New Age" varies from country to country. The term New Age is still common in the UK, the most secularized country of the three compared here. In the field of religious studies, almost all the academic books published in English with the term New Age in the title have been written by authors in the UK.[7] In contrast, in the US, where there has been a remarkable revival of religion since the 1980s, the frequency of use of "New Age" is lower than in the UK. The term "spirituality" is used more often because it can be used in a Christian context. For example, there are twelve conceptual uses of "New Age" and six of "spirituality" in the British Association for the Study of Religion Annual 2012 Conference programme.[8] Two of the usages of "spirituality" relate to New Age, three to "indigenous religion", and one to Jehovah's Witnesses. In contrast, in the programme of the American Academy of Religion 2012 conference,[9] there is only one use of "New Age" but thirty-three mentions of "spirituality", thirteen of which relate to Christian spirituality, and none to New Age spirituality.

Judging from the statistical data, Japan may seem to be the most secularized country, but this is not true. People in Japan practice various behaviours related to established reverence for gods, spirits and ancestors based on their personal preferences, without being aware that they are engaged in a substantively defined concept of "religion". The foreign term "New Age" has not taken root because it cannot describe matters concerning indigenous religious culture, including Shintō, which is recognized as "old" rather than "new". The word "spiritual" can hint at personal individualistic participation in traditional religious practices without membership. The term "spirituality" is used in religious studies, medical care, nursing and psychotherapy, but is not firmly established generally.

NEW AGE AND SPIRITUALITY IN STATISTICAL DATA

"Non-religious" spirituality in Japan, the US and the UK

In light of this discussion, let us examine the statistical data in detail. Table 6.1 is drawn from the online data analysis provided by the World Values Survey. Japan is apparently the most secularized country, since 87.9 per cent identify themselves as "not a member" of a church or religious organization. The US seems to be the least secularized, with only 33.7 per cent "not a member". The second part of the table shows the answers to the question of how religious one considers oneself. Respondents were given three answer options, namely, "a religious person", "not a religious person", and "a convinced atheist". The options are exclusive: that is, one who chose "not a religious person" had to be neither "religious" nor "a convinced atheist". Such a person might not belong to any religious organization, but they could believe more or less in some divine or spiritual being. This attitude corresponds to the well-known category "spiritual but not religious". According to the table, 62.1 per cent of people in Japan consider themselves "not a religious person", compared to 40.9 per cent in Great Britain and 24.4 per cent in the US. Hence, of the three countries compared here, Japan has the most people whose beliefs are potentially akin to "spiritual but not religious".

Table 6.1 Data from the online data analysis of the World Values Survey.

$n = 3328$		Country			
Weight [with divisions]		Total	Great Britain	United States	Japan
Active/inactive membership of church or religious organization	Not a member	60.10%	63.30%	33.70%	87.90%
	Inactive member	18.50%	17.50%	28.50%	7.60%
	Active member	21.50%	19.20%	37.90%	4.40%
	Total	3328 (100%)	1030 (100%)	1239 (100%)	1059 (100%)
$n = 3163$		Country			
Weight [with divisions]		Total	Great Britain	United States	Japan
Religious person	A religious person	50.10%	48.70%	72.10%	24.20%
	Not a religious person	41.10%	40.90%	24.40%	62.10%
	A convinced atheist	8.80%	10.40%	3.60%	13.70%
	Total	3163 (100%)	1009 (100%)	1196 (100%)	958 (100%)

Selected countries/samples: Great Britain (2006), US (2006), Japan (2005). Data from www.wvsevsdb.com/wws/WVSAnalize.jsp.

As shown in Table 6.2, this order does not change when it comes to the questions concerning impersonal spiritual beings or power: 56.3 per cent of Japanese feel "something greater than human power in nature" (Yomiuri Shinbun 2008), while 40 per cent of British believe that there is "some sort of spirit or life force" (Eurobarometer 2005) and 15 per cent of Americans believe in "a universal spirit or higher power" (Gallup 2008). On this evidence, Japanese people, even though they seem to be the most secularized, are the most likely of the three nations to believe in something "spiritual". Nevertheless, such "spirituality" is not necessarily understood as "New Age" in Japan. Many Japanese will be satisfied to hear that it falls into a category of folk and traditional spirituality, not "new", and that it does not take the definite form of "religion". The word "religion" (*shūkyō*) was invented as a translation of the Western concept of "religion" at the beginning of Japan's modern period (Shimazono & Tsuruoka 2003; Isomae 2003; Josephson 2012). Japanese are more familiar with non-religious "folk spirituality" than with organized religions.[10] That is why more than half of them confess themselves "not a religious person" but simultaneously not "a convinced atheist".

Table 6.2a *Yomiuri* newspaper's 2008 survey on the religious view of Japanese.

Do you believe in any religion?	Yes	No	DK/NA
	26.1%	71.9%	2.1%
Do you sometimes feel something greater than human power in nature, or not?	Yes	No	DK/NA
	56.3%	39.2%	4.5%
Do you have a sentiment of veneration toward your ancestor, or not?	Yes	No	DK/NA
	94%	4.5%	1.5%

n = 1,837. DK/NA = don't know/no answer.

Table 6.2b Gallup (2008) survey on belief in God in western USA.

Believe in God	78%
Believe in a universal spirit or higher power	15%
Don't believe in either	6%

Table 6.2c Eurobarometer (2005) UK responses to the question "Which of these statements comes closest to your beliefs?"

I believe there is a God	38%
I believe there is some sort of spirit or life force	40%
I don't believe there is any sort of spirit, God or life force	20%

New Age, religiosity/traditionalism, and secularization

For an illuminating cross-cultural study on the relationship between New Age and religious traditionalism (what I call "*old* age" spirituality), it is important to refer to the debate between Houtman and Aupers (2007) and Houtman *et al.* (2009) on one side, and Flere and Kirbiš (2009) on the other. Flere and Kirbiš argue that one can hardly recognize a significant difference between religiosity in general, New Age and religious traditionalism. General religiosity was measured by five questions concerning belief in God, soul, life after death, heaven and hell. Traditionalism was measured by the degree of importance attached by the respondents to traditional customs, guidance of life[11] and the wisdom of ancestors. New Age was measured by belief in individuals' higher spiritual self, holism of unified spiritual energy, and millenarianism in respect of the coming New Age (Flere & Kirbiš 2009: 163–4). The authors sampled students on four different university campuses in four religiously diverse locations, listed in order of high general religiosity scores: Bosnia-Herzegovina (Muslim environment), US (predominantly Protestant), Serbia (Eastern Orthodox) and Slovenia (Roman Catholic). According to Flere and Kirbiš, "across all environments, the associations between religious belief, New Age beliefs, and traditionalism are positive and significant" (ibid.: 166). They concluded that New Age is a phenomenon associated with both religiosity and traditionalism. They also suggested that it is "a contemporary form of popular religion" that supplements official religion, which I would call "folk spirituality". However, according to their factor analysis, general religiosity, New Age and traditionalism were independent factors, even if they correlated significantly (ibid.: 164–5). One should not therefore conclude that there is one complex attitude that contains the three factors at the same time.

Flere and Kirbiš admit the limitation of their own definition of New Age. It lacks features such as syncretism, expressivism and narcissism which are often used to distinguish it from general religiosity or traditionalism. However, these features are not contents of belief, but specific forms of belief which assume moral or ethical implications. For example, syncretism is confronted with purism, expressivism is confronted with dogmatism, and narcissism is confronted with collectivism. Those three features are therefore opposed to a specific type of religiosity that cannot encompass "general religiosity". In contrast, Flere and Kirbiš defined New Age, religiosity and traditionalism using the contents of propositions or objects of faith, and investigated the correlations among them. Their research design is simple and persuasive. They were right in that they did not include unnecessary intervening variables derived from a specific dogmatic religious attitude. If they had done, they could not have measured precisely the relationship among beliefs.

Houtman, Aupers and Heelas (2009) argue against Flere and Kirbiš to defend their conception of New Age, which is to be distinguished from theistic religiosity and traditionalism. According to them, Flere and Kirbiš's "general religiosity" is not the same as their "theistic religiosity". The former included belief in God, soul and life after death. Such a belief is supported not only by theistic religiosity, but also by New Age spirituality. They then pointed out that the concept of traditionalism that Flere and Kirbiš adopted was characterized by idealization of the past. According to Houtman et al., this type of traditionalism is supported by new agers too (it corresponds to the "old age" spirituality as mentioned before). Traditionalism should therefore be measured by the degree to which one values individual liberty and self-expression, a traditional moral hierarchical relationship between parents and children or male and female, and forms of sexuality. Indeed, Houtman and Aupers found "substantial negative relationships between this type of traditionalism and post-Christian New Age spirituality" (Houtman *et al.* 2009: 171).

One should be aware that Flere and Kirbiš's definition of religiosity and traditionalism differs from Houtman *et al.'s*. The latter is related to particular established social norms (seemingly patriarchal), while the former could include older pre-modern (even "lost" or "alternative") religious and cultural sources and resources, on which some new agers like to rely. Houtman et al.'s definitions had moral implications, but those of Flere and Kirbiš referred only to the objects of faith or contents of propositions, which were not necessarily patriarchal. Houtman et al.'s measure of traditionalism referred to the actual patriarchal human relationships to which today's "fundamentalists" or "evangelicals" would hold. Flere and Kirbiš's traditionalism permitted idealization of the older past in general, including not only the dominant Christian tradition, but also the notion of a "lost tradition" or "perennial wisdom" that was once suppressed by the dominant religion and is now re-evaluated by new agers.

Houtman *et al.* (2009: 173) go on to examine the condition under which Christian religiosity and New Age spirituality co-related by analysing the Religious and Moral Pluralism (RAMP) survey. RAMP is a survey conducted in European countries in the late 1990s. It had four options:

1. I believe in a God with whom I can have a personal relationship (PersonalGod)
2. I believe in an impersonal spirit or life force (Spirit/LifeForce)
3. I don't believe in any kind of God, spirit, or life force (Don'tBelieve)
4. I really don't know what to believe (Don'tKnow).

The RAMP survey designers added to these the fifth response: I believe that God is something within each person, rather than something out there (GodWithin). In order to measure theistic Christian religiosity, they use eight factors: belief in the Bible as God's word, belief in Jesus as God and man, belonging to a church, frequency of church attendance, frequency of prayer, self-identification as religious, belief in salvation, and belief in life after death. They call this measure "Mean Christian religiosity".

Consequently, Houtman et al. found that the size of the gap between PersonalGod and Spirit/LifeForce was relatively small in countries where "Mean Christian religiosity" scored highly. Similarly, the size of the gap between PersonalGod and GodWithin was smaller in highly Christian countries such as Poland and Portugal than relatively secularized countries such as Great Britain, Sweden and the Netherlands, where the "Mean Christian religiosity" was low. They argued that the previous study by Houtman and Aupers (2007) indicating that New Age spirituality was high in the secular-ized societies (those with low theistic religiosity) is not contradicted by Flere and Kirbiš's finding that there were positive relationships between New Age, traditionalism and general religiosity. Houtman *et al.* seem to place Flere and Kirbiš's samples in Bosnia-Herzegovina, the US, Serbia and Slovenia into a category of less secularized societies. Blending them together in their analysis of RAMP data, Houtman *et al.* suggest that, in the least secularized countries, "much of what may at face value look like post-Christian New Age spirituality is in fact quite closely related to theistic Christian religios-ity" and that "New Age spirituality is less closely related to what remains of theistic Christian religiosity in the most secularized countries" (Houtman *et al.* 2009: 177).

Through their discussion, one can see that the more secularized the society is, the bigger the gap between New Age and religious traditional-ism becomes. On the other hand, in less secularized countries, more people believe not only in the theistic personal God but also in the spiritual force or the God within. What makes the matter more complicated is the differ-ence between Protestantism and Catholicism. In a European context, what Houtman et al. call secularized societies are mainly Protestant: UK, Sweden and the Netherlands. The emphasis on absoluteness of the Personal God sharply contrasts with the belief in GodWithin and would be in tension with too much emphasis on Spirit/LifeForce.

Flere and Kirbiš's cross-cultural study was not limited to Christian culture but encompassed the Muslim environment. Islam puts more importance upon God's absoluteness and obedience to a religious code of behav-iour. Nevertheless, their Muslim samples in Bosnia-Herzegovina showed the highest scores in the New Age factors. They found that community-based religious practices might at least permit, or even encourage, "belief in individuals' higher spiritual self, holism of unified spiritual energy, and Millenarianism of coming New Age" (the authors' New Age factors). In other words, the monotheistic belief system does not necessarily exclude those ideas. As is known in the case of Sufism, Islam includes some types of mysticism with the idea of spiritual growth and unity with God, folk beliefs and worship of the saints.[12] In daily prayers, Muslims try to listen to God's voice, putting their hands by their ears. The idea of a "Coming New Age" could therefore be understood in the context of Muslim eschatology.[13]

However, Muslims will not hold specific cognitive contents of New Age teachings concerning extra-terrestrial beings or reincarnation. And new agers would disagree with Muslim conservative attitudes towards sex and gender. Narrowly defined New Age is inherently inconsistent with the Islamic belief system. On the other hand, the New Age factors isolated by Flere and Kirbiš do not contradict those of Islam on a certain general level. That is their significant finding. Spiritual growth, spiritual energy and cosmic evolution are not limited to the narrowly defined New Age. Rather, these ideas belong to the wider sense of "spirituality", which new agers will recognize as the core conviction shared by the world's major religious traditions.

In this case, what are the conditions under which New Age and religious traditionalism conflict with each other? Houtman *et al.* conclude that it lies with the decline in Christian theistic religiosity. They did not find serious conflicts in less secularized (in fact, Catholic) societies in the European Union. According to Flere and Kirbiš's research, that also held true in Muslim environments. Their research also showed a positive relationship between New Age spirituality and religious traditionalism in the US. The US was a Protestant environment but was not so secularized as their European Catholic sample in Slovenia, judging from their scores in religiosity. Generally speaking, secularization in the sense of decline in Christian religiosity is an important condition in which New Age and religious traditionalism come into conflict.

Hence the significance of Japan, which is seemingly the most secularized country in our comparison, with a high percentage of people selecting the answer "not religious". However, as discussed earlier, in Japan "religious" practices are deeply rooted as life customs, but not as "religion". It is not secularization, but Western modernization, that is criticized by the revived "old age" spirituality in Japan. If the enquiry set invented by Flere and Kirbiš were applied to Japanese samples, the result might be a combination of *low* religiosity and *high* New Age spirituality that has a positive relationship with traditionalism. There are two reasons for this. First, it can be said that the high degree of "secularization" in Japan is the basis of awareness of difference between religion and non-religious spirituality. At the same time, it is also possible to say that traditional practices and folk beliefs are still alive enough to revive indigenous spirituality as a force against modernization. That is the second reason. Thus, it is presumed that a more complex reaction would occur in Japan than in Europe, due to the resistance to the modern Western conception of "religion", combined with high uptake in ritual practices. Many Japanese reject "religion" but they observe "religious" practices without being aware that they are concerned with religion. That is, they do not confess that they believe in "religion" even when their ritual behaviour is clearly associated with "religion" in the sense of a substantive definition of this term. One of the reasons for this attitude is that the word "religion" in questionnaires reminds them of new religious groups. From the practitioners' point of view, ritual practices are categorized as traditional social customs, not as religious activities. As we have seen, more than half of Japanese are categorized as non-religious but performatively "religious", and they prefer folk and traditional "spirituality". Therefore, one cannot presuppose without evidence that there will be positive associations between New Age, traditionalism and religiosity.

THEORETICAL CONSIDERATIONS: NARROW NEW AGE AND BROAD SPIRITUALITY

Hypothesis: coexistence, separation and reintegration

What has been discussed above is only a correlation among data for New Age spirituality, religious traditionalism and various degrees of secularization. The statistical data themselves do not explain why this is so. Here, I would like to posit the following hypotheses for future detailed investigation.

1. In a country where secularization has not progressed, world religions and folk religions stand side by side as "great traditions" and "little traditions" (R. Redfield 1956). It is the community-based religious practice that connects these two layers. There is room in communal practices to mix in a faith with a different nature from the doctrine of the world religion.

2. When the community is weakened and when people separate from their native religious life, the individual has to decide their position. Some may confess their faith and choose to be members of a particular religious group; religion thus becomes a matter of preference (Berger 1979). At the same time, some may prefer to be detached from any religious group. Others prefer to be not "religious", but to adopt or consume various religious cultural resources eclectically. Religion therefore tends to be either a dogmatic *group* recruiting newcomers on the one hand, or a set of *cultural resources* on the other hand. Individualization thus leads to a double-sided concept: "religion as group" and "religion as culture" (Horie 2003). New Age has been opposed to "religion as group" but has adopted eclectically the various religious cultural resources to build up a universal spirituality beyond the differences of religions.

3. A form of "folk religion" is separated out from collective ritual and becomes a commodity for personal use. The latter results in New Age forms appearing in the marketplace (Roof 1999) as, for example, belief in magical power, various types of divination and shamanistic practices.

4. Religious groups have an option to "take in" New Age without becoming dogmatic (e.g. Kemp 2003). To that end, the term "spirituality" is useful to practitioners because it can refer in their understanding to both the "essence" of the religion in terms of the mysterious and experiential part, or to the magical and miraculous part promised by New Age. Therefore, "spirituality" can be used to express not only traditional religion, but also New Age issues.

5. It is not that the US and Japan have not yet become secularized, but it might be that religion in these countries is shifting to spirituality or the spiritual after having gone through a certain degree of secularization.

Houtman *et al.* (2009: 177) also point out the possibility of "spiritualization of theistic religion", such as Sufism, Pentecostalism, evangelicalism and the Catholic charismatic movement.

In phase (1), religion and folk belief and practice are largely undifferentiated and exist in a state of layered coexistence. In phases (2) and (3), religion and New Age are separated in the age of modernization and systematization of "religion". Now, in the latest stages, (4) and (5), they are becoming reintegrated in the form of discourses and practices on "spirituality".

Teething problems: distinguishing "New Age", "new spirituality" and "spirituality"
Therefore, it is necessary to distinguish spirituality from New Age. They have different relationships with religion. New Age is opposed to religion in the modern sense, particularly to its authoritarianism and traditionalism, in expectation of the arrival of a new era. Spirituality is also anti-authoritarian but may be thought of as the "essence" of religion: for example, as Christian spirituality or Buddhist spirituality. In those cases, "spirituality" is used to refer to that essence of the particular religion which is neglected in organized forms. Thus, "spirituality" is not always opposed to religion. When the archaic, the primitive, or the marginal parts of religion are praised in terms of romanticism or revivalism, it is the "spirituality *in* religion" that is referred to.

To further complicate matters, a middle ground exists between New Age and spirituality. An eclecticism of spiritualities from various religious traditions has emerged to meet the needs of the times. We may collectively call these forms the "new spirituality". Of course, there has already been an attempt to extend the meaning of New Age to include what is called spirituality, and I do not deny its strategic effectiveness. For example, Paul Heelas defined New Age as follows:

> the New Age is a highly optimistic, celebratory, utopian and spiritual form of humanism, many versions … also emphasizing the spirituality of the natural order as a whole … And more analytically, as an internalized form of religiosity the New Age is … detraditionalized. That is to say, autonomy and freedom are highly valued; and autonomy lies with the experience of the Self or, more broadly, the natural realm.   (Heelas 1996: 28–9)

According to this definition, New Age refers to a combination of a certain kind of spirituality and internalized religiosity. Such a definition may subsume under New Age not only non-religious spirituality but also the "spirituality *in* religion" defined above. However, if it includes traditional religiosity it will weaken the critical counter-cultural motif of the New Age: namely, being against "old age" religiosity. Conversely, some religious persons who evaluate spirituality in their own tradition might feel that to be called "New

Age" would be a form of labelling, since it remains a controversial term (in Christianity, for example).

Susumu Shimazono (2004, 2007), a Japanese researcher, criticizes the concept of New Age and proposes a concept called "new spirituality movements" or, more recently, "new spirituality culture". He draws attention to what has not historically been called New Age, but nevertheless still attaches great importance to "spirituality". For example, some articulations of "spirituality" are derived from academic movements such as psychology, medicine, agriculture and ecology, or from such alternative cultural–political movements as paganism and feminism, or from religious organizations preceding New Age such as Theosophy and Anthroposophy, and practices from Asian religions (Shimazono 2007: 36–42). These movements are not called "New Age" on the popular level, but they are close to it. Shimazono includes New Age in these "new spirituality movements" because both propose a new form of spirituality to replace religion (*ibid.*: 50). Shimazono later came to use the term "new spirituality culture" because these are phenomena without the kind of organizational objects or ideals that "movements" would uphold (*ibid.*: 51), and recently he has used only "new spirituality" (Shimazono 2012: 9).

However, I think that a revival of local tradition cannot be described by the term "new". Therefore, as I have argued, I regard *spirituality* without the qualifier "new" as the broadest concept available in the field of terminology under discussion, because it is actually used (by practitioners) to refer also to religious tradition. And I suggest that *New Age* should be used narrowly as a concept that implies a critical distance from religious tradition, because its advocates expect a coming New Age in which the dogmatism and authoritarianism in established religion will be overcome. Between these two, I identify *new spirituality* as a middle field where an interaction between the "spirituality" in traditional religions – what I call "old age spirituality" – and the non-religious New Age occurs.

TOWARDS A COMPREHENSIVE SCHEMA: FOUR TYPES OF SPIRITUALITY

The comprehensive spirituality that includes New Age and new spirituality and still relates to religion would be defined as follows. *Spirituality refers to both belief in what cannot usually be perceived but can be felt internally, and practices to feel it with the whole mind and body, accompanied more or less by attitudes of individualism or privatism, anti-authoritarianism, and selective assimilation of religious cultural resources.*

The first half of this definition virtually corresponds to "religiosity" or "spirituality" as it is often used in the field of psychology of religion, which emphasizes experiential aspects of religion (cf. Paloutzian & Park 2005). My definition is based on an analysis of eighty-four previous definitions in psychological literature from which I abstracted significant common elements of "spirituality" as defined by multiple authors, and synthesized my definition as the available and acceptable one in the field of psychology (Horie 2007). My reference to psychological literature comes from two strategic reasons. One is that psychologists' debates on "spirituality" in today's sense precede other disciplines" and are systematic enough to rely on. The other reason is that psychological points of view and various kinds of therapeutic techniques are also influential in popular marketed spirituality.

The second half of this definition is concerned with the forms of expression of spirituality in political and economical contexts, which was problematized by Carrette and King (2005). They argued that a commodified form of spirituality with a neo-liberalist ideology is taking over religion by psychologizing it. However, as I have discussed, religion is in fact trying to assimilate spirituality by retrospectively identifying it as the foundational experiential nucleus, the hidden essence, or its general feature (as a synonym for "religiosity"). For example, the American Academy of Religion 2012 Program Book already discussed contains "Christian Spirituality" several times, in some cases presented from Christian theological perspectives. Books with the word "Christian spirituality" in their title amount to over 500 in Amazon.com's catalogue.[14] The word "spirituality" itself has its origin in Christianity. In contrast to Carrette and King, it seems that spirituality can function as a catalytic agent that promotes an innovation of religion from the inside.

This comprehensive spirituality must encompass both the global and the local so that one can apply it to each context discussed here: Japan, the US and the UK. The concept of comprehensive spirituality must also include both religion and non-religion, as I pointed out in the first section of this chapter. Therefore, spirituality is classified into four types by these two binary oppositions (Figure 6.1). To conclude the chapter, let us attempt to analyse the situation concerning spirituality in Japan, the US and the UK with the four types as variables.

FOUR TYPES OF SPIRITUALITY, NEW SPIRITUALITY AND NEW AGE

The first is the local and non-religious type. I call it *folk spirituality*. It comes from the local folk religion and is characterized by features such as animism, *mana* or shamanism. "Folk spirituality" plays an elemental role in the New Age spirituality of each country. There is the local popular culture through which the folk spirituality is expressed in various media. It may be said that the Japanese "spiritual" and the American "New Age" are forms of personal consumption of folk spirituality. In the UK, in addition to "New Age", neo-paganism is an important manifestation of folk spirituality.

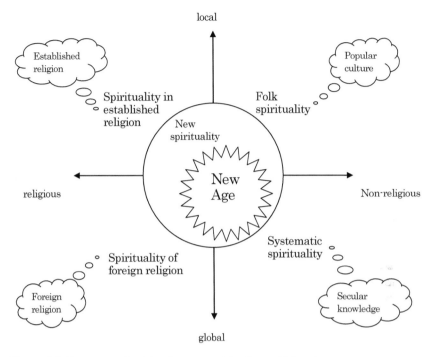

Figure 6.1 Four types of spirituality, new spirituality and New Age.

The second is the local and religious type. I call it *spirituality in established religion*. It orients itself to the revelatory experiences and the miraculous acts of the founder and to the creative re-experience of them under the names of "esotericism" and "mysticism". Outside it is the established religion that inhibits and watches over these expressions of spirituality by lay believers. The extent of the inhibition varies from culture to culture. Conservative Christianity is generally inhibitive, while the liberal denominations are less so; the latter may offer the opportunity for religious practice without an intention to convert the participant. Between the two lies the kind of folk Christianity that is contiguous to folk spirituality. Japanese Shintō and Buddhism are less inhibitive and are extremely open to individualistic participation in their practices.

The third is the global and religious type: that is, *spirituality of foreign religion*. This does not mean organized missions from abroad, but such phenomena as the popularity of a book about an exotic religion without organizational support, or the popularity of a non-native religious practice that can be exercised without learning its doctrine and without being a permanent member. Buddhism and yoga in the US and the UK are good examples. However, most such foreign religions are regarded as traditional religions in their homeland and belong there to the category of *spirituality in established religion*.

The fourth is the global and non-religious type. I call it *systematic spirituality*. It has an intellectual foundation in inter-disciplinary scholarship such as psychotherapy (humanistic psychology, transpersonal psychology, Jungian psychology, mindfulness based stress reduction, etc.), alternative medicine (Andrew Weil, etc.), terminal care (Kübler-Ross, etc.), environmental thought (deep ecology), cognitive science, and religious studies (M. Eliade, J. Campbell, H. Smith, etc.). It is also supported by the expert systems of those disciplines. This systematic spirituality plays a role as a "systematic theology" for the whole spirituality. It is rooted in individualism, psychologism, vitalism and romantic evolutionism. Its characteristics are the theorization of the plurality, fluidity and multilayeredness of the human psyche, the experience of transcendence from within, self-affirmation and self-responsibility, and positive thinking. Systematic spirituality is that intellectual discourse outside established religion which is nevertheless sympathetic toward religion. On the other hand, the discourse belonging to religion can be evaluated as "spirituality" if it shares these characteristics. *Systematic spirituality* plays a role as a filter which discriminates spirituality and gives it authority. Outside it, and standing over against it, there are critical secular scholarships, discourses and institutions against religion. In the US, discourses on systematic spirituality are produced in large quantities and affect not only theology but also the romantic side of religious studies,[15] and it also greatly influences the British New Age. Japan has hardly imported Christianity, which is a foreign religion, but it has received systematic spirituality as a global culture.[16] In this way Japanese "spiritual" authors have learnt how to distinguish what can be classed as "spirituality" from the local Japanese culture.

CONCLUSION: THE CHALLENGE OF "BROAD SPIRITUALITY" TO RELIGIOUS STUDIES

At the core of this schema, where the two axes cross, there exists "new spirituality" that is both post-religious and post-secular and that moves back and forth between the global and the local. New Age can be ideally located at this intersection point. However, it is a part of a richer, comprehensive spirituality. Secularization in this schema can be characterized by the process through which the four types of spirituality are differentiated, opposed to each other, and lack a mutual relationship. Post-secularization would then be the process by which they are reintegrated as a comprehensive spirituality. May it not be said that New Age functions as the catalyst of reintegration? Broad and comprehensive spirituality is individualized, simplified and liquidized in New Age expressions. This process may certainly result in a reduction of historical and cultural variety. However, the units of spirituality represented by New Age can respond quickly to the emergent needs of people and society, and also tease out responses to them by scholars, including theologians. New Age in this sense is connected to all the four quadrants of spirituality, absorbs their elements, and dissolves them in itself. New age elements are in turn taken in to the four quadrants.

However, while New Age stimulates hybridization, it cannot help the essentialization of religion as a cultural resource. There is also a danger of cultural destruction and exploitation, since only a part of a religion may be extracted from its original context, according to a particular requirement, to make "spirituality". Dignity might be lost when New Age is consumed privately, and furthermore, it might be used to justify nationalism and politically conservative forms of traditionalism.

Religious studies relativizes the modern conception of religion by approaching spirituality. Scholars and researchers investigating the ever changing facets of spirituality can prospect alternative possibilities of "religion" beyond its external forms. At the same time, a critical study of spirituality would have to pay attention to the hypostatization and absolutization of spirituality, and the reduction of its historical and regional richness as a result of following people's needs in a market economy. For "spirituality" to be more flexible, more anti-authoritarian, and more dialogical than "religion" in the modern sense, it should permit critical intervention by the discipline of religious studies, including correction of its potential essentialism by the fruits of historical and regional studies together with discourse analysis and ideological criticism.

NOTES

1. See www.gaiasymphony.com/bu/co_guide-e.html (accessed August 2013).
2. See also Michael York's perspective on "paganism as a world religion" (York 2003); he understands Shinto to be a form of "paganism".
3. I conducted an investigation in the UK and the US from 2009 to 2010: in the UK, Glastonbury and Bath (April 2009), Edinburgh (April to May 2009), Findhorn and London (May 2009); in the US, Berkeley and San Francisco (August 2009 to February 2010), Mt Shasta (August and September 2009), Esalen Institute (February 2010) and Sedona (December 2009 and March 2010). I visited various kinds of New Age shops and sacred places, participated in workshops, took field notes and interviewed those whom I met on site: three Japanese visitors, nine Japanese residents, seven British residents and six American residents.
4. See www.efestivals.co.uk/festivals/stonehenge/2009/review-Solstice.shtml (accessed August 2013).
5. See http://uucb.org (accessed August 2013).
6. See www.northbrae.org (accessed August 2013).
7. Below are the books with "New Age" in the titles which are under the category of "Religious Studies" on Amazon.com (accessed 1 September 2012) but which are not theological in nature. The only one written by an American author is Pike (2004). Rothstein (2001) is from Denmark, Hammer (2001) is from Sweden and the others are all from the UK: Prince and Riches (2001), Pearson (2002), Sutcliffe (2003a), Kemp

(2003), Corrywright (2003), Drury (2004), Wood (2007), Heelas (2008), York (2009), and Campion (2012).

8. See www.winchester.ac.uk/academicdepartments/theology/NewsandEvents/ Documents/BASR%20Programme%20for%20Winchester%20Website.pdf (accessed August 2013).

9. See the link to the AAR program book for Chicago 2012 at http://www.aarweb.org/ annual-meeting/past-future-meetings (accessed August 2013).

10. The concept of "folk religion" has already been established in the field of the study of Japanese religion, in connection with folklore study. There is a scholarly society: the Japanese Society of Religious Folklore (Nihon Shūkyō Minzoku Gakkai 日本宗教民俗 学会). There is also a dictionary titled Nihon Minzoku Shūkyō Jiten 日本民俗宗教辞 典 Dictionary of Japanese Folk Religion (Yamaori *et al.* 1998). "Folk religion" refers to a set of manners and customs and the popular beliefs implied in them, which is based on a certain local community and its oral tradition. While it has something more or less to do with the organized religions, Buddhism and Shintō, it has developed independently among people and taken forms of syncretism. However, it is an analytical concept used by scholars, and most of the people do not call it "religion". "Folk religion" consists of collective practices and beliefs, but the local community is dissolving in the course of urbanization and aging. The practices tend to be limited to nuclear families and now are transforming gradually into individualistic participation in occasional ritual events. This trend is widely known in funeral studies (e.g. Inoue 2003) as well as in the mass phenomena of individuals' "power spot" pilgrimages to Shintō shrines, as previously mentioned. Thus, it flows into the realm of non-religious spirituality and creates a category which might be called "folk spirituality".

11. The original question was "Tradition is a major source of guidance at the crossroads in my life". The phrase "guidance of life" is the present author's abbreviation.

12. See Bruinessen and Howell (2007) on Sufism in modern Muslim life in various countries.

13. The belief in the next life is one of the major six beliefs in Islam, and chapters 93 and 99–104 of the Quran illustrate Muslim eschatology. The "coming New Age" can be understood as referring to the time in heaven after Judgment. "And the Hereafter is better for you than the first [life]" (93:4, http://quran.com/93).

14. Searched on 3 May 2013.

15. To give just one example, the State University of New York series in Transpersonal and Humanistic Psychology lists in its catalogue more than fifty books by authors who are academically trained and also practically engaged in spirituality.

16. Cf. Horie (2003) and Horie (2007). Discourses on spirituality in Japan are imported in the fields of (1) transpersonal psychologists or psychotherapists, (2) practitioners of spiritual care (terminal palliative care), and (3) sociologists of religion.

7. DOLPHINS AND OTHER HUMANS: NEW AGE IDENTITIES IN COMPARATIVE PERSPECTIVE

Mikael Rothstein

Present-day popular religion offers a variety of expressions and ways that are typical to the open minds and loose structures of devoted New Age *entrepreneurs*. Scholars of New Age agree on most characteristics: syncretistic belief systems, lack of institutionalization, counter-cultural engagements, experiential disciplines of esoteric and occult kinds, links to popular culture in general, scientist perspectives, emphasis on individual experience and transformation, and a high degree of individualism – to mention the most obvious. These phenomena are often understood to be elements in a particularly modern or even postmodern reality.[1]

On that account it will come as no surprise to the reader that an obliging and embracing woman in her early thirties, with no hesitation, may remind you that she is in fact a dolphin. I am referring to an actual event during a so-called Body, Mind, Spirit bazaar in Copenhagen, Denmark, in 2004, which I attended for fieldwork purposes. The woman offered her services as a clairvoyant with the following credentials on full display: "Formerly incarnated on Venus". Lecturing me about life on that distant planet, and blaming me for my rational and definitely "non-spiritual attitude", she triumphantly said, taking her hands to her breast: "Mind you, I'm a dolphin!" Compared with the average self perception of Euroamerican females in their thirties, this is a remarkable statement, and our immediate analysis is simple: Her self-perception is best interpreted as a detraditionalized notion, driven by a mythology born of a fragmented, individualized, experimenting culture void of tradition. Or rather, this is at least what some scholars would say.[2]

However, proclamations of a similar nature are also known from very different cultures where concepts of modernity and postmodernity have no relevance at all. In a famous description of his nine months' captivity among the Tupinambá of today's eastern Brazil, Hans Staden, in a book from 1557, refers to a local man who declares: "I'm a jaguar". Similarly, ethnographies of the Bororo of the Brazilian Amazon record that these people consider themselves to be intimately related to red macaw parrots, to an extent where human and avian identities merge – thus the proclamation: "I'm a red macaw parrot".

By comparing these three examples – dolphin (usually *Tursiops truncatus*), jaguar (*Panthera onca*) and red macaw parrot (*Ara chloroptera*) – I shall propose an alternative interpretation of *humanimal* identities in New Age conceptions, and challenge modernity or postmodernity as the primary reference for understanding. Discussions of a much broader kind have lingered since Bruno Latour (1993) made the claim that "we have never been modern", insisting that the separation between ourselves as moderns, and the rest of the world, is basically mistaken. In doing so Latour takes on the entire fabric of contemporary thinking, and all current modes of living, but my ambition is more modest: I simply wish to make the point as a historian of religions that our understanding of New Age religion will be improved by means of comparative methodology which takes into account very different religious traditions, and that such an analysis will show that what is often seen as distinctly modern or postmodern may in fact be quite typical to humans in general. Thus my comparative examples will be drawn from cultures far from being either modern or postmodern, a fact indicating that *humanimal identities*, the human notion of being an animal, or at least sharing significant features with species from non-human zoological taxa, including the notion of trans-species communications, is far from restricted to contemporary Western New Age doctrines. This aspect of New Age cosmology has more to do with well-known and widespread religious points of view than with modernity or postmodernity specifically. Radical religious promulgations, be they New Age announcements or those of more traditional cultures, are often less spectacular than initially indicated.

"I'M A JAGUAR"

In 1550 Hans Staden, a young sailor and gunner of Homberg, employed by the Portuguese crown, was captured and enslaved by the Tupinambá, a people living not far from present day Rio de Janeiro, Brazil. During his four months of captivity, he was given the opportunity to observe the ways of his masters, and upon his rather miraculous return, he published in 1557 a book in German about his adventures: *The True History and Description of a Country Populated by a Wild, Naked, and Savage Man-munching People, Situated in the New World, America*. Staden was among the first to record a kind of New World ethnography, and his narrative attracted considerable attention, not least because it offers detailed descriptions of cannibalistic activities. This is not the place to discuss the multitude of interesting elements in this important text. We are only interested in a single detail, the ritual transformation of a man-eating *human* into a man-eating *jaguar*. Referring to his temporary master and owner, Konyan Bebe, Staden writes:

This same Konyan Bebe had a great basket full of human flesh in front of him. He was eating a leg and held it to my mouth, asking whether I also wanted to eat. I said: "a senseless animal hardly ever eats its fellow; should one human then eat another?" He took a bite saying: Jau ware she [linguistic transcription: *Jauáre iche*]. I am a jaguar; it tastes well. With that, I left him.[3]

Attempts have been made to dispose of accounts such as this as an expression of deceitful colonial propaganda, but comparative anthropology has documented beyond doubt, that cannibalism lies within the ranges of normal human behaviour (Sanday 1986). Thus the text depicts a man, Konyan Bebe, who, during the act of munching human flesh, proclaims himself to be of another species: a jaguar in fact. The reason for this pronouncement is not totally clear, but it appears that in order to engage in the eating of humans, the devouring Tupinambá must himself (or herself), at least in some cases, transmute into something else – a carnivorous species, a jaguar. Although the ingestion of humans, according to Staden, is indeed a luxurious and highly appreciated meal to the Tupinambá, it is also a ritualized behaviour which makes it more than a mere fulfilment of alimentary needs. Staden's account describes in various ways how the victim is prepared and processed for consumption, a ritual procedure that directly involves the impending eaters.[4] Gobbling human flesh was no trivial pursuit to the Tupinambá, and those partaking were, as clearly indicated in Staden's surprisingly detailed delineations, under ritual control observing a line of taboos and restrictions. The precise nature of that control, however, is impossible to define on the basis of the sources at our disposal, but the point is clear enough: the ritualized circumstances seem to transform a human identity into an animal identity with respect to the specific act of eating a human. In effect this case leads us to a curious conclusion: humans did not eat humans in Tupinambá society; humans were consumed by jaguars. As always when South American native peoples are concerned, concepts and paradigms are very complex and usually difficult to comprehend, and we are to some extent facing the same challenges as the early European intruders. As expressed by Sabine MacCormac, when Konyan Bebe in his capacity of eating a human being explained that he was in fact a jaguar, he thereby afforded "a glimpse into Tupí perceptions of identity that … for the rest remained deeply opaque to Europeans" (MacCormac 1999: 117).

There is, however, a philological detail which to some extent rebuts the point I wish to make: in the language of the *guarani*-speaking present day Kaiowá Indians, who are culturally and linguistically linked with the ancient Tupinambá (the Kaiowá used to live in relative close proximity to the place where Staden was held captive), the word *jagua* (as transcribed in the dictionary referred to below) means either "a carnivorous mammal" or "a dog". Considering the linguistic overlaps of the old Tupinambá and the Kaiowá tongues, we may suggest that Konyan Bebe's reply to Staden could be alternatively rendered: "I am a dog; it tastes well", indicating that he, contrary to Staden, considered himself to be omnivorous, just like dogs. Should this be the case, the example loses its power in the present discussion as the human–animal correspondence would change from identity (being a jaguar) to similarity (behaving like dogs). On the other hand, the Kaiowá expression *jaguarete ava* (still in *guarani*) means "a person who has been transformed into a carnivorous mammal by means of sorcery" (de Assis 2000: 38)[5] – which immediately takes us back to Staden's text, which seems to describe just that: a human, Konyan Bebe, ritually transmuted into a carnivorous feline. As it appears, the possibility of changing people into big cats still exists among the modern, albeit distant, kinsfolk of the Tupinambá, at least in linguistic terms, which in turn supports our initial interpretation of Konyan Bebe's proclaimed self perception. At the very least the relation between what is human and what is animal is blurred.

This is also where we approach an understanding of why at all this transformation is supposed to happen in Tupinambá society: In his study of the Areweté, Eduardo de Vivieros de Castro convincingly argues that these people figuratively incorporate their enemies into their own being whereby the boundaries between interior and exterior are broken down and social harmony created. One way of doing this is to eat one's enemies. As the Areweté are culturally linked with the Tupinambá, de Casto believes the recent case to cast some light upon the older:

> Asked about what he was eating, the Tupinambá warrior defined his perspective: he was a jaguar, because his food was a man. If the leg he ate was from an enemy, the mouth that ate it (and spoke) was of the Enemy ... when one is a cannibal like Chunhambebe [Konya Bebe], one is the Other – a jaguar, that inedible cannibal. Naturally, a civilized jaguar: he ate cooked flesh – a jaguar with fire.
>
> (de Castro 1992: 271)

But more importantly, he considers the concept of "jaguar" to designate a *quality* of the act (cannibalism) rather than a *substance*, and indicates that although the actual transformation is unreal, the notion of something happening is real indeed (*ibid.*)

We are, in this connection, forced to address a very general question: How does ritual transformation work? Did Konyan Bebe, sitting there with a nicely roasted human leg in his hands looking forward to another mouthful, actually believe himself to be a jaguar? I shall return to this question below. At this stage we shall merely state that his jaguar identity must be interpreted as a *ritual reality*, not a general ontological fact. The *humanimal identity* does not apply in all kinds of social context. It belongs to the specific realm of a transformative ritual. However, the functioning of ritual does not invalidate Konyan Bebe's claim. The ritual condition stipulates it as fact that he is a jaguar.

"I'M A RED MACAW PARROT"

The case of the Brazilian Bororo was made famous by Claude Levi-Strauss's discussion in his *Mythologiques* (especially vol. I; Levi-Strauss [1969] 1983) although others had preceded him, but it was Jonathan Z. Smith who made it mandatory reading for any historian of religions through his article "I Am a Parrot (Red)" (J. Z. Smith 1972). The issued debated is this: What is implied in this sentence: "I am a parrot"? What does it mean when the Bororo claim to be *araras*? Already Émile Durkheim and Marcel Mauss had made a point of discussing Bororo semantics. Initially, in 1903 (Durkheim & Mauss [1903] 1963), they stated that "the Bororo sincerely imagines himself to be a parrot", although Durkheim, in 1912, seems to nuance his understanding of this kind of phenomena as symbolical (cf. Durkheim [1912] 1971: 230–31). These scholars clearly based their initial ideas on the 1894 reports by the first ethnographer who studied the tribe, Karl von den Steinen (as summarized by J. Z. Smith 1972: 392–3). Since then new interpretations have been suggested, not least of a symbolist kind. Psychologist Lev Vygotsky, in 1934, identified a special structure in the Bororo language (and similar languages), suggesting that the word (in this case "parrot") does not form or carry a concept: "It is a family name. It is a means of naming groups with concrete objects that are united in accordance with some type of empirical kinship".[6] According to Crocker (1977) only Bororo men say "we are red macaws", while red macaws are owned as pets by Bororo women, on whom the men are dependent in significant ways. He also asserts that both men and macaws were believed to be in touch with spirits. His conclusion was that the identification of Bororo men with red macaws should not be viewed as ontological but as metaphorical, and as a means by which they seek to express the irony of their situation.[7] Smith is more fundamental in his critique of the earlier interpretations, showing that von den Steinen misunderstood his own data, and that subsequent scholars by and large have reproduced his errors. As it appears, the Bororo believe themselves to become red macaw parrots – *araras* – when they die, which means that they perceive of their human state as transitory. This reminds us of one of de Castro's most important assertions regarding the Areweté and the Amerindians in general: they believe themselves to exist in a transitory process between different modes of existence, not rarely anticipating different animal shapes. The Bororo believe that humans are not only potentially *araras*, they are sure to become large red parrots at some point in the future. This certainty, which is nurtured in the Bororo perceptions of origin and death, and thus entertained in numerous religious situations including burials and other rituals pertaining to death, makes the ongoing identification with the birds part and parcel of what it means to be human, and in that sense it is fair to say that humans and *araras* are united as one. Furthermore, Bororo imagination allows trans-species shapeshifting to occur as the religious experts of society, the shamans, may assume the form of various animals, including red macaws. Accordingly there are a number of parallels between the Tupinambá jaguar-conceptions and the Bororo notions of the red macaws.

"I'M A DOLPHIN"

Like the dolphin woman mentioned at the beginning of the chapter Alyse, a mother of two, has come to understand and appreciate herself and her off-spring, Simon, in a new way. Following a divorce, and fighting for her disabled son's well-being, she has "recently found out that my 'home' is where the dolphins come from and that I am a dolphin".[8] More indirectly perhaps, Amelia Rachel Noelle, a girl of six, exclaimed: "I'm *not* a mermaid, I'm a dolphin!", and pondering over her family relationship with her mother, she said: "I'm a dolphin so you're a dolphin too!"[9] Stories of this kind are habitually related in small auto-hagiographies in new age culture where people build their own identities, or in mini-hagiographies, where other individuals, very often the narrators' own children, are formed into something very special. Another example is Muriel Lindsay, who is introduced as "a dolphin-human". She writes:

> I have long suspected I was a dolphin in a human body. I am only completely comfortable in the water. My skin is only normal in the water. Otherwise, I shed my skin constantly – a condition called ichthyiosis. When I was young, I would turn sommersaults for hours in the water to put myself into an altered state, and I have had many dreams of living and breathing in water (tho I know dolphins don't breathe in the water but certainly, they don't worry about breathing while being in the water for such long periods between breaths).[10]

Muriel, in the same text, also relates a dream which is concluded as follows: "I don't remember the rest of the dream except that what happened was I actually gave birth to a dolphin" (*ibid.*). The same basic idea of a correspondence between dolphins and humans is also expressed in statements such as this, by a writer calling herself Ocean who compares the two species: "They [dolphins] give birth and feed young with milk. They breathe air. They take time for recreation. They have humor and creativity. Pairing is for them not only a strictly reproductive mechanism, but also a game."[11]

The dolphin–human connection is clearly taken for granted, but implicitly important mythological references with explanatory functions, are at work. Lemuria, Atlantis and extraterrestrial worlds, are generally evoked as cradles of the dolphin–human tie-in, and it is impossible to understand the personal narratives of human dolphins without this mythological backdrop, which is expressed in many different ways. One example is a narrative about a distant world, Sirius B, allegedly told by the well-known guru Sathya Sai Baba, which serves to promote a magical substance, *Blue Dolphin Essence*. This substance is endorsed, by the way, by Archangel Michael, Jesus, Bim the Avatar Whale, Djual Kuhl [*sic*], Mary, Lulu the Avatar Dolphin and Vywamus "a tender of the earth grid of Christ Consciousness", and based on the wisdom of the Lemurians (including the blue dolphins of that world): "Sirius B is a 5th dimensional place of loving, higher consciousness. It is an ocean planet and in the oceans live mer people who are part human and part dolphin. The oceans are also populated by many species of dolphins and whales."[12]

In relatively similar ways, in 1989, channeller and New Age worker, Maia Christianne, according to her home page, received a message from certain "Venusian Hesperu Dolphin Masters", informing her that dolphins (and unicorns) are working for the benefit of humanity on Earth, and that dolphin and human forms are interchangeable (the esoteric concept of "inner earth" is not explained):

> Within the inner earth domain there are dolphins who are overlayed by "Hesperus" – a specific type of Venusian beings. The dolphins with the Hesperus overlay are "Dolphin Masters." Some of the inner earth Dolphin Masters do assume human form for periods of time. Their dolphin bodies have exceptionally large craniums. In the mid-1990's the Dolphin Masters began to sending a coupling signal out into their Tribe of the surface seas. Since that time, surface-earth dolphins are carrying the signal of the inner earth Dolphin Masters into the outer domain.[13]

In keeping with the scientistic inclination of most New Age-ideologies (Hammer 2001: 201–2), the human–dolphin correlation is presented as a scientific fact: A biochemical DNA-level unknown to "surface science" is revealed, and an entirely new biological reality exposed:

> The Children of the Wave – those dolphin-twined in spirit, bring to the Earth a signal for union. This is a union of SPIRIT, yet it also gradually transforms the DNA to accommodate the physical reflection of that spiritual union. Understand[ing] the "union" of which we speak is not completed with the merging of the dolphin and the human tribes. This is only the first stage of a greater reunification that the dolphins hold in their field for humanity ...

> What is the role of the Children of the Wave, the Dolphin Ones among us? There is no one role, for each soul moves within the streaming of its own birth canal in the great Universal Ocean, and yet is a part of the whole Hologram of Being. In essence, however, a holistic view of the working of the Dolphin Children could be seen as touching into the deepest part of the LOVE that the dolphins see in humanity, and recognizing it as a bridge between the two species. This bridging is physically contained in the crystalline structure of the DNA, which is almost identical in dolphins and humans. When we say "crystalline structure" we refer to the most refined level of the DNA that is not yet in evidence by the current science of the surface earth.[14]

While this particular idea surely would be repudiated by scientists, the appeal to the authority of science is plain. Another scientistic notion of dolphin–human relations is argued by means of a supposed theory of human origins, the so-called "Aquatic Ape Hypothesis". Although refuted in the scientific community, the theory that early humanoids, contrary to other apes, took an evolutionary turn into a life in water before reemerging as a land-living creature, enjoys some interest in the New Age dolphinist sub-culture. Other branches of current dolphin theology see dolphins and other whales as agents of extraterrestrial visitors, if not themselves extraterrestrials in Earth-bodies. One particularly clear example is the aforementioned Ocean[15] who claims that she "some time ago ... was handed over a video from two former top employees of NASA". Apart from containing testimonies to the existence of UFOs and alien beings, and frequent contacts between army commanders and extraterrestrial beings, pictures were allegedly shown "of the contacts with a dolphin-like man with a human body and a dolphin head".[16] It appears that notions of cross-breeding between humans and dolphins have also entered the UFO strain of New Age mythology.[17]

But dolphins in New Age contexts are not simply dolphins. From a scientific point of view, dolphins are divided into seventeen genera comprising around forty different species, but "dolphin" in New Age perceptions, whether expressed through narratives or iconography, is almost exclusively of one particular kind; the common bottlenose dolphin (*Tursiops truncatus*). This may be partly explained by the fact that the bottlenose is the most common and familiar species, but considering the romantic vision of cetacean mythologizing, the appealing facial expression of the animal is likely to be the chief cause. From an *emic* point of view, all qualities attributed to bottlenose dolphins are reflected in the animal's enchanting physiognomy. It simply appears smiling, friendly and humorous, hence the abovementioned Muriel's greeting: "With dolphin smiles". Furthermore, dolphins are often interested in human company, they are very intelligent, easy to train, they have a complicated system of sound signals indicating high awareness of the surroundings, and they have a high degree of individual personality, while being at the same time very social animals. These facts totally supersede the aggressive or competitive nature of the species which is also occasionally expressed. In New Age contexts the captivating features almost wipe out the animal nature of the species. Spinner Dolphins (*Stenella longirostris*), another appealing kind, rank as a less frequent second choice. There is little doubt that the human identification with dolphins starts with an appreciation of the animals' human-like traits, the significant "smile" and the social behaviour. From a cognitive-psychological point of view, humans seem to use dolphins to mirror and reinforce their own ideals and virtues.

The notion of being a dolphin, to sum up, is a fairly recent construct. In their early summary of cetaceans in New Age speculations, J. Gordon Melton and his co-writers (Melton *et al.* 1991: 381–4) make no mention of humans who believe themselves to be dolphins one way or another, presumably because the idea had not surfaced in the dynamic New Age mythologies yet. The precise explanation behind the rise of human-dolphin identities in New Age thoughts is uncertain, but a diffusion of general socio-cultural influences is not at all unlikely. Notions of trans-species mutations occur in other realms of popular culture, for instance in the famous Harry Potter novels. In an Internet wiki expounding the Harry Potter universe, the concept of "Trans-Species Transformation" is described as "a sub-type of Transformation magic in which (presumably) one organism is either fully or partially Transfigured into another or a different species".[18] Another possible source of inspiration, although less likely, are the many cartoon characters that criss-cross the boundaries between the human and the animal realm such as Mickey Mouse and his numerous colleagues. It is possible that science has also inspired this aspect of New Age thinking. Psychologist Gay Bradshaw, for instance, writes about her work on trans-species psychology: "The *trans* affixed to psychology re-embeds humans within the larger matrix of the animal kingdom by erasing the 'and' between humans and animals that has been used to demarcate and reinforce the false notion that humans are substantively different cognitively and emotionally from other species".[19] New Agers will easily accommodate this understanding, and include a dynamic, transformative physical realm as a common ground. Other scientific sources of inspiration could stem from the fact that animal tissue is used experimentally to substitute human organs, that genetic science is manipulating the boundaries of single species in laboratories, and that certain animal rights groups campaign in order to achieve legal rights for certain animals compared to those of humans ("human rights" for animals, so to say), more specifically the larger primates and cetaceans. The issue of "non-human personhood" is developing, especially with reference to the greater apes, but also dolphins are promoted as persons with legal rights, quite comparable to humans, in projects involving scientists as well as concerned activists.[20]

THE SOCIAL-PSYCHOLOGICAL CONTEXT

Belief systems outside Euro-American brands of Christianity, not least New Age mythologies, are often frowned upon or seen as ridiculous, and the spectator may wonder "if they actually believe in – this or that?" What we should consider, however, is whether people actually believe in things in the way they *say* they do. Did the woman at the Copenhagen fair, for instance, really consider herself to be a dolphin, or is her *de facto* understanding more nuanced than the simple wording suggests?[21] I would pose a counter-question: Why ask? Would we question the statements of the Tupinambá man-jaguar, or the Bororo man-parrot in similar ways? Certainly not. We would, as demonstrated above, try to understand the deeper semantics of their assertions in order to comprehend a socio-cognitive equation quite different from our own. We would, in fact, *expect* to identify some kind of rationality that would disentangle the strange claim we had encountered, and we are not surprised when we learn that human identities in such alien cultures are negotiable, ritually defined, based on kinship, created through initiations, related to sex and trade, and interchangeable between different individuals, be they human or animal. Hence Smith's question, as follows, arises out of a recurrent methodological problem in the history of religions: "How should the historian of religion interpret a religious statement which is apparently contrary to fact?" (J. Z. Smith 1972: 393). So, returning to our examples, we may ask if the individual Hans Staden spoke with actually believed himself to be a jaguar, whether the Bororo factually sees himself as a large, red parrot and whether the dolphin woman really understands herself to be a cetacean?

From a cognitive point of view it is highly unlikely, as demonstrated with great clarity by Smith in his analysis of Bororo conceptions and their interpretations. The Bororo cannot fly, they have no beaks, no feathers and no capability of laying eggs or uttering incredible cries – but they engage, as we have seen, in a mythology that claims an intimate interchangeability between people and birds. The Bororo, consequently, are – at best – parrots on imagined levels, in terms of ethics and social identities, but not in biological reality. It would be a gross underestimation of the Tupinambá or Bororo to say that they are not themselves aware of this fact, and certainly the initial theory (posed by von den Steinen) that they were unable to discern between humans and animals has been proven wrong (as summarized by Smith, *ibid.*). Semantics does not necessarily refer to a biological or physical reality, and the human mind is capable of distinguishing between various levels, especially in religious contexts where imagined or metaphorical realities are crucial: despite the identity claims of the Copenhagen dolphin woman, there was no water, no clicking sounds, no blow-hole splashing and no feasting on fish or squid. The dolphin was, in concrete terms, a human, as are Alyse, Amelia, Muriel and all their counterparts referred to above, although something more complex according to their religious imagination. Humans often

126

operate on more than one cognitive level at the same time. However, Smith's analysis shows to what extent scholars have failed to identify the complexity of the man-bird relation underlying the Bororo statements. As mentioned already, the notion of being *araras* has primarily to do with future, post-mortem forms and thus with human transgression in a larger perspective. A no less complex analysis has been offered by de Castro in his discussion of the Areweté as mentioned above: Only after a meticulous examination of symbolism and semantics in language and behaviour was he able to identify the epistemological and ontological categories of these people, and his analysis may indirectly enlighten us regarding the Tupinambá. Of special importance is the fact that physical reality is only one level of the actuality people live in, and the ability to transform status and identity – including trans-species morphing – seems to be of decisive importance in the ritualized process of relating to other people, whether you incorporate them into your being by devouring them (Tupinambá), or relate to them through complicated social structures (Bororo). At any rate, the above examples point in one direction: the *humanimal* identity has to do with the balance between one self and "the other", and the human dolphin in the Euro-American context seems to express a similar relation.[22] As we have seen the dolphin people need to pose as such in order to "find themselves", and only when they are well established with their apparently paradoxical identity are they able to interact harmoniously with others. Their web-page self-narratives show how people have come to terms with their "inner dolphin" after a period of confusion and alienation, and adopted a way of life that allows them to act accordingly.

Two things, however, seem to distinguish the dolphin woman from the two other *humanimal* examples: First, her self-perception is constructed within a subcultural minority with no wider societal recognition. Second her special identity is not only created within a ritual or semi-ritual framework, but also within a distinct millennial macro-historical configuration. As pointed to by Garry Trompf, "members of new religious movements typically share a heightened sense of cosmic significance by believing their activities are crucial for human history", including its culmination in the millennium, the end of times or something similar. According to Trompf, who has accentuated the term macro-history in this connection, the expression denotes "the writing and envisaging of the past as a whole, and doing so usually entails explaining present conditions and presaging momentous events in the future" (Trompf 2012: 63). According to New Age macro-history, that the world is currently experiencing the advent of the Age of Aquarius, the dawn of a new era, and the rise of "dolphin consciousness", or the merging of humans and dolphins, cannot be understood detached from this notion. It happens as an element in the creation of the new world (although the balance between cause and effect is difficult to determine) and indeed a number of parallel ideas have emerged simultaneously, the appearance of so called Indigo Children, Star Children or Crystal Children being the most obvious.[23]

This does not mean that time is irrelevant in the case of the Tupinambá and the Bororo (in fact the Bororo have a very complicated concept of time and space, cf. Fabian 1992) but it is only in the New Age context that the *human-imal* identities usher in a transformed world. In both South American cases, on the contrary, the merging of human and animal features serves to reinforce the prevailing order of things.

If we combine these observations – that dolphin identities are used to establish a certain kind of self awareness, and a certain kind of relations to others, and that it takes place within a millenarian vision of time – a clearer picture emerges: people of the New Age become dolphins due to their engagement in what they believe to be a cosmic transformation. Tapping into general New Age beliefs they see themselves as heralds of the new world, and while everything belonging to the dying age disappears they will join the millennium in reshaped identities. Assuming dolphin identity means to be part of the New Age. In that sense it is possible to establish a parallel between the Tupinambá jaguar, the Bororo parrot and the New Age dolphin: In all three cases people acquire an animal identity in order to transgress what is (in simple terms) human. The jaguar is able to transgress the boundary between the self and "the other" by devouring a human being, the parrot paves the way into what New Agers may term "the next step of the ongoing transition of the self", and the dolphin rides the waves into the Age of Aquarius. The human animals are themselves transmuted, but the process is ignited by a structural need for transformation on a societal or cosmic level. In order to accomplish a transformation, people themselves need to be transformed, and as the transmutations take place in social settings (be they official or subcultural) we may add that the formation of *humanimal* identities are societal rather than individual enterprises. Although not always.

"I REALLY WOULD LIKE TO BE A CAT"

In order to stress the religious balance of trans-species metamorphoses, I will offer a small excursion to the case of a human animal who, lacking a meaningful contextualization, ended "off-track".

Sometimes the transformation from human to animal transcends the realm of imagination and interpretation. One remarkable example was the late computer programmer, Stalking Cat, originally called Dennis Avner (1958–2012). Stalking Cat, also known as "Cat Man", according to his own narrative, was inspired to "follow the way of the tiger" by a native Huron elder.[24] And so he did, by gradually shapeshifting into a pseudo-feline by means of surgical modification of his entire body. A simple search on the Internet will divulge brief texts and astonishing photos of the Cat Man, who made a point of posing as a tiger, or rather, as he imagined a tiger to appear. Avner's parents, who are of Huron and Lakota descent, reportedly said "that altering oneself to resemble one's own totem is an ancient Huron tradition", thus defending Dennis's life project and contextualizing it within a specific religious tradition. Their son, however, was all but well contextualized. Disregarding his individual motivations, it seems to have been impossible for him to identify a social context where his shapeshifting made sense. I have been able to locate only one relevant reference that confirms "cat" as a totem animal with respect to Huron religion, but I have found no reference to cross-species transformation at all (Vogel 1986: 14). I would deem it quite doubtful that this example reflects an actual tradition. The Cat Man, consequently, was deprived of the mythological and social references that would accord his identity meaning in the eyes of others. Contrary to the human jaguar, parrot or dolphin, he operated on his own, rather desperately searching for the kind of social support or recognition that would bestow some kind of workable cat-identity upon him. He was, for instance, trying to finance his costly surgery by collecting money from people on the Internet in order to further advance his bodily transformation. The fact that he was alone and deconstructed from ordinary society with no place to go in his quest for recognition, however, testifies to the fact that *humanimal* identities such as those briefly explored in this chapter totally depend on the cooperation of the transforming individual and his or her surroundings in order to make sense and become workable. While Stalking Cat remained a freak in the eyes of his wider community (and probably eventually ended his own life), Konyan Bebe, the Bororo kinsman and the woman at the Copenhagen New Age fair are totally intelligible to the groups they refer to. Furthermore, Stalking Cat's example shows that the outer appearance of the human transformed into an animal is of no consequence: he did (at least superficially) look more of a feline than the others look like jaguars, parrots or dolphins, but lacking cultural approval, it did not count.[25] What makes the transmutation happen is the cultural framing, be it specifically ritualistic or socially implicit.[26]

CONCLUSION

I am not arguing that New Age is devoid of particularities, but I would like to soften the idea that something very peculiar or special is taking place. By comparing one particular feature, which may appear radical or extraordinary at first glance, to a few very different cases, I have tried to show that the religious creativity of New Agers has its obvious parallels in societies of a very different kind. This indicates that basic tenets of New Age are quite intelligible even if concepts of modernity or postmodernity are disregarded. We should not be deluded and think that New Age cosmologies have reintroduced magic, mystery and myth into society. Religious imagination never left. It has been there all along, either in the shape of Christianity, or embedded in the age old esoteric-occult traditions of Europe and the United States, which have been rekindled by the emergence of New Age interests during the past decades. I would prefer to conceive of this as a phenomenon comparable to other religions, rather than something exceptionally typical to the place and age in which we live. In doing so I am inserting New Age into the context of religion as such, thereby challenging current theory, which too often sees this particular strain of human religiosity as a very special modern or postmodern kind. Obviously any religious notion is fostered by a particular societal condition. The idea of somehow being a dolphin does not emerge just anywhere at any time. But neither would the notion of being intimately linked with jaguars or large red parrots. Why, then, consider modernity or postmodernity to be the crucial facet in the construction of the human dolphin? Why not look for broader social-psychological capacities in humans that allow and enable people to build trans-species identities? My suggestion is that the fertility of the modern or postmodern soil in which New Age religion is believed to thrive is sometimes exaggerated, and that modernity or postmodernity are insufficient references if we wish to understand phenomena such as human dolphins in Copenhagen.

NOTES

1. References may be superfluous as all important New Age studies since Paul Heelas's 1996 volume *The New Age Movement. The Celebration of the Self and the Sacralization of Modernity* contribute along rather consistent lines, oscillating between modernity and postmodernity as the meta-analytical focal point. For a general comment on these positions in New Age studies, see Partridge (2007: 233–6) which includes references to scholars (James Beckford, Marion Bowman and Michael York not least) who see New Age as a phenomenon epitomizing postmodernity, although Partridge himself (*ibid.*: 236), as Heelas (1996: 216–17), favours modernity as the best reference point.

2. See note 1 above.

3. This translation is taken from Whitehead and Harbsmeier (2008: 91). The word "jaguar", in Hans Staden's original German account, is "tiger", presumably the closest he could get to translate the name of the unfamiliar feline mentioned by Konyan Bebe into his own language (what, more precisely, "tiger" meant to Staden and his European readers remains unclear).

4. There is no single reference, as descriptions are scattered throughout Staden's text. However, most incidents are described in chapters I and II (cf. Whitehead & Harbsmeier 2008: 21–2).

5. This is supported by my personal fieldwork experiences in the Kaiowá Dourados, *aldeia*, Mato Grosso du Sul, Brazil 2007.

6. Quotation taken from J. L. Martin (2011: 154).

7. Formulation taken from French (2011: 77–8). The Bororo, apparently, recognize the fact that macaws are owned by women with mixed feelings.

8. No year is given, but presumably these events refer to the mid 1990s. See: http://paulapeterson.com/Dolphin_Children.html (all web references in this chapter were accessed during July 2012, and where mentioned, April 2013).

9. In order to calm the child's desire to be aquatic, her father had wrapped her legs in order to make her appear as a mermaid, but this clearly was not the identity she wished to assume. Apparently this was in the year 2002. See: www.heathermacauley.com/dolphin-children.htm.

10. See http://paulapeterson.com/Dolphin_Children.html.

11. See www.dolphinglobaltrust.be/swimming-with-dolphins/messengers-of-love.

12. See www.bluedolphinessences.com/Endorsements/History_Sai_Baba.htm.

13. See www.spiritmythos.org/earth/mer/dolphins/nehologram.html.

14. See www.spiritmythos.org/earth/mer/dolphins/dolphchild.html.

15. Ocean's home page gives the following information, though: "20 years ago she was initiated by Melchizidek that she is the ambassador for the dolphins in the Nederlands, she could not believe that she was chosen by the dolphins for this amazing gift, but since ever then the dolphins where the high light of her life". See www.dolphinglobaltrust.be/introduction.

16. The text, by the way, continues with reflections over the rediscovery of Atlantis in the Bermuda Triangle, believed to be predicted by Edgar Cayce more than fifty years ago. See www.dolphinglobaltrust.be/swimming-with-dolphins/messengers-of-love.

17. A good example is the article "The Role of Dolphins in Extraterrestrial Affairs" by Angelika Whitecliff at www.exopoliticsinstitute.org/conference-sem-Angelika-Article-1.htm.

18. See http://harrypotter.wikia.com/wiki/Trans-Species_Transformation.

19. See the home page of Animal Visions at http://animalvisions.wordpress.com/2010/09/17/trans-species-living-an-interview-with-gay-bradshaw.

20. See, as an example, www.aldf.org/article.php?id=2013.

21. We may expand the comparative perspective, and ask if Christians truly believe the Eucharist to be the actual flesh and blood of their man-god? The answer is no, but they believe the miracle of transubstantiation to be real. The cognitive, sensorial experience of bread and wine, however, is unchanged, which relegates the religious claim that something else is going on to a special ritual realm in which it becomes operational.

22. Again a Christian parallel is evident: the Eucharist, the incorporation of the godhead in the human body, is an ultimate expression of the merging of "self" with "the other".

23. The best academic overview I have been able to find is the online *Sceptic's Dictionary*, which has a full account of these concepts with good references. See www.skepdic.com/indigo.html.

24. This quote, and the one pertaining to Avner's parents below, were taken from his now defunct web page. A reference confirming his own statement, however, is available at www.dailymail.co.uk/news/article-2232523/Stalking-Cat-Daniel-Avner-dead-possible-suicide-years-transforming-face-look-like-feline.html (accessed April 2013).

25. It should be noted, though, that Avner was accepted by a number of individuals who were close to him: see his Internet memorial site at http://dennis-stalking-avner.gonetoosoon.org (accessed April 2013).

26. It is possible that the urge to become a certain animal is a special form of a psychological condition known as *body dysmorphic disorder*, where the patient is unable to accept his or her human form. This may be the case with Stalking Cat, but as nothing seems to disturb the anthropoid form of the human jaguar, parrot or dolphin, there is no need to consider pathological explanations in these cases.

8. NEW AGE, SAMI SHAMANISM AND INDIGENOUS SPIRITUALITY

Trude Fonneland and Siv Ellen Kraft

Prior to the late 1990s the New Age spiritualities of Northern Norway differed little from those found elsewhere in the country and in the areas of their origin. Since then, a Sami version of neo-shamanism has been established, along with a new focus on the uniqueness of the arctic north, and expressed through New Age courses and events, as well as through various secular or semi-secular tracks. Reborn as the wisdom of indigenous people in general and the Sami in particular, Sami shamanism caters for spiritual needs, but also for the more mundane needs of tourism, place branding and entertainment, and – last but not least – for Sami nation building and the ethno-political field of indigenous revival.[1]

On one level the story of particular developments in a specific place, Sami shamanism also belongs to broader tendencies in contemporary post-secular society. It will in this chapter serve as a case study through which to explore two issues of general relevance. We are concerned, first, with the interplay between secular and spiritual dynamics, inside and outside of the New Age market. The broader influence of New Age spiritualities tends to be limited to hybrid products – products whose New Age components are open to different interpretations – with or without spiritual references, and which are ascribed at least one function of a more prosaic or secular character (Kraft 2009a). Second we are concerned with the relationship between New Age spiritualities and indigenous peoples, places and ideas, including what we refer to as *indigenous spirituality*. We define this as a discourse concerning the essentialized nature and identity of indigenous people and traditions, forwarded by representatives of the indigenous people's movements, the UN and legislation, tourism and popular culture, academics and activists, and New Age and neo-pagan movements. A close and spiritual relationship to nature is crucial to this discourse, along with sacred landscapes, healing and holism, links to a pre-Christian past, and practices such as animism and shamanism.

The discourse of indigenous spirituality has, we argue, contributed in important ways to the framing of New Age innovations among the Sami as a development within an ancient indigenous tradition, and accordingly legitimated as traditional and authentic. These innovations at the same time support the vaguer discourse on a common and pan-ethnic indigenous spirituality, by providing "live" examples of continuity with the "spiritual inclinations" of the past.

CASE STUDY: THE DEVELOPMENT OF SAMI SHAMANISM

Today known as the founder of the Norwegian neo-shamanic movement, Ailo Gaup participated in demonstrations against the damming of the Alta Kautokeino river in the County of Finnmark, northern Norway, in the late 1970s. Generally regarded as the beginnings of the Sami cultural revival movement, these demonstrations served as premises for what Gaup has referred to as the "78-generation" – the Sami version of the 1968 generation.[2] The latter consisted of young people who to a large, although varying, degree had been cut off from the Sami culture and language of their parents; a generation whose parents had shielded their children from a cultural baggage they considered as shameful, in order to secure for them a better life and more positive prospects. In Gaup's case this break was absolute. Gaup was sent from Kautokeino to a foster family in Oslo as an orphan, and thus lost access to the homeland of his birth.

The early phase of the Sami ethno-political revival was concerned with rights and politics, as well as identity issues, but religion was not among the identity-resources drawn upon. Rather, the reindeer, the *lavvo* (Sami tent) and the *kofte* (traditional Sami clothing) were selected as ethnic symbols and markers. In contrast to these traditional ingredients of Sami culture, Christianity – the main religion of the Sami – carried little potential as a boundary marker against Norwegian surroundings. Meanwhile, the pre-Christian Sami religion was no longer there, and was in addition controversial among Christian Sami. Precisely when Christianity was introduced to the Sami is unclear, but grave excavations reveal that the cross was associated with Sami burial practices from the thirteenth century. From the sixteenth century the building of churches became part of a more conscious colonizing effort in regard to the Sami area, and by the seventeenth century a systematic and active mission was established (Kristiansen 2005). During the mid-nineteenth century a conservative Lutheran revival movement, later to become known as Læstadianism, spread among Sami communities. Læstadianism is still the main religion in Sami core areas and perceptions of the pre-Christian religion as heathen (if not demonic) have in these circles been widespread.

Since the 1990s, a more positive view of the pre-Christian past has gained ground, along with attempts to bridge the gap between *then* and *now*. What Henry Minde refers to as "the preservation theses" has been important to this process (Minde 2008). In contrast to scholars claiming that Læstadianism was the final stage in the Christianization of the Sami, supporters of the preservation theses interpret it as a form that protected Sami traditions, including religious or folk-religious traditions. The old Sami religion, according to radical and romantic versions of this model, never actually disappeared, but lived on under the garbs of Læstadianism.

Similar ideas of hidden yet unbroken traditions and continuity with the past proved important to the development of Sami shamanism. The career of Ailo Gaup – later to become the first professional Sami shaman – was clearly influenced by this theme, and at the same time contributed to its further spread and institutionalization. Gaup's semi-autobiographical publication *The Shamanic Zone* (2005) tells the story of his personal spiritual development, including his interpretation of scholarly literature on the pre-Christian Sami religion. Partly inspired by such studies, Gaup claims to have travelled to the core Sami area of Finnmark in search of his Sami roots, of traces of shamanism, and – last but not least – of a *noaide* (the Sami pre-Christian specialist) who could teach him the art of trance journeys. What he found, at the Tourist Hotel in Kautokeino, was a Chilean refugee called Ernesto, with practical knowledge of trance journeys. Gaup's first ritual visit to the spirit world of his ancestors took place, then, by way of Chilean traditions, and accompanied by an African djembe-drum (Gaup 2005: 86–98).

The second and more decisive step in Gaup's training took place through several extended stays at the retreat centre Esalen in Big Sur, California, where he received training from Michael Harner, the founder of the Foundation for Shamanic Studies. Having thus been trained in Harner's practice of "core shamanism" (Harner 1980), Gaup settled in Oslo and established himself as a professional shaman – a guide to the spirits of the underworld and teacher of an evolving group of Sami shamans. The Norwegian Shamanic movement was, during this first decade (including the version practised by Gaup), more or less a copy of that developed by Harner in the US. The broader New Age scene, similarly, differed little from counterparts in the US and elsewhere in the world. Fieldwork conducted by Andreassen and Fonneland in the New Age milieu in Tromsø in 2002 found few, if any, references to the pre-Christian Sami religion or to local place-specific elements (Andreassen & Fonneland 2002–3). A content study of the leading New Age magazine *Alternative Network* covering the 1990s concluded, similarly, that references to the Sami were more or less absent from the otherwise extensive material on shamanism, paganism and indigenous people (Christensen 2005).

Approximately five years into the new millennium, this scenario shifted. Professional neo-shamans like Ailo Gaup and Eirik Myrhaug were from this period on depicted as representatives of an ancient Sami shamanic tradition

(Christensen 2007), and the Northern Norwegian New Age scene was increasingly filled with Sami shamans, symbols and traditions along with a new focus on local and place-specific characteristics unique to the Northern region, particularly in terms of the domestic geography. The annual New Age fair in Tromsø has since this period included pre-Christian Sami symbols on its advertising material. Sami *lavvos* are placed outside the market hall, indoor market stands offer traditional Sami handwork (*duodji*), and Sami shamanic trance journeys are represented among the selection of spiritual offerings, along with seminars on *joik* (a traditional Sami form of song) and Sami story-telling (Fonneland 2007).

By 2012 Sami shamanism had become a core subject of northern Norwegian New Age. A new generation of professional Sami shamans has been established, and a wide range of new products has been developed, including courses on Sami shamanism, on the making of ritual drums (*runebomme*), guided vision quests in northern Norway, healing-sessions inspired by Sami shamanism and – to mention one of the latest innovations – the Sami shamanic festival Isogaisa, first held at Bardufoss, an hour's drive from the city of Tromsø, and in August 2012 at Fjellkysten in Lavangen. The various products and information about them are available through advertisements, local media coverage, facebook groups, homepages on the Internet and local shops. A variety of Sami ritual drums are, for instance, today offered in tourist shops, at the New Age markets annually arranged in cities all across Norway, as well as on the Internet home pages of Sami shamans (see Fonneland forthcoming).

Indicative of the success of this new movement, the "official" support of Sami shamanism has been rather extensive. The Sami People's organization (Samisk folkeforbund) and Norgga Sáráhkka (a Sami women's organization) have since 2006 served as co-organizers of the New Age market in Tromsø mentioned above, and in March 2012, a local shamanic association concerned with the preservation of Sami and Norse shamanic traditions was granted status as a separate religious community by the County Governor of Troms. This means, according to the laws regulating the religious field in Norway, that members of the association may perform religious ceremonies like baptism, weddings and funerals, and in addition gain financial support relative to membership. This group of practising shamans is now working on developing a ceremony repertoire which will form the basis for the association's rites of passages. For Isogaisa 2012 members also arranged a board election voting for chairman and board members. Interestingly, this shamanic association appears to have been created in order to meet the criteria required for obtaining the rights of Norwegian religious communities; national jurisdiction thus inspired a diverse group of professional entrepreneurs to join forces and organize themselves. It is, at the same time, likely that the Sami ethnic dimension of these endeavours contributed positively to the Governor's decision.

Precisely how, then, does this new construct differ from its US origins in Harner's core shamanism? In terms of basic ideas and practices little appears to have changed: Gaup has followed a route laid out in Harner's syncretic teachings. Having identified what he considered to be the key ingredients of indigenous people's religious notions and practices, Harner urged indigenous people to trace their own particular roots, and thereby to contribute to the global reservoir of shamanic resources. This, one might claim, is precisely what Gaup and his colleagues have set out to achieve. The results are visible on several levels of their enterprises. It is, for instance, common to use terms and symbols from the pre-Christian Sami religion – Gaup's shaman school is known as Saivo Shaman school (*Saivo* being a Sami name for the underworld); the local shamanic organization is called *Skaidi* (a Sami name picturing a scenery were rivers meet), and the festival Isogaisa is named after a mountain in the region of Bardufoss. Meanwhile, the northern Norwegian fauna has resulted in a broader register of power animals like the reindeer and the lynx, and shamanic books, web pages and courses refer to great Sami shamans of the past – both male and female, along with stories of their suppression, of forced assimilation and of current revival.[3] Gaup also provides vision quests to the landscape of his birth, and his colleague Eirik Myrhaug offers shamanic courses at a local Sami sacrificial stone in his hometown, Gratangen.

However, although coloured by local raw material, the teachings and practices of Sami shamanism differ little from those developed at Esalen. We have, as Stephen Prothero in a different empirical context has argued, a change of vocabulary, but continuity in terms of basic ideas: a Sami lexicon built upon a neo-shamanic grammar (Prothero 1996).[4] This construct, moreover, makes sense from the perspective of the broader ethno-political search for a Sami identity and in regard to the Sami's connections to indigenous peoples worldwide and trans-historically. It also makes sense in economic and marketing terms. Sami versions of shamanism are today presented as more authentic than Harner's American Indian version, partly – some actors claim – due to commercialization of the latter.

SECULAR DYNAMICS AND HYBRID ENCOUNTERS

In the wake of Sami shamanism, a variety of hybrid products have been established, catering for broader audiences and for a variety of needs, including tourism, regional development and entertainment. References to Sami shamanism are today represented within experience-oriented and entertainment institutions like museums, festivals, theatres, within the film and tourism industries as well as in the form of products of a more tangible nature like books, video games and food. They are offered by professional Sami shamans and secular agents, and by Sami and ethnic Norwegians alike, and they draw on trends in the spiritual milieu as well as in the experience economy.[5] Secular and spiritual actors and institutions share an interest in landscapes of wilderness and opportunities to experience the past, and they draw – to some extent – upon the same vocabulary. The phrase "arctic magic", for instance, has during the last decade been established as a common ingredient in tourist and cultural promotional material of various sorts, with the northern Norwegian region constructed as an arctic region, situated near the borders of civilization (Bæck & Paulgaard 2012).

Since approximately the turn of the century, various versions of hybrid Sami shamanism have been included among the offers of the tourist industry, many of which involve an experiential dimension. At Sápmi Park, a tourist theme park in the village of Karasjok in Finnmark, tourists are offered virtual encounters with the *noaide* (Mathisen 2010). At the festival Isogaisa, Sami shamanism is listed and marketed as both entertainment and as an important tool for self-development. In the recently launched Sami video game "Sáivu", children are encouraged to design their own shaman drums, which upon beating, produce a magic helper. Next, after having successfully solved a task and found certain Sami items, both tasks and items are to be handed over at a *sieide*, a Sami sacrificial stone.

The spiritual entrepreneurship of Esther Utsi in Tana, Finnmark, illustrates many of the tendencies referred to above, and is in addition perhaps the most elaborate example in our material. Today in her sixties, Utsi in 1997 resigned from her job as head of the local social department in Finnmark County to set up Polmakmoen Guesthouse – a venue designed to meet the needs of spiritual seekers, tourists and companies in search of an inspirational break and facilities for team-building. The premises consist of several Sami turf huts equipped with all mod-cons, a large hut used for meals, entertainment and spiritual practices, an Indian style sweat lodge, and a house used as conference venue. The hostess collaborates with various local tourist entrepreneurs and her business is supported by Innovation Norway, the Norwegian Government's most important instrument for innovation and development of Norwegian enterprises and industry (see Fonneland 2012b).

At Polmakmoen Guesthouse visitors are welcomed with narratives about Utsi's own spiritual calling and development, including communication with Sami ancestors and Native Canadian Indians. During dinner, which she herself cooks and serves, she entertains guests with tales from Sami traditions, and there are meditation sessions accompanied by Sami folk music. Outside of meals, guests can choose between various products typical of the New Age scene, but here presented as rooted in Sami shamanism, including crystal therapies, individual healing sessions and self-development courses – the latter offered to groups as well as to single persons.[6]

Guests who wish to explore further the local area or their own inner depths are invited to take part in the pilgrimage "The Seven Coffee Stops" by foot, on skis or by car – according to the season.[7] The pilgrimage is based upon the tracks of Utsi's reindeer-herding forefathers, from inland to coast and from winter to summer pasture, and is led by Utsi herself and a local guide. The "seven coffee stops" at one level refer to particular places in the landscape where a chosen story connected to Sami reindeer herding traditions is performed. Utsi has created a repertoire of stories from her own family's life and work on the Varanger plateau, all of them focusing on key tasks and challenges related to the work of the reindeer herders and their families. At another level the pilgrimage refers to the seven chakras of the human body, with the pilgrimage perceived as a journey starting at the root chakra and ending at the crown chakra. In the words of Utsi:

> So every coffee stop then has a theme which describes the culture, the nature, food and history, so that the guests will learn more about the area. This is the first dimension. The second dimension is the human body's seven chakras that you are helping to open when you travel through the coffee stops.[8]

The seven coffee stops thus involve old wisdom and more recent mythology, along with wild life experiences and the physical challenge and joy of walking. And it involves, last but not least, a link between the Sami herders of the past and late modern pilgrims (see also Coats 2011: 122), with the Varanger plateau changed from pure geography to a scene where the Sami past is unfolding, through links to both New Age core values and to a Sami heritage. According to Utsi each "coffee stop" constitutes the starting point of an inner journey with wilderness experiences, meditation, healing, and Sami shamanism as catalysts (Fonneland 2012b).

Perhaps the single most interesting ingredient of Utsi's business, is the almost complete lack of the criticism usually granted to New Age entrepreneurs. As elsewhere in the Western world, New Age is situated low on the Norwegian scale of "real" religions. The news media in particular, tend to depict New Age entrepreneurs as cynical and greedy on the one hand, and naive and silly on the other (Kraft 2011). Utsi, in sharp contrast to the status of her New Age colleagues, has established herself as a media-darling and a local hero. She has several times been nominated for the title "Finnmarking of the year", based upon votes to local candidates on the basis of personal achievements, and both local and national media portray her as courageous and creative: an entrepreneur whose novel projects and ideas have helped put Finnmark on the map.[9] In the words of her local newspaper, "Utsi is a driven woman in the travel industry in eastern Finnmark. She runs both Kjølnes lighthouse and Polmakmoen Guesthouse. And the number of this year's visitors has been overwhelming".[10]

This then, is the image of a creative woman, able to keep alive the traditions she has inherited and adjust them to the needs of modern society. In line with this image, the spiritual dimension of her endeavors is commonly referred to as shamanism or Sami spiritual traditions. Placed in the traditional surroundings of Polmakmoen Guesthouse, even well-known New Age markers – like crystals, pendulums and chakras – are perceived by the media as a natural part of ancient Sami traditions. As a Sami woman, she is expected to be close to nature, the traditions of her ancestors and their ancient spirituality. Utsi, in other words, is interpreted according to the framework of what we below refer to as *indigenous spirituality*.

"INDIGENOUS SPIRITUALITY"

Kraft has in previous publications described indigenous spirituality as a civil religious dimension of Sami nation building, concerned first and foremost with identity-issues – with the Sami as distinct from Norwegian/Western surroundings, and as a part of the broader international family of indigenous people. Richard Perard and Robert Linder have suggested five functions typical of civil religions. First, people widely accept a shared sense of their nation's history. Second, the society is related to a realm of absolute meaning, and third, it is perceived as in some sense special. Fourth, civil religions provide a discourse that ties the nation together. Finally, a collection of beliefs, values, ceremonies and symbols contribute to an overarching sense of unity (Pierard & Linder 1988: 22–3). Sami nation building exhibits all of these functions (see Kraft 2009a, 2009b). Like civil religions in general, its spiritual references tend to be vague and inclusive, and like nationalist orientations they are concerned with the relationship between *then–now*, and *here–us* – with a mythical space where *we* were once defined and later can search for ourselves (Eriksen 1999). In the words of Anne Eriksen: "Nationalist history has been concerned not merely to document that a given nation is old, but to an equal degree that throughout its extensive history it has preserved a cultural distinctiveness; that 'we' are still the same" (*ibid.*: 71; our translation). Unlike nation states, indigenous cultures often lack a state territory, and where nation states typically define themselves in terms of their own uniqueness, indigenous cultures increasingly situate their uniqueness within the framework of indigeneity as a global phenomenon (see Kraft 2009a).

This new global identity is partly a result of UN meetings and regulations, including laws that have helped standardize certain assumed qualities by translating them into rights. In contrast to the "freedom of beliefs" promoted by human rights discourse, the beliefs of indigenous people tend, for instance, to be explicitly connected to particular landscapes. To cite one example: ILO Convention 169 (Indigenous and Tribal Peoples Convention, 1989), ratified by Norway in 1990, claims that governments must "respect the special importance for the cultures and spiritual values of the peoples concerning their relationship with the lands or territories" (Article 13, 1). Regular references to indigenous people as children of Mother Earth are similarly common in UN fora, along with references to a holistic worldview.[11] A key symbol in the discourse on indigenous spirituality, forwarded primarily by New Age circles from the 1970s,[12] Mother Earth has come to symbolize all of the qualities discussed above, and in addition a view of her "children" as crucial to her saving. In the words of the above mentioned ILO convention 169, the spiritual relationship of indigenous peoples to the land are important to *humankind as such*. The convention calls attention to "the distinctive contributions of indigenous and tribal people to the cultural diversity and social and ecological harmony of humankind and to international co-operation and understanding" (page 1). As Sami scholar Harald Gaski in more poetical (and essentialist) terms has formulated it: the Sami constitute "the modern natural man, still hearing and obeying the heartbeats of the Earth itself", and are – due to their high level of modernization – "particularly suited to mediate between a Western alienation from nature and an indigenous holistic thinking" (Gaski 2004: 371).

To some extent a reversal of the primitivism of the past, the discourse on indigenous spirituality qualifies for Michael Shermer's notion of "the myth of the beautiful people" (Shermer 1997). Characteristics that once placed indigenous people on a lower level of the evolutionary scale today account for their position as peaceful, wise and noble caretakers of environmental wisdom. As anthropologist Jonathan Friedman has put it:

> [The] indigenous is now part of a larger inversion of Western cosmology in which the traditional other, a modern category, is no longer the starting point of a long and positive evolution of civilization, but a voice of Wisdom, a way of life in tune with nature, a culture in harmony, a *gemeinschaft*, that we have all but lost.
> (Friedman 1999: 391)

Indigenous spirituality depends upon this broader reversal of established categories, with the relationship to nature as boundary marker. Indigenous people have a close and spiritual relationship to nature, according to this discourse, based upon ancient traditions and holistic worldviews. Western societies lack such wisdom, are alienated from nature, do not experience themselves as part of its holistic connections, have historically exploited and abused them, and appear – accordingly – as place-less. The category "indigenous", as Peter Beyer has noted, is local by definition: "It is what was 'here from the origins', as opposed to that which came here 'from somewhere else, relatively recently'" (Beyer 2006: 103). The West, in contrast, is associated with mobility and capitalism – with claims to ownership of the Earth, and with exploitation of its resources.

Christianity belongs to the "West" according to this logic, as an example of that which "came here relatively recently", and collaborated with Western state regimes in the colonialization of that which was "here from the origins" (*ibid.*). For this reason, one may assume, and despite its position as the religion of the Sami since the seventeenth century (Kristiansen 2005), Christianity has largely been left out of the indigenous nation building project. Cultural distinctiveness has been rooted in the pre-Christian past, while Læstadianism has accounted for its continuing presence, the motif that *we are still the same*. Læstadianism, according to the theme of preservation and hidden traditions, provided room and shelter for ancient Sami ideas and practices. In the words of professor of pedagogics Jens Ivar Nergård, the most prominent voice of this perspective, "the old nature religion entered a kind of inner exile, disguised under Læstadian Christianity" (Nergård 2006, our translation). From this exile it has served, and still serves, as a repository of wisdom and a buffer against forced assimilation.[13]

An example of what Olav Hammer (2001: 85–200) has referred to as "the appeal to tradition", the theme of exile provides a historical base to the idea of an essential "Sami-ness" across time and place, while at the same time adding authenticity to the current generation of Sami shamans. Indicative of this process, the so-called "reader" – a Læstadian religious expert and healer – is frequently synonymized with the shaman and the *noaide*. The profiled actor and shaman Mikkel Gaup has, for instance, in media interviews regularly referred to his grandfather, who was a well-known Læstadian reader, as a shaman, and claims – moreover – to have been offered to take over his vocation. Like in the case of Esther Utsi, the media accepts such stories and practices as typical of a Sami tradition that was for a long time hidden, but now finally is coming into the open.[14]

Scholars like Jens-Ivar Nergård have contributed in important ways to the semi-factual status of the "theme of exile" and recent revival of an ancient religion, and of this type of religiosity as typical – if not integral – to the concept of indigeneity and indigenous people, including the Sami. As to the wider spread of such ideas, popular culture like music and film have no doubt been important. Historian of religion Cato Christensen has in several articles explored the history-making significance of Sami films, with particular focus on two feature films by the Sami film-maker Nils Gaup: *The Path Finder* (1987) and *The Kautokeino Rebellion* (2008) (Christensen 2012; Christensen & Kraft 2011). *The Path Finder* was the first Sami feature film, was nominated for an Oscar reward, and is generally regarded as important to the international development of indigenous film. Gaup's representation of a pre-historic Sami community, guided by its pathfinder, the *noaide*, was in addition a commercial success, and has been acknowledged in Norwegian public discourses as not only a good film but as important to understanding Sami history and the Sami people.

In *The Kautokeino Rebellion* Gaup moves on to the Christian era, with an adaption of a traumatic event in Sami history – a violent conflict in the village of Kautokeino, where a group of Sami reindeer-herders killed the local chief of police and the village's merchant (Christensen & Kraft 2011). At one level an attempt to redress cultural memories, Christensen argues, the film represents the killings as the inevitable outcome of the evil regime of Norwegian church representatives (Christensen 2012). At another level, of more explicit relevance to the "preservation theses" and secret traditions, *The Kautokeino Rebellion* provides a portrait of a Læstadian community equipped with the key ingredients of indigenous spirituality: nature spirituality, a holistic worldview, and a few – but significantly placed markers to the repertoire of the *noaide* religion of the past. References to *Noaidevuohta* (the Sami pre-Christian religion) are, at the same time, vague enough not to upset the Læstadian community, among which the Sami pre-Christian religion is still controversial. As the folklorist Thomas DuBois comments, in an article on *The Pathfinder*:

> *Noaidevuohta* (shamanism), the divinatory drum, and other aspects of Sami pre-Christian religion carry little charm or allure for many members of Gaup's insider community. While Scandinavians further to the South may dabble in neopaganist explorations of shamanic rituals and worldview with seeming impunity, many Sami in the late 1980s remained ambivalent or opposed to this aspect of their culture's past. The old religion continues to be viewed as illicit among many Nordic Sami Christians, who belong to either the Lutheran church or the Læstadian sects within it and who often view pre-Christian traditions as irreligious and idolatrous.   (DuBois 2000: 268)

Although to some extent still controversial, opposition to aspects of the Sami pre-Christian religion, such as the *noaidie*, the drum, *joik* and shamanism seem during recent years to be limited to their presence on church ground, as part of Christian liturgy and ceremonies.[15] Ideas and practices related to Sami shamanism are today common in tourist enterprises controlled by the Sami and in semi-official institutions like museums. In Norwegian media and popular culture, Sami shamanism is commonly referred to as *the religion of the Sami* – historically and today, and frequently with a lack of distinction between the two.

It seems, then, that what a decade ago emerged as a New Age-style innovation has to some extent been established as part of the cultural revival of the Sami – as a revival of past traditions rather than an invention of new ones. It seems clear, moreover, that this process depended on the broader discourse of "indigenous spirituality" – on a discourse that revolves around similar ideas to that of neo-shamanism, but lacks the negative connotations of the latter. Sami shamanism, at the same time, today serves as a live example of the strength and continuity of Sami traditions, thus – one may assume – adding positively to the pool of ethnic markers.

Both an identity concept and a political resource, indigenous spirituality belongs to the ethno-political project of building a positive identity and to the political sphere of rights and regulations. It is expressed through popular cultural forms, as well as through local and national media (see Kraft 2009b), and it has – to some extent – entered the world of official legislation and political decision-making. In 2004, to name one example, plans to build a ski-trek on Tromsdalstinden, a mountain in the outskirts of the northern Norwegian town Tromsø, were cancelled in the wake of evidence that it was once a sacred Sami mountain and the site of ritual performances (see Kraft 2010b). An example of what John L. Comaroff has referred to as "theo-legality" and the "rise of legal theology" (Comaroff 2010), the Sami ethno-political movement – like religious and particularly indigenous religions around the world – draw upon "rights and rites" in their search for a viable identity. We have, in these instances a "politics of recognition" that translates "into rights", or to phrase it differently – contexts in which "the discourse of rites is elemental to the discourse of rights … and vice versa" (*ibid.*: 194).

CONCLUSION: NEW AGE, INDIGENEITY AND SECULAR DYNAMICS

The choice of a narrow versus a broad concept of New Age obviously has crucial implications for evaluations of its present status. In our case a narrow version would exclude both the touristic and marketing tendencies we have explored, the discourse on indigenous spirituality, and perhaps even Sami shamanism. As to the latter, it is hard, in the landscapes explored in this case, to distinguish clearly between "New Age" and "neo-paganism", and not necessarily fruitful to do so. These operate on the same market and draw upon similar ideas of self-development and self-realization. Many of them also combine techniques and therapies connected to both New Age (in a narrow sense) and neo-paganism (in a narrow sense). In the case of entrepreneurs like Esther Utsi, the status of her offerings as "Sami shamanism" clearly has more to do with her ethnic background than with her actual practices. We have here a spiritual entrepreneur focusing mainly on self-help therapies such as crystal therapy and healing, and in addition, a tourist enterprise combining elements from local Sami traditions and New Age pilgrimage, and offered to spiritual seekers and "ordinary" tourists alike. In order to make sense of this type of spiritual setting, it is – we have argued – crucial to take into account the interplay between secular and religious elements and include what we have referred to as "hybrid" products.

The development of Sami shamanism and indigenous spirituality calls for similar allowance for hybridity and fluid boundaries. The tendency in

scholarly research has been to distinguish rather sharply between the interests of New Age entrepreneurs on the one hand, and the traditional practices of indigenous peoples, on the other.[16] The noble savage, according to
this view, depends upon maintaining some distance – be that in geographic
or temporal terms (Bowman 1995). It is a concept of New Age discourse,
connected to the romantization of primitive "others", and as such it is a late
modern contribution to older traditions of Western colonialization.

There is no shortage of convincing examples to support charges of cultural theft and demeaning practices. Current conditions are, at least in the
case of the Norwegian Sami, far more complex than those depicted in the
scenario of indigenous victims of New Age abuse. Such a scenario fails to
account for the presence of indigenous people within these same scenarios, including Sami shamans and the voices of indigenous spirituality. An
example of what Harald Prins has called "the paradox of primitivism", the
reproduction of primitivist themes is no longer limited to "Western" circles.
Primitives themes are explored also by indigenous actors, some of whom
recognize the primitivist formula, and some of whom actively draw on it
as a cross-cultural "structure of comprehension and imperatives for action"
(Prins 2002: 56). Their motives may be economic, spiritual, connected to
the search for a meaningful ethnic identity – or all of the above. Indicative
of the hybrid character of New Age spiritualities, they belong to primitivist
traditions as well as to recent processes of cultural revitalization and local
meaning-making.

NOTES

1. The Sami people are the indigenous people inhabiting the Arctic area of Sápmi, which
   today encompasses parts of Sweden, Norway, Finland and the Kola Peninsula of Russia.
   The Sami are recognized under the international conventions of indigenous people, and
   are the northernmost indigenous people of Europe.
2. See the newspaper *Klassekampen* ("Class Struggle"), 11–12 March 2006.
3. See for instance *Eirik Myrhaug. Sjaman for livet* (Brynn & Brunvoll 2011), *The Shamanic
   Zone* (Gaup 2005), *Samisk Shamanism* (Eriksson 1988).
4. Prothero developed the model in a study of Henry Steel Olcott, co-founder of the
   Theosophical Society in 1875, and the first US citizen to convert to Buddhism. His
   argument is based on the notion of creolization, a term borrowed from comparative
   linguistics, where it refers to the process by which languages and dialects come into
   contact and fuse in colonial contexts. Olcott's faith, Prothero argues, was a "'Buddhism'
   of his own invention … a Buddhist lexicon informed by a Protestant grammar and
   spoken with a theosophical accent" (Prothero 1996: 69).
5. Pine and Gilmore (1999) define the experience economy as a concept which
   encompasses all types of branding and is about engaging consumers through personal
   stories and images that are meant to give each individual customer access to a unique,
   memorable and extraordinary experience.
6. Polmakmoen Guesthouse is used as a site for conferences and courses by different firms
   such as Statoil and Volvo, by the Norwegian Government as represented by some of

its ministries and by the Sami parliament. Though not taking part in organized New Age courses, these firms and politicians are all introduced to Utsi's standard repertoire concerning her spiritual experiences and can be said to exemplify how a New Age spirituality has taken root within the public domain of business organizations (compare the Dutch case study in Aupers and Houtman 2006: 211–14; this article is reproduced in the present volume).

7. A "coffee stop" is a local measurement related to three factors: distance, time and relationships. Traditionally, a coffee stop referred to selected sites of rest in the landscape where one stopped to take a break and boil coffee on the fire. These sites were also viewed as social gathering places where relationships were created.

8. Interview with Esther Utsi, November 2010; our translation.

9. See the local newspapers *Nordlys*, 17 October 2010; *Finnmark Dagblad*, 23 July 2010; *VG*, 15 February 2009.

10. See *Finnmark Dagblad*, 23 July 2010; our translation.

11. Mother Earth has even been granted a particular day: 22 April, referred to as International Mother Earth Day, after a resolution in the UN in 2009.

12. For a study of New Age initiatives behind the discourse on indigenous people as children of Mother Earth, see Heath and Potter (2004).

13. For a more detailed review of Nergård's perspectives, see Kraft (2007). For a critical account of neo-romantic perspectives in research on Læstadianism, see also Drivenes and Niemi (2000). For a discussion of neo-primitivism in indigenous research, see A. Geertz (2004).

14. Folklorist Marit Anne Hauan interviewed Mikkel Gaup during the 1970s, and claims that during this period he served in the role of "læser" and healer, and referred to himself by this title (information from a research seminar at the Department of Religious Studies, University of Tromsø, spring 2008).

15. Theologian Hanne Beate Stenvaag at theUniversity of Tromsø is working on a PhD thesis focusing on developments within Sami church life in the Church of Norway. Her fieldwork points to current discussions and also to changes regarding opposition to the use of *joik* and the Sami drum *(runebomme)* in church contexts. While the *joik* and the drum still are controversial in core Sami areas, these symbols to some extent have been included in the liturgy in the south Sami area, and also in celebrations connected to the Sami people's day, 6 February, in the capital of Oslo.

16. These accounts have also been met with resistance. For example, Suzanne Owen (2008) and Christina Welch (2004, 2007) emphasize that simple accusations of neo-colonialism elide the complexity of indigenous agency in cultural encounters.

9. THE HOLISTIC MILIEU IN CONTEXT: BETWEEN TRADITIONAL CHRISTIANITY AND FOLK RELIGIOSITY

Dorota Hall

This chapter addresses the holistic milieu and spiritual practices in Poland. It aims at highlighting local peculiarities of holistic phenomena related to the strength of traditional models of religiosity in this country. It goes on to claim that due to the lack of explicit challenge posed to the Catholic Church and Catholicism's dependence on mainstream religious patterns, the examples of the wider milieu discussed here cannot be understood as promoting a fully alternative spiritual culture. They should rather be seen as embedded in Catholic folk religiosity.

My argument starts with a discussion of the importance of Catholic self-identification for those interested in holism, the minor attention the latter give to modern individualistic trends, and the entrenching of their practices in traditional ways of getting in contact with the sacred. Subsequently, the chapter refers to existing academic considerations on the nature of "New Age" and new spiritualities and shows problems with their applicability to the Polish context, suggesting instead – although with important reservations – the use of the notion of "folk religiosity". The final section returns to the evidence from the researched field on the embedding of new spiritual developments in mainstream religion, in order to show the discursive strategy used by Polish promoters of holism, which reveals their surrender to the authority of the Church.

The chapter is based primarily on materials collected during my ethnographic fieldwork and in-depth interviews among vendors and customers of alternative medicine fairs and esoteric shops in Warsaw and with participants of spiritual workshops and therapies advertised there, as well as with visitors to the Węsiory village in northern Poland where stone circles built by Germanic tribes in the first centuries CE, now considered a "power place", are located.[1] The chapter also refers to articles published in the *Nieznany Świat* [*The Unknown World*], an esoteric monthly magazine popular among interviewees taking part in my project. Furthermore, this paper draws on important earlier research by a Polish scholar Anna E. Kubiak (2005) carried out in the years 1998–2000. Kubiak conducted a survey among practitioners of holistic techniques in various Polish cities (the questionnaire was distributed during meetings, lectures, workshops and esoteric and alternative medicine fairs) as well as a survey of a representative sample of Poles aged 15 and over which contained a question on acquaintance with and practice of holistic techniques. These surveys are unique sources of quantitative data on Polish holism.

The empirical picture of Polish holistic phenomena this paper presents thus refers mainly to the 1990s and the first half of the 2000s. It is possible that individualistic tendencies may become more visible. Nevertheless, the focus of this paper is not on reporting the most recent developments, but rather on highlighting important conceptual issues related to studying holistic practices in local contexts from the perspective of the social sciences.

THE IMPORTANCE OF CATHOLICISM

As revealed by Kubiak's survey among practitioners of holistic techniques, 42 per cent subscribe to Catholicism (Kubiak 2005: 160).[2] This figure for those adhering to traditional religion is higher than the percentages given by Michael York (1995) who studied the audience of the magazine *Body, Mind and Spirit* in the United States (30 per cent considering themselves Protestants, Catholics or Jews) and Dominic Corrywright (2003) who researched the audience of the magazine *The Spark* and participants of the Psychology of Vision workshop in western England (27 per cent subscribing to a traditional religious group). At the same time, Kubiak's representative survey sample of Poles shows that 19 per cent of respondents had practised holistic techniques, for example, bioenergy therapy, radiesthesia (dowsing), yoga, acupuncture, while as many as 90 per cent adhered to Catholicism (Kubiak 2005: 160). This Catholic self-identification was also underlined by those taking part in my research project.

Of course, interviewees mentioned a lot of reservations. They criticized the Catholic Church for the exaggerated sense of guilt it shapes, for presenting itself as an ultimate authority in matters related to religious convictions and morality, and for putting forward theological ideas of suffering and submission. They also disapproved of the Church's pressure in the realm of policy-making and expressed doubts as to the superior moral competencies of the clergy. Still, it seems they felt the need to define themselves as Catholics, even if they noticed inconsistencies in their worldview or declarations. To give an example: "I am a Catholic and at the same time, I believe in reincarnation. It's funny, isn't it?".[3] Another typical declaration was: "I am a Catholic. This is very strange in my case. Because I am attached, I've been raised in this religion ... I don't believe in a God who punishes, as they taught me, I've moved away from this. But still, Jesus has remained, and religious holidays have remained".[4]

To some extent, the willingness to communicate the attachment to Catholicism might be seen within the perennial perspective keenly employed by adherents of today's holism who equalize various religious traditions, and have a tendency to perceive themselves as successors of the perennial knowledge inscribed in all religious currents, no matter what name these currents were given (cf. Heelas 1996: 27–8). However, such an interpretation would somehow neglect the quantitative importance of Catholic self-declarations among Polish practitioners of holistic techniques. It seems that they not only follow the global features of holistic beliefs, but also reflect tendencies typical for Polish society: numerous surveys show that the percentage of Poles subscribing to Catholicism significantly exceeds 90 per cent (Hall 2012), and this is in spite of the criticism towards the Church and its involvement in political issues, since as much as 65 per cent of Poles disapprove of the Church's influence on the policy-making process (Borowik & Doktór 2001: 84). This is also in spite of the inclination to subscribe to beliefs falling outside the scope of the Catholic doctrine, since about 40 per cent of Poles declare they are religious "in their own way", one-third of the society considers God "some sort of spirit or life force" (Hall 2012), and only slightly more than two-thirds of the population endorses belief in Catholic dogmas such as the immortality of soul, an afterlife, heaven and hell and the Final Judgment (CBOS 2009).

As far as the selectivity in accepting Catholic beliefs is concerned, not necessarily or not only does this stand for the trend of individualization self-consciously sanctioned by a significant portion of Poles, but it may also result from a lack of knowledge of Catholic doctrine. Considering this issue, Władysław Piwowarski (1984), a Polish sociologist of religion, dubs Poles "unaware heretics", and it seems such a depiction perfectly conveys the religious condition of Poles which results from historical factors, mainly the period of partitions of Poland (1795–1918) and the communist era, when the sense of identification with the Church, noticeable in the realm of common declarations of adherence and widespread participation in religious rituals, strengthened to spite the authorities – but it was at the cost of the development of intellectual aspects of the belief and spreading knowledge of Catholic theological orthodoxy. Hence, when a person interested in the "energetic" influence of thoughts and words says: "Jesus said that human beings cannot live with bread alone, but they live with every word they speak. Thus everybody should be conscious and aware of every word and thought even the least significant ones".[5] it may either mean she introduces deliberate corrections to the Gospel passage ("human beings cannot live with bread alone, but need every word that God speaks" – Matthew 4:4) and reinterprets the Bible in such a way that it fits to the holistic perspective which underlines the interconnectedness between material and immaterial aspects of the universe, or it may simply demonstrate a lack of familiarity with scripture typical among Poles. Quite probably the interviewee's statement might be situated between the extremes: she does not know, or remember well, the Gospel of Matthew but she freely alludes to it while presenting her holistic worldview.

Furthermore, sociological surveys show that Poles are dutiful in performing religious ritual. Both the declared regular church attendance and regular frequency of praying are at high levels in Poland, amounting to, or even going beyond 75 per cent, as is the case of participation in masses at least once a month (Hall 2012). The importance of public ritual (masses and other church services), as well as private devotion (prayers, arranging home altars, drawing importance to Catholic objects such as crosses, rosaries, etc.) is also visible among Polish adherents of new spiritualities. They commonly visit church buildings, although perceive them in a specific, non-Catholic way as "power places". Some willingly participate in masses, although while doing that, again in an unorthodox way, they focus on beneficial "energies" influencing their meditation: "if a number of people comes at a defined time, the energies are stronger, more intense".[6] Some take Catholic sacraments, including going to confession, but they see this in a very technical way: "[this is] the same cleansing as, for instance, the bowel cleansing on the physical level. I know I just need to cleanse my body and I do that. Sometimes I need to cleanse my psyche. Then, I go to confession".[7] At home, while arranging home altars, they do not forget to place the image of the Mother of God among photos of gurus and other items said to be filled with "positive energetic vibrations", since – as explained by the same interviewee – "[she] has the energy of light". They also incorporate traditional Catholic accessories (rosaries, holy medals exhibiting saints) into the set of amulets they use to protect themselves from "negative energies". The readiness to draw from Catholic practices and objects shows the embedding of the Polish holistic milieu in the mainstream religious tradition.

FOLK DIMENSIONS OF HOLISTIC PRACTICES

Results from the survey performed by Kubiak show that Polish practitioners of holism consider epistemological motivations as the main reason for their involvement in new spiritualities. Kubiak compares her findings with conclusions drawn by Stuart Rose (1996) from his survey research among readers of the New Age magazine *Kindred Spirit* (established 1987) in Great Britain.[8] It appears that, in Great Britain, the will for self-development was the most commonly quoted ground for such involvement. The second most important motivation was the need to change one's life-style, which might also be linked to the idea of self-development – in Poland, in contrast, such a motivation was only at the fourth place in the ranking. Furthermore, in

Great Britain, a substantially lower percentage of people were motivated by the search for healing health problems through the use of alternative medicine; also, fewer people quoted paranormal abilities as the reason for their interest in holism (Kubiak 2005: 151–3). Thus, the Polish holistic practitioners seem to draw significant importance to unconventional medicine and seem to be much more sensitive to extraordinary powers. At the same time, if we compare them with British adherents of new spiritualities, it appears they somewhat reduce individualistic ideas of self-enhancement.

The declared emphasis put on alternative medicine and extraordinary powers, together with the lack of strong support for modern individualistic tendencies, is a very interesting combination. It resonates with the fact that the most common holistic practices in Poland, which are bioenergy therapy, radiesthesia, Reiki, work with chakras and acupuncture (*ibid.*: 150–51), seem to harmonize with traditional modes of operation which are deeply rooted in the Polish religious culture, and are employed in clear tension with the trend of modern individualism. Throughout the years when Polish Catholicism focused on building a common identity opposing various political authorities and fostering mass participation in ritual, much space was given to practices situated on the fringes of the Catholic orthodoxy which cultivated sensual and tangible aspects of the relationship with the sacred: miraculous events, such as Virgin Mary revelations (some of them not approved by the Church), were subject to common fascination, pilgrimages to sanctuaries and holy icons (some of them not approved by the Church) were held, and folk healers continued their activity.

Thus today, when bioenergy or Reiki healers perform their treatments and touch the body in need of a cure in order to transmit sacred energy from above, they allude to practices by folk therapists performed in a very similar way. This is all the more so since bioenergy or Reiki practitioners often ask a transcendent God for this energy – "it is not my energy, it is just the amount that Providence gives me. And the other person will take as much as they need and Providence will grant them this energy"[9] – and, before the healing session, some of them pray using the words of the Lord's Prayer. Furthermore, when Sai Baba devotees are enthusiastic about photos of the master which secrete *vibhuti* – "I even have photos of it, this is an authentic fact! ... She [the interviewee's friend] thought it was dust and she wiped it off again and again. But it continued to appear, this *vibhuti*. ... I was a witness, I lived there, downstairs. And people were coming there, and ... they left flowers"[10] – they implicitly allude to the folk fascination with miraculous, bleeding or crying effigies of Jesus or the Holy Mother (Hemka & Olędzki 1990). When pilgrims to Węsiory touch the ancient stones in order to draw upon the beneficial energy, they make exactly the same gestures as pilgrims to traditional Catholic shrines who touch the holy icon in order to be cured from a disease. When radiesthesians use measuring equipment, not only radiesthetic pendulums, but also dosimeters and thermometers, and display the energetic radiations produced by the stones on special monitors or take "photos of the energy", they allude to the folk fascination with visible manifestations of what is uncanny or sacred. Indeed, Polish adherents of holism might be perceived as successors of the sensual and miraculous dimensions of folk religion.

The idea that Polish practitioners of holistic techniques continue traditional, folk patterns of religiosity is validated by the fact that they are somewhat distanced from modern individualistic trends. They have built their convictions and modes of acting on the traditional worldview and practices, although they employ a new vocabulary: for instance, they give new names, such as the highest energy, *prana*, *mana*, *chi*, and so forth, to the power of God. As such, they are not direct successors of a "subjective turn" in culture, as posited in the "subjectivization thesis" by Heelas and Woodhead (2005), for example. The countercultural revolt of the 1960s, along with the wide promotion of ideas linked to subjectivity and self-actualization, to little extent embraced Poland. At that time, and also within the two subsequent decades, Poles were preoccupied with other issues: they emphasized more the need for the liberation of the whole of society, stemming from the Soviet oppressive influence, than the need for the liberation of individual subjectivities. Thus, when new spiritual proposals came to Poland on a massive scale in the beginning of the 1990s, soon after communism collapsed, they met a society much attached to the Catholic Church and traditional forms of religiosity. They encountered these traditional tendencies, intertwined with them and resulted in the local version of holism. Research carried out in post-Soviet countries suggests a similar pattern in Lithuania (Ališauskienė 2012) and at the Polish–Byelorussian–Lithuanian border (Grębecka 2006).

"NEW AGE" AND "FOLK RELIGIOSITY"

The descriptive and explanatory value of the category "New Age" has been questioned by scholars studying recent forms of spirituality.[11] The application of this term to scholarly considerations on social phenomena is even more problematic in the case of Poland. The Polish holistic milieu cannot be characterized by the strong opposition towards the main religious institution, the opposition so much underlined by scholars studying new spiritualities. The retreat from Christian dualism to holism (seen as one of the main foundations for "New Age" by Hanegraaff 1996, which no subsequent researcher has much questioned) is not their *differentia specifica* either, because contemporary holistic beliefs and practices in Poland draw much from the traditional folk religiosity which already affirms the immanent dimension of the sacred. According to this, God and saints may influence the world through numerous miracles and revelations, God's power may heal, and it is possible to get into tangible contact with the sacred while touching a holy icon or drinking water from a miraculous spring. Hence, no significant "retreat" from dualism to holism makes sense in this context, since in Poland it has for long been socially allowed to employ imagery based on the immanent vision of the sacred, without explicitly confronting the orthodox dualistic Christian cosmology. Finally, modern individualism, the concept so willingly used either by scholars who are (or were) attached to the notion of "New Age" (Hanegraaff 1996; Heelas 1996; and their many followers) or by those who call for the abandonment of the term (e.g. Sutcliffe 2003a), does not seem to be the most appropriate concept to portray the holistic milieu in Poland. This is mainly because Polish practitioners of holism do not seem preoccupied with stressing their disjunction to the mainstream religion, and also, they do not see individualistic ideals as the main driver for their involvement in new spiritual practices.

Perhaps the notion of "folk religiosity" can shed light on how Polish holism might be interpreted. The model of "folk religiosity", constructed as a kind of ideal type, is firmly inscribed in Polish ethnographic tradition. Its main characteristics are "miracular sensitivity" and "sensualism". The miracular sensitivity refers to peculiar religious emotionality, the yearning for miraculousness, and embraces strong attraction to extraordinary or uncanny events (Hemka & Olędzki 1990). Sensualism draws on the conviction that the sacred and the truth are inscribed in their visual representations. To explain this idea, Joanna Tokarska-Bakir (2000) refers to Hans-Georg Gadamer's ([1975] 1989) aesthetical notion of *Nichtunterscheidung* ("indifferentiation" or "non-differentiation") and transposes it into studies of religion. Within Gadamer's perspective, "indifferentiation" stood for a basic ontological disposition which allowed for experiencing a work of art in a way that recognizes a bond between what the work of art presents and the presentation itself. Religious indifferentiation therefore stands for a third category of relation with the sacred, situated between the full identification of the sacred with the profane (as in ecstatic states) and their total separation (as in modern, disenchanted culture). Typically, folk religiosity greatly affirms the disposition to "indifferentiate". As a consequence, the sensualistic folk religiosity highly values all kinds of sensual relation with the sacred realm: it is enthusiastic over eye-witnessed truths and tangible contacts with sacred objects.

However, use of the model of "folk religiosity" demands strong caution for it is entangled in relations of power exercised by ethnographers in their descriptions of "folk people": that is, low educated dwellers of countryside areas, whose religiosity was historically subject to "othering". "Folk people" were by definition represented as exotic in the writings of those who belonged to elites and guarded the stability of social class distinctions. For them, the "folk religiosity" had to represent a set of practices and beliefs which significantly differed from the elite religiosity (Zowczak 2008). Yet, in the course of the twentieth century, attributes of "folk religiosity" came to embrace various social strata, which were related to finer social differentiation and the blurring of the boundaries between social classes in Poland. Besides, as pointed out by Magdalena Zowczak (*ibid.*), the very model was inspired by the history of Western religious studies based in a perspective derived from the cultural context of Protestant denominations, along with their rationalistic distance towards everyday religious practices. Thus, the "folk religiosity" came to bear characteristics opposed to the individual mysticism and reflexive ethics preferred by Protestant cultures: especially various collective and thus supposedly unreflective forms of religious devotion, such as pilgrimages and the cult of holy effigies. It must be noted, however, that the main features of the "folk religiosity" harmonize with the Catholic cultural background. In contradistinction to Protestantism, which is more focused on the individualistic relation with the sacred, the Catholic view admits the presence of divinity in the world, embodied, for instance, in the activity of angels and the intercession of saints. It also accepts use of "magical" means by practitioners for exerting an influence on God and gaining salvation, including rituals, ceremonies and sacraments (Berger 1967).

Linking new spiritualities to folk tradition is not a new idea. In one of the first academic anthologies devoted to the study of "New Age" phenomena in various parts of the world, Mark Mullins (1992: 242) dubbed the Japanese New Age "a new expression of folk religion and a revival of animism" that uses new media: books, cassettes and video recordings. Mullins's discussion referred to the religious situation in Japan which he considered a special case compared to what is at work in the "highly rationalized Judeo-Christian context" where "many features and characteristics of the New Age and religious revival ... may appear cultic and bizarre" (*ibid.*: 240). Nevertheless, the Polish research shows that even within the "Judeo-Christian context", links between new spiritualities and "folk religion" might also be indicated. Yet there is much truth in Hanegraaff's criticism of Mullins which applies not only to Japan, but elsewhere. According to Hanegraaff (2001), while assuming that the New Age has adapted itself to local animistic traditions rather than imposing on them an alien religious system, Mullins placed excessive confidence in ethnocentric theories of religion which refer to "magic", "animism", "the occult" and so forth, without taking into account processes of historical transformations. Mullins apparently followed theories which draw on works by J. G. Frazer or Bronisław Malinowski and treat "animism" or "magic" as universal and static phenomena of human culture – in contradistinction to the dynamic historical phenomena, such as the Judeo-Christian religion, which belong to the culture of the theorists.

The term "folk religiosity" along with its derivatives, such as "miracular sensitivity" and "sensualism", shares the same ethnocentric stigma, especially when considering the fact that the Polish ethnographic tradition which elaborated the notion has for long implemented its colonial ambitions by reflecting not on distant cultures overseas, but on "folk people" at home. The application of the model of "folk religiosity" to practitioners of new spiritualities therefore has potential to re-activate the hegemonic control. Still, it might be used for operational purposes, as a tool referring to cultural currents which are nevertheless subject to transformations, and which are yet linked to the Catholic tradition. It might help to emphasize the hegemony of typically Polish religious patterns, which somehow govern new spiritualities, penetrate them, and impose their worldview, language and modes of action.

The main justification for making an association between new spiritualities as exercised in Poland and the "folk religiosity" deeply inscribed in the Polish religious culture is that such an operation highlights local peculiarities of transnational holistic phenomena. The association is made at the academic level; it is very rare that Polish holistic practitioners themselves consciously refer to the "folk tradition". The asserted linkage between both cultural currents results from putting into practice the ethnographic imagination. This is based on "thick description" which consists in careful study of the "field" through interviews and observations, by means of which an ethnographer digs through successive layers of significance and subsequently represents them by means of a multilayered description:

> If ethnography is thick description and ethnographers are those who are doing the describing, then the determining question ... is whether it sorts winks from twitches and real winks from mimicked ones. It is not against a body of uninterpreted data, radically thinned descriptions, that we must measure the cogency of our interpretations, but against the power of the scientific imagination to bring us into touch with the lives of strangers.
>
> (C. Geertz 1973: 16)

Hence, although new spiritualities manifest themselves in a similar way in various parts of the globe, their manifestations are locally grounded, and in context the same symptoms of the phenomenon (contracting the eyelids) do not necessarily signify the same (they might be winks, or regular twitches). In the case of holistic practices, the action of contracting the eyelids might equally stand for healing with the Reiki technique, or for touching the ancient stones in order to draw beneficial energies. The alternative between winks and twitches refers to different possible meanings inscribed in such practices: in Poland, they are understandable within the folk Catholic context which has given space, for instance, to the activity of folk healers and sensualistic operations by pilgrims to shrines, while in Great Britain and other countries influenced by Protestantism, they might perhaps be interpreted as the testimony of intense efforts to re-enchant a world already disenchanted. Similarly, in Poland, individualistic claims highlighting the need for self-enhancement and individual transformation, if made at all, seem to express only the developing, emancipatory will for individualization, while in Great Britain and other countries influenced by Protestantism, they seem to match the long cultural tradition referring to personal aspects of religious practice.

The association of new spiritualities with "folk religiosity" in the case of Poland does not presume that the worldview and practices by holistic adherents are exactly the same as the worldview and practices by representatives of the traditional "folk religiosity". It rather highlights the fact that both cultural currents refer to the same patterns: they affirm a sensitivity based on the more or less immanent vision of the sacred and support related practical activities. The "folk religion" itself is not static and has evolved throughout the years, and resulted in many cultural phenomena, new spiritualities being just one of their possible contemporary manifestations. Other manifestations embrace, for instance, the fascination with Virgin Mary revelations (as mentioned, not all approved by the Church) reported from various cities in Poland and attracting pilgrims from all over the Polish territory (Czachowski 2003; Zieliński 2004). The link between actions undertaken by adherents of new spiritualities and those by Virgin Mary devotees is acutely visible when comparing photos taken in an esoteric shop in Warsaw and in Węsiory stone-circles, with a photo taken in Okonin, a place of Marian revelations (Hall 2007: 378–9). In the esoteric shop, the photograph shows a woman stretching out her hands to touch a painting displayed at an exhibition of esoteric art said to be filled with positive energies. In Węsiory, pilgrims similarly place their palms in contact with the stone surface. And in Okonin, in exactly the same way, a woman touches a willow tree on which – as believed by pilgrims – the Virgin Mary appeared. However, regardless of such similarities it must be remembered that pilgrims to places of Virgin Mary revelations and Polish adherents of new spiritualities have different viewpoints on the nature of the sacred, the former being much attached to specific Christian imagery (even if they are inclined to greatly value immanent aspects of the sacred), and the latter tending to employ a perennial perspective emphasizing multiple interpretations which employ the notion of "energy" (even if they still highly value the Catholic tradition). Likewise, the two milieus have significantly different attitudes towards various developments of contemporary culture, the former being traditionalistic to a highest degree, hostile towards many aspects of modernization, and feeling that they have a mission to defend Polish Catholics from any news from foreign influences (Zieliński 2004), and the latter being enthusiastic about trends of globalization which provide access to the religious heritage of various cultures.

PAYING TRIBUTE TO THE CHURCH

The hegemony of the Catholic Church in Poland is visible when taking into account the Church's strong position in the political realm, evidenced, for instance, by bishops' successful attempts to influence legislation on societal issues: for example, abortion and the privileged teaching of the Catholic religion in schools. Catholic domination manifests itself not only in the strong position of Church high officials, but also as the permeation of societal attitudes by historical religious patterns. Even if there is only weak social approval for the Church's influence on policy making in Poland, the Church and the Catholic religion are still considered an authority, and the ordinary Poles' identification with Catholicism mirrors this fact. At the same time, the dominant model of religiosity is ambiguous when it comes to accepting orthodox Catholic tenets of belief.

While commenting on the sociological survey on the religiosity of Poles conducted at the end of the 1990s, Irena Borowik estimates that, taking into account their endorsement of the Catholic worldview, nevertheless about 10–15 per cent of Poles are unreligious, even if they declare their belonging to the Church. The same percentage make up persons representing the most coherent picture of Catholic religiosity in terms of compliance with Church teachings: they see themselves as Catholic and devout, and they are consistent with regards to belief in a personal God, the divinity of Christ, the vision of afterlife, the interpretation of the Holy Scripture and salvation. But 70 per cent of the Polish population might be situated between such extremes. Members of this majority believe in God and Christ, declare themselves Catholics, attach importance to religious ritual, but simultaneously they selectively accept Catholic beliefs (Borowik & Doktór 2001: 123–4). 70 per cent of Poles characterized in such a way create a friendly environment for innovative religious ideas, provided, however, that these ideas do not explicitly deny the existence of God or Christ, do not unambiguously criticize Catholicism and do not desecrate its symbols, and in addition, that they render great value to the ritualism so much glorified by Poles. It seems that ideas and practices promoted by the Polish holistic milieu fit these characteristics. The environment is all the more friendly since the Polish Church hierarchs do not decidedly condemn beliefs and practices that draw on Catholicism yet are not quite in line with Catholic orthodoxy: for instance, they allow the functioning of Radio Maryja which builds its message on xenophobic sentiments contradicting the achievements of the Second Vatican Council.[12] The standpoint of the institutional Church towards new spiritualities is more uncompromising, but is also not free from ambiguities. It is somewhat symptomatic that one of the first Reiki masters in Poland was a Catholic nun, while the Archbishop emeritus of Lublin promotes radiesthesia, bioenergy therapy, and an anthropology of the body based on notions of "energy", *chi*, *prana*, and so forth, in his statements (Pylak 2003).

Since the beginning of the 1990s, many Christian books criticizing holistic and new spiritual practices, such as Reiki or Silva Mind Control, have been published in Poland. They provoked a response from promoters of holism, for instance, from the editors of the *Nieznany Świat* ("The

Unknown World") magazine mentioned earlier. It is very interesting how this response was formulated. The editors employed a specific strategy: they did not detach themselves from the Church institution, but instead, they legitimated their views through reference to the authority of clergy open to ideas presented in the magazine. Considering the strong social support for Catholic-related phenomena, it appears to be the only possible tactic capable of attracting Poles to the new spiritual trends promoted by the magazine. It also provides protection from unambiguous criticism from the Church. Not surprisingly, the tactic was employed by the *Nieznany Świat* editors on various occasions.

The first example was in 1998, after the "Letter" Association for Evangelization by Media, a Catholic organization, had published a book titled *Reiki: The Rain of Heavenly Energy?* (Posacki *et al.* 1997). The book contains articles critical towards the Reiki technique, including a "testimony" by a "Reiki survivor", a person previously engaged in Reiki therapy and then converted to Catholicism, two responses sent to periodicals by Reiki masters and a decisive answer to them. The harsh evaluation of Reiki is supported by both the *Catechism of the Catholic Church*, and the opinion of bishop Pawłowicz who was then responsible for investigation of "cults" in Poland on behalf of the Polish Bishops' Conference, and who classified Reiki practitioners as a destructive group. The dissemination of the book overlapped with the death of the Reiki master Mariusza, a Catholic nun acutely criticized by the authors. As a response *Nieznany Świat* published articles both devoted to the nun, and at the same time very critical of the Catholic publication (*Nieznany Świat* 1998[4]). The editors associated the nun's death with the anti-Reiki drive against her activity, labelling it a "crusade". Furthermore, they presented an interview with a Catholic priest who was a Reiki practitioner and the nun's collaborator, and they referred to factual errors committed by the authors of the critique of Reiki. It is symptomatic that the standpoint of the Reiki defenders was tactically supported by *Nieznany Świat* by referring to the authority of a Church representative who was himself engaged in the practice. In other words, an interview with a Catholic priest evidently legitimates the therapy.

Other polemics by *Nieznany Świat* were conducted in a similar way. There was the case of discussion on Silva Mind Control when an interview with a Silva method trainer, a Catholic monk, was quoted (*Nieznany Świat* 1999[2]), as well as the case of the defense of dowsing when priests who practised the technique were recalled (*Nieznany Świat* 2002[3]). The authority of the traditional religion appears to be impossible to overcome outright, but must be engaged strategically. This is not to say that the Polish holistic milieu does not have any potential of "culture criticism", which is Hanegraaff's (1996) key notion of the counter-cultural stance of "New Age". Still, practitioners are located within concrete cultural conditions, and while proposing new holistic techniques and presenting a perennial worldview, they simultaneously pay tribute to Catholicism and the Catholic Church, in various ways expressing their attachment to traditional religious authorities.

CONCLUSION

In Poland, the Catholic Church and the Catholic tradition seem to be evident authorities for people interested in holism. For this reason, and also because of the relatively low support of Polish holistic practitioners for ideals of modern individualism, it is problematic to apply certain scholarly considerations on "New Age" or new spiritualities to the Polish case, especially attributes of self-actualization and culture criticism. The operational employment of the category of "folk religiosity" seems to be more accurate, because it links the holistic practices as exercised in Poland to broader patterns of the historical religious culture. So long as we retain a focus on power relations, this category allows us to adequately discuss the issue by emphasizing the interplay between the perennial perspective and the hegemonic Catholic models of relations with the sacred.

Holistic practices, like any activities emerging in the social field, are embedded in power relations. Actually, the emergence and growing popularity of holistic trends in many countries in North America and Western Europe might be seen as a manifestation of resistance to the power of traditional Church institutions which have for long tried to exert a governing influence on individuals (Heelas 1996; Hanegraaff 1996). It even appears difficult to imagine new spiritualities in isolation from this tension in religious authority: that is, from being in opposition to the Church structures. In Poland at least, however, and perhaps by extension in other Catholic contexts, the situation is more complicated. It seems the Polish holistic milieu has not been able to establish an alternative spiritual culture, opposed to the mainstream patterns of religiosity. This becomes visible if we shift our focus from situating the holistic worldview and practices within the tradition of studies on "New Age" towards placing them within the ethnographic tradition, which underscores the symbolic dimension of the researched phenomena and their local grounding.

NOTES

1. The fieldwork was carried out under my direction in 2000–2004 by students of the Institute of Ethnology and Cultural Anthropology of Warsaw University. Its results are extensively discussed in my PhD thesis (Hall 2007).
2. 656 valid questionnaires were included in Kubiak's calculation.
3. Woman, aged about 30, participant of the meditation group held by the spiritual teacher Ewa May in Warsaw, August 2003, interviewed by Katarzyna Jabłońska.

4. Woman, aged 22, student, customer of esoteric shops and participant of workshops organized there, Warsaw, July 2003, interviewed by Marzena Zera.

5. Woman, aged about 40, bioenergy-therapist and astrologer, customer of the Feng Shui "Chi" esoteric shop in Warsaw, November 2001, interviewed by Anna Nowak.

6. Woman, yoga practitioner, Warsaw, October 2000, interviewed by Błażej Piotrowski.

7. Woman, aged about 50, leader of the Training Center for Development TOR advertised in esoteric shops, Warsaw, Winter 2003, interviewed by Marzena Zera.

8. Kubiak adapted Rose's questionnaire, slightly adjusting it to the Polish context, and items in her questionnaire were almost the same as those used by Rose.

9. Woman, aged about 50, practitioner of Reiki and the Denison technique, Warsaw, February 2001, interviewed by Paweł Jurkiewicz.

10. Woman, aged about 60, Sai Baba devotee, Warsaw, April 2001, interviewed by Małgorzata Śmigierzewska.

11. Cf. Sutcliffe and Bowman (2000) and Sutcliffe (2003a). Also Heelas and Woodhead (2005) drop the category, replacing "New Age" with the terms "holistic milieu" or "subjective-life spirituality".

12. In 2009, the Media Ethics Council criticized Radio Maryja for its anti-Semitic comments. Even this did not mobilize the Polish Bishops' Conference to take any decisive steps against the radio station.

10. NEW AGE AND THE SPIRIT OF CAPITALISM: ENERGY AS COGNITIVE CURRENCY

Lisbeth Mikaelsson

COMMERCIALIZATION AND THE SPIRIT OF NEW AGE

In his classic work linking economy and religion, *The Protestant Ethic and the Spirit of Capitalism* (1920), Max Weber proposed that the Puritan teaching of predestination and its ideals of hard work, moral discipline and frugality combined with rational capital accumulation were determining elements in the successful rise of early modern capitalism.[1] Since this book was first published, capitalism has become the dominant economic system in the world, almost mysteriously dynamic and all-pervading, and economic mindsets and instrumental rationality are increasingly invading areas formerly outside the sphere of financial calculation. While hard work still must be considered conducive to economic success, the other values listed by Weber as "the spirit of capitalism" more or less counteract the consumer capitalism that reigns today. Peter Berger makes the obvious, but fitting comment that values which function well in one period of economic development may not be functional in another period (Berger 1999: 17). Lavish consumption is a cornerstone in Western capitalist economies, and a frugality ethic is obviously not a sustaining attitude for such a system.[2] In a parallel way, the theological exclusivism and morality of Puritanism and its likes are unable to legitimate the multireligious commodification of today. How religious ideas and values influence economic development in a society is a pertinent question. An equally interesting issue, however, concerns how religion is shaped by economic conditions.[3] This seems obvious in relation to New Age, where social interaction now to a large extent takes place within a framework of selling and buying. Is this development connected with the lack of conventional religious organizing in the New Age movement? This lack has been a notorious headache for scholars wishing to define it (cf. Possamai 2007). Guy Redden proposes that it is exactly the market character of New Age that is the reason for the diffuse shape of the movement and the problems of definition (Redden 2005). How its market structure interacts with "the spirit of New Age", and what values and ideas are incorporated in this "spirit", are urgent issues concerning this religious field today. The contention in this chapter is that key New Age concepts and their usage are influenced by the commercial purview and stimulate economic expansion, with the concept of energy being picked out for closer scrutiny.

NEW AGE CAPITALISM

For decades commentators have metaphorically spoken of contemporary religious pluralism as a market (cf. Roof 1999). Gradually the market metaphor has been supplemented with a real market, or rather several markets, in which an astounding supply of "spiritual" products are offered for sale. Facing the profusion of such products, the phrase "New Age capitalism" has come into use (cf. Lau 2000).[4] While the countercultural, small-scale enterprises run by idealists should not be overlooked, the huge markets for self-help books and alternative medicine are far more conspicuous manifestations of commercialization. "Spiritual tourism" and feng shui-influenced architecture and house decoration, are other manifestations (Norman 2011; Rossbach 1983). The spiritual or alternative segment is generally a variety within ordinary trades and services, and products are marketed with references to common requirements and desires: health, longevity, vitality, self-improvement and fulfilment. Dividing lines between the mainstream and the alternative are becoming quite blurred with the increasing success of "spiritual" or "holistic" choices. Steven Sutcliffe indicates the widespread diffusion of *varia* associated with New Age by pointing at "the New Age" president Bill Clinton and the Russian spokesman for "an integrated universal consciousness" Michael Gorbachev, the Body Shop cosmetics franchise, and the London night club "Seed" (Sutcliffe 2003a: 124–5). A particularly blurred field relates to popular culture, which teems with references to religion (cf. Partridge 2004–5; Morgan 2007).

Stars and best-sellers on the spiritual market have earned fortunes, like Deepak Chopra and a number of other authors read by millions such as Paolo Coelho, Robert Redfield, Rhonda Byrne and Shirley Maclaine.[5] It has been estimated that books within the spirituality category constitute between 7 and 12 per cent of the total book sales in the world (Heelas & Woodhead 2005: 70; cf. Heelas 2008: 73). Beside the authors of wisdom and self-help literature, the typical actor on the selling side is an entrepreneur, or a group of entrepreneurs, putting up a business specializing in, for instance, one or more therapies, counselling, training programmes, or a shop with the bric-a-brac assortment of dream catchers, incense, South Asian gods, crystals and tarot cards.[6] Products like management courses are tailored for the business world (cf. Storm 1991: 86–92), but most of the offers are directed at individual consumption. Some entrepreneurs are also touring lecturers who address audiences at alternative fairs. A Norwegian celebrity example is the royal princess Märtha Louise, who runs a self-development business called Astarte Education, publishes books about how to get in contact with angels,[7] and gives lectures at fairs. The big fairs, containing extensive varieties of "alternative" products side by side and thus staging the tolerant ideal of "there are many answers to the same question",[8] appear as the very incarnation of the idea of New Age as a uniform market. There are now fifty alternative fairs arranged in Norway every year, attracting about 100,000 visitors.[9] In a population consisting of five million people, where around 80 per cent belong to the Church of Norway, the number is indicative of the penetrating power of New Age ideas and practices. The largest fair, near Oslo, offers "everything in the field of spirituality, self-development, alternative therapy, holistic philosophy, life style, healing, divination and mysticism", according to a newspaper advertisement (Mikaelsson 2011: 80). The list is indicative of the items included in umbrella concepts like "the alternative/spiritual market" and the fair is a fitting symbol of how buying and selling has become a central kind of social interaction in the field of New Age spirituality. Both participants and visitors at Norwegian fairs include people with varying levels of involvement. If we imagine the involvement structures as a model of concentric circles in which the spiritual expert inhabits the central, small circle, that expert will very often be a person selling a certain spiritual product and interacting with people ranging from dedicated clients and disciples to the outermost circle of stray customers (cf. Gilhus & Mikaelsson 2005: 13).

The popularity of these fairs in Norway pertains to a general issue of great importance: how New Age spirituality co-exists with traditional Christian denominations in the host society and affects the overall religious field (cf. Heelas & Woodhead 2005; Possamai 2007). Should it be understood as fitting into the categories of "folk", "vernacular" or "lived" religion unfolding alongside established churches which provide rituals of passage and communal identity to spiritual seekers and the cultic milieu as well as to their own congregations (cf. Selberg 2011; Bowman & Valk 2012; McGuire 2008)? Although reliable figures are lacking, a large number of Norwegian visitors at the fairs, readers of New Age books and clients using alternative therapies belong to the Lutheran Church of Norway, or probably to a lesser extent, one of the other Christian denominations. However, their participation in non-commercial projects and organizations is rather modest. The membership organization Holistisk Forbund [Holistic Federation] rooted in the Alternativ Nettverk has only attracted around a thousand members since its start in 2002.

The relationship between church religion and alternative spirituality has continually been discussed by Norwegian scholars.[10] The market character of New Age is likely to be a main reason for more or less active members of Christian denominations to allow themselves to be involved with it. If New

Age had entered the Norwegian scene in the overall shape of a conventional religion, it would have been perceived as a competitor to Christianity and would probably been met with much more reserve. It is no coincidence that conservative Christian apologists in Scandinavia and elsewhere, fearing the influence of individualistic and Asian-inspired spirituality, have insisted that New Age *is* a religion and consequently should be attacked as a rival and dangerous faith (Mikaelsson 2008). Rather than being an obstacle, the diffuse character of the movement is the formula for success which has secured its footing in Norwegian and other societies across established dividing lines.

SOCIAL AND ECONOMIC PREMISES FOR NEW AGE CAPITALISM

A number of wider changes explain the development of New Age capitalism. Jeremy Carrette and Richard King argue that what is going on is a "silent takeover of religion" by the corporate word of business, turning religious traditions from many parts of the world into vague and saleable "spirituality" in tune with Western individualism and neoliberalism (Carrette & King 2005). The authors point to the prevailing psychological paradigm, naturalized and part of everyday commonsense as it is, as a foundation for individualist self-absorption and what they think is a lack of social ethics and political concerns in New Age capitalism. Without subscribing to all their viewpoints and criticisms, the focus on psychological privatization of religion within dominant economic structures is highly relevant. The expanding therapy culture, marked by therapeutic discourse and practices, is rooted in psychology. As described for instance by Eva Illouz in her book *Saving the Modern Soul*, therapy has become a cultural framework which now orients people's self-perceptions and conceptions of others, both in American society and beyond (Illouz 2008: 12; cf. Madsen 2010). "The therapeutic is a site within which we invent ourselves as individuals, with wants, needs and desires to be known, categorized, and controlled for the sake of freedom", explains Illouz (2008: 3). Such a cultural mega-trend in the Western world throws light on the enormous growth of alternative therapies. Catherine Albanese points at how healers apply therapies that at once psychologize and spiritualize, while professing love as the panacea for human ills: a testimony of the influence of psychology (Albanese 1999: 318–19).

Another general premise has to do with the development of the so-called "new economy", which is a number of trends, enterprises and economic arenas associated with the decades around the turn of the millennium – such as IT, biotechnology, Internet trade and the experience economy. Emphasis on culture is central in the experience economy, which includes trades like tourism, event management, retail trade and heritage industries (Löfgren & Willim 2005: 1–2). To a considerable extent New Age capitalism can be categorized as "new economy". A characteristic element is the demand for personally meaningful occupations. Paul Heelas and Linda Woodhead use the concept "soft capitalism" for "new economy" enterprises emphasizing human creativity and personal development, and they point to a new work ethic attached to this which they call the "self-work ethic". The idea is that people do not work just for the sake of income; they look for personal and psychological rewards as well (Heelas & Woodhead 2001: 54–5). In a similar vein Albanese refers to the increasing professionalism accompanying increasing commercialization in the New Age market. In contrast to the nineteenth-century spiritualist or folk healer, a contemporary alternative practitioner has been through training programmes, may have an advanced degree, belongs to a professional network, attends conferences and keeps up with relevant publications (Albanese 1999: 320). A Norwegian study of entrepreneurs within alternative therapy confirms the self-work ethic thesis. The study showed that personal fulfilment was important to the informants, and that their ideas of self-realization also emphasized helping other people (Stavrum 2009). This indicates that both the demand and supply side concerning New Age spiritual products might be explained by similar general features.

Overlooking the greed sometimes displayed by Christian churches through the centuries, European societies dominated by Christianity often look with suspicion on people making money from religion, tending to view them as impostors or hypocrites. In Norway, Märtha Louise has for instance been severely criticized for charging money for her angel courses, since angels according to common opinion belong to a sacred dimension that should be kept unpolluted by profit making (cf. Kraft 2008). No doubt there is good reason to look upon present-day hedonism and commodification of religion with a critical eye. However, being such a large and complex phenomenon, New Age capitalism calls for a variety of theoretical and empirical approaches.[11] The approach in this chapter concerns some central tenets, attitudes, and cognitive mechanisms that can explain why there seems to be so little ideological resistance against the commercial drive in the New Age field.

SIGNIFICANT IDEAS AND ATTITUDES

One trail leads to the historical background of New Age in Theosophy, since an inheritance from this movement is the relativistic approach to established religions. Religious plurality is cherished as different paths to the same truth, but for Theosophists the obligation to truth is a higher imperative than loyalty to any religious faith. This kind of relativistic and selective ethos allows a person to take from a religious tradition what she likes and ignore the rest. There is an anti-authoritarian element in this position which was fully spelled out by Jiddu Krishnamurti (1895–1986), the Theosophical messiah who in 1929 turned away from Theosophy and denounced all organized religion. In the following decades Krishnamurti taught large audiences in the West that "truth is a pathless land" where everyone has to find his own way, and that authority of any kind is destructive (Godwin 1994: 367). Even without the full-fledged individualism of Krishnamurti, Theosophical doctrines and their like stimulate eclectic and open-minded attitudes which are manifested in people's willingness to listen to unusual messages and to try new things. Such a mentality is a prerequisite for the kind of New Age capitalism that reigns today.

An empirical study that is relevant in this context is Nurit Zaidman's investigation of preferences for religious objects among two groups of Israeli sub-cultures: one new agers, the other pilgrims at local Jewish shrines. The pilgrims looked for product authenticity – they wanted objects that had some connection to the saint and the shrine. The new agers, however, did not care for authenticity, but looked for products that could create a good atmosphere and were pretty, interesting or new. The newness of things was important to them. They also tended to attribute a personal meaning to the objects they bought, for instance by using their intuition. In other words, as customers the new agers were less oriented towards tradition and more individualistic than the pilgrims. Zaidman makes the important observation that when product authenticity is not emphasized, the market is free to expand and is open to anyone (Zaidman 2003: 355). Product authenticity, then, may function as a limiting factor on the market, while the focus on newness and individualism stimulates product growth.

Individualism and skepticism towards external authorities are elements in the "seeker" mentality which has long been analysed as typical of New Age spirituality (cf. Sutcliffe 2003a; Redden 2005; Possamai 2007). It may well be asked whether the seeker mentality is actively stimulated by the commercial market. Seen from a seeker perspective a rich selection of "alternative" products and freedom of choice and obligations are as attractive in this field as in any other when norms about religious exclusivism, commitment and duty have weakened (cf. Bruce 2002: 90). If this analysis is correct, an important function of the commercial market is to stimulate seekership through institutionalizing a social role as spiritual consumer. This is the standpoint taken by Guy Redden, who emphasizes that commercial actors provide "the arrangements that allow for seekership roles to be played out" (Redden 2005: 236).

HOLISTIC MONEY

Money in the modern sense is the precondition for capitalism. In the prosperity teachings of New Age, money itself has become a vehicle for spiritual self-development. This circumstance invites reflection on what money is, especially given its ubiquitous presence in daily life makes it almost a matter of course. However, modern money is a cultural construction with a long history that can be traced back to ancient Greece. Coinage was instrumental in the development of a monetary system, and the earliest known coins, dating back to 600 BCE, were found in the city of Ephesos in Asia Minor (Ferguson 2008: 24). Coins and banknotes are material objects like sea shells and other things that people have used as money but, as the classicist Richard Seaford says, money is both a thing and a relation; its relational character, however, tends to be disguised by its materiality (Seaford 2004: 1). According to Seaford, ancient Greek money was fundamentally changed when coins were stamped with a sign of their monetary value. In his opinion, the pragmatic effectiveness of this symbolic invention contributed to marginalize other values ascribed to the coins in the ancient Greek city-states (*ibid.*: 6). In the modern monetary system money does not have any use-value as a thing. Consequently its sole pragmatic function belongs to the economic system, although currencies can still have cultural value, as for instance national symbols. With the arrival of digital electronic transactions the perception of money is changing. When not having any embodiment whatsoever, money becomes a pure sign, and consequently its relational, abstract character is more apparent than before.

The basic purpose of money is to signify numerical value so that it can function as a medium of exchange and payment, and a vehicle for storing wealth and measuring value (Ferguson 2008: 23; Seaford 2004: 2). Seaford's ingenious analysis of early Greek culture maintains that the impersonal and uniform monetization that developed here created the first thoroughly monetized culture – a development transforming social relations and conceptions of life, especially because the monetized society was projected onto the cosmos. This projection partially explains Presocratic ideas about an impersonal, all-powerful substance in place of the anthropomorphic pantheon, creating a philosophical cosmology of tremendous importance for later development of Western civilization.

The argument in this chapter is that the character and function of money is projected onto the concept of energy in New Age. This becomes particularly visible in prosperity teachings, which have become increasingly important since the 1960s (Heelas 1999: 60–61). Prosperity teachings propose that money is energy and that handling money is therefore a question of using energy laws, like "flowing" and "magnetism". One of the gurus is Stuart Wilde, who declares in *The Money Bible* that a prosperity-seeking person has to be in tune with the energy flow of money, which means being "flexible, fluid, and fast on your feet" (Wilde 1998: 14). According to the well-known spiritual counsellor Shakti Gawain, the magnetic law of energy is such that energies with particular properties or vibrations attract similar ones (Gawain 1992: 22). Therefore money "likes" other money or people with prosperity consciousness. Interestingly, the prosperity teachings deviate from the prevalent impersonal mark of money by making money an extension of personality, not just in a symbolic sense, but literally through a psychologized concept of energy. The result is a particular combination of individualism and holism. The idea of holism can have a radical political potential, but it is a flexible concept, with no built-in barriers against economy or money-making as such.[12] The implementation of holistic thinking in various commercial therapies and techniques is now characteristic of New Age. In prosperity teachings, holism is coupled with hedonism and self-development in a manner concurrent with a capitalist and therapeutic culture. In this context money itself has become a key spiritual symbol, linked on the one hand with the psychological development of character and consciousness, and on the other with understandings of the dynamic nature of the cosmos. Money is presented as a mirror reflecting the kind of persons we are. Wilde sums this up: "Big heart = big money. Little heart = little money" (Wilde 1998: 8). The truly affluent person is therefore not only rich, she also has a healthy emotional life: loving herself, being generous, vital and self-confident. This teaching argues that such persons are more in tune with the nature of the cosmos than poor and dissatisfied individuals (Mikaelsson 2001: 104). Chopra and other prosperity authors fall into line: human abundance has the same origin as "a cluster of nebulas, a galaxy of stars, a rain forest, or a human body", and the laws of money are eternal and natural, Chopra proclaims in *Creating Affluence* (1993: 17f, 48, 52). Roman and Packer describe the spiritual laws of money as universal energy laws that create abundance. These energy laws affect a mix of physical and psychological phenomena: "principles of ebb and flow, unlimited thinking, giving and receiving, appreciation, honouring your worth, clear agreements, magnetism and more" (Roman & Packer 1988: xxvi). Louise Hay suggests that we think of the universe as a cosmic bank in which we can make mental deposits in the shape of realizations of one's creativity, through meditation and affirmations (Hay 1993: 143). The word "abundance" is often used in a "holistic" manner to describe a totality of material prosperity, mental and spiritual well-being in harmony with the universe at large.

The increasing dominance of electronic money means that viewing it as an energy system becomes even more appropriate, and this new type of monetary physicality makes it possible to figure out a new bodily contact with money. Wilde reminds his readers of the millions of dollars that are electronically passing through a person's hands every day, and suggests that you make an imaginary flick of the hand "to stop some of that loot in the transit, so it sticks in the palm of your hand" (Wilde 1998: 4). When money is transfigured into an unseen, immaterial, but still immensely powerful force, one can imagine that the project of manipulating it with consciousness-changing techniques becomes even more plausible to many people. The logic of the holistic prosperity-creating project means that a person is tapping into cosmic forces as well as evolving his own self liquidity. Most people need assistance to develop prosperity consciousness, however, and they are helped by a large number of manuals suggesting psychic techniques like manifestation, visualization, meditation and reading. In contrast, ordinary hard work seems out of the question. In this way dysfunctional feelings and attitudes are corrected and abundance created from within. The distance from the Protestant ethic of hard work and frugality ordained by a transcendent godhead could not be greater.

Conceiving energy through the lens of money and the monetary system has consequences for the construction of the concept. The monetary system is both man-made and therefore social, and yet also impersonal, and these properties are reflected in the conceptualization of energy. While Mammon once was the divine ruler of the monetary system, the New Age energy concept does not readily make room for a godhead governing the world through personal force and commandments. Rather, energies of various kinds are conceived as being at everybody's disposal, and if you know the nature of relevant energies and how to use them, you can change your own existence, in much the same way that wealth allows people the freedom of lifestyle and choices.

COGNITIVE MODES

The cluster of attitudes, values and ideas described so far are not just a stock of more or less divergent items. Quite the contrary: taken together, they constitute "a spirit" or ethos that have potential to stimulate economic development given the right surroundings and conditions. The main ingredients in this cluster are open-mindedness towards religious plurality, elastic and prosperity-friendly holism, positive attitudes towards material well-being, and priority of a seeker mentality together with inducements to develop the self along various dimensions – spiritually, mentally, socially and economically – a "spirit" that goes well with therapy culture, "new economy" and the self-work ethic. A further stage in the argument is that this package of ideas is underpinned by certain cognitive mechanisms, which help to transform religious and magical items into commercial products, and vice versa.

These cognitive mechanisms are *translating* and *disembedding* procedures linked together. Primary vehicles in these operations are key New Age concepts from its *lingua franca* such as "self", "spirituality" and "energy": all of them detraditionalizing tools that are able to absorb practices, symbols and ideas from disparate religious traditions and launch them within New Age mindsets. Marion Bowman and Steven Sutcliffe suggest that spirituality can be understood as an emic repacking of popular and vernacular religion to suit the conditions in our society (Sutcliffe & Bowman 2000: 8), and the same is true of "self" and "energy". Carrette and King suggest that the construction of the modern idea of spirituality is the main vehicle for assimilating religious phenomena into a psychological frame of reference, and that this concept of psychologized spirituality serves the interests of capitalism (Carrette & King 2005: 65). A similar critique is directed at the psychological concept of a unified self, which they reject as an illusion benefitting capitalist markets. In their view, the unified self is the veritable "market subject" or "consuming agent" (*ibid*.: 80). New Age musings on the self and its development are clearly deeply influenced by psychology and rooted in the Human Potential Movement. Its idea of an essential, individualistic and spiritual human self that can be stimulated and developed by practices and insights taken from disparate cultural traditions undoubtedly prepares the ground for many lines of business.

In the final section of this chapter, the concept of energy will be picked out for closer scrutiny, since this concept seems to play a significant role in the adaption of New Age to economic structures and thinking, behaving in certain ways like an economic currency. The concepts of both self and spirituality are related to the person and therefore carry some inherent cognitive restrictions. Energy, however, seems to be without any limits in its application – it is as slippery and ubiquitous as money itself. Through the energy concept, New Age capitalism explains techniques as well as effects, and thereby makes commodities for Western customers accessible both in a cognitive and in an economic sense.

THE CONCEPT OF ENERGY

A conception of energy which is both experiential and explanatory is dominant in New Age discourse today. At the same time energy functions as a popular metaphor in other areas. For example, Löfgren and Willim points to the metaphors of "heat" and "energy" overflowing in media and management handbooks to describe an economy warming up, and the hectic activities on the stock exchange (Löfgren & Willim 2005: 3). In spiritual discourse, energies can be felt and handled by sensitive people and we learn that everything has an invisible energy aspect: places, times, gods, objects, bodies, souls, as well as relationships, actions and communications. "Spirit" is energy of a subtle, changeable nature, while the energy of matter is more coarse and compact (cf. Gawain 1992: 22). Souls and consciousness are seen as intelligent forms of energy. While religious traditions often localize divine forces to a separate sacred sphere manipulated by priests and other experts, energies are everywhere, the spiritual ones intermingling with the others. A human being consists of both positive and negative, spiritual and gross energies in various proportions. People´s energies decide whether they are healthy, happy, well-functioning and affluent – or the contrary. Illness is caused by energy imbalance, blockage or drain, resulting from detrimental life styles, false ideas or bad treatment. Energies are being absorbed, balanced, strengthened, transferred, exchanged, stolen and leaked through the procedures of ordinary life. This popular energy concept has become all-embracing. It is used to explain all sorts of phenomena, and is now a unifying cognitive category in alternative spirituality. Energy appears as the standard explanation of why healing, therapies, and many other spiritual practices function. The main sources of this development are quantum physics, Theosophy and Western occultism, and Asian teachings about invisible forces of life, such as the Chinese concept *chi* and the Indian *prana*, which underlie popular practices like acupuncture, t'ai chi, feng shui and chakra healing.

The human body is conceived as an "energy body", sometimes referring to the Theosophical doctrine of the seven bodies constituting a human being, or perhaps more often understood in a similar way to David Spangler's concept of "the wide body": that is, an "incarnation pattern" which consists of a person's body, memories and mental dispositions, relationships to other people, the place one lives and works, and participation in ultimate reality (Spangler 1996a: 53, 64). The individual body is conceived as an integrated part of a greater whole which it both affects and is influenced by. The "wide body" pattern can in turn be changed through using manifestation techniques. According to such views, the individual human being is a compound energetic node in a holistic network of energy exchange, involved in continuous interplays and processes with all the layers of existence, from the world of atoms to the surrounding universe (cf. Mikaelsson 2004: 368–9).

As the list of meanings and usages illustrates, "energy" has come to function as a widespread cognitive currency. This is not just a metaphor. The way the energy concept behaves on the New Age market actually has such money-like properties that it can be viewed as a cognitive currency. Both money and energy are disembedding technologies, with similar ways of functioning in the creation of commodities. While it is common to think that being saleable somehow reduces the value of many things, commodification as such does not regularly transform an object into something different. A doll for sale is still a doll. As a commodity, however, the doll has an additional, economic value which is linked to a number of features the doll shares with other commodities, like having a price and being exhibited for sale. Saleability involves "translation" into an economic system. This system operates through specific principles which are more or less in harmony with other systems that determine the handling of objects in the social world. Similarly, energy symbolism invests phenomena with a physical dimension, without robbing them of their phenomenal and ideational distinctiveness. For instance, in the *lingua franca* of New Age, a magic doll is said to transfer indigenous energies to its owner. The doll is defined as a magical object and simultaneously integrated in the explanatory system of New Age. Or another example: a person believing in feng shui might place a Ganesha figure in a room to secure beneficial energies there, although the energy principles of feng shui have nothing to do with Hinduism.

170

Money and energy thus transpose objects into another system through allocating systemic values: that is, money value and energy attribution. A cognitive handling of diversity is inherent in such translation processes which is probably important for the success of the energy concept. Both money and energy are able to combine difference and unity, and their unifying principles seem to have an endless capacity to incorporate heterogenous phenomena. In Western capitalist society more and more areas of life have to adapt to the forces of economic calculation and saleability. In a similar manner, energy holism is able to integrate differences of faith, practice, and doctrine from all parts of the world in a cosmic-personal vision, which functions as a symbolic capital for spiritual entrepreneurs to tap, since the traditional religions are "resources without copyright", in the words of Guy Redden (Redden 2005: 239).

The easy, fluent, all-encompassing character of energy holism dulls the sharpness of difference between religious traditions while the appeal of the exotic is retained – thereby making products with an Indian, Chinese or native American background acceptable for Western customers. The foreign-ness of things tends to be attractive in contemporary culture, a fact which is particularly apparent from the popularity of various national cuisines and mass tourism. Cultural difference creates interest and pleasure, but only if it is, as Stuart Hall says, "commodified, sanitized, and thus *neutralized* for easy consumption" (cited in Lau 2000: 11–12; cf. Salamon 2001: 164–6). Similarly, vagueness and ignorance secure the smoothness of many energy attributions. Detailed information could spoil the market value of an object. If it was announced that the magic doll had got its power from an animal sacrifice or sinister invocations, its economic potential on the New Age market would probably be harmed. Energy on sale to a certain public must serve the values of that public.

When viewed as energy the sacred becomes less sacred, less exclusivist, and less above the trivial pursuits of ordinary life. One spiritual practice can be as good as another since in the end they both control energies. The threshold against commercial use of religious assets becomes lower, which is illustrated by expanding New Age capitalism. The apparent conclusion is that creating spiritual commodities and viewing phenomena in energy terms are mutually reinforcing processes. The resulting convergence makes money a very pertinent symbol of energy holism, a fact which is demonstrated so clearly in the prosperity teachings of New Age.

One aspect of the cosmification of money as energy is that the bad reputation money has through its association with social evils like injustice and greed is cleaned away. Instead, the money gospel – for several propagators a lucrative message indeed – becomes a noble thing to bring forward. Besides, it is repeatedly maintained that there is no shortage of money in the world, everyone can have a fair share, and growing rich does not imply that someone else becomes poor, since prosperity is an expanding process. The discourse represents a capitalist world with seemingly inexhaustible possibilities for the individual with the right mental approach, while references to the social world of class, work, and economic structures generally minimize its conditioning role for the individual person. At this point, the marriage of spirituality and neoliberal capitalism is consummated.

CONCLUDING REMARKS

New Age capitalism is more than its prosperity teachings, and its many aspects are not exhausted by viewing it through the lenses of a market model alone. The impact and meanings of the New Age concepts of spirituality, self and energy are definitely not sufficiently described through a unilateral economic perspective. That said, New Age capitalism is a most interesting development in today's religious field both through its impact on and links with general economy, therapy culture and everyday life, and because its co-existence with established churches in Western countries brings new religious dynamics into these societies.

The popular energy concept sketched above is central for the spirit of New Age capitalism. Materialism and desire for profit become spiritualized, and spirituality commodified, through its application. The vagueness, flexibility and neutrality of the concept means that it can be continually redefined and applied to any number of new products. Energy as currency seems without limits in its capacity to integrate indigenous and local religious material that might still be undiscovered by spiritual entrepreneurs through the conjoined processes of disembedding and translation discussed above. Evidently the energy concept will not restrain development toward further commodification and prosperity thinking, or contribute to reorienting New Age in the direction of a conventional religious organization.

NOTES

1. A simple explanation of capitalism is that it is an historical economic system in which capital (money, machinery, goods etc) is used with the primary object of self-expansion. Capitalism therefore involves the desire to accumulate more capital (Wallerstein 2003: 13–14). Historical capitalism resulted in widespread commodification of processes attached to exchange, production, distribution and investment that had previously not been performed via the market (*ibid.*: 15).

2. In his ingenuous account of the historical background of contemporary consumerism, *The Romantic Ethic and the Spirit of Modern Consumerism* (1987), Colin Campbell takes his point of departure in Weber's theory. In contrast to Weber, who was concerned with the early stage of capitalism when Puritanism was dominant in English society, Campbell traces the increasing religious and cultural acceptance of hedonism after the decline of Puritanism, constructing a historical lineage of consumerism which comprises Puritanism-Sentimentalism-Romanticism.

3. The fairly young discipline of economics of religion is grounded in the works of Adam Smith and Max Weber, and dominated by two theoretical approaches: market-based and rational choice theory. As *The Oxford Handbook of the Economics of Religion* (McCleary 2011) makes clear, a great variety of issues are investigated within the discipline. Larry Witham's broadly laid-out book, *The Marketplace of the Gods: How Economics Explains Religion* (2010), applies an economic model of human beings in the study of how economics and religion interacts. The economic model presumes that the individual seeks to gain more benefits than costs, and does this by using rational calculation (i.e. rational choice) (Witham 2010: 8). However, the influence of economy on religion and *vice versa* is such a complex subject that a number of approaches are called for.

4. Lau concentrates on economic flourishing in the US within the fields of aromatherapy, macrobiotic eating, Yoga and t'ai chi.

5. According to Carrette and King (2005: 150) Deepak Chopra has produced over thirty books which have sold in more than ten million copies in twenty-five languages. Chopra's enterprises also include sales of herbal products and massage oils.

6. Cf. Carolyn Morrow Long's *Spiritual Merchants: Religion, Magic and Commerce* (2001), a detailed study of the development of the African-based belief system in the US and its evolution during the twentieth century into a spiritual products industry.

7. *Møt din skytsengel* (2009), co-authored with Elsabeth Samnøy, and *Englenes hemmeligheter* (2012), co-authored with Elisabeth Nordeng. The books are translated into other languages.

8. Translation of the Norwegian poster headline announcing the alternative fair in Bergen in 2000.

9. See www.alternativ.no (accessed August 2013). The company Alternativt Nettverk (Alternative Network) has had a key role in the formation of the New Age field in Norway since the 1990s. It was established as a network organization in 1992, and transformed into a company in 1997. It publishes the magazine *Visjon* with a circulation of 15,000 copies, and arranges courses, conferences and fairs. Its range of interests includes alternative medicine, ecology, global consciousness, self-development and alternative worldviews. The organization is thus a fitting example of scholarly understandings of New Age as a spiritual market.

10. Cf. Botvar 1993; Engedal and Sveinall 2000; Lund-Olsen and Repstad 2003; Aadnanes 2008; Botvar and Schmidt 2010; Engelsviken, Olsen and Thelle 2011.

11. A recent example of the usefulness of various perspectives is a study by Norwegian scholars Dag Øistein Endsjø and Liv Ingeborg Lied, *Det folk vil ha* [what people want] (2011). The authors focus on various commercial sub-areas in popular culture, like the Eurovision Song Contest, advertising, pleasure parks, film and interior decoration, demonstrating the *modus operandi* of religious ideas, symbols, narratives and artefacts in these spheres.

12. "Holism" belongs to the standard repertoire in alternative circles and is a frequent theme in the scholarly literature about New Age. See William Bloom's *The Holistic Revolution: The Essential Reader* (2000) for a survey of the important themes, authors and texts. Western dualism between body and soul, matter and spirit is generally criticized, coupled with an emphasis on the interconnectedness of everything.

11. BEYOND THE SPIRITUAL SUPERMARKET: THE SOCIAL AND PUBLIC SIGNIFICANCE OF NEW AGE SPIRITUALITY

Stef Aupers and Dick Houtman

In most of the social-scientific literature, New Age – or "spirituality", as increasingly seems the preferred term – is used to refer to an apparently incoherent collection of spiritual ideas and practices. Most participants in the spiritual milieu, it is generally argued, draw upon multiple traditions, styles and ideas simultaneously, combining them into idiosyncratic packages. New Age is thus referred to as "do-it-yourself-religion" (Baerveldt 1996), "pick-and-mix religion" (Hamilton 2000), "religious consumption à la carte" (Possamai 2003) or a "spiritual supermarket" (D. Lyon 2000). In their book *Beyond New Age: Exploring Alternative Spirituality*, Sutcliffe and Bowman (2000: 1) even go so far as to argue that "New Age turns out to be merely a particular code word in a larger field of modern religious experimentation", while Possamai (2003: 40) states that we are dealing with an "eclectic – if not kleptomaniac – process ... with no clear reference to an external or 'deeper' reality".

This dominant discourse about New Age basically reiterates sociologist of religion Thomas Luckmann's influential analysis, published about forty years ago in *The Invisible Religion* (1967). Structural differentiation in modern society, or so Luckmann argues, results in erosion of the Christian monopoly and the concomitant emergence of a "market of ultimate significance". On such a market, religious consumers construct strictly personal packages of meaning, based on individual tastes and preferences. Indeed, in a more recent publication, Luckmann notes that New Age exemplifies this tendency of individual "bricolage": "It collects abundant psychological, therapeutic, magic, marginally scientific, and older esoteric material, repackages them, and offers them for individual consumption and further private syncretism" (Luckmann 1996: 75).

Luckmann emphasizes that those personal meaning systems remain strictly private affairs: by their very nature, and unlike traditional church-based Christian religion in the past, they lack a wider social significance and play no public role whatsoever. Writing thirty years ago, the late Bryan

Wilson has made a similar claim about the post-Christian cults, stating that those "represent, in the American phrase, 'the religion of your choice', the highly privatized preference that reduces religion to the significance of pushpin, poetry, or popcorns" (Wilson 1976: 96). And more recently, Steve Bruce has characterized New Age as a "diffuse religion", noting "There is no ... power in the cultic milieu to override individual preferences" (Bruce 2002: 99).

Accounts such as those are found over and over again in the sociological literature, as Besecke (2005: 186) rightly observes: "Luckmann's characterization of contemporary religion as privatized is pivotal in the sociology of religion; it has been picked up by just about everyone and challenged by almost no one." Work done in anthropology and the history of religion nonetheless suggests that this orthodoxy is deeply problematic (Hammer 2001, 2004a; Hanegraaff 1996, 2001; Luhrmann 1989). And indeed, from within sociology itself, Heelas (1996) has demonstrated convincingly that New Age spirituality is remarkably less eclectic and incoherent than typically assumed. Our aim in the current chapter is to elaborate on those dissenting voices and demonstrate that this sociological orthodoxy is not much more than an institutionalized intellectual misconstruction. More specifically, we criticize three related arguments that together constitute the privatization thesis:

1. that New Age boils down to mere individual "bricolage";
2. that it is socially insignificant, because "the transmission of diffuse beliefs is unnecessary and it is impossible" (Bruce 2002: 99); and
3. that it does not play a role in the public domain.

We finish by summarizing our findings and briefly elaborating on their theoretical significance.

We base ourselves on data from a variety of sources collected during the first author's PhD research in the period 1999–2003 (see Aupers 2004). Besides literature on New Age and a variety of flyers and websites of Dutch New Age centres, we especially draw on in-depth interviews with two samples of New Age teachers. Focusing on this "spiritual elite" rather than on people who only vaguely identify with labels such as "spirituality" or "New Age" enables us to study the worldview of the spiritual milieu in its most crystallized and "pure" form. Besides, these are of course the very people who communicate this worldview to those who participate in their courses, training and workshops. The first sample consists of spiritual trainers who work for Dutch New Age centres in the urbanized western part of the country.[1] The centres have been randomly sampled from a national directory of nature-oriented medicine and consciousness-raising (Van Hoog 2001) and the respondents have next been randomly sampled from those centres' websites. Eleven of those initially contacted – a very large majority – agreed to be interviewed.[2] The second sample consists of trainers at Dutch New Age centres that specialize in spiritual courses for business life. Apart from this theoretically imposed restriction, the sampling procedure was identical to the one just described. Nine in-depth interviews were completed with, again, almost no refusals.[3] Finally, we rely on data from a theoretically instructive case study of the Dutch company Morca that has embraced New Age capitalism. Within the context of this case study, the first author has conducted in-depth interviews with Morca's president-director, his spiritual coach, four employees who had participated in the company's spiritual courses, and three employees who had not. Unless indicated otherwise, we draw on data from the first sample of spiritual trainers in the following section, then, on data from the second sample of trainers and finally on the case study of Morca.

THE ETHIC OF SELF-SPIRITUALITY

> Diffuse religion cannot sustain a distinctive way of life.
>
> (Bruce 2002: 94)

As the sociological orthodoxy suggests, teachers of Dutch New Age centres combine various traditions in their courses. One may use tarot cards in combination with crystal-healing and Hindu ideas about chakras; another may combine traditional Chinese medicine, Western psychotherapy and Taoism into another idiosyncratic concoction. There is, in short, no reason to deny the prominence of "bricolage" in the spiritual milieu.

What is a problem, however, is that whereas scholars of New Age typically assume that this "bricolage" or "eclecticism" is the principal characteristic of New Age, *none* of the interviewees feels that the traditions on which s/he bases his or her courses are at the heart of one's worldview. As the Dutch New Age centre "Centrum voor Spirituele Wegen" argues in one of its flyers, "There are many paths, but just one truth". This *philosophia perennis* or "perennial philosophy" derives from esotericism – and especially from Blavatsky's New Theosophy (Hanegraaff 1996) – and has influenced the first generation of New Agers in the 1970s through the work of Daisetz Teitaro Suzuki and Aldous Huxley. According to this perennialism, all religious traditions are equally valid, because they all essentially worship the same divine source. Perennialism's virtual omnipresence in the spiritual milieu can be illustrated by means of the following explanations by three of the interviewed New Age teachers:[4]

> I feel connected with the person of Jesus Christ, not with Catholicism. But I also feel touched by the person of Buddha. I am also very much interested in shamanism. So my belief has

nothing to do with a particular religious tradition. For me, all religions are manifestations of god, of the divine. If you look beyond the surface, then all religions tell the same story.

That is important: you can find spirituality in every religion … In Christianity you"ll find Gnosticism, in Hinduism it is the philosophy of Tantra, in the Jewish tradition it is the Kabbalah. The fundamentalist versions of religion are divided: only Allah, only Jesus Christ. But the esoterical undercurrent is almost the same!

For me it is easy to step into any tradition. I can do it with Buddhism from Tibet, with Hinduism, and I can point out what is the essence of every religion … I am dealing with almost every world religion … There is not one truth. Of course there is one truth, but there are various ways of finding it.

More fundamental than "bricolage", in short, is perennialism: the belief that the diversity of religious traditions essentially refers to the same underlying spiritual truth. Accepting this doctrine, people become motivated to experiment freely with various traditions to explore "what works for them personally". As already briefly indicated above, Heelas has done path-breaking work in laying bare the precise nature of this underlying spiritual truth, pointing out the primacy of the doctrine of self-spirituality:

Beneath much of the heterogeneity, there is remarkable constancy. Again and again, turning from practice to practice, from publication to publication, indeed from country to country, one encounters the same (or very similar) *lingua franca* … This is the language of what shall henceforth be called "Self-spirituality" … And these assumptions of Self-spirituality ensure that the New Age Movement is far from being a mish-mash, significantly eclectic, or fundamentally incoherent.
(Heelas 1996: 2; original emphasis)

In the spiritual milieu, Heelas explains, modern people are essentially seen as "gods and goddesses in exile" (*ibid.*: 19): "The great refrain, running throughout the New Age, is that we malfunction because we have been indoctrinated … by mainstream society and culture" (*ibid.*: 18). The latter are thus conceived of as basically alienating forces, estranging one from one's "authentic", "natural" or "real" self – from who one "really" or "at deepest" is:

[T]he most pervasive and significant aspect of the *lingua franca* of the New Age is that the person is, in essence, spiritual. To experience the "Self" itself is to experience "God", "the Goddess",

> the "Source", "Christ Consciousness", the "inner child", the "way
> of the heart", or, most simply and ... most frequently, "inner
> spirituality".
> (*Ibid.*: 19)

This, then, is the binding doctrine in the spiritual milieu: the belief that in the deeper layers of the self one finds a true, authentic and sacred kernel, basically "unpolluted" by culture, history and society, that informs evaluations of what is good, true and meaningful. Those evaluations, it is held, cannot be made by relying on external authorities or experts, but only by listening to one's "inner voice": "What lies within – experienced by way of "intuition", "alignment" or an "inner voice" – serves to inform the judgements, decisions and choices required for everyday life" (*ibid.*: 23).

Like traditional forms of religion, the idea of self-spirituality consists of a well-defined doctrine of "being and well-being" (Goudsblom 1985) or a "theodicy of good and evil" (Weber 1920). A "mundane", "conventional" or "socialized" self – often referred to as the "ego" – demonized as the "false" or "unreal" product of society and its institutions, is contrasted with a "higher", "deeper", "true" or "authentic" self that is sacralized and can be found in the self's deeper layers. In the words of our respondents:

> I experience god, the divine, as something within me. I feel it as being present in myself. I connect with it as I focus my attention on my inner self, when I meditate. ... It's all about self-knowledge, being conscious about yourself. ... It has nothing to do with something that's outside of you that solves things for you.

> I think spirituality is something that lives inside of you. It has a lot to do with becoming the essence of who you are and being as natural as possible.

> I am god. I don't want to insult the Christian church or anything, but I decide what I'm doing with my life. ... There is no "super-dad" in heaven that can tell me "You have to do this and that, or else ..." I am going to feel!

This sacralization of the self is logically tied to an understanding of social institutions as evil. Modern bureaucracies, for instance, are generally regarded as "alienating", "nonsensical", "inhumane", and "without soul", while excessive identification with career, status and pre-structured work roles is regarded as a major source of personal problems. More generally, the subordination of the self to pre-given life orders is held to inescapably result in frustration, bitterness, unhappiness, mental disorder, depression, disease, violence, sick forms of sexuality, and so on. The sacralization of the self, in short, goes hand in hand with a demonization of social institutions to produce a clear-cut dualistic worldview (Aupers & Houtman 2003):

> If you cannot find yourself in your work ... If you don't have pleasure in your work, then you start to think about yourself negatively and that's a bad thing. Then you become physically and mentally ill.

> It can make people really ill. You should know how many people have psychological and psychosomatic complaints because they are imprisoned in a role, a role where they are not at home. I meet many of these people in this centre.

> "I am my work." I hear that a lot. When people retire they fall into this black hole. "I do not exist anymore." Because "I am my work, my status. I am the director." ... That's hard! Things go wrong then. They will become bitter and unhappy. Sometimes they die soon.

This dualistic worldview constitutes the heart of the doctrine of self-spirituality. Motivated by perennialist philosophy, participants in the spiritual milieu freely use various concepts to describe the spiritual essence of human beings and "follow their personal paths" towards their deeper selves by delving into various religious traditions. They may speak, for instance, about the "higher self" of Theosophy, the "divine spark" of Gnosticism, the "soul" of Christianity, the "Buddha nature" of Buddhism or the "inner child" of humanistic psychology. Notwithstanding those essentially trivial differences, the underlying doctrine of self-spirituality is uncontested.

The emergence of a pluralistic spiritual supermarket confirms Luckmann's classical prediction, in short, but has simultaneously blinded many observers to the commonly held doctrine of self-spirituality – the belief that the self itself is sacred. It is this doctrine that paradoxically accounts for the staggering diversity at the surface of the spiritual milieu – an inevitable outcome when people feel that they need to follow their personal paths and explore what works for them personally – and simultaneously provides it with ideological unity and coherence at a deeper level. The common characterization of New Age as "pick-and-mix-religion" or "diffuse religion" is not plainly wrong, then, but rather superficial. If it is believed that the sacred resides in the deeper layers of the self, after all, what else can be expected than people following their personal paths, experimenting freely with a range of traditions in a highly heterogeneous spiritual milieu? The diversity of the spiritual milieu *results from* rather than *contradicts* the existence of a coherent doctrine of being and well-being.

THE SOCIAL CONSTRUCTION OF SELF-SPIRITUALITY

As we have seen, the spiritual milieu is in fact more doctrinally coherent and hence less diffuse than typically assumed. It remains to be seen, therefore, whether "spiritual socialization" really is an oxymoron, because "the transmission of diffuse beliefs is unnecessary and it is impossible" as Bruce (2002: 99) claims. To study this, we analyse the biographies of the spiritual trainers of our second sample. They have been strategically selected because they specialize in spiritual courses for business life and in fact all prove to have started their own careers there. How and why did they make this remarkable shift from "normal" jobs, such as clerk, president-director or manager, to the spiritual world of shamanism, aura reading, tantra and channelling? More specifically: what, if any, was the role played by socialization?

Alienation as the key: who am I, really?
In obvious contrast to the way Christian identities are typically adopted, only one of the nine respondents developed an affinity with spirituality due to parental socialization during his formative period. Contrary to Bruce's suggestion, however, this does not mean that socialization plays no role at all, although this process only started after they got motivated to get involved due to the experience of identity problems. Through excessive identification with the goals set by the companies they worked for, with their pre-structured work roles and well-defined task descriptions, they increasingly felt alienated. This raised questions of meaning and identity: "What is it that I really want?", "Is this really the sort of life I want to live?", "What sort of person am I, really?"

The case of Chantal, who now works in the New Age centre Soulstation, is exemplary. She studied economics, rapidly made a career in the business world and, she explains, completely identified with her work. Looking back she states that she was "marched along the paths set out by society" and adds: "I studied marketing and sales, but had never learned to look in the mirror". Like most others, she points out that her identity crisis began with an "intruding conversation" with a consultant:

> I was working at MCR, a computer company, and I was the commercial director. A big team, a big market, and a big responsibility for the profits. Much too young for what I did. But that was my situation: You did what you had to do. Then I was invited by a business partner to visit a consultant. I sat there talking for two hours with that man. It was an inspiring visit and suddenly he looked at me intrudingly and said: "I hear your story. It sounds perfect, looking at it from the outside, but where are you?" In other words: "The story is not yours. It is the standard 'format'

of the company you are presenting, but where is your passion? What makes you Chantal instead of Miss MCR?"

The latter question marks the beginning of an identity crisis and an enduring quest for meaning. She adds:

> I thought: "Shit, I have no answer to this question and I have to do something with that." The result of this conversation was a burnout that lasted almost a year. That's a crisis, you know! In the evening hours I started to do coaching sessions, I started thinking about the question: "Who am I, really?" You start to look in the mirror. And then, at a certain moment, you can no longer unite your private life with your position at work. It's like your skis are suddenly moving in opposite directions. And that's definitely not a comfortable position: before you realize, you're standing in a split.

The suggestive metaphor of "standing in a split" between the demands of business life and private life applies to most of the respondents. The more they become involved in "soul searching", the more they alienate from their working environments. "Being true to oneself" becomes an imperative and, in the end, becomes incompatible with the demands of business life. This cognitive dissonance is the main reason why respondents eventually resign from their regular jobs. Marco, founder of New Age centre Merlin, specialized in Enneagram trainings (the Enneagram is a psycho-spiritual model to increase self-knowledge) and shamanistic courses, states in this respect: "That is why I left business life. When I felt that I had to work on the basis of my intuition, or my feelings, this became a problem. ... It was just not accepted that such a thing as intuition existed. I had to base my accounts on numbers and figures. I couldn't bear that any longer. Now I want to do work that feels right."

Yet another respondent, Marie-José, worked for nineteen years as a consultant, a manager and, finally, a director. She started working on "intuitive development" in her personal life but felt increasingly that she could not reconcile these private practices with her public task as a director. These were, she explains, "two incompatible languages":

> Finally I ended up in a sort of dull routine and realized that the organization was only interested in its own survival. ... The only thing that counted was that one could legitimate one's decisions to the outside world. I severely began to disconnect from the company. ... It became clear to me that I performed a certain role that fitted the formal position I had in that company. Like "This is my role, so this is the way I act and what I feel is something

I let out when I am at home." Then I thought: "I have to leave this company, because I can't stand it no longer to act as if I feel nothing, while in fact I am overwhelmed by my emotions." ... I figured: "What will happen when I express my feelings in the office? Should I cry?"

The process of "soul searching" that follows should not be misconstrued as a strictly personal quest for meaning. Although a latent sense of unease or discomfort may well have been present beforehand, it is indeed quite telling that it typically became manifest only after a conversation with a consultant or coach. Remarks like "He touched something within me", "Something opened up" or "The light went on" indicate that due to this contact latent discomfort becomes manifest and triggers a process of searching the depths of one's soul.

What follows is a process of socialization in which three mechanisms validate and reinforce one another:

1. acquiring a new cognitive frame of interpretation
2. having new experiences, and
3. legitimating one's newly acquired worldview.

These mechanisms, Tanya Luhrmann (1989: 312) demonstrates in her study on neopaganism, are the pushing powers behind an "interpretive drift": "the slow, often unacknowledged shift in someone's manner of interpreting events as they become involved with a particular activity".

Spiritual careers: knowledge and experience shifting in tandem
Initially, the process of soul searching has a secular character. Motivated by their identity crises, respondents start describing their selves in vocabularies derived from humanistic psychology. Emotions are permitted and valued positively, but are not yet defined as higher, spiritual or sacred. Although they generally start out with humanistic psychological self-help books and courses, they eventually end up doing more esoteric types of training, such as shamanism, aura reading and the like.

Daan comments on his relentless participation in various courses as "a sort of hunger that emerges in yourself. You start to nourish and feed it. And so you hop from course to course." By satisfying their "hunger" on the New Age market, the respondents acquire alternative frames of interpretation, new vocabularies and symbols to interpret their experiences. They learn to label weird, out-of the-ordinary experiences as spiritual. *Vice versa*, these experiences validate the acquired frame of interpretation. In the words of Luhrmann: "Intellectual and experiential changes shift in tandem, a ragged co-evolution of intellectual habits and phenomenological involvement" (Luhrmann 1996: 315). The story of Marie-José provides a good illustration:

> We were walking on a mountain. ... And I was just observing, thinking what a beautiful mountain this was and suddenly everything started to flow within me. This was my first spiritual experience. ... I felt like: "Now I understand what they mean when they say that the earth is alive." I began to make contact and understood that I am like the earth, a part of nature, and that my body is alive.

The formulation "Now I understand what they mean when they say" illustrates that knowledge precedes experience and, perhaps, shapes its specific content. A similar story is told by Chantal. During her stay at Findhorn she learned about the existence of auras, chakras and streams of energy inside and just outside the body. This resulted, she argues, in "spiritual experiences":

> When I was there, someone said: "You have a healing energy around you and you should do something with that." Well, I had never heard of these two words, "healing" and "energy". So I was like: "What do you mean?" She said: "I'll give you an instruction." After that I started practising with a friend of mine. I moved my hand over her body and I indeed felt warm and cold places. And I felt sensations, stimulation. Then I became curious.

Chantal began to delve deeper in the matter of healing and increasingly felt streams of energy around people. After a while she started to actually see these fields of energy: "After this I began to see auras, colours around people. At that time I still worked at this computer company and – after three months [at Findhorn] – I returned to the office. During meetings I was really staring at people; like, 'I have to look at you, because you have all these colours around you.'"

Respondents voluntarily internalize a spiritual conception of the self in the process and radically re-interpret their personal identities in conformity with it. On the one hand, a new image of the self in the present emerges: undefined emotions and experiences are now understood in spiritual terms and the new identity is understood as profoundly spiritual. On the other hand, they start to re-write their biographies: they break with their past identities, now understood as "one-dimensional", "alienated" or "unhappy". As one respondent argues: "I now know that I was structurally depressed without being aware of it". Statements such as those exemplify the cultural logic of conversion: they have "seen the light" and now re-interpret their past lives as "living in sin". As with classical conversions, they follow the logic of "Then I thought ... but now I know." The more our respondents became immersed in the spiritual milieu, the more these considerations were reinforced, to eventually reach the point of successful socialization, "the establishment of a high degree of symmetry between objective and subjective reality" (Berger & Luckmann 1966: 183).

Legitimations

Having left their regular jobs and having started new careers as trainers and teachers in the spiritual milieu, it is hardly surprising that our respondents regularly encounter resistance and critique. They are well aware that they are seen by many as "irrational", "softies", or "dreamers" and that their way of life is perceived by many as "something for people with problems". How do they deal with these and other forms of resistance? A core element in their legitimation strategy is a radical reversal of moral positions: they argue that it is not themselves, but the critical outsider who has a problem, although he or she may not be aware of this. Following the doctrine of self-spirituality, resistance, critique and moral opposition are taken as symptoms of a deeply felt anxiety that cannot (yet) be directly experienced. Critics, our respondents argue, project an unresolved "inner problem" on the outside world. In the words of Marie-José "People who have such strong resistance secretly have a strong affinity with spirituality. Otherwise they wouldn't be so angry. They just can"t break through their resistance. Obviously they have a problem. Why else would you make such a fuss about something that doesn't concern you?"

Daan tells a similar story:

> People are projecting it on the outside world: they get angry. There is obviously something in themselves they are not satisfied with. And then it's easier to get angry with others than to say: "This is jealousy in me" or "This is greed". "No, let's not take a look at that, let's project it on the outside world." To handle these problems takes loads of strength and efforts. ... To enter a process of spiritual growth, you have to be very strong. As we can read in the Vedic literature: it is much easier to conquer seven cities than to conquer yourself.

Marco, who, among other things, works with the Enneagram (a psychospiritual model to increase self-knowledge), explains his strategy in dealing with resistance and critique during his courses as follows:

> Of course, in my trainings, I regularly meet people who show resistance but I can easily trace that back to their personality. Then I say: "You see, this is your mechanism of resistance that is now emerging." ... Then I say: "I can fully understand you, I know the reasons why you are saying this". Then they say: "It is useless debating with you!" I say: "But what can I do about it? ... It is part of the type of person you are, as explained by the Enneagram."

Our interviewees normalize their positions and pathologize criticism by outsiders by "reading" it as a symptom of psychological fear, anxiety or insecurity, in short. As a consequence, the "inside" group is portrayed as courageous and free (because they choose to face their "demons"), while the "outsiders" are labelled as alienated because they are disconnected from their deeper selves.

The process of socialization unfolds as follows, then. First, latent feelings of alienation become manifest after a conversation with a consultant, raising problems of meaning and identity – "What is it that I really want?", "Is this really the sort of life I want to live?", "What sort of person am I, really?" Second, during the process of soul searching that follows, people are socialized into the ethic of self-spirituality, with knowledge and experience shifting in tandem. Third, after successful socialization, standardized legitimations are deployed, further reinforcing the ethic of self-spirituality. Those findings are strikingly consistent with those of Hammer (2001), based on a content analysis of a sample of New Age texts in his case. In his book *Claiming Knowledge: Strategies of Epistemology from Theosophy to the New Age*, Hammer (2001: 366–7) also demonstrates that several cognitive and social mechanisms are operative so as to make New Agers conform to a set of unwritten norms (see Hammer 2004a, for a very brief summary of the argument as well as Hanegraaff 2001, for a similar type of analysis): "Labeled spiritual rather than religious, experiences are presented in numerous New Age texts as self-validating and primary. Thus, attention is turned away from the fact that the frame of interpretation is culturally constituted, and that ritual forms and collective practices fundamentally shape individual experience."

This process of socialization into a spiritual discourse about the self reveals that participants in the spiritual milieu are less authentic than they typically believe they are. After all: how authentic are those concerned, when they have in fact been socialized into a shared emphasis on the primacy of personal authenticity? New Agers' self-claimed authenticity rather reminds one of the classical scene in Monty Python's *Life of Brian*, in which a crowd of followers enthusiastically and literally repeats Brian's words with one voice when he desperately attempts to convince them to go home and leave him alone: "We are all individuals!" they shout, with only one astonished dissenter muttering "I'm not ...".

It is striking to note that, apart from the latent feelings of alienation that trigger it, the process of socialization into a spiritual discourse about the self is basically identical to that revealed by Howard Becker in his classical study of marihuana users. In that case, too, acquired knowledge underlies the recognition and positive evaluation of experiences, just as in both cases "deviant groups tend ... to be pushed into rationalizing their position" by means of standardized legitimations (Becker 1966: 38) so as to neutralize critique from outsiders and reinforce the adopted way of life to insiders.

SELF-SPIRITUALITY'S PUBLIC SIGNIFICANCE: BRINGING "SOUL" BACK TO WORK

"Sociologists rarely study spirituality in the workplace", Grant *et al.* (2004: 267) observe. Although some substantial studies have been done in this field (e.g. Heelas 1996; Mitroff & Denton 1999a; Nadesan 1999; Roberts 1994; Salamon 2001),[5] this blind spot is probably due to the received wisdom that spirituality lacks public significance, remaining confined to "the life-space that is not directly touched by institutional control" (Luckmann 1996: 73) and failing to "generate powerful social innovations and experimental social institutions" (Bruce 2002: 97). But obviously, the very rarity of studies of spirituality in the workplace precludes any premature conclusions to the effect that spirituality fails to affect our "primary institutions", modern work organizations. "[I]f it appears to sociologists that spirituality cannot take root within secular bureaucracies, it may be because their theories have not yet allowed it", as Grant *et al.* (2004: 281) rightly note. And indeed, notwithstanding common claims to the contrary, it is difficult to deny that spirituality has in fact entered the public domain of work organizations.

New Age incorporated
In the 1980s, business organizations became interested in the worldviews and practices of the New Age and, *vice versa*, New Age began to turn towards business life (Heelas 1996; Nadesan 1999). Renowned management magazines such as "People Management", "Industry Week" and "Sloan Management Review" publish articles on the opportunities of spirituality for business life on a regular basis (e.g. Baber 1999; Berman 1999; Braham 1999; Hayes 1999; Mitroff & Denton 1999b; Neal 1999; Traynor 1999; Turner 1999; J. Welch 1998). Indeed, on a basis of 131 in-depth interviews and 2,000 questionnaires in American companies, Mitroff and Denton demonstrate that employees and managers feel a great need to integrate spirituality in business life. In *A Spiritual Audit of Corporate America* they conclude:

> This age calls for a new "spirit of management". For us, the concepts of spirituality and soul are not merely add-on elements of a new philosophy or policy. … No management effort can survive without them. We refuse to accept that whole organisations cannot learn ways to foster soul and spirituality in the workplace. We believe not only that they can, but also that they must.
> (Mitroff & Denton 1999a: 14)

Most of the spiritual ideas, initiatives and practices that are applied in business life can be labelled as self-spirituality: "The inner-individual orientation is what most people, including the majority of our respondents, mean by spirituality" (*ibid.*: 26).

Examples of large companies that have become interested in New Age training are Guiness, General Dynamics and Boeing Aerospace – even the US Army has adopted them (Heelas 1996). It is hard to tell to what extent New Age affects American business life, but there are some indications. Naisbitt and Aburdene (1990: 273) refer to a survey held among five hundred American companies, at least half of which had at one time or another offered "consciousness-raising techniques" to their employees. They estimate that companies in the US spend at least four billion dollars on New Age consultants annually, which is more than ten percent of the total of thirty billion spent on company trainings every year (see Barker 1994; Nadesan 1999; Swets & Bjork 1990: 95).

Since the 1990s, the shift of New Age towards business life has become clearly visible in the Netherlands, too. A prime example is Oibibio in Amsterdam, founded in 1993. Oibibio's business department offered training in spiritual management, such as "Team management and the soul" and "Management in astrological perspective", to keep companies "ready for battle" in times in which "dynamic streams of production, services and information increasingly put pressure on organisations and managers". They make the following claim in their flyer "Our trainers are builders of bridges: they speak the language of business life and pragmatically know how to implant the spiritual philosophy in your organisation; they do so in cooperation with your employees."

Oibibio's bankruptcy in the late 1990s did not trigger a decline of New Age capitalism in the Netherlands. Instead it marked the birth of many other, more successful New Age centres such as Metavisie, Soulstation, Being in Business and Firmament. Metavisie, probably one of the largest players in this field, claims to have offered in-company training to seventy-five of the one hundred most renowned companies in the Netherlands.[6] The list of clients on their website comprises more than two hundred national and international companies and institutions, among them many of the major Dutch banks and insurance companies (ABN Amro, ING, Generale, Rabobank, Aegon, Amev, De Amersfoortse, Centraal Beheer, Interpolis, Zwitserleven and Delta Lloyd) and IT companies (Cap Gemini, CMG, Compaq, Getronics Software, High Tech Automation, IBM Nederland, Oracle and Baan Software). Internationally renowned Dutch multinationals such as Ahold, Heineken and telecom company KPN are also on the list, as well as remarkably many government-sponsored institutions such as the national welfare organization UWV-GAK and the University of Amsterdam, and the Ministries of Finance, the Interior, Trade and Industry, Justice, Agriculture and Fisheries, Transport and Public Works, Welfare, Health and Cultural Affairs, and Housing, Regional Development and the Environment. This is, indeed, convincing evidence that New Age is penetrating the public sphere. More than that, the list indicates that especially organizations producing immaterial services rather than material products provide their employees with spiritual in-company training. Especially the post-industrial service sector seems hospitable towards New Age, then. What is the goal of the spiritual in-company training in all of these organizations?

The interviews with trainers of New Age centres that specialize in spirituality in business life and those centres' websites reveal that their courses aim primarily at deconstructing the typically modern separation between the private and public realms, by trying to impose the logic of the former upon the latter. This complies, of course, with the ethic of self-spirituality: the centres aim to make the rationalized environments less alienating and more open to "authenticity" and "spirituality". By doing so, it is argued, they seek for a win/win situation or, in the terms of Heelas (1996), "the best of both worlds". In the following accounts, "authenticity" is held to result in both well-being *and* efficiency and "spirituality" in happiness *and* profit, while "soulful organizations" are portrayed as successful:

> Organisations are in movement. The pressure increases. People want dedication. There is a call for a new sort of leader. A leader that takes business results *and* human potential into account. ... Metavisie helps to create these leaders of the future. Together we cause a paradigm shift in society. A society that is not primarily obsessed with money and profit but a society that celebrates the quality of human life. Where it is the highest goal to be your most authentic self.
>
> (www.metavisie.com, accessed November 2005)

> The mission of Being in Business is to build a bridge between organisations and spirituality to make businesses more successful. Success, then, is not primarily defined as making more profit, but also as increasing well-being for you and your employees. Being in Business shapes this spiritual dimension in your organisation by providing services that will increase consciousness, vitality, fun, pleasure and energy. Spirituality is profit. Because profit is nothing more than materialised energy. The more energy your organisation generates, the higher the profit. And spirituality in your organisation is of course much more.
>
> (www.beinginbusiness.nl, accessed November 2005)

> People who develop personal mastership steadily become more capable to live their authenticity. In such a situation, one can put all one's natural talents in the world and do what one is really good at. The more authentically one lives, the more effective one's actions. Authenticity therefore has a large impact on productivity within organisations.
>
> (www.soulstation.nl, accessed November 2005)

188

Firmament strives towards unlocking, developing and reinforcing the unique potential and inspiration of individuals. By doing
so, they bring back the soul into your organisation. It is our
experience that vital and soulful organisations, where employees
recognise their personal goals in the goals of the organisation,
operate powerfully on the economic market.

(www.firmamentbv.com, accessed November 2005)

Although bureaucratization may pose all sorts of practical obstacles to the
introduction of spiritual practices in the workplace (Grant *et al.* 2004), this
should not blind us to the fact that it also paradoxically underlies attempts
to bring "soul" back to work – to break with "alienating" bureaucratic organizational structures and pre-given work roles. As we have seen, this seems
to apply especially to organizations in the post-industrial service sector,
probably because the highly skilled and specialized work in this sector is
much more difficult to rationalize and control from without, and because
attempts to nevertheless do so are likely to meet with fierce professional
resistance.

Indeed, the "best of both worlds" approach that dominates the concomitant discourse suggests that tensions between bureaucratic demands on
the one hand and opportunities for spiritual practices on the other may in
fact be less severe than typically assumed. Organizational goals are typically taken for granted and remain strictly instrumental, after all, while the
"inner lives" of employees are considered valuable assets that enable firms
and organizations to strengthen their positions in highly competitive and
demanding environments. Although it is hard to deny that spirituality has
entered the public realm of work, then, what is badly needed is good ethnographic research into whether and how tensions between bureaucratic
demands and spiritual practices emerge and, if so, how those are dealt with
on an everyday basis.

Self-spirituality in action: "Grow or I'll shoot!"
We finally present the findings of a case study of a company that has to
a large extent institutionalized the ethic of self-spirituality. This case is
not typical of contemporary business life, but is theoretically instructive.
Whereas people enter the spiritual milieu freely and voluntarily, driven by
problems of identity caused by alienation, as we have seen, the employees
of this particular company find themselves in a setting in which the ethic
of self-spirituality is more or less imposed upon them. Its functioning as
a binding social norm – as a "social fact" in the classical sense of Émile
Durkheim – thereby becomes more visible and easier to study, precisely
because not all employees are equally enthusiastic about such an imposition
of a spiritual regime. As such, this case study enables us to further illustrate
the claims made above about the existence and nature of a coherent spiritual

doctrine of being and well-being and about the dynamics of socialization into such a spiritual discourse about the self.

The company in case is Morca, a producer of bathroom equipment with branches in various countries in western Europe.[7] Geert, its president-director, is deeply involved in New Age and provides in-company training for his employees. On a personal level, Geert is motivated to implement spirituality in business life because of his own biography. The development he went through exactly matches the analysis in the previous section: he went through an "enormous personal crisis", made contact with his current spiritual coach, followed various New Age courses and increasingly embraced the ethic of self-spirituality. He discovered – in his own words – that he is both "the question and the answer" and "the painter and the canvas".

Marcel, his coach and spiritual mentor, takes care of the courses at Morca. Marcel works with various religious traditions (Christianity, Taoism, Buddhism), embraces the "perennial philosophy" and emphasizes the primacy of self-spirituality: "The spiritual leader knows that self-knowledge is the source of all wisdom". Three questions are at the heart of his courses: "Who am I?", "What do I want?" and "How do I get it?". The president-director explains the goal of the courses as follows: "I want to provide the opportunity for employees to find themselves in their jobs. And it is my conviction that if you 'follow that path', you"ll end up encountering your inner spirituality. And when people get inspired they are inclined to make beautiful things. And we all profit from that."

Like the New Age centres, then, Morca aims for the "best of both worlds". It aims to transform the public realm of the organization into a private sphere where employees can express themselves fully because "authenticity is the most important thing in the world". By doing so, Morca expects its employees to be more happy and, hence, more effective, so as to increase productivity and profits.

It is important to note that participation in the courses is *formally* a free choice. Geert claims to have abandoned his former missionary attitude "Grow or I'll shoot". Having learned that people cannot be forced into a spiritual lifestyle he now argues (like his coach): "Pulling the grass will not make it grow faster". As we will see, however, employees in Morca are in fact subject to social pressure to participate in the in-company trainings, producing mutual distrust, critique and a divide between participants and non-participants.

Participants: "It takes guts!"

All of the interviewed who have participated in the training are people in mid- to top-level management positions. They are extremely positive about the training, because it has given them the opportunity to solve personal problems ("stones in your backpack") and to grow spiritually. They emphasize the influence of Geert and Marcel in making them participate. In the words of Mark, an assistant group controller: "I am doing it because someone gave me a kick in the butt to participate. That's how it feels. That one is Geert." The latter's influence is perceived as stimulating. Originally, they were sceptics and thought it was all "vague" and "irrational". In compliance with the analysis in the previous section, they now label these forms of scepticism as "psychological resistance" or "fear of growth". Beforehand, they were just not aware of their problems in private and working life, thinking "Private is private, don"t bother me about that!" This attitude changed while participating. Arthur was the first to "break through his resistance" during the courses. He explains:

> A lot of shit from the past entered my consciousness. When you become emotional and start to cry in front of the group – and not just a little bit, but letting loose completely ... That takes guts! You need that guts. If you don"t have those, well, then it gets tough. Everybody thought: "I am sitting here with my colleagues, I have to work with them tomorrow, I am not going to cry!" So there was this mechanism of resistance: "I don't want this." I was one of the first who dealt with a serious emotional problem. ... Once I did it, others showed the courage to follow.

This statement exemplifies the legitimations discussed in the last section. "Opening up" to colleagues and showing emotions is now understood as a sign of "guts", while defending the boundary between private and working life is understood as a symptom of fear. Frank is another participant who entered the world of self-spirituality through the courses:

> I am very rational and before I started the course I told Marcel this: "What I know about myself is that I have the feeling that I don't really have emotions." However, the first session we did, I was filled with tears, overwhelmed by emotions. In a certain situation Marcel told me: "I thought you had no emotions?" Then I thought: "Well, I obviously have them but they are normally hidden somewhere where I cannot reach them."

In short, the stories of these employees exemplify the breakdown of the modern separation between private and public life produced by the shift towards self-spirituality in the organization. They are convinced that this approach works: it helps them to solve personal problems and to be more open and expressive at the office. This in turn, they argue, stimulates a sense of fellowship and community: "We have become much more open towards one another. We have become a group. We really trust each other." Under the influence of the president-director and his coach, then, self-spirituality has become an organizational asset. But how do those who did not participate in the courses evaluate all of this?

Non-participants: "I don't feel like doing that!"

The interviewed who have not participated in the training are mainly people who occupy lower positions in the organizational hierarchy (production, administration and the like). Moreover, they are supervised by the participants discussed above. Their accounts mirror those of the managers who have participated and who have become involved in spirituality in the process. They experience the influence of the president-director not as stimulating, but as pressure. Taking a more conventional stance, they reject the privatization and spiritualization of public organizational life and wish to preserve the divide between private and public. Personal issues, Johan argues, are out of place in a working environment:

> I think courses like this are disturbing. I mean: I am not against it, but I would never do such a thing with colleagues. I've heard that it revolves around showing your personal feelings and emotions. That frightens me. ... To really let yourself go, you need to know people very well. You need to trust people. ... In this respect, I really want to keep my private life private.

Martijn tells a similar story:

> At a certain moment it was explained what the course was all about. How you had to act, what you had to do and how you had to open yourself up to others. Then I thought: "Do you really have to do that in front of your fellow-workers?" Actually, I don"t feel like doing that. It's not that I have to keep everything as a secret, but it "runs deeper", they say. And then I think: "Do I want that?"

These employees paint a completely different picture of spirituality in business life: they defend the modern boundary between private and public and perceive the sharing of emotions with co-workers (especially superiors) not as courageous, but as frightening; the influence of the president-director not as stimulating, but as pressure. Moreover, they disagree with the participants that the courses result in a stronger sense of unity. On the contrary:

> In a company like this you get two camps, because there are people who participate and those who do not. And, to be honest, I think that the people who participated have changed. How do you say that? These were people who already had high self-esteem. That became stronger during the course. Maybe that is the power of the course: "Believing in yourself". But it's not nice to feel better than others and treat them that way.

The other interviews confirm that there are two camps in the company. The spiritual group argues that the others would better join in, because otherwise "They'll miss the connection". The secular group "feel(s) less than the others", feels that they "don't fit in" and "are not respected". These quotes nicely illustrate the tension that has built up around the courses and, more generally, around spirituality in the organization. In her critical study on "New Age spiritualism" in business life, Nadesan (1999: 19) claims: "Those who reject the (spiritual) discourse or those who fail to achieve success get labeled as unwilling to take care of themselves or, worse, as reaping their karmic rewards."

As we have demonstrated, spirituality is widespread in Dutch company life and is considered a valuable asset to enhance both meaning *and* effectiveness. We are not dealing with mere hype or the latest management fashion. After all, the discussed developments began already in the late 1980s, blossomed in the 1990s, and have remained salient ever since. More substantially, our data indicate that especially organizations in the post-industrial service sector are hospitable towards self-spirituality. Highly educated professionals working typically in mid- to top-level management are, in comparison with production workers, more oriented towards intrinsic motivations, goals and rewards. They give priority, Mitroff and Denton (1999a: 212) demonstrate on the basis of their survey, to "interesting work" and realizing their "full potential as a person". Indeed, from an organizational perspective, this makes it profitable to break with alienating bureaucratic structures and incorporate issues like self-understanding, identity and self-spirituality in corporate culture. This elective affinity between the post-industrial service sector and New Age spirituality further strengthens our conviction that spirituality in public organizational life cannot be dismissed as mere hype or the latest management fashion.

The case of Morca, again, is not typical of spirituality in the public realm, but it does demonstrate convincingly that substantially more is at stake than individuals exploring their own spirituality. More specifically, it demonstrates that self-spirituality is a well-defined doctrine with a strong potential for socialization: people at this company learn the importance of rejecting external authorities and making contact with their "deeper selves". Although exactly the same occurs in the spiritual milieu, as we have seen above, it easily remains unnoticed there. This is because participants who enter voluntarily to work on their personal problems are likely to experience this process of socialization as a strictly personal and authentic delving in the self's deeper layers.

CONCLUSION AND DISCUSSION

In his defense of secularization theory, Steve Bruce (2002) criticizes authors such as Rodney Stark (1999; see also Stark & Bainbridge 1985) and Grace

Davie (1994), who argue that secularization is *by definition* accompanied by religious innovation. Stark, Bruce explains, makes *a priori* assumptions about religion as a universal human need, while Davie argues from a similar perspective that there will always remain a "believing without belonging". We agree with Bruce that such claims about humans as "essentially" religious beings are "nonsociological" (Bruce 2002: 104). More than that: they are metaphysical, we would argue.

We also agree with Bruce that much research into spirituality is sociologically naive and immature. This not only applies to the research of those who are overly sympathetic to spirituality and hence cannot resist the temptation of "going native", as our colleagues from anthropology say. Perhaps surprisingly, it equally applies to the work of those who are highly critical of it (see Woodhead 2010 for examples). Because of his own tendency to criticize other people's ideas about spirituality as "nonsociological" (Bruce 2002: 104) or "bad sociology" (Bruce 1998), Bruce himself perhaps provides the best example. Attempting to hammer home the radical individualism of the spiritual milieu, he writes:

> Findhorn, one of Europe's oldest centres of New Age thought and teaching, *requires* of those who take part in its various forms of group work that they confine their talk to "I statements". The point of this is to establish that, while each participant has a right to say how he or she feels or thinks, *no-one has a right* to claim some extra-personal authority for his or her views.
>
> (Bruce 2002: 83; emphasis added)

To be sure, those observations do much to underscore the radical individualism of the spiritual milieu. But simultaneously, and ironically, they do more than that. They also demonstrate how this very individualism operates as a socially sanctioned obligation of personal authenticity, revealing precisely the social significance of spirituality that Bruce denies. Arguing that allegedly "diffuse beliefs" such as those cannot and need not be transmitted (*ibid.*: 99), Bruce's failure to capture and satisfactorily theorize this ambiguity of the spiritual milieu's "individualism" causes him to overlook that people are socialized into compliance to the doctrine of self-spirituality.

What Bruce has on offer, then, is a mere sociologically naive reproduction of New Age rhetoric about the primacy of personal authenticity rather than a mature and critical sociological analysis. The assumption that people all by themselves develop their strictly personal and authentic spiritualities is obviously sociologically naive, since "as good sociologists, we all know that there is no such thing as an isolated individual" (Besecke 2005: 194). Besecke also criticizes the received conception of "privatized religion", arguing that it results in a conception of religion "as almost an exclusively psychological phenomenon, with very limited and indirect social consequence" (*ibid.*:

187). As we have demonstrated, spirituality is in fact less unambiguously individualistic and less privatized than most sociologists hold it to be.

The conception of spirituality as embraced by Bruce (and, to be sure, most other sociologists of religion) inevitably coincides largely with the self-image of the spiritual milieu. It is hardly surprising, after all, that the spiritual practitioners interviewed by Heelas and Woodhead (2005: 27) also deny in every possible way that the doctrine of self-spirituality is socially constructed, transmitted and reinforced: "Time and time again, we hear practitioners rejecting the idea that their relationships with their group members or clients have anything to do with pre-packaged … ways of transmitting the sacred." But even if spiritual practitioners do not "[tell] their group members or clients what to think, do, believe or feel" (*ibid*.: 28), they do tell them that they should take their personal feelings seriously, that a one-sided reliance on thinking at the cost of feeling is detrimental and that one should follow one's heart.

The task to be taken up in the years that lie ahead, in short, is a radical sociologization of research into New Age and spirituality. What we need is research that critically and systematically deconstructs emic rhetoric to document how precisely spirituality is socially constructed, transmitted and reinforced in the spiritual milieu and how, why, and with what consequences it is introduced at the workplace.[8]

ACKNOWLEDGEMENT

This chapter was first published in 2006 as "Beyond the Spiritual Supermarket: The Social and Public Significance of New Age Spirituality" in *Journal of Contemporary Religion* 21(2): 201–22. It is reprinted by permission of the publisher, Taylor & Francis Ltd., http://www.tandf.co.uk/journals.

NOTES

1. This is the so-called "Randstad," which is where most Dutch New Age centres are situated.
2. Those interviews were conducted by Inge Van der Tak, our research assistant. Interviews lasted about ninety minutes on average and were tape-recorded and typed out verbatim (see Aupers *et al.* 2003 for a report of the findings). The same procedure was followed for the two rounds of interviews conducted by the first author (see below).
3. Those interviews were conducted by the first author in 2003.
4. Unlike the remainder of this section, these three quotes are taken from interviews with the second rather than the first sample of spiritual trainers. However all respondents from both samples adhere to this type of perennialism.
5. Substantial fieldwork on New Age and business organizations has also been done in Denmark by Kirsten Marie Bovbjerg (2001).
6. These claims made by Metavisie were found on their website www.metavisie.com (accessed November 2005). We have not contacted the companies on the website to validate whether they indeed contracted Metavisie to provide in-company trainings.

7. To safeguard anonymity, the name of the company and names of the president-director, the spiritual trainer and the employees interviewed are changed into pseudonyms.

8. Obviously, it is important to study whether normal participants in the spiritual milieu, just like the spiritual elite studied here, also adhere to the doctrine of self-spirituality. Furthermore, it is preferable to study the process of socialization by means of participant observation. An obvious drawback of the methodology used for the current chapter (i.e. interviewing those who have completed the full process after the fact) is that biographical data thus obtained are inevitably coloured by the newly acquired spiritual identity. It should however be noted that, given the nature of this identity (self-spirituality, primacy of authenticity, anti-institutionalism, etc.), the approach used here seems biased *against* the finding that processes of socialization do occur. Another drawback of our approach here, and hence another advantage of participant observation, is that only the latter enables one to study the role of resistance to socialization into a spiritual discourse as a reason for abandoning a course.

12. FROM NEW AGE TO NEW SPIRITUALITIES: SECULAR SACRALIZATIONS ON THE BORDERS OF RELIGION

Frans Jespers

In the 1960s the first signs of what would be called "New Age" appeared in the Netherlands. Then in the 1990s the holistic practices and beliefs associated with New Age seemed to transform into new spiritualities. In this chapter, I would like to reconstruct what happened during this half century in the field of these holistic practices and beliefs, drawing on empirical examples collected in the Netherlands. For this purpose, I will summarize descriptions and interpretations of the main events and complement these with some case studies. Moreover, I would like to develop another direction for the definition of most New Age and new spiritual activities and ideas – a direction that does not perceive them to be self-evidently "religious", but as various forms of "secular sacralizations". I am convinced that a careful exposition of some Dutch cases can clarify what can be called "religious", and what can be seen as "secular", but with a religious connotation: what I call a "sacralization". This means that I concentrate on the levels of persons – their practices, beliefs and experiences – and of their organizations. My approach is that of the comparative study of religion.

First, I present an overview of the main New Age and spiritual phenomena of the past half century in the Netherlands, with special attention to three case studies. In the second section I analyse this Dutch situation with the help of accepted scholarly characterizations. Next, I reconstruct the transition from New Age into new spiritualities. In the fourth section I develop a typology for New Age and new spiritual practices, especially in relation to religion and secularity, with the help of my Dutch examples. Finally, I discuss secular sacralizations.

EXAMPLES OF NEW AGE AND NEW SPIRITUALITIES IN THE NETHERLANDS

The history of New Age and new spiritualities in the Netherlands has been described in several sociological and anthropological studies, most of them in Dutch but also a few in English (Aupers & Van Otterloo 2000; Aupers 2005; Aupers & Houtman 2008; Meester 2008; Jespers 2009a; de Hart 2011; Hense *et al.* forthcoming). Here I summarize the main points and complement them with three small case studies.

The start of New Age in the Netherlands is usually situated around 1965. In the cities, some alternative leaders introduced meditation and esoteric symbolism, sometimes along with the use of drugs. Exotic gurus such as Bhagwan and Maharishi Mahesh Yogi found a following. An iconic moment was the opening of the *Kosmos* in Amsterdam in 1969: this former youth centre became an alternative institute for yoga and spiritual growth. It evolved from the then quite lively countercultural milieu, and was a model for many similar centres elsewhere. In the period until 1990 more than one hundred centres of various kinds were established all across the country. They often took the form of an alternative shop for books about yoga, therapies, magic or Asian religions, and for incense, divination cards and precious stones. In their publications (books and magazines like *Bres* ["Breach"] and *Onkruid* ["Weed"]) the idea of an imminent New Age was common. Many of these texts had been translated from English, and a few from other languages – an indication that most ideas came from abroad. However, the core term "New Age" often remained untranslated; the English term was in vogue. Some Dutch authors and teachers attained the status of a spiritual leader (Aupers 2005: 187–90; Aupers & Van Otterloo 2000: 53–67). Although most centres were and are still situated in the cities, a series of centres also appeared in rural areas, even quite isolated. Some of them were organic farms, while others were schools for alternative therapists. Magic, shamanism, Asian meditation and human potential training belonged to their main practices.

About 1990 changes occurred: the countercultural milieu decreased, whereas some former parts of it, such as heavy metal music or divination, became respectable and popular. The term "New Age" disappeared almost completely. Centres and book shops of the "holistic milieu" (Heelas & Woodhead 2005) presented themselves less as "alternative" and more as appealing to the public at large. In 1991 a big annual festival was launched under the name *Eigentijds Festival* ("Contemporary Festival"). Alternative medicine, merged with esoteric ideas and indigenous practices (of Siberian shamans, or Chinese healers), became popular. Furthermore, due to the nationwide rise of paranormal fairs a new audience was attracted, mainly lower-working-class women (Jespers 2010: 58–77). Another fresh sector was that of spiritual business training courses as a version of the human potential movement (Aupers & Houtman 2006). After 2000, various television programmes about the paranormal and divination appeared as well. Many Internet websites show the activities, tools and books which are on offer.[1] One of the most popular current practices is mindfulness, which is presented both as a form of psychotherapy, and as a means for individual spiritual growth.

In the same period the term "spirituality" came into fashion in the afore-mentioned milieus of popular paranormal or healthcare activities. Previously, spirituality was also a Christian pious practice, especially in Roman Catholic monasteries, which also took advantage of this new interest. Furthermore, spirituality was partly associated with the practice of Spiritualism, propagated already in the second half of the nineteenth century. Now, in the holistic milieu, combinations of "old spirituality" (from Christianity, Buddhism, Indigenous Religions and Spiritualism) and "new spirituality" (from alternative medicine, divination) were made. New forms of Buddhism ("Western Buddhism") were developed, mainly through forms of meditation (van der Velde 2009). In addition, many Pagans began to call their way of life "spiritual". Furthermore, spiritual beauty and wellness treatments came on offer, for instance in successful glossy magazines on spirituality (e.g. *Happinez*). International self-help authors like Eckhart Tolle, Wayne Dyer and Rhonda Byrne (*The Secret*) are now widely sold. Also, a Dutch cardiologist called Pim van Lommel received a kind of guru status with his book *Eindeloos bewust-zijn* ("Consciousness beyond Life", 2010) on near-death experiences, in which he develops a holistic spirituality. It can be argued that even many Dutch humanists include a spiritual dimension within their worldly "art of living", more or less identical with holistic health in its attention to a balance of body, mind and spirit with nature and the cosmos (Meester 2008: 137–59).

Three other recent developments are: spiritual books for children and education, the spiritual shop as a gift shop, and spiritual shops in quarters of cities where many immigrants live (for instance Rotterdam-Zuid). These are variously indications that the new spiritual beliefs are passed on to the next generation, that a larger audience sympathizes with them and that this is no longer an exclusively ethnically white occupation. Another sign of this joint process of acculturation and diversification is the fact that some general, large book shops have their own department for "esotericism" or "spirituality". Furthermore, small shops for special sectors have started up: for fantasy, Wicca, Tibet – also on the Internet.[2]

I will complement this short history of Dutch New Age and new spiritualities with three brief case studies. The first is Reiki. The Usui Shiki Ryoho Reiki branch was introduced in the Netherlands in 1984 (Jonker 2012). It was presented as an Eastern healing treatment. In the years after 1990 more branches of Reiki appeared, up to thirty. Probably more than ten thousand people were initiated in the lower levels of Reiki, and a few hundred achieved the Master's degree. Many alternative healers apply Reiki as one of the most popular techniques. The peak of Reiki activities (treatments, courses, initiations) seems to have been between 1995 and 2000. Since then, Reiki is usually presented as a spiritual path, stressing inner-life. Some masters even talk openly about their mystical experiences, although they do not consider Reiki to be a religion. Jojan Jonker discovered that most of the symbolism of such mystical experiences is "holistic": light, energy, a higher presence, special messages; the effects are strong positive emotions (rapture) and sometimes special insights or paranormal knowledge (*ibid.*: 304–8).

Another case is related to a small organization called Mannenwerk ("Menwork"), officially a foundation (Weerd 2011). It offers short courses and counselling groups for men, mainly gay and bisexual men. In the core group some eight volunteers cooperate, and about sixty to eighty men participate in the activities annually. At the start, in 1979, it had the political aim of gay liberation. The methods used in activities were counselling and group dynamics. Providers and participants would not relate the organization to New Age, but rather to a therapy, or to the human potential movement. Over the years the objective of self-empowerment of (gay) men remained the same, but the methods gradually changed. After 2000, sacred stories and symbols ("enlightenment", meditation, candles) were introduced. From 2008 the concept of spirituality found a (modest) place in the programme, mainly inspired by ideas of Eckhart Tolle. A course or a discussion group of Mannenwerk offers diverse means (respect, confidence, safety, humour, play) for participants to discover their true personality and to empower it by restoring the relationship with "the Undercurrent of life" (*ibid.*: 19–21).

Finally, the very popular daily television show *AstroTV* is part of a large eponymous firm which offers many divinatory services, mainly with more than fifty personal consultants called "spiritual specialists", most of them women.[3] Daily television broadcasts started in 2004 and grew steadily. The "specialists" present themselves on the website of the organization with a short biography, a list of their qualifications, and some explanation of the divinatory techniques they use and of the expected outcomes. About a quarter of them give religious references in their biography, whereas all show a holistic worldview with its symbolism such as karma, chakras and energy fields. AstroTV gives a rather commercial impression, but actually the prices are moderate in comparison with other professional counsellors such as psychotherapists and social workers. The predominantly female clientele generally takes both the holistic worldview and the religious symbolism for granted (Jespers 2009b: 186–92).

THE MORPHOLOGY OF DUTCH NEW AGE AND NEW SPIRITUALITIES

Can we discern some main features in these case studies? I would like to portray Dutch New Age and new spiritualities with the help of the main studies on New Age and new spiritual groups in the Western world (Hanegraaff 1996; Sutcliffe 2003a; Kemp & Lewis 2007; Heelas 2008; Knoblauch 2009). Five important aspects can be discerned:

1. practices and methods;
2. objectives;

3. social structure (participants, organization);
4. beliefs; and
5. sources of knowledge.

The *practices and methods* (1) in New Age and new spiritualities are very diverse, which helps to explain the use of the plural form "spiritualities". In the Netherlands, most practices are small-scale activities of healing or therapy (e.g. Shiatsu, Reiki, hypnotherapy), meditation (yoga, Zen) or divination (Tarot, astrology). Many practitioners work independently but some of them cooperate in a centre. Such centres can specialize in alternative medicine, spiritual growth, or wellness (Heelas 2008: 67–74; Knoblauch 2009: 100–120). Most practitioners have several therapies to offer, from which the client can select (Aupers & Van Otterloo 2000: 81–9). Tools and books, including self-help books, are for sale in special shops. Furthermore, festivals or paranormal fairs attract a great deal of interest (Sutcliffe 2003a: 107–30, 174–94). All in all, the Dutch holistic milieu is as much oriented to the peculiar needs of the clients as it is in the rest of the Western world: the promise of individual experiences are crucial in such practices (Heelas 2008: 136, 153).

The primary *objective* (2) is often to gain empowerment or to regain personal balance, both called "spiritual growth". Thus, subjective development and well-being are central, and authenticity must be the guide, especially when a person has serious problems. A first requirement is achieving a new (self-)consciousness, a fresh awareness of body, spirit, and the relationship with others and with life or the universe. Finally, a transformation has to take place in order to attain balance or "holistic health" (Heelas 2008: 17, 130–32). A secondary objective can be contributing to a new world – which is a core element of New Age *sensu stricto* (Hanegraaff 1996: 331–61). All these characteristics can be recognized in the Dutch situation.

The *social structure* (3) consists in the dimension of organization and participation. Although there are many groups, centres and practitioners, a large organization does not exist. Mainly local groups and loose networks function. Participants just meet each other at local centres, weekend activities, courses or a festival. Some recent Dutch surveys show that around 2 per cent of the population is active as a provider or steady believer, 8 per cent participates occasionally, and 29 per cent sympathizes (Kronjee & Lampert 2006: 176–80; de Hart 2011: 164–84; Berghuijs *et al.* 2013: 20–27). They are chiefly middle-class people, with a majority of women, usually well educated and middle-aged. All this corresponds to British figures, for example Vincett and Woodhead (2009: 320).

The general characterization of New Age and new spiritualities as "holistic" stems from their *beliefs* (4). Individual adherents or groups express their own, quite different ideas or accents, but these appear to be variations of a more or less standardized set of holistic beliefs. One can distinguish a worldview (or cosmology), a view on the person (anthropology), and a view on society. According to the holistic cosmology, our world has (at least) a material and a spiritual dimension (Hanegraaff 1996: 119–68). Spiritual energies flow everywhere, connect everything and can incite material reactions. Many believe that there must be a kind of divine "life force" or universal "source of love" that governs the cosmos. Everything happens for a reason. Everyone is born with a destination and "lessons to learn". Each person has three main components: body, mind and spirit (or "soul"). Someone whose spirit is developed sufficiently can incite and control spiritual energies (*ibid.*: 204–24; 256–63). Finally, in our society just a small vanguard knows that a New Age is breaking through, in which the feminine plays an important part (Sutcliffe 2003a: 222). Some other groups do have an intuition of the spiritual world, but they stick to limited (traditional, dogmatic) religious representations and authoritarian organizations. Thus, most participants in new spiritualities call themselves "spiritual and not religious" (Vincett & Woodhead 2009: 320). These ideas can be found in various ways in the Dutch spiritual milieu (Berghuijs *et al.* 2013).

Finally, when we look at the *sources of knowledge* (5) of these practices and beliefs, we find again a great diversity. The basic beliefs belong to (5a) the Western esoteric tradition, from early Gnosticism via Hermeticism and Spiritualism to Theosophy. Next, many beliefs are derived from (5b) channelling and mediumship, personal messages or other experiences that are said to be received from "the other side" such as ascended masters, angels and other entities. A third source is (5c) the collection of wisdom from the religious traditions of the world, especially the traditions of Asian and indigenous religions (Native American, Nordic). All such beliefs are enhanced by selected interpretations from sources in the natural sciences and psychology. Although this knowledge appears rather disparate, participants see it as one comprehensive tradition of perennial wisdom (Hanegraaff 1996: 411–513; Vincett & Woodhead 2009: 321–2). Again, all this is present in the Dutch groups.

THE TRANSITION FROM "NEW AGE" TO "NEW SPIRITUALITIES"

Up until now, New Age and new spiritualities were taken to be more or less identical: for instance, in the influential account by Heelas (1996). Thus some authors write about "New Age spiritualities", suggesting that this combination encompasses the whole range of activities (Aupers & Houtman 2006). Other scholars assert that new spiritualities are actually the successors of New Age, situating the transition around 1990 (Melton 2007: 95–6), 1980 (Knoblauch 2009: 102, 111) or 1995 (Vincett & Woodhead 2009: 326–7). Although we can detect no big differences between these two currents, their sociocultural situation is not the same. New Age emerged about 1968 as a typically countercultural phenomenon in which the expectation of an imminent New Age expressed aversion to the dominant bourgeois society. Most adherents were highly educated and very critical of the dominant culture (Hunt 2003: 143). Around 1990 such practices and ideas grew more popular and developed a more positive attitude towards dominant society. Since then, new spiritualities belong to mainstream culture, and people from both lower social strata and the elite participate (Knoblauch 2009: 111). Sutcliffe establishes that after 1990, the term "New Age" becomes more of a (rather vague) scholarly label which is barely recognized in social reality and emic discourse (Sutcliffe 2003a: 129, 197–9). Hubert Knoblauch even concludes that nowadays in Germany, "New Age" is a foreign attribution (*Fremdzuschreibung*; Knoblauch 2009: 101).

So what exactly did change in the Netherlands in the years 1990–1995, apart from the relative disappearance of the term "New Age"? I refer back to the five aspects described above. In the field of *practices and methods*, the paranormal fairs and the television programmes on astrology were introduced. Divination itself was not new, but its presentation in mass media was. Four more fields of new spiritual practice were women's beauty and "pampering", wellness, self-help books, and business training courses. In the case of *Mannenwerk*, after 2000 the first religious symbolism (myths, meditation, "the Undercurrent") was introduced. With Reiki, mystical experiences of a higher "presence" have been added to the practices. Next, in the field of *objectives*, only a few forms of spiritual growth were introduced. Some humanists included it as an important aspect of their naturalistic art of living and, in the therapy of mindfulness, the notion of spirituality is sometimes mentioned. In contrast, on the level of *social structure* a big shift took place. Whereas New Age was a fringe movement with adherents who had a countercultural attitude and chose an alternative way of life, the new spiritualities received more recognition, both among lower social strata (who gravitated towards paranormal fairs and psychic television programmes) and among social elites (who preferred mindfulness or Western Buddhism). In short, the new spiritualities belong to mainstream culture (Kronjee & Lampert 2006: 184–6). In contrast, in the field of *holistic beliefs* in the world, person and society, there was no big change. Finally, the *sources of knowledge* have one striking addition: near-death experiences, which may be a part of the general increase of belief in miracles and paranormal experiences (van Lommel 2010; Berghuijs *et al.* 2013).

The English term "New Age" was somewhat appropriated in the Dutch alternative milieu between 1970 and 1990, but afterwards the Dutch translation "Nieuwe Tijd" became more fashionable. However, Aupers and Houtman (2008) argue that the basic rule of authenticity obliged all adherents to proclaim their personal way, so that they would seldom count themselves among a general "New Age movement". Moreover, there can be a difference between Anglophone countries, where the concept of New Age originated, and other European regions where the concept was used both in translation and in English (e.g. in the Netherlands, Germany), but as a general outside indicator (whether scholarly, social or commercial) only in English (Bochinger 1994). For instance, Wouter Hanegraaff based his standard book on New Age exclusively on the analysis of emic English literature, in which the concept was not even very strong. My conclusion is to continue the use of the term New Age for the period 1970–90 (or 1995), but to remain aware of the predominantly etic character of the term.

No less intriguing is the sudden popularity of the term "spirituality". It is definitely an emic term, used by almost all adherents (in contrast to the term New Age). Spirituality is generally combined with the personal and with authenticity. Almost all groups aim for spiritual growth, but in their own way, which produces a plurality of "spiritualities". Moreover, for a scientific analysis it is useful to distinguish such spiritualities from the traditional religious ones, and therefore to add the adjective "new". This is primarily an etic, scientific specification, whereas the adherents themselves believe that their spiritualities have ancient roots and form a part of perennial wisdom (see the section "Morphology", above). As a scholarly definition of spirituality, I propose to adopt that of the *World Spirituality* series:

> The series focuses on that inner dimension of the person called by certain traditions "the spirit". This spiritual core is the deepest center of the person. It is here that the person is open to the transcendent dimension; it is here that the person experiences ultimate reality. The series explores the discovery of this core, the dynamics of its development, and its journey to the ultimate goal. (Cousins 1996: xii; see Jespers forthcoming).

This definition has proved to be adequate for many religious and secular types of spirituality.

The most important aspect of the transition from "New Age" to "new spiritualities" at the social level can be indicated as *popularization*. In his excellent German study Knoblauch showed that this popularization occurred both in traditional Christianity and among the new spiritualities. One explanation for this is that traditional (European) folk religion appropriated aspects of New Age. I myself suggested it reflected a historical shift from folk practices of manipulation of powers for immediate solutions (in both Christian and secular contexts) to new spiritual practices, in which esoteric, Asian, indigenous and psychological elements were added (Jespers 2010: 71–3). Sutcliffe recognizes in New Age a popular *habitus*, based in a routinized way that common people "do" religion (Sutcliffe 2006: 298). However, Knoblauch differentiates between "folk" religion (*populare Religion*) and "popular" religion (*populäre Religion*). This last adjective indicates that something new happened to both traditional and new religions: namely, the use of the media in order to reach the masses. An intriguing effect of this "mediatization of religion" is a tendency to spread forms of "banal" religion, which actually occurs in some new spiritualities (Hjarvard 2011: 128–30). According to Hjarvard, this tendency is caused by the mediatization of religion in general, but I think that the real cause is the demand of the masses for "banal" religion, which demonstrates the influence of popularization. Thus, this "popular turn" of religion implies both a kind of resacralization and banalization, which is a complex development.

TOWARDS A TYPOLOGY OF SECULAR SACRALIZATIONS

My systematic question is this: in what respect are New Age and new spiritualities forms of "religion"? I begin with the main positions and arguments in relation to this question. Subsequently I present my concept of religion and my typology, followed by a discussion.

The first position is held by some scholars who consider New Age and new spiritualities to be religion. For instance, Aupers and Houtman take "New Age spirituality" as a prototype of a "religion of modernity", because it recognizes the sacred deep within each person: "New Age can be understood as a veritable religion of modernity because its participants collectively sacralize the long-standing modern value of individual liberty, and especially the ideal of an authentic self that distances itself from allegedly alienating institutions and traditions" (Houtman & Aupers 2010: 15). In this way, these authors represent a clearly Durkheimian stance.

The second position states the opposite: New Age and new spiritualities are not religion, but secular practices and ideas. Most traditional Christian, Muslim and other believers and theologians take this position (Kemp 2007: 455–62). Also a sociologist like Stephen Hunt is inclined to call New Age a cultic milieu, a "mix 'n' match religiosity", in short a "quasi-religion", meaning not a "real" religion, but an imitation or a derivative form (Hunt 2003: 132–3, 222).

The third position lies in between the above. For instance, Heelas stresses the religious ingredients – belief in a higher reality, evidence of sacralization of the Self – displayed by many self-identified "spiritual" activities, so that they cannot be flatly designated as secular. At the same time, most practices show secular features, such as humanistic ethics (Heelas 2008: 73, 76, 167, 172–4). Heelas' indication of the sacred within new spiritualities takes the form of a universal or perfect life-force (*ibid.*: 127). Knoblauch shows the same ambivalence by stressing that new spiritualities address themselves to a great transcendence and therefore have a religious core; their practices, however, are subjective and often pantheistic (Knoblauch 2009: 129, 159, 185). His solution is to establish that the borders between religion and the secular are being blurred, especially in many new spiritualities (*ibid.*: 267). Sutcliffe shares this position (Sutcliffe 2003a: 11, 224).

Hanegraaff takes a fourth position, asserting that New Age and new spiritualities are secular forms of religion. He defines religion in general as "any symbolic system which influences human action by providing possibilities for ritually maintaining contact between the everyday world and a more general meta-empirical framework of meaning" (Hanegraaff 1999: 371). Most concrete historical religions offered people a social institution for expressing religion, so institution is characteristic for traditional religions. But the secularization of Western culture undermined such institutions, whereas the sacred continued to fulfil its part, nowadays as an immanent meta-empirical framework experienced by persons within their inner self (*ibid.*: 373–4). Hanegraaff identifies spirituality as "the individual manipulation of symbolic systems" directed towards such an immanent sacred fulfillment (*ibid.*: 372).

I am not inclined to join the broad Durkheimian first position, in which almost every collective activity can be called religion, nor the second one, which is too theological. Yet neither do the third and fourth positions match my analysis of New Age and new spiritualities, because these positions lack a clear concept of the secular, as I will discuss in the next section. Although all participants share more or less the same holistic beliefs, some of their practices look like religion, for instance devotions and incantations, while others are similar to secular psychotherapies or corporal treatments. What does this mean?

Firstly, we need clear practical definitions of "religion" and "the secular". On the one hand, functional definitions of religion appear to be too broad, because they include too many currents and activities; in our case they include all new spiritualities (see position one). On the other hand, strictly substantive, theistic definitions leave out too much (position two). As a middle course I propose to use the description of the sociologist Martin Riesebrodt, which is not meant as a sharp definition. He describes religion as practices and beliefs of people who expect a kind of salvation by higher powers for their life problems: "Thus religious practices everywhere are addressed to superhuman powers that influence or control something beyond human control. All religions claim the ability to address misfortune, crises, and salvation" (Riesebrodt 2010: 89). By "religious practices" he means forms of worship and institution. Next, "salvation" (as a translation of the German *Heil*) is primarily averting misfortune, healing disease, resolving crises and restoring well-being. Opposed to religion I situate a secular way of life and worldview in which the things and people within this world suffice to make human life meaningful and to solve life problems. This secular way of life and worldview can take various forms, for instance naturalistic, humanistic or hedonistic, according to the values that are important for individual persons. Thus I do not take the secular in its historical primary sense as the non-religious way of life, but as the result of a life which finds fulfilment within this world (Taylor 2007: 5–12).

On this basis, from my examples of Dutch New Age and new spiritualities I can establish that only a few practices can be called "religion". It is most obvious in the case of Pagans; and many have no problem with their "spirituality" being perceived as a restored version of indigenous religion. Next to them, some esoteric Christians combine Gnostic ideas with church membership and worship. Both groups merge old veneration of gods with new spirituality. Furthermore, many new Buddhists appear to believe in higher powers without referring to a personal God. They tend more to holism than to theism. However, they include forms of worship (of Buddha as a sacred person). Thus, within the field of religion, we can distinguish (traditional) theistic views and practices (Pagans, esoteric Christians) from holistic ones (new Buddhists; see Figure 12.1, below). However, when they have no worship and a low level of institution, I am inclined to call that way of life "secular". For instance mindfulness is typically presented as a psychological practice, but it is often also seen as a "spiritual" activity, usually without worship or larger institution. Therefore in my typology it is defined as "secular".

My second demarcation is related to the holistic secular field. Maybe there are a few very devout mystics, for example in new Buddhism. They lead a rather austere, far from busy daily life. Riesebrodt uses for such people Weber's term *virtuosos*, because they develop their personal world-rejecting type of religiosity apart from the community, and often opposed to popular religiosity (Riesebrodt 2010: 122–48). This qualification of the *virtuoso* is also suitable where such special people can be found in secular holism (see Figure 12.1). However, most participants in new secular spiritualities lead a normal civil life and are only involved part-time in "spirituality". For this popular engagement, I distinguish three subcategories of the functioning of spiritual practices, with decreasing intensity (see also Jespers forthcoming).

The first and most visible subcategory is where spirituality works as a religion. Participants are quite intensely involved, because they expect it to offer some kind of salvation, especially from a (super-)natural power. However, they do not venerate this power. But they can have meetings, authoritative persons and texts, meditation or healing practices, religious symbols, and moral rules. I call this type of spirituality a *functional equivalent* of religion. A nice example is Reiki: for many Dutch masters it provides a deep well-being. Other examples are mindfulness, or the belief in near-death experiences. Such activities and ideas function for many people as a religion, but they lack the core aspect of cultic veneration, and the adherents themselves deny it to be religion.

The second subcategory is related to incidental spiritual practices. People come together for a course, a weekend, or a meeting, where they invoke and experience something extraordinary. This experience is brought about by the use of religious symbols or rituals, such as meditation and healing. This is what happens during an hour in a course of *Mannenwerk*, or in a spiritual business training course. With the help of a religious myth, or incense, music and a mantra, something like "your divine self" or the presence of the "source of the universe" is invoked and experienced. I call this type *moments of sacralization* in which the participants experience a kind of collective exalted mood, although they more or less individually determine the sacred meaning of the symbolism (if they do so at all). Such moments can also appear on other occasions, for instance with public expressions of mourning after a violent incident.

The third subcategory is even thinner. It is the level of short references to the sacred, for instance in a television programme on astrology. Sometimes the hostess talks about destination, reincarnation, spirits that you can invoke, or messages from "the other side". The same goes for the symbolism on tarot cards or magical objects, and in their use, or in some novels, computer games or works of art. I call this *fragments of sacralization*. The reference can provide an experience of something extraordinary or enchanting. Usually this experience happens individually, whereas the collective experience belongs to the previous subcategory of *moments of sacralization*. A large part of all the things called "spiritual" in our times belongs to this subcategory: for instance, wellness spirituality and divinatory practices.

Finally, I have put all my categories into a scheme (Figure 12.1) which is mainly meant to categorize phenomena in the border regions of religion and the secular. I consider the categories as descriptive and non-normative *ideal-types*. They enable us to recognize spiritual practices as minimally religious parts of secular activities and beliefs, which can appear on various levels of sacralizing intensity. However, these types are more convenient to comprehend individual situations where we know the details of a person's experiences with something sacred, whereas we should be careful with applying such characterizations to groups.

RELIGION	Theistic virtuoso religion	Popular theistic religion and old forms of spirituality
	Holistic virtuoso religion	Popular holistic (new) spiritualities
SECULAR	Holistic virtuoso spirituality	Popular secular spirituality: (1) functional equivalents of religion (2) moments of sacralization (3) fragments of sacralization

Figure 12.1 The border regions of religion and the secular.

DISCUSSION: SACRALIZATION AND RELIGION

In my categories the concept of *sacralization* needs some clarification. Its normal meaning is: the action or fact of endowing with sacred qualities (*Oxford English Dictionary*), that is to make or to recognize something or someone as "holy". This concept is also the central qualification of Heelas for New Age, for instance with "celebration of the self and sacralization of modernity" (the subtitle of Heelas 1996). In his later book *Spiritualities of Life* he withdrew this indication, replacing it by the holistic term "life" or "life-itself and the fulfilled experiential life" (Heelas 2008: 26, 17, 32). Nevertheless, his presupposition remains that this immanent life force is the sacred core of a religion in a Durkheimian sense, and that sacralization must therefore be religious as well (*ibid.*: 114, 127). That brings him to the uneasy conclusion that some "spiritualities of life" are religious and others are secular, without explaining which ones and why. In the same vein Knoblauch lacks clear concepts. However, starting from my own concepts of religion and the secular in the preceding section, sacralization means to bring something or someone into a direct connection with supernatural powers (to make holy/powerful and to consecrate, for example by means of a ritual) or to recognize that something or someone has this relation with the supernatural (to call it holy, and to bless it).

Elements of religion can be exported out of the strictly religious domain: for instance through rituals (lighting candles before a statue), in concepts (the divine, reincarnation), and by means of symbols (angels). Outside of the strictly religious domain, the application of such elements still can be called "sacralization" (maybe in the diluted form of "blessing") because a reference to a supernatural dimension or a special order is made, but the content itself remains secular. In that case however, the elements lose (more or less) their religious impact and meaning, so that their reference at the same time goes in other directions (towards the extraordinary or enchanting) and is more superficial or "banal" with regard to religion (Hjarvard 2011). Moreover, even a reference to the sacred can be differentiated by a literal religious meaning ("angel" referring to some supernatural powerful figure) and a metaphorical meaning ("angel" referring to a beloved person). After all, the word "sacred" also has both a literal meaning (that which is connected with supernatural power) and a metaphorical meaning (that which is very important or special). Aupers and Houtman mix up both meanings by calling "individual liberty" and "non-institutionalized authenticity" "sacred" in the literal sense, whereas in new spiritualities these expressions are actually used in a metaphorical sense.

It is obvious that "moments" or "fragments" of sacralization in my typology are secular. They have their religious associations, but function in a religiously limited way within a secular environment. For instance, when people who had a near-death experience bear witness to meeting a clear light, there is an association with divine presence, but many witnesses usually continue enjoying this life without any religion (van Lommel 2010). In this respect Hanegraaff's description of new spiritualities as "secular religion" is rather misleading, because he only wants to stress that we are encountering individual, non-institutionalized forms of religious ideas and practices in these phenomena. Actually, his definitions of religion(s) and spirituality are too broad while his explanation of secularity is too narrow. In his definitions of religion in general, of "a religion", and of spirituality, the higher dimension is indicated as "a more general meta-empirical framework of meaning". But this formulation can be applied to all kinds of abstract meaning systems: for example, to nationalism, communism or humanism, or in an individual way to hedonism or to a psychotherapy like mindfulness. Thus, these definitions have the disadvantage of most functional definitions of religion. Hanegraaff's differentiation between "religion" (in general) and "a religion" (or "religions") is not adequate either, because the factor of institutionalization would be the decisive criterion to distinguish traditional religions (with collective character) from secular ones (taking individualized forms).

Hanegraaff has a point in differentiating between religion-in-general and concrete religions. However, I propose to use the concept of "religiosity" (religiousness) for religion-in-general: religiosity in both a social and an individual sense, and in both a pre-secular and a secular sense. For concrete "religions", I prefer to use Riesebrodt's definition, because it is more precise and narrow than Hanegraaff's. Thus, I can call some forms of holistic spirituality a "religion" if there is some form of worship of the supernatural and a collective institution, and the moments or fragments of sacralization in other new spiritualities "forms of religiosity" although they are secular. Actually, both my approach emphasizing moments or fragments of sacralization, and Hanegraaff's approach emphasizing spirituality, stress the crucial level of practice and experience. However, Hanegraaff takes as the most characteristic practice in spirituality "manipulation" or magic, exerted on the symbolic system of the meta-empirical framework. For my part, spiritual practices can be diverse so long as they are connected with "spirituality" in the sense of Cousins's definition adopted earlier. Finally, my major objection to Hanegraaff (and also to Aupers & Houtman) is that their qualification of new spiritualities as essentially individual is exaggerated, as others have pointed out (Sutcliffe 2003a: 208–13; Heelas 2008: 61–78).

CONCLUSION: THE SIGNIFICANCE OF SECULAR SACRALIZATIONS

My first task in this chapter was to examine the history of New Age and new spiritualities and to explain the transition between these currents of religiosity. Dutch New Age during the period from 1965 to around 1990 appeared to be quite similar to the qualifications and aspects of New Age in the West in general. In the early 1990s a gradual transition occurred into new spiritualities. I mentioned some new practices (wellness, self-help, business training courses), objectives (an attentive life), different social positioning and status (increasingly mainstream and popular), and the introduction of new beliefs and sources of knowledge (near-death experiences). The main effect of this shift has been a popularization of the "holistic milieu": the masses were reached, with the help of mass media, with a more moderate message of salvation.

My second question was how to differentiate the practices and beliefs in new spiritualities in relation to religion. I proposed distinctions between religious (in the strict sense) and secular forms of spirituality, and for the latter a decrease of religiosity in three subtypes: functional equivalents of religion, moments and fragments of sacralization. I illustrated this typology with examples of Dutch new spiritualities. These show that the shift in the direction of popularized spiritualities does not imply a linear process of further secularization, but a complex pattern of the co-existence of more traditional religious expressions (Paganism), holistic religion (Western Buddhism), functional equivalents of religion (Reiki, mindfulness) and moments and fragments of sacralization (divinatory invitations, wellness practices). We need more qualitative research and comparative studies to get better insight into the complex forms of these new spiritualities. My main aim in this chapter has been to present a practical typology based on empirical case studies to assist in this task.

NOTES

1. For instance, www.kd.nl, especially its "agenda", and http://spiritualiteit.startpagina.nl (both last accessed August 2013).
2. These developments have been reported by students in small fieldwork studies between 2006–2010 in the Religious Studies Department of Radboud University, Nijmegen.
3. See www.astrotv.nl (last accessed July 2011).

13. COGNITIVELY OPTIMAL RELIGIOSITY: NEW AGE AS A CASE STUDY

Olav Hammer

THE "MODES OF RELIGION" THEORY

In a number of well-known publications, Harvey Whitehouse proposes (2000, 2004a) that religious practices and concepts are transmitted by one of two fundamentally different modes: the imagistic and the doctrinal. The "modes of religion" theory has attracted considerable scholarly interest, and only the bare essentials need to be summarized here. The theory is based on the observation that religious elements, in order to survive, must be committed to memory, and that there are two distinct forms of memory with divergent properties that profoundly influence the nature of those religious elements.

Episodic memory stores single, salient events. We remember specific details from our last birthday or what we did when we heard of the attacks on the iconic date of 9/11. Semantic memory allows us to recall general knowledge, procedures and routines. This is what enables us to remember as a general fact that Moscow is the capital of Russia, and makes us able to easily recall what we usually eat for breakfast, whereas we presumably don't remember how we found out what the Russian capital is called, or what we specifically had for breakfast on a random day several years ago.

The sheer fact that religious concepts and ritual actions, like any other information, need to be stored in memory and recalled implies that religions are subject to the strictures inherent in each of the two memory types. Imagistic religiosity depends on single events with considerable emotional impact being stored in episodic memory. Doctrinal religiosity relies on one's ability to memorize general knowledge about one's religious traditions: how to pray, or what the gods' postulated properties are.

Each mode comes with a set of further predicted characteristics. Imagistic religion is intensely emotional. Typical examples from the literature involve painful ordeals, for instance when a cohort of youngsters goes through a frightening and agonizing ritual of initiation. The experience itself will be remembered for the rest of their lives. By contrast, the ordeal may involve relatively little explicit verbalizing about the meaning of the experience. Whatever reflection on what these salient events may signify will often be spontaneous, vague, and vary from one initiate to another. The social bonds forged by participating together in the initiation ritual are more important than whatever doctrinal content may be transmitted. Those who made it through the agony and humiliation will feel linked by their common experience. From this basic fact other properties follow: in particular, in order to succeed in fostering this feeling of bonding, the groups that participate cannot be too large, and for the emotion to be sufficiently intense, the experience must not be repeated too often.

Doctrinal religiosity is the converse of the imagistic mode. In this mode, the details of doctrines and the significance of rituals are of paramount importance. The amount of material to commit to memory may be very large, the specifics are often hard to learn, and easy to forget. For members of a religious tradition to be able to remember such a mass of details, extensive socialization is required. This typically takes place through rote learning or very frequent participation in communal rituals. Occasions for memorizing the material need to be organized, and resources have to be mobilized for large-scale rituals to take place. The bulk of doctrinal knowledge can be so great that only a few members of the community can be expected to master it. Doctrinal religion therefore demands a considerable degree of institutionalization in order to succeed, and typically differentiates between the lower degree of learning of the masses and the specialized insight of a priestly class. On the other hand, emotional intensity and close bonding are much less important. Institutions that transmit doctrinal religion (such as churches) can have very many members, who barely know each other. Doctrinal purity, on the other hand, is vital, and the borders of the acceptable can be policed with exceptional zeal.

It is easy to find real-world examples that illustrate Whitehouse's modes of religion theory, but the dichotomy between imagistic and doctrinal religiosity has also been critiqued (in particular in the contributions in Whitehouse & Laidlaw 2004). First, it is far from always clear whether a specific element of actual religious behavior should best be classified as doctrinal or imagistic. The two modes should probably be seen as ideal types, and it is easy to find examples of religious events with doctrinal as well as imagistic characteristics. The Muslim pilgrimage to Mecca, the hajj, is an apt example. For most participants, the hajj is a once-in-a-lifetime experience. The ritual as a whole is emotionally intense, and there are several peak moments that will no doubt be recalled in detail by the participants: circumambulating the Kaaba, perhaps catching a glimpse of the black stone or even coming close enough to touch it; symbolically stoning Satan at Mina; standing in prayer on the plains of Arafat. Such elements would seem typical of imagistic religiosity. On the other hand, the hajj is an extremely large-scale and highly scripted event. The number of pilgrims has vastly increased over the years, and approximately 2.5 to 3 million people participated in the 2011 hajj.[1] Obviously, any one pilgrim will only get to know a tiny fraction of all the other participants, and the intense social bonding predicted by Whitehouse's theory is simply impossible to achieve outside that group. Each participant furthermore needs to assimilate a vast amount of information about the hajj. On the one hand, there are narratives linking the individual elements of the hajj to a mythological past, connecting sites and actions during the hajj with a fund of doctrinal knowledge. Even more importantly, there are innumerable minutiae that need to be mastered in order to perform a correct hajj. Ritual actions are prescribed in detail: the clothes one is allowed to wear in order to maintain ritual purity, the words to be chanted when proceeding between precisely defined geographical points at specific times during the days that the hajj lasts, the exact number of pebbles that one should use during the symbolic stoning of Satan, and so forth. In preparation for the hajj, those who intend to participate will study instruction manuals and get ready in other ways for the upcoming events.

A second point of critique, and one that is crucial for the present purposes, is that one easily finds examples of rituals that have too little explicit "theological" content to fit the category of doctrinal religiosity, but are also too emotionally low-key to serve as examples of the imagistic mode. This is explicitly noted by Whitehouse (e.g. Whitehouse 2004b), who suggests that there is a third "mode": the *cognitively optimal*. In short, some concepts are easier to memorize than others, some trains of thought seem more comfortable or natural than others. This fact also implies that doctrinal religiosity in particular is inherently unstable. Although people may learn less-than-obvious doctrines or ritual behaviors through memorization, there is a tendency to drift back from "theologically correct" concepts towards cognitively more optimal ideas.

Whitehouse (*ibid.*: 190–93) summarizes some of the research conducted in this area, and in particular discusses four ways in which cognitive optimality affects religious concepts. *Anthropomorphism* is pervasive, and makes it is easier to imagine the postulated superhuman agent as a "grey-bearded man" than, for instance, as an omnipresent being who cannot be adequately described in any terms that apply to human beings. The insistence of theologians of some traditions that the divine cannot be described in ordinary human language or understood as anything remotely resembling mundane creatures may be a workable basis for the *via negativa* of a religious elite, but will in everyday forms of religion soon be replaced by anthropomorphized conceptions of the deities. Under the heading of *ritualization* Whitehouse discusses the ways in which religious rituals will function cognitively better if they involve already existing mental structures. For instance, because it is biologically adaptive for humans to avoid contamination, evolution has presumably hard-wired a drive in us to avoid sources of potential pollution. A series of ritual actions can be hard to memorize and perform correctly, but chances of successful performance and transmission are greater if the rituals are associated with ideas regarding purity and impurity. The survival rate of ritual actions will also increase if these rituals involve *chains of causal reasoning* that are routinely invoked in people's attempts to intuitively understand ordinary actions. Just as "everyday" actions are readily understood in terms of an agent carrying out an action by means of an instrument, the superhuman being putatively involved in a ritual can be conceptualized as an agent, patient or (presumably more rarely) instrument. *Narrativity*, finally, has to do with the role of well-formulated stories in transmitting religious concepts and practices. A myth with a good plot is simply more memorable than a bare-bones statement of doctrine.

This chapter intends to explore the concept of cognitively optimal religion in somewhat greater detail. If, as Whitehouse (*ibid*.: 192) maintains, his two "modes of religiosity ... are created against a background of more intuitive, cognitively optimal ways of thinking and behaving", we may inquire what that background is. As the title of this chapter suggests, "New Age" religiosity offers valuable clues to answering that question. Under the "New Age" rubric, one finds a number of related forms of popular religiosity in the modern West that have neither imagistic nor doctrinal characteristics, yet are efficiently transmitted and thrive despite little institutional backing. A closer look will show that these religious phenomena do match Whitehouse's four ways of making religion cognitively optimal, but will also allow us to construct a more detailed list of traits.

"NEW AGE" RELIGIOSITY AND THE MODES THEORY

As is well known, the label "New Age" is used to encompass a range of very diverse phenomena, including aura reading, astrology, Bach flower remedies, chakra balancing, channelling, crystal therapies, Earth mysteries, holistic health, I Ching divination, the belief in reincarnation, Reiki healing, swimming with dolphins and tarot reading. Such a list may give the impression that the "New Age" age label is so diffuse that anything goes. I would argue, however, that this partial catalogue actually points at just the opposite. Note, firstly, that venues that cater to "New Age" interests tend to include much the same inventory of items: whether in San Francisco or Stockholm, book shops and festivals will market paraphernalia and titles on precisely the range of topics listed above. Second, the range of variation within each category is quite constrained. Reincarnation comes in many different culturally specific versions (Obeyesekere 2002). New Age theories on reincarnation rarely acknowledge classical Hindu suggestions that rebirth is a tragic reality, or the pan-Indian belief that all sentient beings, including humans, animals and spirits, are connected via the mechanism of reincarnation. For

New Agers, the prospect of living yet another life is generally a happy one, and there is an almost universal conviction that the human soul can never regress to a "lower" life form. Third, all New Agers are not equal: there are authority figures who write books, hold workshops, appear in the media and suggest innovations in the religious repertoire, with precisely the net effect that a relatively small number of concepts and practices are spread throughout the New Age milieu. In sum, some New Age elements are very successfully transmitted, a fact that needs to be accounted for.

However, the "modes of religiosity" theory in its classic formulation with two distinct modes only goes some way in explaining the spread of "New Age" religion. Some socialization into complex doctrines does indeed exist. Divinatory systems such as astrology require some level of expertise, such as knowing what interpretations are typically given to the twelve signs, the ten celestial bodies that astrology classifies as planets, the aspects (angles between planets), and houses. Another method of divination, tarot cards, requires a substantial amount of memory work if performed with no textual aids: there are seventy-eight cards, each of which is associated with a range of symbolic associations. Unsurprisingly, tarot card reading is very often done by non-expert practitioners who consult textbooks. Thus even in the case of divination, doctrinal expertise is supplemented with the cultural memory available in books.

A few systems of complementary medicine also require extensive expert knowledge, and here memorization is common among professional and semi-professional alternative therapists. Methods of healing based on theories of Chinese origin, in particular, are very complex and can take months or years of study and practice in order for the practitioner to become proficient. With such methods, there is a major qualification to be made: only those who practise the methods in question have this expert knowledge, their clients normally do not.

There are also examples of the imagistic mode in contemporary folk religiosity. A few decades ago the use of hallucinogens provoked intense experiences conducive to formulating religious explanations. Literary models such as Aldous Huxley's *The Doors of Perception* (1954) could be consulted by those who wished to understand these experiences. Although by no means defunct, hallucinogens are nowadays hardly part of "mainstream" New Age. There are a few other contexts, as well, where fairly intense experiences are involved. Among these are "uncanny" situations: seeing ghostly apparitions, or witnessing the apparent transformation of a person into the channel of a superhuman being. Other examples include intense and striking imagery that at least some individuals experience in the recall of putative past life experiences.

Most experiences provided in the New Age milieu are much less intense. A successful consultation with the astrologer, a session with the aromatherapist or Reiki healer, a sense of being immersed in a spiritually uplifting book

– that is about as dramatic as it gets. However, as the subsequent sections will show, whereas New Age religiosity largely lacks complex doctrines and intense experiences, it survives because of its cognitive optimality.

WHY COGNITIVE OPTIMALITY?

The diverse list above, with elements ranging from auras to the tarot, may make New Age religiosity look more anarchistic that is actually warranted. I have elsewhere (e.g. Hammer 2006) argued that a number of shared presuppositions can be reconstructed from the mass of New Age data. For the present purposes, only two such presuppositions are important:

- There are better ways to get to understand the world we live in and our own place in it than via the intellect. These alternative epistemological tools can include intuition, feelings, altered states of consciousness, or various divinatory techniques such as astrology or the tarot.
- Valid understanding is not arrived at by accepting doctrines formulated by others, but rather by a highly individual quest, that should be based primarily on personal experience.

The distrust of the formal and normative modes of rationality espoused by the institutional pillars of society, and the preference for more intuitive ways of assessing the validity of any given practice, together provide the rationale for following cognitively optimal pathways of thinking and behaving. In New Age contexts, the idea is essentially that if something feels right, it is right. If I feel that there is something wrong with me, I visit a Reiki healer, and after a few sessions consider myself to be in good shape, that is sufficient evidence to accept not only the practice of healing, but presumably also to admit of the existence of the invisible cosmic energies that the healer is said to transfer into my body. Standard biomedical interventions are tested in a way that differs dramatically from this scenario (for instance, by involving double-blind randomized testing with a control group receiving a placebo) in order to avoid the cognitive pitfalls that, according to scientific norms, are involved when one relies on such subjective validation.

What makes Whitehouse's "modes of religiosity" theory so appealing is, as shown above, that it addresses several issues in one fell swoop: most crucially, why some religious elements survive and are transmitted, while others die out. Without rote memorization and without intense experiences, most doctrines and most sequences of ritual actions are too complex or too unexciting to be firmly committed to memory, and will over time die out. A considerable added bonus is that the "modes" theory also explains the social formations surrounding the two modes. Thus imagistic religion goes with tightly knit, small-scale groups where the feeling of emotional bonding is more important than the propagation of clearly defined religious concepts or the performance of complex rituals. Conversely, doctrinal religion goes together with larger social groups, where the sense of social cohesion may be weak and the primary function of the group is precisely to ensure that religious concepts are familiar to all and rituals are correctly carried out. As we will see, the concept of cognitively optimal religion has the same kind of explanatory power. It not only provides a model for how non-rote and non-imagistic religious elements can, in fact, survive extremely well, but also suggests the particular kinds of social formations where this type of religion will tend to thrive.

THE NUTS AND BOLTS OF COGNITIVE OPTIMALITY

A fundamental presupposition underlies the following discussion: it assumes, as does most of the current scholarly literature, that religion is not a *sui generis* phenomenon. In other words, there is nothing "special" about religion: the way we reason about religious concepts and actions is not fundamentally different from the way we reason about mundane concepts. The list of specific cognitive mechanisms presented here is equally applicable to everyday reasoning. This listing could be made quite extensive, but the purpose of the remainder of this chapter is merely to provide a few examples.[2]

The first of the mechanisms in our brief sample is the *clustering illusion*. Humans have a tendency to assume that there are significant patterns in events and may for instance see a causal relationship between events that co-occur. Our ability to see patterns and draw the conclusion that one event causes another is crucial. Without it, we would not be able to understand our environment and to make rational decisions. If we see dark clouds we may draw the conclusion that it will soon rain, and a suitable response can be to take an umbrella or to stay indoors. The term clustering *illusion* signifies that our ability to detect such correlations is not particularly well calibrated: we tend to see causal connections even when there presumably are none.

This is a fitting place to begin to understand New Age as cognitively optimal religion, since very many New Age practices hinge on the detection, and perhaps over-detection, of patterns and causal relations. One form of clustering illusion partly explains the success of divinatory systems such as astrology or the tarot. The astrologer examines the birth chart, and then offers a character analysis that to the clients appears to make sense. The story fits memories that the clients have about their lives. Since chart and narrative appear to correspond, it is easy to conclude that the symbols and the narrative present an unproblematic match, and that the diviner's ability to weave a meaningful story about the client's life is directly *caused* by his or her understanding of the symbols of the chart, and of the celestial events depicted by those symbols. Hence, a consultation will typically be experienced as a confirmation of the validity of astrology and conversations with people interested in astrology typically uncover how a first encounter is perceived as the cause of a continuing fascination with divination.

Healing provides a somewhat different example of this effect. Common healing systems such as Reiki have only to a limited extent been investigated according to the norms of clinical testing, and the results have hardly been an overwhelming success for advocates of healing.[3] Nevertheless, healing continues to be widely practised, and clients can report that the effects have been beneficial. There is a ready explanation for this apparent discrepancy. While the success of astrology typically depends on clustering two discrete events (the natal chart representation and the astrologer's narrative), healing also involves a statistical phenomenon, *regression to the mean*.

What this means is basically that one's moods, states and performance vary over time, as do most chronic conditions for which people seek treatment. Pains increase and decrease, emotional states change over time, and so forth. But, as numerous experiments have shown, our cognitive capacity is very poor when it comes to understanding statistical correlations. A person with, say, a chronic pain can visit a healer. At some later time, the pain will be milder. From this basic fact, it is easy for that person to conclude that the improved conditions were caused by the treatment.

Another important mechanism involved in healing is *suggestion*. Subjects tend to experience what they expect to experience. The perhaps most familiar version of suggestion and the one most relevant here is the placebo effect. For as yet poorly understood reasons, patients who undergo biochemically ineffective treatments can find their symptoms relieved. Pain is diminished (Graham 2004), depressions are alleviated to a degree that matches the effectiveness of antidepressants (Mayberg *et al.* 2002), and even Parkinson's disease can be treated with placebo injections (Graham 2001). There are obvious implications for cognitively optimal religiosity: even relatively mild levels of social reinforcement allow individuals to find their beliefs validated by firsthand experience.

Confidence in astrology, healing and numerous other New Age practices can be bolstered by *memory limitations*. Both of Whitehouse's modes of religiosity are, as we have seen, correlated with the way our memory functions. Cognitively optimal religiosity is, as well. People remember selectively, and events as they actually took place in the past are converted into a narrative that at times only indirectly reflects those events. Even the flashbulb memories that according to popular belief engrave salient events indelibly upon our minds are according to more recent research (Talarico & Rubin 2003) remarkably unreliable. Striking events are in fact not recalled more accurately than more run-of-the-mill incidents, but the confidence in their veracity is greater.

Much of the folk religiosity described in this chapter is dependent on narratives: tales spun about the course of an illness and the interventions of a healer; stories about a visit to the astrologer and the remarkable fit between the chart reading and one's personal background; anecdotes about an uncanny dream that later turned out to be an accurate premonition. The actual course of events that underlie such narratives is, obviously, almost impossible to reconstruct. If research on memory in more mundane situations is any indication, a prior commitment to a New Age-inspired worldview would encourage people to construct accounts that are not always quite accurate, but which are nevertheless felt to be precise renditions of the past. The encounter with the healer may not have led to any decisive improvement of one's symptoms, but over time a rosy account is created via regression to the mean and memory limitation, that makes recovery appear to be the causal outcome of the treatment. The astrologers' attempts at judging their clients' personalities and life histories may actually have been quite mediocre, but in hindsight suggestion and (again) memory limitation combine to make their accuracy seem truly amazing. Memories of the seemingly prophetic dream may have been considerably modified in view of subsequent events, or the dream may even have occurred after the event, but memory glosses over discrepancies and rearranges the chronology.

The correlations that we believe we perceive; the suggestions that we follow; the selective memories around which we weave narratives of past events – all of these in turn are supported by our *prior beliefs*. Not everybody is equally prone to experiencing a ghostly haunting; a previous belief in the existence of ghosts is a key factor if the suggestion is to take hold. The effect of prior belief is ubiquitous in religion, where beliefs and practices tend to mutually reinforce each other in clusters (Hammer & Sørensen forthcoming). The perhaps best-known example from the ethnographic literature concerns the Azande of central Africa (Evans-Pritchard 1937). Illnesses and social problems are believed to be caused by witchcraft. While witches themselves are usually not aware of their malevolent influence, their identity can be revealed by means of oracles. Ritual precautions can then be taken to counteract the magical forces. Should the problems persist, there are ready explanations: perhaps the witchcraft was in this particular case too powerful to be counteracted by the measures deployed. Since magic is an integral part of an existing cluster of concepts and rituals, it resists disconfirmation.

The way in which the Azande view of magic is impervious to disconfirmation is an example of the more general tendency to seek to have our opinions confirmed. *Congruence bias* affects the way we go about judging whether a hypothesis is correct. Most likely, we will devise a simple test that can be presumed to confirm the hypothesis (Baron 2008: 171–7). The benefits experienced from healing can be tested by visiting the healer once more. The validity of the visit to the astrologer can be confirmed by rummaging through one's memory for further, confirming matches between past experiences and the diviner's narrative. Other hypotheses that might explain healing or divination are not even countenanced.

The most dramatic effects of congruence bias can be seen when people are confronted with disconfirming data, but actively use input that goes against their favoured hypotheses to reinforce the opinions that they already hold. Subjects in one study (Lord *et al.* 1979) were selected for their strong opinions for or against capital punishment. Each subject was then presented with two carefully balanced reports, one for and one against the death penalty, and was asked to assess them. Those who were initially opposed to capital punishment felt that the arguments that supported their own point of view were well constructed and relevant, whereas the report presenting opposing data was perceived to be deficient. Those who were in favour of capital punishment were equally convinced that the report supporting their own point of view was more convincing. Ultimately, both groups of subjects managed to process the disconfirming data in a way that allowed them to become even more entrenched in their respective opinions.

In New Age settings, ways of defending one's cherished beliefs against counterarguments are easy to elicit: those who voice doubts about New Age propositions are often said to lack the personal experience necessary to pass a judgment, or to be blinkered by their materialistic presuppositions, or to have yet to reach the same level of spiritual evolution as their New Age interlocutor. Although people can and do change their opinions, even on matters of deep conviction, belief thus has a considerable persistence. New Age attitudes that have been internalized are only with great difficulty dislodged by opposing beliefs.

A final, important element in this short overview of mechanisms contributing to cognitive optimality is the difficulty in accurately monitoring one's own ability to form and test hypotheses. We all tend to overrate ourselves, and will probably also overrate how accurate we are in our judgments. Perhaps the best illustration of this cognitive weakness is the statistically illogical tendency of the average person to believe he or she is more competent than the average human being in a wide variety of fields (Dunning *et al.* 1989). Most people think that they are better parents and spouses than most others. Automobile drivers think they drive more safely than most others, managers believe their business skills are above average and teachers pride themselves on didactic skills that exceed that of their peers. It is hardly surprising if we happen to be convinced of the rationality of our own religious or secular worldview, and the folly of that of others.

Paul Heelas (1996) argues that a defining characteristic of New Age religiosity is its message that there is something wrong with us, and its offer of various ways to remedy our failings. The fact that New Age and Self-Help books often share space in bookshops confirms Heelas's picture. Although this is an open hypothesis in need of testing, one particular aspect of inadequate self-monitoring seems likely to play a significant role in the conflation of new age religiosity and self-help. There is evidence that those who are less competent on any given task have more difficulty recognizing their true level of ability than do more competent individuals (Kruger & Dunning 1999). In experimental settings, it can also be shown that even artificially induced self-serving attributes are nearly impervious to disconfirming evidence. People who in a first phase of an experiment were made to believe that they had above-average interpersonal skills were not swayed by the careful debriefing procedure carried out by the researchers in the second phase of the experiment (Nisbett & Ross 1980: 176–9).

If one can extrapolate such findings to New Age milieus, those who buy significant amounts of self-help literature or who enroll in self-improvement courses will have considerable difficulties in accurately assessing whether their efforts actually boosted their abilities. Even if self-help literature may induce a feeling of making progress in a variety of personal areas, their actual performance may quite possibly be as paltry as before reading the books or following the course. In fact, if their level after the course is truly dismal, their tendency to overestimate their newly acquired skills will be all the greater. In sum, there is significant research that suggests self-help literature does not deliver what it promises (Wiseman 2009).

SOCIAL FACTORS IN COGNITIVELY OPTIMAL RELIGION

The fact that our reasoning and our experiences are largely formed by our prior beliefs leaves us with a fundamental question: where do these prior beliefs come from? Answering this question requires us to return to Whitehouse's doctrinal mode of religiosity. As noted above, few aspects of New Age religiosity involve the rote memorization of vast bodies of theological materials. On a more modest scale, however, there is certainly an element of learning pre-existing doctrines, and these doctrines will interact with cognitively optimal mechanisms to confirm that New Age concepts are valid.

A central presupposition of New Age religiosity is, as we have seen, that one need not follow authorities: the most important test for any idea or practice is that it should be experienced as "true" by us. This individualistic imperative (Hammer 2010: 49) clashes with a sociological truism: we are not free-floating individuals, but are socialized into a society where there is already a mass of practices and opinions that to a large part dictate how to behave and what to accept as "true". Such socialization can certainly be found in New Age religiosity. As mentioned above, a survey of afterlife conceptions from around the world reveals an astonishing range of beliefs. However, New Agers appear to prefer a particular version of reincarnation, as if this were the only option to a materialistic belief that the demise of our physical bodies puts an end to our existence, or to Christian perspectives on life after death. In fact, people who profess belief in reincarnation can only do so because they know that this option exists. Without trend-setting books, from older titles such as *The Search for Bridey Murphy* published in 1956, to more recent ones such as Ian Stevenson's *Twenty Cases Suggestive of Reincarnation* (second edition 1974), and Brian L. Weiss's *Many Lives, Many Masters* (1988), or books about Edgar Cayce (Sugrue 1973; Langley 1968), few people would have heard of reincarnation other than, perhaps, as an exotic component of Hindu and Buddhist traditions. Reading about past lives in a book and accepting reincarnation as a possible explanation of what will happen in the afterlife may be a truly minimalist version of doctrinal religiosity, but it does fulfil a basic criterion of Whitehouse's doctrinal mode: purported facts are received in an emotionally low-key setting and are committed to memory.

For a smaller group of people, the theory of reincarnation can be tested by means of the preferred New Age epistemological route: personal experience. Past-life regression is offered by a number of therapists, and is essentially a technique by which people can be made to perceive vivid internal imagery. These scenarios can be quite striking: the images perceived in the mind's eye can take on a life of their own, and with a minimum of coaxing one feels transported into the biographies of medieval knights, Native Americans, soldiers in the Napoleonic wars, Chinese monks or ancient Egyptians. When tested by such means, prior belief in reincarnation can be reinforced by means of the cognitive mechanisms already mentioned.

The New Age milieu provides particularly clear opportunities to assess the evidence through cognitive mechanisms such as congruence bias. The very name "past-life regression" privileges one particular account above all others, as do leading questions posed by the therapist ("what did you look like?", "what language did you speak?", "what was your name?") . There is a body of literature that promotes naturalistic perspectives on such experiences (see, for example, Spanos 1996: 135–42). These works are published in academic journals or by academic publishers, are little known to the general public and are promoted precisely by the institutional experts that elicit distrust among many New Agers. Alternative explanations suggesting that the visual imagery produced in these ritual settings are fantasies rendered particularly vivid as the result of role-playing therefore have little opportunity to dislodge emic explanations.

The fact that the New Age explanation is frequently the most readily available account creates the kind of cluster of mutually reinforcing concepts and actions mentioned above. The vivid images are presented as memories of past lives, while the belief in past lives provides a plausible explanation for the images. In this way, a firsthand experience becomes a privileged way of transmitting socially constructed doctrines. The social components can be so powerful that they seem to counteract otherwise well-documented cognitive biases. Even anthropomorphism, one of Whitehouse's examples of cognitively optimal religion, is undermined by a widely disseminated suggestion that the superhuman agent is an "energy" or "force" rather than a person.[4] One can argue that speculation about the nature of the divine plays a minor role in New Age religiosity: generally, theological reflection is subordinate to the kind of practical activity that takes place when clients consult diviners and healers.

SOCIAL CONSEQUENCES OF COGNITIVE OPTIMALITY

Each mode of religiosity goes hand in hand with particular social formations and cognitively optimal religion is no exception. How are these doctrines and practices disseminated, and by whom?

The belief that certain exotic experiences are due to memories of past lives seems at first sight to be due to a kind of vague "consensus opinion". No large, organized religious institution supports this belief or sponsors the associated rituals. I have suggested elsewhere (Hammer 2010: 56–60) that in several contemporary Western countries three types of informal loci of religious production and distribution complement the role traditionally played by churches: personal networks, markets and media. To briefly summarize my argument, personal networks are important because the close social bonds with friends and family make their opinions appear reliable. New Agers have shifted authorities: they rely not on the threatening, negative knowledge of institutional experts, but on the insights of close kin and friends. These networks are not self-contained: new elements are continually introduced, especially via the more popular or entertaining sectors of the media, for instance popular television shows, or best-selling books.

Doctrinal religion in this particular shape, that is doctrines passed on through personal networks, media and markets, lives in symbiosis with cognitive optimality. Market forces and the impact of "infotainment" presented by the media combine to introduce products of popular religious culture that, in Clifford Geertz's well-known terminology, serve both as models of and models for popular discourse. They are "models of" in the sense that the most influential products reproduce preexisting interests. They are "models for" by combining, rephrasing and repackaging these interests in a novel and appealing form.

The social consequences are largely those seen in Colin Campbell's classic description of the cultic milieu (C. Campbell 1972). Rather than via the dominant institutions that promote doctrinal purity, or the tightly knit groups of people sharing intensely emotional experiences, cognitively optimal religion is in the West spread through loose networks of people who tolerate a diversity of opinions and interests, and have little incentive to provide detailed doctrinal accounts of their beliefs.

COGNITIVE OPTIMALITY AND THE SCEPTICAL POSITION: TOWARDS A NATURALISTIC EXPLANATION

Readers acquainted with sceptical literature will be familiar with the cognitive and social biases mentioned here, as well as many others. Their deployment in this chapter as explanatory mechanisms may therefore provoke the uneasy feeling that we are entering into a polemical field that we should avoid. There are, however, crucial differences between the way sceptical literature invokes these mechanisms, and the present suggestion that they be incorporated into a naturalistic, explanatory model of cognitively optimal religiosity.

Sceptics will often draw moral conclusions from identifying the mechanisms cited above. In the sceptical position, such explanations are typically juxtaposed with two other explanations that are closely related to each other, but are incompatible with the naturalistic model presented here. The first is the argument from pathology. According to this mode of reasoning, there is something fundamentally wrong with people who believe in "pseudo-science". They must be unusually naive, deluded or irrational. The second is the argument from immorality. This mode of reasoning affirms that there is something ethically wrong with New Age practices, since practitioners charge a fee for a service that "does not work".

However, the cognitive explanations proposed in this chapter for behaviours and ways of reasoning that do not accord with normative standards of rationality are not intended to convey any such implications. It is just the case that human beings are hard-wired with certain cognitive traits. Practices that indicate the operation of such traits merely illustrate an interesting facet of the human mental apparatus which underpins all representations. These traits exist in us all, which is precisely why it requires strong social mechanisms to counteract cognitively optimal belief and impose doctrinal or imagistic forms. For this reason, as well, a detailed theory of cognitive optimality provides a necessary addition to Whitehouse's two modes.

NOTES

1. The figures are taken from not entirely consistent media reports of the event. The *Telegraph* reported 2.5 million pilgrims (www.telegraph.co.uk/news/worldnews/middleeast/saudiarabia/8867639/Hajj-pilgrimage-2011-by-numbers.html#, accessed August 2013). For the 3 million figure, see the *Daily Mail* online edition at www.dailymail.co.uk/news/article-2058284/Eid-al-Adha-2011-3m-Muslims-attend-annual-hajj-pilgrimage-holiday-begins.html (accessed August 2013).
2. The literature on such mechanisms is vast. A useful recent survey with extensive references to earlier publications is Baron (2008).
3. There are a few tests listed in databases such as PubMed. These clinical trials appear to provide little or no support for the efficacy of Reiki. For examples, see www.ncbi.nlm.

nih.gov/pubmed/18991519 and www.ncbi.nlm.nih.gov/pubmed/22021729 (both sites accessed August 2013).

4. Thanks to my student Jakob Larsen for pointing out this seeming counter-example to the suggestion that anthropomorphism should be the result when religious representations revert to a cognitive optimum.

14. THEORIZING EMOTIONS IN NEW AGE PRACTICES: AN ANALYSIS OF FEELING RULES IN SELF-RELIGION

Shu-Chuan Chen

NEW AGE PRACTICES IN TAIWAN

This chapter provides a sociological analysis of emotions and feeling rules in New Age practices about self-transformation. Based on ethnographic field-work, it employs a social constructionist approach to examine the issues of emotions with regard to self-transformation in two New Age healing practices in Taiwan: A Course in Light (ACIL) and Divine Will (DW). I argue that it is important to insert the issue of emotions into New Age discourse because it is the key element to understanding the experiences of self-transformation for participants. In particular, I look at the way participants manage and change their emotions in New Age practices in terms of self-reflexivity and of feeling rules. Participants in New Age practices deal with emotions at both personal and interactive or interpersonal levels. At the personal level, participants experience the transformation of emotions through the reflexivity of the self, which involves a process of emotional identification, experiences and displays. In respect of the interactive level, emotion work is used in practices such as ACIL to deal with emotional conflicts between participants.

Since the 1970s sociologists have done abundant research regarding the position of emotions in social life and on the influence of emotions on human interaction. In a review of the literature Jonathan Turner and Jan Stets have identified seven types of sociological theory of emotions, which are (1) dramaturgical and cultural theories, (2) ritual theories, (3) symbolic interactionist theories, (4) symbolic interactionist theories incorporating psychoanalytic ideas, (5) exchange theories, (6) structural theories, and (7) evolutionary theories (Turner & Stets 2005; Stets & Turner 2007). Each of these approaches focuses on emotions in social life in different dimensions.[1]

However, empirical research in the sociology of emotions reveals a curious lack of focus on religion and "spirituality" with the exception of the recent milestone publication of *A Sociology of Religious Emotions* by Riis and

Woodhead (2010). My purpose in this chapter is to introduce the study of emotions in "New Age" practices.[2] The elements of emotions and embodiment are strongly involved in healing practices in New Age circles in Taiwan (Chen 2008); therefore, I hope to enhance a sociological understanding of emotions with regard to personal transformation through a study of ACIL and DW.

Historically, the idea of the New Age was introduced from the US to Taiwan in the early 1980s and has subsequently developed into a fluid social movement. The preference for a sacralized "Self" and self-transformation by means of healing has been attracting a growing number of followers within the Taiwanese spiritual marketplace (*ibid.*: 75–107). ACIL and DW are spiritual practices which require studying written materials and practising a particular kind of "light meditation" in order to achieve self-transformation. ACIL was introduced to Taiwan in the mid-1980s by a Taiwanese American, Vicki Young, who started translating the materials into Chinese from 1993. DW is a course derived from the spirit guides Orin and DaBen and was first introduced to Taiwan in the late 1990s; participants use the original English version as there is no Chinese translation (*ibid.*).

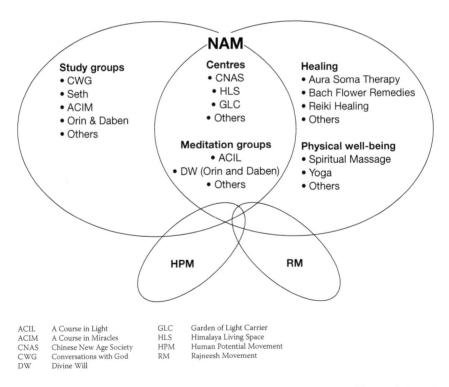

ACIL	A Course in Light	GLC	Garden of Light Carrier
ACIM	A Course in Miracles	HLS	Himalaya Living Space
CNAS	Chinese New Age Society	HPM	Human Potential Movement
CWG	Conversations with God	RM	Rajneesh Movement
DW	Divine Will		

Figure 14.1 A diagrammatic scheme of the New Age movement in Taiwan (adapted from Chen 2008: 14).

THE SOCIAL CONSTRUCTION OF EMOTIONS IN "SELF-RELIGION"

One of the key sociological theories about the New Age Movement (NAM) in modern society is "Self-Religion", proposed by Paul Heelas (1988, 1993, 1996) in his analysis of the development and operations of New Age ideology and practice. He regards New Age spirituality as an "internalised form of religiosity" because the manifestations of spiritual wisdom for New Agers depend on "going within" to find eternal truth (Heelas 1996: 29). According to Heelas (*ibid.*: 18–20), "self-spirituality" is the heart of New Age ideology, consisting in three primary tenets: "your lives do not work", "you are Gods and Goddesses in exile", and "let go/drop it". The logic or "doctrine" of self-spirituality (Aupers & Houtman 2006) is therefore to teach people to believe that their lives do not work because they are conditioned by ego/traditions and ignore the truth of the authentic (divine) Self; to obtain "salvation" is to let go of all limitations which prevent people from assessing this inner truth.[3] In addition to these three main elements, some other characteristics of the NAM which express Heelas's idea of Self-spirituality are unmediated individualism, the Self-ethic, self-responsibility, personal freedom and perennialism. The NAM in Taiwan also displays these characteristics.

Heelas (1996: 137–8) suggests that one of the major problems derived from modernity is the problem of identity. Since this may cause some people to isolate themselves from modernity, he views New Age as a spirituality of modernity in the sense that "it provides a sacralised rendering of widely-held values" such as "freedom, authenticity, self-responsibility, self-reliance, self-determination, equality, dignity, tranquility, harmony, love, peace, creative expressivity, being positive and, above all, 'the self' as a value in and of itself" (*ibid.*: 169). In other words, the appeal of the New Age is related to "the culturally stimulated interest in the self, its value, capacities and problems" (*ibid.*: 173), and to the fact that "[the New Age] is positioned to handle identity problems generated by conventional forms of life" (*ibid.*: 174).

In fact the most prominent medium in which New Age helps participants deal with the problem of self-identity is embodied healing practices. As Heelas indicates, "in a general sense of the term, the entire New Age has to do with healing", including healing the Earth, healing the "dis-ease" of the capitalistic workplace, healing the person, and healing bodily disease and illness (*ibid.*: 81). It is the latter two dimensions of healing that particularly concentrate on the self, which in turn shifts the focus to issues of emotions and embodiment in relation to participants' transformational experiences.

From the perspective of social constructionism, emotions are regarded as learned rather than inherited behaviours or responses. Social constructionists tend to identify and trace the ways in which norms and expectations relating to the emotions are engendered, reproduced and managed in specific sociocultural settings, and the implications for selfhood and social relations of emotional experience and expression (Lupton 1998: 15). Social constructionists view emotions as conceptually constituted by language, beliefs and social rules, which is quite different from evolutionary theories of emotions which tend to regard them as natural phenomena (Armon-Jones 1986: 32–3).

The first step in approaching emotions is to obtain a proper understanding of how various emotion-related vocabularies are used in different cultures (Harre 1986: 5). Emotion vocabularies are thought to give cultural meaning to emotional states and, therefore, to dictate what we are expected to feel in certain cultural or social contexts. In the case of New Age, I pay attention to which emotional vocabularies participants use during practices. In addition, the interactive dimensions of social life should be considered when examining emotions and embodiment. As Lyon and Barbalet (1994) argue, emotions are dynamic, making the body itself become active, and are also communicative expressions of the self. That is, emotion is not only embodied but also fundamentally social – not an inner thing but a "relational process", because many emotions can exist only in the reciprocal exchanges of a social encounter.

Dramaturgical and cultural theories are useful when examining the "relational process" of emotions in New Age practices because they focus on the interactive dimensions. The relational process emphasizes "the importance of culture as providing a script, the presentation of the self on a stage in front of others who constitute an audience, and the use of props and other staging devices to achieve not only dramatic goals, but also strategic ends" (Turner & Stets 2005: 26–7). Interactions between actors are guided by a "script" written by culture, in which the actors are aware of the "norms, values, beliefs, and other symbolic elements that direct how they are to talk, act, and otherwise play their roles" (*ibid.*: 26) in a specific situation. In addition, actors not only play roles and interpret the script, but also engage in strategic behaviour as they manage their presentations of self.

When examining New Age practices, I will focus on Hochschild's ideas of emotion work (1979), which is regarded as a major perspective in the interactionist accounts of emotions and enables us to examine the complex relationship among feeling rules, ideology and social structure. According to Hochschild (*ibid.*: 561), "emotion work" refers to "the act of trying to change in degree or quality an emotion or feeling". It often becomes an object of awareness when people's feelings do not fit into a situation (*ibid.*: 563). Emotion work functions through "feeling rules" which are the public side of an ideology based on social rules or norms that deal with the affective dimensions of social life. People are expected to express proper emotions in certain situations according to relevant rules. Emotion work, in this regard, is a type of "emotion management" that people undertake to cope with feeling rules.

In her research on flight attendants, prostitutes, social workers, debt collectors and sales workers in modern society, Hochschild concludes that the number of "emotion workers" has been rising since the early twenti-eth century and that the management of emotions has become increasingly commercialized. She sees the phenomenon as amounting to "the commer-cial distortion of the managed heart" (Hochschild 1983: 22). Although her theory about "emotion work/labour" is largely centred on a specific arena (the service industry) and doesn't specifically refer to religious or spirit-ual emotions, Hochschild has recently asserted that her theory applies to all social phenomena, and it is in this light that I apply her theory to the study of New Age practices: "The idea of emotional labor – and of a sociol-ogy of emotions in general – helps illuminate the hidden injuries ... of all the systems we study, including the latest versions of sexism, racism, and capitalism" (Hochschild 2008: 80). I argue that the spiritualities that sup-port New Age practices include beliefs that offer participants "feeling rules" to "manage" their emotions in their interactions with others. However, I also note that one of the goals of New Age activities for adherents is to free themselves from the limitations of traditions and thus to live the "real self", which on the face of it is opposite to the case of "managing hearts" in labour markets. Therefore, exploring the way in which New Age par-ticipants manage their emotions and what feeling rules they learn in their practices will provide new insights into connections between "managing" (difficult) emotions and expressing "authentic" emotions. In this way, my case studies show the social construction of emotions within the practice of "Self-Religion" in a way that is anticipated, but not fully demonstrated, by Heelas (1996: 191–2).

OBSERVATION AS A COMPLEMENTARY WAY OF SEEING EMOTIONS

The empirical data employed in this chapter are adapted from my qualitative fieldwork conducted in 2003, 2004 and 2008 in Taiwan. In addition to in-depth interviews with practitioners, I employed observation as an alterna-tive approach to examining emotions for two reasons. First, most research on emotions in sociology is limited to some form of "self assessment" by asking people to locate themselves on an emotion scale. Interviewing people about their opinions or experiences of emotions is thus a method that very much depends on subjective verbal reports. However, because it has been noticed that what people say and what they feel are often inconsistent, espe-cially when defence mechanisms have been activated, it is important to be able to obtain data that can identify and explore this inconsistency. Second, sociologists such as Turner and Stets (2005: 316) have noticed that observa-tions are rarely used in social psychological research on emotions in par-ticular. A more rounded picture could be achieved if qualitative researchers could also use their eyes and ears rather than only participants' verbal or written reports to extend the range of sociological data on emotions.

Participant observation is therefore crucial because interactions and dialogues between people in a social situation would not be possible without "embodiment". Although emotions involve mental processes, people do not notice (or confirm) each other's emotions or feelings until they are embodied as bodily gestures such as facial expressions, postures, behaviours or speech during interaction. In addition, social psychological research on emotions has concluded that facial expressions of certain emotions are universal, such as happiness, fear, anger and sadness. These are called "primary emotions" (Turner & Stets 2005: 11–13; Thamm 2007), and they are differentiated from "secondary" emotions, which are learned through socialization and expressed in a culturally relative way (Turner & Stets 2005: 13–21). In other words, although there are cultural differences in the way in which some emotions are expressed and interpreted, certain primary emotions are universal among humans. Therefore, by means of participant observation the researcher can see, hear and feel how people deal with or express their emotions in a specific situation. In this regard, empathy and reflexivity are skills that the researcher must apply when looking at the "soft" side of human interactions. In other words, although most sociological research on emotions uses measurements such as emotion scales and interviews, qualitative observations should be added as a complementary method when looking at how people deal with their emotions in interactions, such as are found in the learning and practice of the New Age courses ACIL and DW.[4]

REFLEXIVITY AND EMOTIONS IN NEW AGE PRACTICES

Practices such as ACIL and DW appear to generate similar reports of self-transformation for participants as related practices in the NAM. Often, energy flows were reported to play an important element as an expression of transformation. Participants also learn the appropriate way of expressing their emotions freely and positively as well as cultivating the skill of applying self-reflexivity in their daily life. The connection between reflexivity and emotions in New Age practices is therefore key to understanding the transformational experiences for participants.

Take ACIL as an example. This is a spiritual practice in which people meditate by means of visualizing twelve colours of light energy relating to five subtle bodies and twelve energy centres.[5] The practice aims to cleanse and purify the different "subtle bodies" in order to achieve transformation (Moltzan 2001: 5–7). ACIL strongly focuses on the reflexivity of the self. Participants usually share their feelings and thoughts with other people, either in weekly group practice or by electronic communication. Normally participants regard emotional talk or emotional reactions as a process of cleansing based on their emotional experiences in daily life.

During the period of my participation, an event of emotional conflict between two members occurred in the eighth lesson of the "Planetary Level 1" section of ACIL. The theme of this session was the light energy of the colour orange. In the beginning, the session proceeded as usual: sharing and studying, with the group teacher reminding members that they might encounter criticism this week, in the form of either self-criticism or criticism from others. A few minutes later, member B suddenly stood up and wanted to change her seat from being next to member A. Member B felt that she was becoming dizzy after member A joined the session. The group teacher and another member, C, explained that it was because member A had not been very well recently. The teacher encouraged member A to share with group members the challenges she had encountered recently. Quite unexpectedly, member A directed an emotional outburst towards member B, who also reacted aggressively and angrily to member A. It was obvious that member A was uncomfortable and upset. She expressed the view that everyone seemed to blame her for passing negative energy to member B; at the same time, member B clearly had an emotional and angry reaction towards member A. The atmosphere was uncomfortably chilly, and everyone retreated into silence for a while. The group teacher said nothing about the conflict but continued to explain the way in which the energy field works through our life, offering her own experiences.

The next day, all participants in the group (me included) received the following email from member A:

> From: A
> Subject: Thanks to B ~~~
> Date: Friday, July 09, 200~~~
>
> Hi B,
>
> It's A. I am sorry to bother you with this email. I would like to tell you that I am very grateful for your contribution to me last night; you helped me evoke my feelings that have been repressed, that is, feelings of being misunderstood and of being rejected. Thus, I was encouraged and motivated to freely express such feelings that had been deeply buried in my heart.
>
> Although I was very annoyed at that time (in the group meeting), when I stepped out of the classroom, leaving the aura there, I knew immediately that I was in the process of "Fa" [cleansing].
>
> Therefore, thank you!
>
> I would like to tell all my classmates: do not be afraid, the process of cleansing in light meditation is just as our teacher said, it is

just like the process of peeling an onion; the point is to be aware of ourselves. Thanks to my classmates and thanks more to B.

Thank you!
A

To interpret what is happening here it is helpful to refer to Rosenberg's explanation of the process in which emotions can be transformed by means of the reflexivity of the self into a state completely different from merely physiological experience:

> The internal features that constitute the foundation of the emotions are physiological or bodily sensations. ... Reflexivity is exemplified by taking these experiences as objects of one's own reflection or control. Once the internal state of arousal comes to be "worked over" by these reflexive processes, they acquire a totally different character. (Rosenberg 1990: 3–4)

Rosenberg's central argument is that cognitive reflexivity changes the physiological nature of human emotions. He proposes three dimensions in which the reflexive process transforms emotions (ibid.: 4–11). "Emotional identification" is a product of cognitive reflexivity and takes place when an internal state of arousal is ambiguous. When this self-reflexivity operates at the level of action and through the interpersonal process for expressing or hiding certain emotions, it is termed "emotional display". Finally "emotional experiences" involve two ways of altering feelings: through cognitive work and through bodily work. The former is used to control our thoughts in order to manage our emotions via a form of mental self-manipulation. The latter is a way of acting on our body to control our emotions (Rosenberg 1991).

In the case of the event at ACIL mentioned above, the three dimensions of transforming emotions rely on the reflexivity of the self through a kind of emotional awareness. It is not possible to begin transformation until the self is aware of its emotional experiences and makes appropriate identification of what is going on. In the process of self-reflexivity, member A became aware of her emotions, and then she labelled her emotional outburst as a process of "cleansing", which can be regarded as an emotional identification. In addition, such changes remain at an inner level that remains invisible until feelings are expressed through an emotional display, as we saw from the email by member A.

I noticed that the teacher and other participants neither tried to stop verbal conflict between participants nor managed to calm their emotions. The group members tried to ignore what was happening in the session, which otherwise continued as usual as participants kept on sharing thoughts with each other. In this case, the "emotion work" for the other participants, to use Hochschild's (1979) phrase, was to pretend that nothing special or unpleasant was happening; it is a form of acting as if out of "ignorance". However, such "emotion work" is performed in order to encourage members A and B to feel free to express and display what they were feeling, instead of repressing their emotions. In other words, emotional conflict between members was accepted and positive meaning was given to it. This embodies the point of view about emotions shared by most interviewees, that it is not necessary to repress, reject or lacerate our negative emotions such as anger, loneliness, grief, hate and emptiness. Although these emotions make us suffer, this is temporary. The following quotation from an interviewee represents this view of emotions:

> I felt that a good person would not show anger; we should be nice to people. But when I had learned to accept my emotions and to look at my anger, I found that very often the reason hiding behind my anger is a state of imbalance. For example, this pattern might be learned from our parents. They might hope that you could live up to their expectations, and they would be upset if you disappointed them. Therefore, we would repress our anger, right? ... But when I learned that this is a part of me, I accepted it and looked at the way my parents had treated me, I got the sense of it and finally forgave them.

For these practitioners, each kind of feeling has its own messages and meanings that are waiting for them to explore. In the case of ACIL, participants learn how to bring consciousness to their emotions and to freely express feelings. Through practising the light meditation they learn that the flow of emotions is a process of cleansing. As the text of ACIL states, when "all of the emotional reactions to life, all the feelings that have been harboured and contained ... are exposed to the light, there is a tremendous clearing that becomes apparent as you witness your emotional reactions becoming much stronger" (Moltzan 2001: 103). This process of "release and clearing" in ACIL involves learning the rules pertaining to the identification and expression of emotions which is an important part of New Age culture.

EMOTION CULTURE IN NEW AGE PRACTICES

I explained in the previous section that people experience changes of emotions by exercising reflexivity of the self. Now I would like to explore in greater detail how people learn to experience the changes of emotions in New Age practices through a process of interaction among participants. It is in this interactive process that what Hochschild calls "feeling rules" manifest themselves which reflect the emotion ideology of the practice and in turn help people learn the correct way to transform their emotions. Let us take another session in Divine Will as an example, entitled "Transforming Your Emotions". During my participation in the group all the members were encouraged by the group teacher to host one session. I volunteered to host this one, and therefore had the advantage of being able to analyse the emotion ideology and feeling rules based on the course texts. I will also discuss my observations of the way participants learned, understood, interpreted and applied those feeling rules during the session.

According to Hochschild (1979, 1983), there are two types of norm in emotion culture. The first is "feeling rules", which are based on emotion ideology and govern the intensity and the duration of emotions. The second is "display rules", which involve "surface acting" that "specifies when and how the overt expression of emotions in a situation is to occur" (Turner & Stets 2005: 36). Hochschild defines "feeling rules" as "guidelines for the assessment of fits and misfits between feeling and situation" (Hochschild 1979: 566). The way in which people identify and respond to feeling rules varies between different societies or groups. In DW, we will see what participants learned from the group meeting about the correct way of transforming their emotions, and how they interpreted their feelings by learning a set of feeling rules.

For the "Transforming Your Emotions" session, I followed the normal procedure of the group meeting: sharing, studying and meditation. At the beginning of the session the group teacher offered information about following a healthy winter diet through Chinese medicine. I then began leading the session according to the course material. First, I asked members to share their feelings on the day before they joined the group. Then I gave everyone a handout on the topic "The Way to Transform Your Emotions".

During the stage of sharing, participants talked about how they felt and expressed their feelings in daily life. For example, one group member shared the way in which she dealt with her negative emotions:

> When I feel happy, people tend to notice my emotions. However, if I have some negative emotions, I am very aware of such feelings and situations; people would not notice my negative emotions because I would hide them and avoid bringing them to others. I might also choose to be alone. As for feeling other people's emotions, such as from my family, I think that one of the most useful ways is to let people express their feelings. I would feel their state of emotions more or less, but I cannot really tell what is going on with them if they do not express anything.

This extract shows that the person valued positive emotions as well as the importance of expressing them; however, she "managed" negative emotions, which is also a kind of "emotion work" in Hochschild's term. Another participant described emotions as a flow: "Yesterday I suddenly got some insight into emotions, I felt that emotions are something very lovely. … I felt emotions are a flow. … *And I felt that we should not resist our emotions but fully accept and enjoy them; and let them flow.*"

These extracts reveal a central element in the emotion ideology of DW: there is a connection between energy and the concept of "emotion flow". There are two principles in the emotion ideology of DW: "working on energy" and "working on love". In respect of "working on energy", DW participants learn to become aware of the state of their emotions in terms of energy, especially energy around the "emotional body". This is described by teacher Sanaya Roman (1986a: 104) as "a restless, constantly vibrating flow of energy around you". Moltzan explained further that in ACIL, "the emotional body consists of energy made up of your feelings. The emotional body can affect your health, wealth, and happiness if your emotions harbour unresolved issues" (Moltzan 2001: 5). For participants in DW, the first step towards transforming emotions is to raise their "vibrations" from low to high, and to cleanse the "energy" and purify it.

DW teaches participants that the most efficient way to raise their vibrations is to work on love. Why is love related to the changes of emotions? According to Orin, "Love is a place that exists as energy you can tap into whenever you have a loving thought of anyone. You literally pull up your own vibration" (Roman 1986a: 86). Participants are also trained to express and experience "unconditional love" because it indicates that "love transcends the self": "Any time you express unconditional love, from your deepest being, and any time you receive it, you assist many more people in achieving it also" (*ibid.*: 86–7). ACIL also stresses this element: "It (unconditional love) is not required that you like the personality of any individual, nor must you like anything about any individual. What is desired of you is that you love the soul of all individuals" (Moltzan 2001: 167–8).

The theme of "working on love" for DW participants also includes cultivating three qualities and displaying them in daily life: compassion, acceptance and gratitude. Compassion is "the ability to put yourself in the other person's shoes" (Roman 1986b: 78) and "coming from compassion means coming from truth" (*ibid.*: 82). It reminds people about "focusing upon not what you want from them, but how you can assist them in their unfolding and growth in whatever direction is to their highest good" (Roman 1986a: 87). For cultivating the quality of acceptance, Roman says that "every time you recognise the love you have, you increase it. One of the laws of receiving is that recognising when you have gotten something increases it in your life, and every time you do not acknowledge something you make it so much harder to have more sent to you" (*ibid.*: 93). For the final quality, "gratitude", the text says "when you say thanks, and appreciate your life, acknowledging people, events, and the higher forces, the pattern of energy that represents your emotional body begins to rearrange itself into a higher and finer vibration" (*ibid.*: 104).

FEELING RULES

So far we can see that the emotion ideology of New Age practices such as DW is based on the principles of "working on energy" and "working on love". However, in order to transform emotions, participants have to learn how to align themselves with the divine will through the practice of meditation. The goal is to let emotions flow smoothly in daily life. My analysis of the feeling rules that DW teaches shows that the following two guidelines are dominant:

1. keeping emotions in stability and balance;
2. increasing positive emotions and reducing negative emotions.

DW teaches participants to become aware of their emotions and to remain in a state of peacefulness. Such a state is described in this way: "as you reach higher planes of reality, your emotions become so calm they are like the still lake that reflects back every cloud and tree" (Roman 1986a: 125). A male participant expressed how he felt about practising the DW: "I felt that I experienced many changes in the mental body and the emotional body. I can keep my emotional body in a state of stability; it helps me think positively. It provides me with love and joy, and helps me view everything from a higher point of view." Most interviewees who have participated in DW or other forms of meditation which are part of the Orin systems mentioned the way in which they have learnt to keep their emotions in a state of balance and stability. A female interviewee told me:

> We are human beings, it is impossible to live without any emotions; but they [emotions] have become a smooth flow. You are aware of each kind of your emotions when they come; then, when they go, you know it. That is it. I feel that it [light body] helps me to be free quickly from those emotions.

There is also a method practised for keeping oneself in a state of balance when interacting with others, as the following extract of messages from Orin indicates:

> Stability comes from an attitude of balance ... Observe those situations in which your balance is disturbed by another's lack of balance. The next step is to tell yourself that you can keep your balance ... As his (imbalance) energy comes into you ... see that you are resonating with that unbalanced part in him. To stop responding in this way, send him love.   (Roman 1986a: 123–4)

In addition to keeping emotions in stability and balance, participants learn three points about maintaining positive emotions and reducing negative emotions. The first is to increase positive emotional vocabularies and decrease negative vocabularies. This reminds people that their attitude and perspectives create their own reality: "your attitude determines how you experience the world. ...Your attitude is the words you use when you talk to yourself" (*ibid.*: 123). I asked participants to share what kind of negative and positive emotions they are aware of in their daily life. The most common negative emotions were "anxiety, sadness and depression" and the most common positive emotions were "love, peace, calm, happy and delightful". Focusing on positive emotions as part of transformational experiences is also reported by many of my interviewees in other New Age practices. For example, a female interviewee from A Course in Miracles said that "the experience of transformation for me is in the aspect of emotions ... I would feel harmony and calm".

Second, DW teaches participants to relax their body by deep breathing, which is often practised in guided meditation at the final stage in a group meeting. In the session "Transforming Your Emotions", participants worked with the seven "divine wills" – to initiate, unify, evolve, harmonize, act, cause and express – using seven steps. They are taught that each of the steps aims to achieve purposes such as purifying the emotional body, absorbing and expressing positive emotions, achieving emotional balance and understanding one's soul's desires (Roman 2001: 19–22).

The final point about transforming emotions from negative to positive for New Age participants consists in using affirmations to increase positive feelings, because "the ability to make yourself right rather than wrong will help you grow faster" (Roman 1986b: 92). Participants can obtain different themes of affirmation from the website of Orin and DaBen under the subheading "Daily Affirmation Room".[6] The following examples are linked to the theme of "flowing emotions"; I have categorized them into sub-themes to emphasize specific feeling rules discussed above.

- Acceptance of Self
  "I love all my emotions. I let my emotions flow through me.
  All my feelings are a part of myself. I accept all of them".
- Emphasizing positive feelings
  "My body is filled with joy and aliveness.
  I choose my emotions. I choose to feel calm and good".
- Self reflexivity
  "My fears are the places within me that await my love.
  I listen to any messages that my emotions are giving me".
- Maintaining stability in relationships
  "I am aware of other people's realities. I stay centered in my own calm, clear energy.
  Joy flows through me and radiates out to others. I lift the burdens of others through my radiance of joy".

CONCLUSION

Working with emotions is an extremely important element of the practice of self-transformation in New Age ideology. In this chapter I have examined the operation of emotions and feeling rules in one part of New Age culture from a social constructionist perspective. My observations and discussions in relation to two typical New Age courses in Taiwan, ACIL and DW, are an extension of the theory of "Self-Religion" by Paul Heelas. The social constructionist approach provides a useful perspective which views emotions as learned rather than inherited behaviours or responses. In addition, explanations of "emotion culture" by Hochschild and Rosenberg are used as a theoretical framework to examine the process of self-reflexivity for these New Age participants.

At the personal level, I have argued that the three ways of changing emotions (emotional identification, displays and experiences) rely on the reflexivity of the self. At the interactive or interpersonal level, emotion work – such as the act of ignoring outbursts – is used in the New Age practices examined here to deal with emotional conflicts between members. Participants are encouraged to be mindful of their emotions as well as to express their feelings, and to give their emotions positive meanings. My analysis of the session on "Transforming Your Emotions" showed that two principles, "working on energy" and "working on love", represent the emotion ideology of the DW. They are regarded as the foundation of the two key feeling rules: "keep emotions in stability and balance", and "increase positive emotions and reduce negative emotions". Participants were encouraged to follow these feeling rules with the aid of the meditation in DW, and in so doing, they reported changes in their emotions: that is, the normative experiences of self-transformation taught and endorsed by New Age authorities. In this way ACIL and DW serve as an "alternative" expert system (Chen 2008: 170) for managing uncomfortable feelings under the conditions of late modernity, and for converting these feelings into new expressions of "self-spirituality".

NOTES

1. In addition, Gillian Bendelow (2009), Randall Collins (2005), Arlie Hochschild (1983), Theodore Kemper (1978) and Thomas Scheff (1990) have contributed to the growth of emotions theory in specific social arenas, including health care systems, material relationships, the service industry, politics and social movements.
2. I follow a social constructionist approach to the "New Age" and "New Age Movement" in Taiwan, in which my definition of the concept (as a secondary construction by the observer) is based on the primary construction of participants. See also Chen (2007, 2008).
3. However, the idea of salvation is absent in New Age spirituality in Taiwan. (Chen 2007). Instead, New Age participants prefer focusing on the more practical goal of healing.

4. I participated in ACIL learning sessions from November to December 2003 and again in July 2004. I participated in DW in twelve sessions from November 2003 to January 2004.
5. In ACIL the physical body is understood to consist of five "subtle bodies": emotional body, mental body, perceptual body, astral/etheric body and soul body. The twelve colours of "light energy" are white, gold, blue, emerald green, violet purple, ruby red, orange, pink, amethyst, mint green, scarlet and black.
6. See www.orindaben.com/db/dbaffirm/affirmations.php (accessed August 2013).

15. DOING THINGS WITH ANGELS: AGENCY, ALTERITY AND PRACTICES OF ENCHANTMENT

Terhi Utriainen

NEW AGE AS ENCHANTMENT

There is a very concrete question motivating this chapter: what do contemporary people *do with angels*?[1] In more general terms the question points to *making things happen* in life and, more particularly, in the religious field that we might call New Age. Here is one example of the kind of setting I have in mind: a group of women are taking part in an evening course "The World of Angels". The course takes place in a private home, and the organizer plays soft music in the background and leads us in guided meditation – a visualized journey that takes us to meet our own angels so that we can ask them for something important we need in our lives. Accompanied by butterflies we walk along a winding sandy path and through a meadow and a secret garden to meet our angel in an imaginary house of our liking. We sit down with him/her, hold hands and have a long intimate chat. Soon our angel gives us a gift (a word, an object, a symbol) after which we are slowly led back along the same path to where we started. We quietly return to the everyday world and start to share our experiences of our personal angels with each other and begin interpreting the message of the gifts we received and what we could do with them.[2]

What happens in a setting like this, where the important elements are the following: *doing, with* and *angels*, that is, *practice, relation* and the meta-empirical *other*? In order to link these elements with each other, I attempt to complement theoretical insights from practice approaches with those from phenomenology. This combination is fragile and risky, but I propose that it is worth trying for various reasons. First, a religion like this is about practice in many ways. Second, it is about humans *relating* and *doing things with* an "other-something" (see also Utriainen 1999–2000). Finally, it is also about various other beings or powers. These three aspects ask to be connected.

New Age is about doing things within a religion which means that it is about religious agency: that is, making things happen in a religious field or with the power of religion. In her research on Catholic women who identi-fied themselves as woman-conscious, Laura Lemming (2007: 749) defines religious agency as the "personal and collective claiming and enacting of dynamic religious identity". I claim however that religious agency is not always only about claiming or enacting (religious) identity, but about doing many kinds of things and making changes in worlds. In some contexts (and perhaps more so within conservative religious settings, such as Lemming's) identity ("who one is") may become the most important field and aim of reli-gious agency whereas in others (in relatively liberal and eclectic settings, like New Age) something else may be at stake. This something else might be, for instance, personal healing or enacting so as to bring about a transformation of the whole universe. Sometimes agency in the New Age context would seem to be a way, or style, of sensing oneself and the world around oneself a little differently.

New Age is a slippery and debated category. Whatever it is, it illustrates and epitomizes a religiosity that is relatively open-ended, democratic and non-institutional, and eclectic, practical and lived. New Age, it might be argued, constitutes part of today's "folk religion" although a lot of practition-ers do not embrace the concept at all. As part of my ethnographic studies I conducted a survey at a lecture-style event given by one international angel-guru Lorna Byrne in October 2011. Only four of the 263 people who filled in the questionnaire ticked "New Age" as their self-identification. The most frequent choice was "spiritual person". Thus, at least in this particular sub-field of New Age, which very much borders on Christianity, people are not attracted by that appellation. Rather, "spiritual person" seems to work as a much more open and inclusive identity category.

Not everything that we find in New Age is new but is similar to more tra-ditional forms of folk religion. However, there is something new besides its location and profile (Sutcliffe & Bowman 2000: 11): how, in what contexts, and by whom this religiosity is articulated and communicated in the modern context. Thus, even if we want to approach New Age as a loose title for folk religion that also often selectively combines religions, one formative condi-tion of this kind of religiosity is its wider modern context of (post-)seculari-zation, individualization and neoliberalization and the changes these trends bring to both religious and secular lives. New Age religiosity is enacted in relation with this complex modern condition that presents itself as multiple paradoxes between choices and determinism, as I will argue in this chapter.

New Age can be approached either as a reaction to or as one possible product of the disenchantment brought forth by the Protestant-driven his-tory of the Western world. Robert Orsi (2005: 12) writes that "the modern world has assiduously and systematically disciplined the senses not to expe-rience sacred presence; the imaginations of moderns are trained toward sacred absence". In contrast to this, New Agers cultivate life-worlds where other than human beings and forces (angels, fairies or energies) can – in favourable circumstances – act and make a real difference. For example, Matthew Wood (2007: 66) claims that "supernatural entities" are important to a lot of New Age practices. Contacts with these entities often take place as more or less subtle forms of possession (*ibid.*: 163–6). This world of multiple and heterogeneous acting forces can be called *enchanted* (Partridge 2004–5; Salomonsen 2002; Utriainen 2011): that is, endowed with an aesthetic, sensuous and effective spell and fascination with something not seen or felt by all, and all the time. Thus there is something invisible or something that tends to evade the senses but that can be contacted and made close and intimate as a resource for everyday living. Contacting the other world requires skills, and it can be argued that a big part of New Age is learning, teaching and cultivating these skills as an everyday pragmatic and enchanted stance towards life. This particular art of enchantment includes various kinds of practices and detailed techniques of imagining and relating with the "other". It is important to learn how to *meet* and very concretely to *feel* angels and other powers that are considered not quite from this world, but that are nevertheless attributed some kind of causal power and efficacy.

One dilemma to solve is how to approach and talk about this "other" with which these practices engage. Should we talk about "otherness"? "Other than human" entities or actors/actants? The "transcendent"? The "supernatural"? The "meta-empirical"? Or should I simply stay in the world of my research participants and talk about angels (and other spirits and things if and when they come along)? Even if there is a very rich variety of these actors in the world I study, and even though one would not wish them to be colonized by Western epistemological categories, I want to find a relatively general yet elastic and philosophically grounded way to conceptualize this aspect of practice, which is conceived as part of the everyday world by my research participants but also as making a very special difference in it. I will explore how it could be approached through phenomenological concepts of otherness and alterity. In this chapter, I will thus sometimes write "angels" but, also, "angel-others" or "alterity" when wanting to point out this more general aspect.

Furthermore, angels are not a simple and equivocal category in themselves but a good example of something complex and quite unstable. An angel may be understood as a symbol or metaphor – but it can also appear as an ontologically "real" energy or spirit that prompts quite concrete changes in the world. Sometimes angels are not taken to be that different from humans but in other instances they are something very unlike humans. These shifts back and forth between mere metaphor and magical efficacy – as well as the likeness and difference between angels and humans – are movements that call for attention. In particular the movement from metaphor to magic and back indicates that *something important happens* in this shift whereby angels become more or less concretely "present". It is also of importance to note that ways of conceiving of angels and relating to them differ from case to case as well as from one narrative context to another. Even one single interview may contain different approaches to the other-worldliness of angels. In one interview with two angel-healers, one of them said that she saw angels with her own eyes, whereas the other interviewee drew quotation marks in the air with her fingers when she uttered the word "angel", thus signalling that to her angels are not "real" in any simple way but are at least partly metaphoric or imaginary. Another example of this ontological complexity is when, at the angel-healer course, we were actively encouraged to *imagine* angels if we could not otherwise easily contact them or believe in them.

Angels become even more complex and unstable objects – and less and less one single and well-defined category – within the modern context of reflexivity and doubt. Many of my research participants articulate their awareness of the fact that most people do not share their belief in or contact with angels, even though they also claim that their experiences and prac-tices are becoming increasingly shared and public today. Sometimes their intimacy with angels becomes so active and concrete that it endangers their friendships and partnerships. However, at times they themselves express reservations saying "I don't know if I really believe in them" or "I don't know if angels really exist". One interviewee said that she did not want to reflect too much on whether the healing power she felt during channelling came from inside herself or outside: "I have actually stopped thinking [about where the power comes from] because thinking may stop channelling from working". This context of a shifting critical distance and reflexivity – and the need to find ways to stay in contact with less religious worlds where one's relations to angels are not often understood – is of course also present in the interview situation. We are thus dealing with "more religious" worlds (and positions and rhetoric within those worlds) that are densely interwoven with "less religious" worlds.

PRACTICE-BASED APPROACHES TO RELIGION AND AGENCY

Theories of practice aim at analytically describing and/or explaining the social world and its actors and agents in terms of practices. In the study of religion these approaches take religious practice as the focus and treat "belief" or "experience" as something that evolves from practice and is learned and cre-ated to a large extent through and by it. For instance, Catherine Bell (1992) approaches ritual from the perspective of Bourdieu's theory of praxis and focuses on how ritual as the practice of power produces particular kinds of bodies and positions needed in the social and sacred economy.

However, in contrast to overly deterministic accounts, many practice approaches also give space to agency. Indeed, it can be argued that practice constructs agency – especially if by agency we do not mean only individual efficacy, but a shared socially and culturally mediated capacity to act or to make a difference or to transform things (Ahearn 2001: 118). This would make agency into something that is not attributable to one sole actor (like the individual) but to a composition of actors. This composition, or network, would always be born out of varieties of relations; in religious contexts like New Age, these relations often include non-human others like angels. To borrow the approach of the anthropologist Laura Ahearn, it is "important to ask how people themselves conceive of their own actions and whether they attribute responsibility for events to individuals, to fate, to deities, or to other animate or inanimate forces" (*ibid.*: 113). Thus when researching into how to make things happen – like how to heal – ethnography and interviews are very good approaches. The analysis should not, however, be limited to the level of individuals even though we start with their accounts. As Karlyn Campbell (2005: 5) writes, we should take the individual or author as one important "point of articulation" of agency, but also take notice of all the other kinds of actors and structural factors.

On the one hand angels are something humans relate to, and on the other hand they are something different/other than human – thus, using Taves's terminology, they are *something special*.[3] Relating to angels can happen spontaneously (as when angels come to rescue one from dangers or to console one in distress), but in the New Age context access is very often constructed by means of practices that can be actively learned and endlessly cultivated and refined. This distinction between spontaneous experiences and cultivated practices is, of course, relative. The key issue is thus only partly the fact that angels are different kinds of entities than human persons. It is at least as much the fact of the practice itself and how it is learned and cultivated. I therefore suggest that the angel-other is only relevant at all via relational practices. Thus a practice approach becomes the frame within which I want to place phenomenological insights about otherness or alterity.

In many respects, religious practice such as doing things with angels resembles many other relational practices, but in some ways it also differs from them. It is possible to talk with angels and make them your best friends. In some ways, however, relating to angels differs from other social relations and one needs to learn how to build and cultivate them so that one acknowledges this difference. This is something discussed and learned in and through such meaning-making practices as literature and courses.[4] For instance, one has to learn and become sensitized to the special methods angels use when they try to reach you and tell you something – by using such signs as feathers suddenly appearing everywhere, a peculiar feeling of a pressure of air or change of temperature on some part of your body, or repeatedly and irresistibly being drawn by particular colours. One also needs to learn certain methods for actively contacting angels – such as the meditation described at the beginning of the chapter, angel oracle cards or various angel-healing techniques. Oracle cards are one popular and relatively easily learned method for consulting angels: one can draw a card, look at the image and read the interpretation in an accompanying book.[5] The sessions of the angel-healing course in which I participated often ended with dealing out and reading cards. By learning these kinds of practices and techniques one gradually becomes increasingly familiar and sensitive to the very special relational and communicational partners that angels are, as well as what can be done with them.

One class of religious practices and agency is pedagogical techniques of the body: that is, embodied practices that teach how to contact and construe the otherworld with its forces and entities, and how to cultivate the contacts thus created. Marcell Mauss's insights ([1935] 1979) about techniques of the body have been further elaborated especially by anthropologists like Talal Asad (1993) and Saba Mahmood (2005) who focus on the impact of pedagogical and moral religious practices in the formation of subjectivities and agencies and the ways they are built through bodies. Another example of religious body pedagogics can be read in Rebecca Lester's (2005) ethnography on young Mexican postulants who, during their postulant year, learn to transform their secular teenage bodies into passionately religious Catholic bodies. Chris Shilling and Philip Mellor (2007) display the body pedagogics of Taoism and Charismatic Christianity and show the ways whereby these two religious cultures discipline bodies that become capable, in the first case, to adjust to the cosmos or, in the second, to break free to meet the transcendent. Shilling and Mellor want to emphasize that in the contemporary world the bodies demanded and constructed by globalizing technologies will confront the challenge of various kinds of bodies framed and moulded by religion. Religious body-practices teach the embodied subjects to construct relations with Jesus, God, power, angels, the inner self, nature, or something else. However, these embodied agents will not act only inside their religious worlds but also in many kinds of more or less accommodating or clashing relations with more secular worlds.

One important aspect of these enchanted pedagogical practices is their materiality: the fact that they become very concretely and sometimes enduringly imprinted in bodies and the bodily habitus. Sometimes habits and habitus can be said to embody and carry religion: that is, to make it both materially real to oneself and visible to others. An obvious example would be making the sign of the cross (Kupari 2011). However, Matthew Wood (2007: 162) argues that New Age as a non-formative religion does not construct a distinct habitus, since it involves so many authorities that they compromise one another. This is an interesting and insightful claim: my research participants, apart from not proclaiming a New Age identity, did not profess using any distinctive material or gestural signs. Another aspect is that enchanted body pedagogics often actively engage with imagination. Imagination, like dreaming and art, is often so heavily present in religious practices that it can be claimed to be an integral part of them (Taves 2009: 156–60). Sometimes religious imagination is called visions or revelations. In the angel setting the very word imagination is often used with a poignantly positive emphasis: namely, imagination is believed to create things in the sense of making them true and real. This coming together of materiality and imagination makes a strong basis for enchantment and this is precisely where some crucial trans-formative shifts between mere metaphor and the efficacy of magic happen. An excellent example of this is photographing angels: angels (metaphorical figures of light) are sometimes seen in photographs as balls of light called "orbs".[6] Two of my interviewees showed me their albums and websites full of what for them are materializations of angelic energy. Digital cameras have become an invaluable technical and material device for enchantment: making the invisible visible when human senses are not enough.

Embodied pedagogies of enchantment are present throughout angel practices and other New Age techniques, even if perhaps in less demand-ing and complex forms than in some other contemporary religions, such as paganism with its more demanding, time-consuming and elaborate ritu-als (e.g. Luhrmann 1996; Salomonsen 2002). One example of pedagogies of enchantment is the working of angel-healing. In the angel-healer course we repeated over and over again the practice of invoking the archangels one by one by slowly and smoothly spreading our arms over the healée in imi-tation of the wings of angels. We were taught to become sensitized to the most subtle sensations that accompanied this bodily practice and learn to interpret it as a touch of this or that angel. What is created in this bodily and imaginary coming together of the healer, healée and angels is a subtle and porous layer of healing magic over the quotidian bodies of the practitioners. I suggest that it may be precisely this practically co-created enchantment that is understood to heal (Utriainen forthcoming). This layer of magic is so porous and light that it lets secular life filter through and does not com-pletely isolate itself from it. Rather, it works as a film that makes secular life shine through in a somewhat transformed way. If we thus ask – slightly modifying Vincett, Sharma and Aune (2008: 11) – "where ... do our [reli-gious] bodies end and the [secular] world begin?" – we must answer that, in the case of angel-practices, an important layer of magic simultaneously and gently separates and mixes the two together. This thin layer is something that both belongs to our bodies and is *other* to it.

FROM THE WHOLLY OTHER TO INTIMATE ALTERITIES

In her chapter "Encountering Otherness", Morny Joy draws a helpful map of the landscape of philosophies of otherness, difference or alterity which have been an important preoccupation of phenomenology and continen-tal philosophy. Even though this preoccupation with otherness is heterodox and complex – are we talking about God(s), the face of the other, the other sex or perhaps difference in a very general and generative sense? – otherness is most often understood as some "external entity whose own claims need to be taken into consideration" (Joy 2011: 221–2). According to Joy, "most often this extraneous entity takes a human form, but the challenge can occur at both the experiential and conceptual levels. [And] the diverse attempts to depict this dimension of otherness can take either a positive or negative form" (*ibid.*: 221). Otherness or alterity is, thus, always a relation to something.

Alterity can be understood at least in ontological, theological, political and ethical terms. Often ontological and ethical ways of conceiving alterity are addressed by phenomenology whereas the political understanding is delegated to critical, post-structural and post-colonial theory. In traditional phenomenology of religion, the ontological (and theological) understanding of Other as God or Transcendent has dominated although philosophy of religion has also interested itself with the ethical other.[7] I propose that if we approach a religious formation like New Age as a field of relational practices of enchantment, we find that these enchantments involve very intriguing relations with alterity – or alterities in the plural. I claim further that this otherness is sometimes construed as ontological otherness (cosmos or God) by practitioners themselves. However, otherness can also be understood by practitioners and conceptualized by researchers in pluralized forms – especially as ethical and intimately embodied relations. What is important here is that alterity always implies and presupposes relational practices in more or less material or imaginary forms.

For Mircea Eliade religious experience was, following Rudolf Otto, a relation to the wholly other, the ultimate ontological reality (Strenski 2006: 309–36). This reality was primary and external to humans but at least fleetingly within their reach either in spontaneous experiences or by using proper ritual practices whereby people take part in the primordial world-order. The fundamental relation humans had with this otherness was awe and submission. Since Eliade attributed ontological reality to this very serious and big Other, a reality more fundamental and compelling than social or material reality, he has been excluded from much of today's study of religion for doing theology instead of serious (social) scientific research of religion. Also an ethnographic critique of Eliade is legitimate, since angels (for example) at least often appear on such intimate terms with practitioners that they cannot be considered only as *wholly* other, but as something more concrete and close.

But what if alterity was instead understood in ethical terms in the study of religion? The famous figure of ethical alterity is the face of the other (human being) in Emmanuel Levinas's work. For Levinas, the face of the other is precisely that "external entity whose own claims need to be taken into consideration" (Joy 2011: 221–2) all the time and in every situation. Each subject is inevitably and pre-reflectively related to the face of the other. If asked what would be the kind of (religious) practice that gives us this kind of alterity, Levinas's answer is responsibility. This responsibility happens particularly in emotionally intensive moments of transcendence, such as joy and pleasure (e.g. Bergo 2011; Joy 2011: 222–5). Levinas's philosophy is one of the "[self] being affected by an other, whose arrival cuts through my concerns about the world and my own mortality" (Bergo 2011: 67). Some may call this affective transcendence "God".

Levinas's emphasis on ethics, inter-subjectivity and affectivity instead of abstract ontology makes alterity into something that might help us understand some aspects of communicating with others like New Age angels. As companions of life, angels are something both human-like and god-like. Practices aim at building conditions and spaces where angels can be encountered face-to-face. And even though it sometimes seems that New Age angels are there merely to serve humans and run their errands, their otherworldly face (angels are understood to come from cosmic or divine light) poses limits and transcends human aspirations and actions. Furthermore, contacts with angels are often described in very sensuous and affective terms: angels give rise to pleasure and surprise. Thus there is ethical responsibility and affective transcendence in this interaction.

Thomas Luckmann's sociologically framed phenomenological understanding brings alterity even further down to earth and closer to everyday life, especially in his 1990 article "Shrinking Transcendence, Expanding Religion". He uses the word transcendence for what I call alterity, and what is something not-quite-the-same, not-quite-tangible or not-quite-here, and significantly he writes about transcendences in the plural. He also completely disconnects alterity/transcendence from its theological underpinnings and writes about a scale of transcendences from smaller to greater. In this phenomenological thinking, alterity is rooted in universal human experience and has different aspects or instances according to our position as perceivers and actors.

One example that Luckmann gives is sleep and dream: both are transcendent to waking experience. The example of temporal alterity is the future: it is unknown and other to the present moment. Transcendence also has a spatial dimension: anything behind my back or around the corner is transcendent to what is before me. Other people are also part of the experiences of transcendence: they are "not-me". Language is a most important source and means of transcendence when it makes absent things present (Berger & Luckmann 1981: 54–5). Luckmann (1990: 129) claims that "human experience is a continuous flow of transcendence" in which dreams would be examples of smaller transcendence while religion is a big transcendence:

> When an experience presents itself as pointing to something that not only cannot be experienced directly (as long as the experiencing self remains in everyday life) but in addition is definitively

not part of the reality in which things can be seen, touched, handled by ordinary people, one may speak of the "great" transcen-
cences.   (*Ibid.*: 129)

With Luckmann we are thinking about alterity as something unknown yet
quite human, mundane and embodied – and also as something like a precondition of perception, action, orientation and reflection. Many instances
of transcendence would not be directly relevant to religion or the study of
religion or even in any strong sense figure, in Joy's terms, as an "external
entity whose own claims need to be taken into consideration" (Joy 2011:
221–2). Following Luckmann, religion would be only one – historically
influential, but also precarious and unstable – way of acknowledging alterity
or providing practices by which it becomes elaborated. Kelly Besecke (2005)
suggests that for Luckmann, religion is ultimately a particular kind of *communication* of transcendence, and she argues against Luckmann's privatization theses with her own research on discussion groups in the US: not only
private meaning-making but also shared societal conversations about transcendent meaning are still very much part of modern life.

   As far as I can see, there are no inherent and stable dividing lines between
religious and non-religious transcendences and every society has its own
ways of articulating and communicating human experiences of transcendence so that they become parts of (religious) collective memories and social
realities (Luckmann 1990: 130). In Luckmann's historical scheme of the privatization of religion, "the 'sacred cosmos' of modern industrial societies …
is no longer articulated as a consistent thematic whole. It consists of assort-
ments of social reconstructions of transcendence" (*ibid.*: 134). Today, only
some of these reconstructions of transcendence are traditionally and insti-
tutionally "religious". On the contrary, many are this-worldly and minimal,
"shrunken" transcendences that are very much "rooted in the cultivation of
immediate sensations and emotions" (*ibid.*: 136) and articulated and communicated by markets, media and popular culture instead of through "traditional" religious institutions. New Age (with its angels, fairies and energies)
is an example of this kind of easily accessible and multiply communicated
assortment of transcendences and alterities, as Luckmann concludes in his
article.[8] If accompanied by Joy's short definition of alterity, angels and similar
relational agents can be seen to pose at least some such claims which people
feel they need to take into consideration in their lives. Angels as instances of
alterity often become intimate parts and participants in people's embodied
everyday lives, in their relations with others as well as in their expression of
sensations and emotions.

   So what might be the relationship between embodied intimacy, alterity
and religion? To tackle this question I turn to the ethnographically rooted
phenomenology of Thomas Csordas. Csordas (2004) builds his approach
to religion on the phenomenology of the body of Maurice Merleau-Ponty

in connection with Pierre Bourdieu's habitual body, and explicitly grounds alterity in embodiment and intimacy. He focuses on alterity with a minimal distance from the experiencing subject, but in contact with her relational world. Following Csordas, alterity should be seen as an aspect of the embodied and relational open structure of human experience: our changing bodies, other people, desire and suffering, imagination, always orientating towards "what-is-not-there" in either a large or small, frightening or adventurous, sense. This alterity would also be the "kernel"[9] of religions: religions would stem from a fleshy and relational open structure of human experience to otherness that Csordas describes as *displacement*: that is, transformation, endless change and dislocation, in order to accentuate that it is not any kind of stable object, but a process, relation and orientation. Religions could thus be understood to have been grown and worked out of this general source of embodied alterity. Other kinds of (institutionalized) elaborations of alterity would be, for instance, art and politics. Even if Csordas's articulation about religion working with "alterity in and for itself" is a little bit vague, I find the following lines illuminating:

> When alterity is elaborated as oppression of the other we are in the domain of politics; when it is elaborated as striking beauty, we are in the domain of aesthetics; when it is elaborated as competition we are (perhaps) in the domain of athletics; but when it is elaborated as alterity in and for itself, we are in the domain of religion. (Csordas 2004: 173)

Csordas does not refer to Luckmann, but I find a common motif in their respective treatises of alterity in that they root it in the human body and relational interaction. One benefit of this kind of approach is that it connects the alterity that we find in religions with alterity in a much more general but also variegated everyday sense. This approach also helps us to understand the kind of practices and agency with regard to alterity that are cultivated in New Age, where the scope of alterity varies from greater to smaller, where it is sometimes about God and the whole of the universe, but at other times something this-worldly, intimately inter-subjective and interwoven with the human body and its senses. And where it sometimes becomes very close to a mere play of imagination and metaphorical displacement.[10] This understanding of alterity helps me to show how angels can appear varyingly as distant and grandiose heavenly or planetary bodies, or as one's intimate soul-mates and best friends; how they are sometimes present as a subtle change of bodily sensations, and at other times metaphors of mercy, beauty or inspiration. Furthermore, angel practices are sensitive to the socially and epistemologically shifting contexts of modernity that sometimes allow religious presences and at other times strictly forbid and expel them and leave space only for spiritualized aesthetic images – or even just quotation marks. Sometimes alterity is expressed by my inter-viewees very simply as a sentiment that "it was not me who made it happen". This very basic articulation of religious subjectivity was put into words by one of my informants, a singer and songwriter, like this: "One day these songs just appear from somewhere, just like out of the blue … as if some-body was guiding me".

CONCLUSION: AGENCY AND DESTINY IN NEW AGE

Several scholars have noted a peculiar sense of disembodiment and even absence produced in religious sensibilities under conditions of secular modernity. Robert Orsi, as stated earlier, claims that modernity delimits or downplays the possibilities of felt religious presence, and Talal Asad (1993) writes that our modern bodies simply have not been taught the special tech-niques with which to reach for the divine the our way pre-modern bodies were instructed. Also Mellor and Shilling's (1997) sociological treatment of various historical re-formations of the Christian body recounts a story of the disenchantment of our embodied lives. Religion in modernity – espe-cially Protestantism but also modernized Catholicism – is often depicted as a sphere of life cut off from bodies, senses and everyday agency. However now it seems that the narrative of secularization and disenchantment does not completely hold water, as alterities – understood as various kinds of others – make their way back in through New Age and similar practices of enchantment. Even secular theories of feminism have begun to take notice of this (Braidotti 2008); a welcome move considering the continuous preva-lence of women in religions, especially in New Age spiritualities, as well as religions' involvement in sexual and gendered lives (e.g. McGuire 2008: 159–83; Aune *et al.* 2008).

A combination of practice-based approaches and insights from phenom-enology, as argued in this chapter, might help to delineate different levels and aspects of alterity with regard to contemporary religion and agency. It might especially help in understanding such religious agencies that aim at enriching and complementing everyday modern life and people's lived embodiment by cultivating enchanting and intimate relations to alterity. This chapter is therefore a contribution to approaches that model religion – including New Age as a key example – not as a stable object but as a multidi-mensional process, and as something that is not categorically isolated from other human and social experiences and phenomena, but as both interwo-ven with them and also complicating them. Religion (in modernity) is not one: it can be as much about change and transformation as about secu-rity and stability. In Thomas Tweed's (2006) words, religions can be about both *crossings* and *dwellings*. Religions are very much about doing things with multiple others (also Utriainen 1999–2000): actively moulding worlds, locations, subjectivities and agencies. Alterity can be conceived as a start-ing engine – "the kernel" – in this play of dislocations and transformations.

In this chapter I have described what happens within relational practices of enchantment and how these relate to alterity, using angel practices as a case study. I intend this to serve as a starting point for a further ques-tion: what are the possible subjective and cultural trajectories taken today with these practices and the invisible powers that they nurture? I propose that New Age more widely could be seen as a non-stable set of enchant-ing imaginary-practical technologies: as an art for crafting lives and futures. More or less explicit practices of New Age and holistic spirituality operate in contemporary everyday life where people try to combine individual agency and something like destiny or guidance with alterity. In popular idiom this combination is sometimes called "finding my own path".

The concrete and material practices of "my own path" would allow people to connect the modern value of individual choice with another kind of value: that is, the feeling of being part of something larger, a plan or script that helps one to direct one's own life. Even though Anthony Giddens (1991: 109–43) writes that destiny has given way to a risk-calculating ethos in modernity, within New Age practices we can witness a desire for a sense of direction or purpose in life, but along with something that can be felt as, at least to some extent, the individual's own choice (Utriainen *et al.* 2012). "My own path" – or destiny – would thus be a flexible combination of Luckmann's "little" and "great" transcendence as expressed in the vibrant contemporary combina-tion of angel practices.

NOTES

1. Angels are becoming increasingly visible entities and representations in the con-temporary religious field. According to Gilhus (2012a), in Norway, for example, they are important border-markers between Lutheranism and New Age. For the Lutheran Church, contemporary ways of dealing with angels are not properly Christian even though angels are an important aspect of the Christian imagination.
2. My ethnographic research on angel practices in Finland is part of the project "Post-secular culture and a changing religious landscape in Finland" at Åbo Akademi Uni-versity, Turku, Finland (see Nynäs *et al.* 2012).
3. The starting point of Ann Taves's 2009 book is that religious "things" are just one subcategory of more general "special things".
4. These are provided for instance by such international figures as Doreen Virtue, Diane Cooper and Maria Zavou. They have all published books and provide courses, which can be seen on their Internet sites.
5. According to my interviewees, both Doreen Virtue and Diane Cooper have designed very popular packs of angel oracle cards along with, for instance, unicorn cards or goddess cards.
6. See www.dianacooper.com/orbs (accessed August 2013).
7. Grace Janzen's work is a good example of this (e.g. Janzen 1998).

8. Luckmann critiques part of New Age as "egoistic and hedonistic" (Luckmann 1990: 138). His argument would work very well without this unnecessary (and patronizing) moral assessment.

9. Csordas also writes of the phenomenological "origin" of religion. Perhaps this choice of the word was one thing that led to the relatively critical reception of his article by commentators.

10. One paradigmatic dilemma is whether embodiment as described by phenomenology can be translated into embodiment as understood in a more naturalistic (or cognitivist) sense. This is one issue that critical responses to Csordas's article in *Current Anthropology* revolved around. Csordas took a reserved stance towards this linking. In her recent book, Ann Taves is positive about the benefits of this translation. She suggests that transcendence – the "urge to make sense of things" and distinguish both ideal and anomalous things from ordinary ones – might somehow be rooted in human biology (Taves 2009: 38). However, this would not imply that the analysis of religion has to work only on the biological level. For myself, I leave the question open.

CONCLUSION: NEW AGE SPIRITUALITIES – "GOOD TO THINK" IN THE STUDY OF RELIGION

Ingvild Sælid Gilhus and Steven J. Sutcliffe

In this book we have drawn on the data of new age spiritualities in order to try to rethink the general category of religion. Since the basic prototype of religion seems largely to have remained undisturbed when the terms "new religions" and "new religious movements" were introduced from the 1970s, especially in the context of undergraduate teaching programmes and every-day "common-sense" understandings, it is time to reassess and if possible to alter this situation. Two main questions have arisen over the course of this volume: in what ways do new age data ask questions of the dominant category of religion; and what is the analytical potential of a renewed general category of religion that includes new age phenomena among its integral components? In short, in what ways is new age "good to think" in the study of religion, to employ Levi-Strauss's apt phrase?

NEW AGE SPIRITUALITIES AND THE RETURN TO "ELEMENTARY FORMS"

When the academic study of religion was created in modern research universities in the later nineteenth century, the pioneers were preoccupied with finding basic motifs and components of "religion". In the words of Émile Durkheim in 1912, the aim was to identify "the elementary forms of religious life".

Several of the contributors to this volume look back to classical theories and engage more-or-less directly with some of the pioneers. In some respects we find a desire to return to the roots of the study of religion: to go imaginatively "back", behind and beyond the world religion prototype, and to found a new beginning in comparative studies. Paul Heelas, for instance, continues Durkheim's line of thought by re-visiting the relationship between the secular and the sacred which he translates into the language of the imperfect and the perfect, re-thinking the sacred as a state of utopian perfection. Other contributors challenge the received wisdom of

256

a clear sacred – profane dichotomy. For example, Liselotte Frisk criticizes Stark and Bainbridge for perpetuating a strong dichotomy against the grain of evidence from new age spiritualities, which suggests a mutual imbrication of "sacred" and "profane" elements of different depths and intensities in the fabric of everyday life.

In the present context, however, the project to isolate "elementary forms" is not directed towards so-called "primitive" religions, but is based in studies of beliefs and practices circulating in modern "Western" societies. In a roughly homologous fashion to Durkheim's use of data from Australian aboriginal practices (while acknowledging its problematic construction and contextualization), contributors to the present volume study the elements or components of new age spiritualities as particular material from which we can also learn something more general about the synthetic phenomenon we call "religion", but now within a different set of cultural geographies, and firmly separated from a colonialist or social evolutionist agenda.

If new age spiritualities point to a more basic level or layer of representations of "religion", how are these forms conceptualized and expressed? "New age" as elementary forms refers to ideas and practices embedded and distributed within broader social and cultural processes. As such, specific content and detail is appropriate to time and place. At the same time a recurrence of form and function beneath the presenting face of sheer variety seems to point to transcultural and perhaps universal propagative mechanisms and adaptive strategies. Over the last twenty-five years, cognitive and biological studies based in evolutionary theory have sought to identify a basic repertoire of forms, functions and mechanisms of religion. New age data appear to provide further grist to this mill. In the present volume Olav Hammer makes a direct connection between new age and cognitive theories when he asks why some religious elements rather than others are successfully transmitted as "cognitively optimal religiosity". A bridge between cognitive and sociocultural theory is also suggested by the contributions of Lisbeth Mikaelsson in respect of energy as "cognitive currency" and Mikael Rothstein in respect of the social psychology of new age human – animal identifications.

Some contributors point towards an emergent catalogue of elementary forms, or at least to key concepts. Ingvild Sælid Gilhus points out that "new age" practices of healing, astrology and divination are among the most ancient and durable forms of religion that exist. Steven Sutcliffe emphasizes a susceptibility to animism and the core practice of "search" among contemporary practitioners. Paul Heelas calls attention to vitalistic currents underpinning values of this-worldly "life", and Liselotte Frisk finds "healing" and "energy" to be central concepts.

NEW AGE SPIRITUALITIES AND SOCIAL AND CULTURAL CHANGE

In addition to questions about elementary forms and universal mechanisms, the volume has also raised more proximate questions about how new age spiritualities interact with contemporary social and cultural processes. Two aspects to this question are worth drawing out: the interaction between new age and secular formations, and the interaction between global new age and local cultural forms.

New age and secular forms

The interchange between secular and religious forms is highlighted in several chapters. Liselotte Frisk points out that, in general, "the borders between mainstream and New Age activities seem to be weakening". In many cases there are simply no clear boundaries. In this light religion is not so much dichotomously "set apart and forbidden", as Durkheim proposed; rather, the "sacred" and "profane" look more like relative positions or intensities on a continuum of representations (Taves 2012: 59).

Terhi Utriainen develops this line of analysis by modelling religion "not as a stable object but as a multidimensional process, and as something that is not categorically isolated from other human and social experiences and phenomena, but as both interwoven with them and also complicating them". Her example is contemporary enthusiasm for angels, who are represented as complex entities with whom practitioners engage on an ontological spectrum from impressionistic metaphor to efficacious agent. In a similar vein, Trude Fonneland and Siv Ellen Kraft describe the products of Sami shamanism as hybrid and argue that the new age components of these productions are open to interpretation – whether they are seen as "religious" or "cultural" (and thereby "secular") depends on the consumer. Scholars' interpretations of the degree of weakening of borders between sacred and profane also vary. Frans Jespers, for instance, proposes that we think of most new age spiritualities as varieties of "secular sacralizations", whereas Paul Heelas considers "spiritualities of life" to represent a subtle but clear "transgression" of the secular order.

Ethnography and historical sources alike suggest that practitioners' attributions of either "religious" or "secular" may waver both in respect of describing different phenomena, and of describing the same phenomena in different contexts. An obvious question arising is whether this interpretative "wavering" characterizes how religion in general is produced, a position which tends to be overlooked in more formative and more abstract representations of "religion". Mikael Rothstein, for instance, seeks to relate new age religiosity to social–psychological capacities and responses in humans, rather than seeing more abstract or higher-order frames of reference as significant variables. In so doing, he stresses that new age belongs squarely in a general anthropological model of religion and should not be seen as a special "modern" or "postmodern" formation.

New age and local religion

When New Age forms acculturate locally, a process of "domestication" takes place in which globalized representations interact with indigenous formations. This interchange between globalized new age forms and local religious elements raises the question of "glocalization". According to Roland Robertson (1992), glocalization means that both universalizing and particularizing tendencies are present at one and the same time. Among new age beliefs and practices there is a sometimes subtle interplay between homogeneity and heterogeneity, so that "paradoxically, the culturally homogenizing tendencies of globalization imply continued or even reinforced cultural heterogeneity" (Meyer & Geschiere 1999: 2).

This process is illustrated throughout the volume but especially in the discussion of Norwegian, Dutch, Polish and Japanese examples. Two chapters in particular discuss the interplay between new age representations and "indigenous" religion in light of this process of glocalization. The question is systematically treated by Norichika Horie, who makes a distinction between globally received new age forms in a "narrow" sense, and the recovery of local folk and traditional formations as part of a "broad spirituality". Horie points out that in the case of Japan there is a reinterpretation of traditional religion in parallel to the encounter with global new age forms, and he portrays the former as "rediscovered *old* age spirituality" in contrast to the incursion of a "new" formation. Trude Fonneland and Siv Ellen Kraft describe how in northern Norway, new age ideas and beliefs have been incorporated into the local Sami cultural revival and have also been taken up into the globalized phenomenon of "indigenous spirituality". They argue that the presentation of Sami shamanism does not differ markedly from the formative neo-shamanism taught by Michael Harner in the Esalen community in California (Kripal 2007), but in displaying a Sami vocabulary "built upon a neo-shamanic grammar", the data strikingly show the imbrication of local and global as "glocal".

One of Dorota Hall's key points is that the new spiritualities are always locally grounded and embedded and cannot be properly understood outside their contexts of expression. She shows that in Poland, where the Catholic Church is strong and Catholic self-identification is culturally important and historically significant, promoters of holistic activities that might elsewhere be more unambiguously identified as either secular or "mind body spirit", tend to communicate their attachment to Catholicism. Holistic spirituality in Poland thus might more fittingly be understood as an adaptation within Polish "folk religiosity". Hall's findings would reward testing in other societies where the cultural impact of Catholicism on new age spiritualities is also strong, such as Ireland (Kuhling 2011), Italy (Palmisano 2010) and Lithuania (Ališauskienė 2012). More research on how new age beliefs and practices are expressed in Catholic contexts would also help to open up the question of whether there might be an implicitly "Protestant" cultural background to "new age spiritualities". This line of enquiry would bring out more clearly the complex historical relations between new age and Christian denominational teachings to add to existing work on the impact of "esoteric" (Hanegraaff 1996) and "Eastern" (C. Campbell 2007) influences.

Certain symbols serve as important instruments in organizing, focusing and translating religious meanings back and forth between a local and a global context. "Cultural translation" is a concept first used by Malinowski (Burke 2009: 55), and the global new age repertoire includes symbolic vehicles that are especially well suited to attract and translate meanings from different traditions. One example is the concept of "energy": Lisbeth Mikaelsson argues that in new age spiritualities the character and function of money is projected onto this concept. She stresses the importance of linking together cognitive mechanisms of translation with the dis-embedding procedures entailed in the notion of energetic "flows". According to Mikaelsson, the symbolic vehicles of self, spirituality and energy working in synchronization "absorb practices, symbols and ideas from disparate religious traditions and launch them according to New Age mindsets".

New age beliefs and practices clearly interact with local "secular" and "religious" cultures in different ways in different places, and strategies of adaptation and resistance consequently vary. Studies of the interaction between globalized new age and localized representations can contribute dynamically to the debate on globalization on the one hand and on cultural hybridity on the other.

FROM A WORLD RELIGION PROTOTYPE TO A PROTOTYPE OF RELIGION

In this book we have tried to turn the category of religion around and to stress religion as something that moves "on the ground" and penetrates various cultural formations. The "lived" experience of religion is always in focus in this type of study, whether explicitly as theoretical object, or implicitly as background frame of reference. For example, working within the terms of an interpretative sociology, Paul Heelas draws attention to vitalistic impulses within new age spiritualities as a pre-eminent expression of "lived" religion. Based on a more empirically oriented sociological method, Shu-Chuan Chen provides a social constructionist account of the production of new age experiences as a form of "self-religion" – a concept pioneered by Paul Heelas – through examination of the emotional components in identity work teachings in Taiwan. These are designed to manage unruly emotions and to promote smooth(er) interactions among individuals from different backgrounds amid the stresses and strains of life and work in an advanced industrial society. In a similar societal context in the Netherlands, Stef Aupers and Dick Houtman argue that a discourse on "spirituality" has penetrated the modern business world. Against claims by earlier scholars that new age represents an entirely "pick and mix" and/or "private" religiosity, Aupers and Houtman show its dissemination in this most public and rationalized of modern sectors of society, via people's exposure to a "doctrine" of "self-spirituality".

If turning away from the world religion prototype – as do all our contributors in one way or another – seems to place less emphasis on institutional forms of religion, this does not mean that "lived" religion is not still dependent on some form(s) of organization. As with the vexed question of authority, it is not that there is *no* form or level of organization or institution in new age representations – just *less formative* forms and levels. Ann Taves and Michael Kinsella claim that research on new age has tended to overlook robust historical evidence for the co-existence of many different kinds of institutional organization. In their chapter they search for the organizational regularities in ostensibly "unorganized" new age phenomena, and how these arrangements relate to the dominant religious formations in society. When new age is entirely reduced to the concept of "self-religion" or "self-spirituality", this epithet can hide the fact that new age beliefs and practices are typically not a set of individual creations or a series of "idiocultures", to use a folkloric concept stressing radical personal customization, but a thoroughly social formation co-constructed by constituent actors through mutual communication and association. Rothstein, for instance, suggests that use of animal identities by humans is bound up with processes of transformation and transgression of meanings that are inescapably collective rather than individual if they are to hold authority and "make sense" at all. There is, in short, a need for more research into the apparently camouflaged social and organizational forms and structures of new age spiritualities.

This book has dealt with data usually thought to comprise a diffuse and semi-institutional form of "spirituality" with a life and trajectory of its own, typically represented as a separate research area, put into dedicated panel streams in conferences, or tagged on to the coat-tails of projects on "new religions". In contrast, studies of new age can show how contemporary social and cultural processes destabilize the traditional institutional structures of "religion". Nevertheless the cumulative aim of the chapters in this volume is not to set up new age *per se* as a new prototype of religion, a position which would merely crudely reverse the prevailing taxonomy, but to contribute fresh data to a common stock of representations towards a more productive general model. In other words, we think that an attentive study of new age can reveal some of the "building blocks" that religion in general is made of (cf. Taves 2012).

New age data therefore hold analytical potential that makes them "good to think" in the study of religion. Thinking seriously about new age data will make some aspects of the field more visible than they have been for some time. Among other things it should contribute to clarifying the following problems:

- "religion" as a mobile social phenomenon not owned or principally moulded by religious institutions, or confined to the prescribed function system;
- "religion" produced in other places and environments than in officially designated institutions or organizations;
- the subtle interplay between "religious" and "secular" attributions, and between global and local forms;
- "religion" as sometimes "thinly spread" (Gilhus & Mikaelsson 2000; Bender 2012) and thus more widely distributed than is commonly represented;
- the basic processes – cognitive, biological, behavioural – that create and form "lived" religion, and which help us to explain the origin and production of "religion" not as a unique event in the dim and distant past, but as a human capacity in the here and now.

In short, the inclusion of new age beliefs and practices has potential to construct a more complete and dynamic model of "religion". In this sense, new age spiritualities are eminently "good to think": among the most stimulating "food for thought" in the modern field.

CONTRIBUTORS

Stef Aupers is Associate Professor, Centre for Rotterdam Cultural Sociology (CROCUS), Erasmus University Rotterdam. His research deals with spirituality in "secular" domains and tendencies of "re-enchantment". His latest books are *Religions of Modernity: Relocating the Sacred to the Self and the Digital* (co-edited with D. Houtman, 2010) and *Paradoxes of Individualization: Social Control and Social Conflict in Contemporary Modernity* (with D. Houtman and W. de Koster, 2011).

Shu-Chuan Chen holds a PhD in Sociology from the University of Warwick. Her research projects have included yoga and healing in Taiwan, and her publications include "Spiritual but not Religious, Transformational but not Salvational: A Sociological Examination of New Age Spiritualities in Taiwan" in *Taiwan Journal of Religious Studies* (2007) and the book *Contemporary New Age Transformation in Taiwan* (2008).

Trude Fonneland is a Postdoctoral Fellow at the University of Tromsø. Her doctoral thesis was on Sami neo-shamanism in Norway and her current project is on spiritual entrepreneurship in northern Scandinavia. Her publications include "Spiritual Entrepreneurship: Tourism, Spirituality and Politics" (2012) and "Isogaisa – Shamanism in Festival Clothing" (2013).

Liselotte Frisk is Professor in Religious Studies at Dalarna University. Her research interests include the mapping of new age spiritualities and holistic practices. Among her publications are *Nya religiösa rörelser i Sverige. Relation till samhället/världen, anslutning och engagemang* (1993) and *Den mediterande dalahästen: Religion på nya arenor i samtidens Sverige* (with P. Åkerbäck, 2013).

Ingvild Sælid Gilhus is Professor of Religion at the University of Bergen. She works in the areas of religion in late antiquity and new age spiritualities. Main publications include *Laughing Gods, Weeping Virgins: Laughter in the History of Religions* (1997) and *Animals, Gods and Humans: Changing Attitudes to Animals in Greek, Roman and Early Christian Ideas* (2006).

Dorota Hall is Assistant Professor at the Institute of Philosophy and Sociology, Polish Academy of Sciences. Her publications include *New Age in Poland: The Local Dimension of the Global Phenomenon* (2007, in Polish) and articles in academic journals such as the *Anthropological Journal of European Cultures*. Currently, she is researching religion and non-heteronormativity in Poland.

Olav Hammer is Professor of the History of Religions, University of Southern Denmark. His many publications include *Claiming Knowledge: Strategies of Epistemology from Theosophy to the New Age* (2001), *The Invention of Sacred Tradition* (co-edited with J. R. Lewis, 2007), *Alternative Christs* (ed. 2009) and *The Cambridge Companion to New Religious Movements* (co-edited with M. Rothstein, 2012).

Paul Heelas has published a trilogy of volumes with Blackwell: *The New Age Movement* (1996), *The Spiritual Revolution* (with L. Woodhead, 2005) and *Spiritualities of Life: New Age Romanticism and Consumptive Capitalism* (2008). While serving as Senior Research Professor in Sociology of Contemporary Spirituality, Erasmus University Rotterdam, he edited a four volume set, *Spirituality in the Modern World: Within Religious Tradition and Beyond* (2012).

Norichika Horie is Associate Professor at the Center for Death and Life Studies and Practical Ethics at the University of Tokyo. His publications include *Psychology of Religion in History: Formation and Constellation of its Ideas* (2009, in Japanese), *The Future of Spirituality* (2011, in Japanese) and "Spirituality and the Spiritual in Japan: Translation and Transformation," (*Journal of Alternative Spiritualities and New Age Studies*, 2009–11).

Dick Houtman is Professor of Sociology of Culture and Religion at the University of Leuven, and was a Visiting Fellow at Yale's Center for Cultural Sociology in 2012–13. His principal research interest is cultural change in the West since the 1960s, including the turn to New Age spirituality. Recent books are *Religions of Modernity* (co-edited with S. Aupers, 2010) and *Things: Religion and the Question of Materiality* (co-edited with B. Meyer, 2012).

Frans Jespers is Senior Lecturer in Comparative Religion in the Faculty of Philosophy, Theology and Religious Studies at Radboud University, Nijmegen. His main field of research is new religious movements and new spiritualities. Among his recent publications are *Nieuwe religiositeit in Nederland* (ed. 2009) and *Present-Day Spiritualities* (co-edited with E. Hense and P. Nissen, forthcoming).

Michael Kinsella is a doctoral student in the Department of Religious Studies, UCSB, where he specializes in the cognitive science of religion and American metaphysical religion. He is currently combining ethnography and experiment in a study of the Near-Death Experience Movement. He is the author of *Legend-Tripping Online: Supernatural Folklore and the Search for Ong's Hat* (2011).

Siv Ellen Kraft is Professor of Religious Studies at the University of Tromsø. She works primarily with New Age spiritualities, and issues related to the Sami religious revival. Recent publications include *Religion i pressen* (*Religion in the Press*, with A. Døving, 2013), *Hva er nyreligiøsitet* (*New Age Spiritualities*, 2011), *Religiøse reiser* (*Religious Journeys*, co-edited with I. S. Gilhus, 2007) and *Den ville kroppen* (*The Wild Body* – *Tattooing, Piercing and Painful Rituals*, 2005).

Lisbeth Mikaelsson is Professor of Religion at the University of Bergen. Her research has focused on Christianity and new religions and she has published numerous works about Norwegian mission literature, women and mission, religion and locality, pilgrimage, Theosophy, and New Age. Among her publications are *Kallets ekko: Studier i misjon og selvbiografi* (2003) and *Religion i skrift: Mellom mystikk og materialitet* (co-edited with I. S. Gilhus, 2013).

Mikael Rothstein is Associate Professor of Comparative Religion, University of Southern Denmark and Visiting Professor at Vytautas Magnus University, Kaunas. Among his English publications are *Secular Theories in the Study of Religion* (co-edited with T. Jensen, 2000), *New Age and Globalization* (ed., 2001), *The Cambridge Companion to New Religious Movements* (co-edited with O. Hammer, 2012) and *Handbook of the Theosophical Current* (co-edited with O. Hammer, 2013).

Steven J. Sutcliffe is Senior Lecturer in the Study of Religion in the School of Divinity, University of Edinburgh. His chief interests lie in the history and ethnography of alternative spiritualities in modernity and in the modern history of the study of "religion". He is the author of *Children of the New Age: A History of Spiritual Practices* (2003) and editor of *Religion: Empirical Studies* (2004).

Ann Taves is Professor of Religious Studies at UCSB. She specializes in the study of religious experience and its role in the formation of religious movements primarily but not exclusively in the American context. Her books include *Fits, Trances, and Visions* (1999) and *Religious Experience Revisited: A Building-Block Approach to the Study of Religion and Other Special Things* (2009).

Terhi Utriainen is Adjunct Professor in the Study of Religions and Gender Studies at the University of Helsinki. She specializes in lived religion, gender, embodiment, suffering and death. She has worked in several interdisciplinary research projects, presently in the project "Post-secular Culture and a Changing Religious Landscape in Finland" at Åbo Akademi University. She is co-editor of *Post-Secular Society* (2012).

FURTHER READING

The following selection presents background reading which we have found to be productive in our own work or which has otherwise had a notable impact in the field. We hope it will encourage further enquiry into the relationship between new age spiritualities and general theories of religion. For reasons of space and accessibility we have limited ourselves to English-language sources, but we are aware of excellent literature in other languages, including Norwegian, Finnish, Dutch, Polish and Japanese, to name just five languages represented by scholars in the present collection, and we hope that this collection will contribute to wider collaboration among scholars of new age in any and all languages.

There are many good sources available, including some excellent research articles, so inevitably we have had to be highly selective. Our choice here consists largely in monographs and edited collections working with a (usually) single controlled topic or theme, in order to encourage the deeper theoretical engagement we call for. In all cases we indicate the volume's methodological approach and interdisciplinary potential where relevant. The selections are grouped into three main areas – theories of religion, new age studies, critical studies of spirituality – to help researchers interested in developing comparative theories of new age spiritualities to read profitably across mutually stimulating fields.

THEORIES OF RELIGION

Beyer, Peter 2006. *Religions in Global Society*. London: Routledge.
Following systems theorist Niklas Luhmann, Beyer sees religion as one of several differentiated function systems characterized by a specific mode of communication. He analyses religion as a dimension of the historical process of globalization, and he locates his data for religion within a functionalist theoretical framework designed to throw light on systemic changes and adaptations in the contemporary world.

Fitzgerald, Timothy 2007. *Discourse on Civility and Barbarity: A Critical History of Religion and Related Categories*. New York: Oxford University Press.
From a perspective of discourse analysis, Fitzgerald argues that religion is a social construction and does not exist as an empirical entity. Conceived on a Christian model as personal belief in revealed truth, "religion" has been falsely exalted into a universal concept. Fitzgerald traces its use in Western pre-modern and modern discourses, and argues that, like the related categories "secular" and "political", "religion" is theologically and politically biased, and serves the interests of modern states.

266

Masuzawa, Tomoko 2005. *The Invention of World Religions, or How European Universalism was Preserved in the Language of Pluralism*. Chicago, IL: University of Chicago Press.
Employing a genealogical analysis within the history of ideas, Masuzawa explores the modern creation of the category "world religion" and its development into a taxonomy of multiple comparable entities based on a Christian prototype. Masuzawa argues that this particular cultural invention was part of a wider European project to create others in the image of itself; its legacy is the historical self-evidence and continuing propagation of the idea of "world religions".

Pyysiäinen, Ilkka 2009. *Supernatural Agents: Why We Believe in Souls, Gods and Buddhas*. Oxford: Oxford University Press.
Working within the cognitive science of religion, Pyysiäinen argues that humans' capacity to attribute desires and motivations to others through our innate "theory of mind" is the basis for belief in supernatural agency. By analysing sources including Christianity, shamanism and Buddhism, he argues that there are recurrent cross-cultural patterns in practitioners' ideas about superhuman agents, and that these representations form the core element in religious formations.

Saler, Benson [1993] 2000. *Conceptualizing Religion: Immanent Anthropologists, Transcendent Natives, and Unbounded Categories*. Leiden: Brill.
Saler is a cultural anthropologist who understands "religion" to be a Western "folk" category rather than a universal scientific datum. He criticizes monothetic definitions of religion based on one substantive feature and proposes instead a polythetic definition of religion based in family resemblances. Saler argues that "religion" has historically been based on the monotheistic prototypes of Judaism, Christianity and Islam and he recommends constructive dialogue between anthropologists and indigenes to identify a more inclusive prototype.

Smith, Jonathan Z. 1981. *Imagining Religion: From Babylon to Jonestown*. Chicago, IL: University of Chicago Press.
The main point in this important collection of essays in the history of religions is that the object of the study of religion is entirely theoretical. This insight is expressed in the famous words: "There is no data for religion. Religion is solely the creation of the scholar's study. It is created for the scholar's analytic purpose by his imaginative acts of comparison and generalization" (p. xi). This repudiation of an essence or fixed nature invites scholars to devise and operationalize their own controlled theories of "religion".

Taves, Ann 2009. *Religious Experience Reconsidered: A Building Block Approach to the Study of Religion and Other Special Things*. Princeton, NJ: Princeton University Press.
Since James's *Varieties of Religious Experience* (1902), religious experiences have often been regarded both as unique and as the evidential basis for religion. Taves is sympathetic to the theoretical potential of "experience" but does not see it as fixed or *sui generis*; rather, as an event attributed "special" meaning, a term she prefers to "sacred". Her multidisciplinary approach combines anthropology, cognitive psychology and sociology in a comparative study of the "building blocks" of "religion", represented as a cluster of "special things".

Tweed, Thomas 2006. *Crossing and Dwelling: A Theory of Religion*. Cambridge, MA: Harvard University Press.
In this locative approach to the history of religions, Tweed takes his point of departure in rituals by Cuban Catholic migrants in Miami. He discusses how practices, artefacts and institutions mark boundaries, and how religion is constituted and reconstituted as a set of spatial movements made across social and geographical borders. This creates a dialectic between "crossing" and "dwelling" which can be used as a template for comparative studies. Tweed connects his analysis of particular local rituals to spatial theories of religion.

NEW AGE STUDIES

Hammer, Olav 2001. *Claiming Knowledge: Strategies of Epistemology from Theosophy to the New Age*. Leiden: Brill.
This book offers a discourse analysis of how European "esoteric" traditions from Theosophy to New Age have adapted to challenges to their authority in the modern world. Hammer singles out three epistemic strategies used to give esoteric formations legitimacy: appealing to a range of traditions from different parts of the world which are represented as "other" and/or "exotic"; claiming scientific status for religious beliefs; and using narratives of experience as an authoritative source of knowledge.

Hanegraaff, Wouter J. 1996. *New Age Religion and Western Culture: Esotericism in the Mirror of Secular Thought*. Leiden: Brill.
Based on textual analysis within a history of ideas approach, Hanegraaff argues that "Western esotericism" formed the historical background for the emergence of new age spiritualities. He distinguishes between new age *sensu stricto* (in a strict sense), referring to millenialistic expectations of an imminent new era, and new age *sensu lato* (in a broad sense), refering to the wider "cultic milieu", later dubbed the "holistic milieu" (for both terms, see entries under "Critical studies in 'spirituality'" below). New age spiritualities are by definition the secularized descendents of an esoteric worldview.

Hess, David J. 1993. *Science in the New Age: the Paranormal, its Defenders and Debunkers, and American Culture*. Madison, WI: University of Wisconsin Press.
From a cultural studies perspective, Hess looks at the "three cultures" of new age, parapsychology and scepticism in the US. He argues that in spite of their variety, these cultures share certain categories, strategies and values focused around questions of science and reliable knowledge. Through these common interests, the "three cultures" effectively co-construct each other; moreover, debates in this "paraculture" about gender and power shadow debates in the mainstream, meaning that these cultural domains are not so different or separate.

Kemp, Daren & James R. Lewis (eds) 2007. *Handbook of New Age*. Leiden: Brill.
This substantial anthology includes many leading scholars in new age studies who examine the history, morphology, practices and influence of new age spiritualities in a broad but controlled overview of the field. It is a comprehensive collection which includes sociological, anthropological and psychological approaches. Presented as a "toolbox" for scholars working on a common research object, the onus is on the discerning theorist to operationalize appropriately.

Lau, Kimberly J. 2000. *New Age Capitalism: Making Money East of Eden*, Philadelphia, PA: University of Pennsylvania Press.
From a cultural studies perspective informed by Marxian ideology critique, Lau discusses the use of non-Western practices such as yoga, t'ai chi and macrobiotics by American service providers to create a profitable commercial market of products and courses. She examines the creation and operation of an "ideology of the alternative" as a life-style stance in Western popular culture, which enables capitalist entrepreneurs to make a profit on what they present to consumers as the "authentic" and "ancient" traditions of other cultures.

Rothstein, Mikael (ed.) 2001. *New Age Religion and Globalization*. Aarhus: Aarhus University Press.
The contributors to this edited volume offer a range of perspectives on new age beliefs and practices relating to the important theoretical idea of globalization. The balance of contrib-

utors is towards sociology and reflects Nordic perspectives in particular. The collection is among the first publications to engage empirical case studies – including UFO groups, healing movements and the spiritualization of money – with explicit theoretical discussion, thus demonstrating the wider intellectual potential of new age data.

Sutcliffe, Steven J. 2003. *Children of the New Age: A History of Spiritual Practices*. London: Routledge.
This book provides a genealogy and social history of new age from the 1930s to the 1990s based in a combination of archival research and ethnographic fieldwork in the UK, especially in relation to the Findhorn colony. Sutcliffe deconstructs the idea of a "new age movement" and maps instead a complex interplay between different emic interpretations of "new age" among groups in the field. He suggests dropping the term as an analytical tool in favour of developing alternative explanatory models, especially the behaviour of "seekership".

Wood, Matthew 2007. *Possession, Power, and the New Age: Ambiguities of Authority in Neo-liberal Societies*. Aldershot: Ashgate.
In a sociological approach combining fieldwork and theory, Wood stresses the role of social authorities and class identities in producing what he calls "nonformative religion", of which new age spiritualities are one particular variety. Wood is critical about the postulated "self-authority" operating in these forms of religion, which he sees as an assimilation from emic discourse, and argues that social authorities are embedded in participants' subjectivities. He criticizes the idealist bias of new age studies and recommends studying practices in their social contexts.

CRITICAL STUDIES IN "SPIRITUALITY"

Bender, Courtney 2010. *The New Metaphysicals: Spirituality and the American Religious Imagination*. Chicago, IL: University of Chicago Press.
Based in ethnography and cultural history, Bender examines the beliefs and practices of contemporary "metaphysical" practitioners in the university town of Cambridge, Massachusetts, and traces the historical roots of this type of American spirituality to the nineteenth century as a cluster of lively, popular traditions. She shows how metaphysical practices are produced and entangled with other social and religious phenomena, as well as with secular institutions.

Carrette, Jeremy and Richard King 2005. *Selling Spirituality: The Silent Takeover of Religion*. London: Routledge.
Employing a critical theory approach in the Frankfurt school tradition, this book attacks the perceived "big business" of contemporary spirituality, including complementary healthcare, Feng Shui and aromatherapy, as well as the use of "spirituality" within corporate business settings. The authors oppose what they represent as a "takeover" of liberal and progressive religious concerns through neo-liberal marketization and privatization, and they expose the mechanisms and profits when religion is "sold" as a commodity on the spiritual market.

Heelas, Paul 2008. *Spiritualities of Life: New Age Romanticism and Consumptive Capitalism*. Oxford: Blackwell.
Heelas is a pioneer in the study of new age "self-spirituality" and his latest monograph stresses the experiential significance and neo-romantic values of new age practices from an interpretative sociological perspective. Heelas defends the gently countercultural attitudes of new age spiritualities against reductionistic economic and political critiques, and he seeks to nuance the debate about "spiritual consumption" through his more positive interpretation that new age practices represent a vitalistic current of "life" returning to the religious field.

269

Heelas, Paul & Linda Woodhead (with Benjamin Seel, Bronislaw Szerszynski & Karin Tusting) 2005. *The Spiritual Revolution: Why Religion is Giving Way to Spirituality*. Oxford: Blackwell. This sociological study is built on fieldwork and questionnaires in the English market town of Kendal. Its theme is the relationship between the (Christian) religion of the "congregational domain" and the (new age) spirituality of the "holistic milieu". The book explores whether spirituality is taking over traditional religion within an overall shrinking religious sector. The posited "spiritual revolution" therefore refers to changes within this religious sector rather than within society at large. Findings are compared with wider evidence from the US and Europe.

Houtman, Dick and Stef Aupers (eds) 2010. *Religions of Modernity: Relocating the Sacred to the Self and the Digital*. Leiden: Brill. This volume is sociologically based and presents the varieties of new age spiritualities as a ubiquitous form of modern religion. The contributors examine how the "sacred" has been relocated to the subjective world of individual selves, and also to the domain of technological objects which epitomize advanced industrial societies. The collection includes case studies related to "invisible religion" and to the construction of spirituality as an individualistic phenomenon, as well as spirituality in relation to science fiction and digital technology.

Kaplan, Jeffrey & Heléne Lööw (eds) 2002. *The Cultic Milieu: Oppositional Subcultures in an Age of Globalization*. Walnut Creek, CA: AltaMira Press. This collection of sociological case studies takes its point of departure in Colin Campbell's important and productive article about the "cultic milieu" (first published in 1972) which is reprinted here as the touchstone of the collection. The volume contains chapters about cultural opposition and dissent across the political spectrum in various American and European contexts: among others, contributors examine far-right groups, radical environmentalists, neo-shamans, the gothic milieu and the anti-cult movement.

Lynch, Gordon 2007. *The New Spirituality: An Introduction to Progressive Belief in the Twenty-first Century*. London: Tauris. From a sociological background informed by theological considerations, Lynch synthesizes a loose movement which he calls "progressive spirituality" from various new age formations. He presents these as a response to four needs in Western societies: for a viable form of modern liberal religion; for a woman-friendly religiosity rejecting patriarchal authority; for a re-sacralization of science; and for an ecologically responsible practice. Lynch's resultant "new spirituality" is a seminal contemporary hybrid whose exclusions are as interesting as its inclusions.

Partridge, Christopher 2004–5. *The Re-enchantment of the West*, vols 1 and 2. London: T. & T. Clark International. This is a rich descriptive overview of how contemporary popular culture and subcultures are permeated by practices, ideas and beliefs which Partridge labels "occulture". He points to its high profile in literature, film, popular music, new religions, healthcare practices and new age spiritualities. On the basis of the persistence and even flourishing of "occulture", Partridge argues that, instead of a decline in religion, we are witnessing a contemporary re-enchantment of "Western" societies supposedly irrevocably secularized.

BIBLIOGRAPHY

Aadnanes, P. M. 2008. *Gud for kvarmann: Kyrkja og den nye religiøsiteten*. Oslo: Universitetsforlaget.

Aagedal, O. (ed.) 1994. *Døden på norsk*. Oslo: Gyldendal.

Ahearn, L. 2001. "Language and Agency". *Annual Review of Anthropology* 30: 109–37.

Ahlin, L. 2007. *Krop, sind – eller ånd?Alternative behandlere og spiritualitet i Danmark*. Højbjerg: Forlaget Univers.

Ahmad, S. 2003. *Great Sufi Wisdom: Bulleh Shah*. Rawalpindi: Adnan Books.

Albanese, C. L. 1999. "The Subtle Energies of Spirit: Explorations in Metaphysical and New Age Spirituality". *Journal of the American Academy of Religion* 67(2): 305–25.

Albanese, C. L. 2007. *A Republic of Mind and Spirit: A Cultural History of American Metaphysical Religion*. New Haven, CT: Yale University Press.

Ališauskienė, M. 2012. "The New Age Milieu in Lithuania: Popular Catholicism or Religious Alternative?" In *Religious Diversity in Post-Soviet Society: Ethnographies of Catholic Hegemony and the New Pluralism in Lithuania*, M. Ališauskienė & I. W. Schröder (eds), 151–67. Farnham: Ashgate.

Altnurme, L. 2011. "Changes in Mythic Patterns in Estonian Religious Life Stories". *Social Compass* 58(1): 77–94.

Anderson, W. T. 1993. *The Upstart Spring: Esalen and the American Awakening*. Reading, MA: Addison-Wesley.

Andersson, M. 2010. "En undersökning kring yoga: Religion eller vetenskap?" Unpublished paper, Högskolan Dalarna.

Andreassen, B.-O. & T. Fonneland 2002–3. "Mellom healing og blå energi: Nyreligiøsitet i Tromsø". *Din: Tidsskrift for religion og kultur* 2002(4)–2003(1): 30–36.

Anonymous [1952] 1981. *Twelve Steps and Twelve Traditions*. New York: Alcoholics Anonymous World Services, Inc.

Anonymous 1957. *Alcoholics Anonymous Comes of Age*. New York: Alcoholics Anonymous World Services, Inc.

Armon-Jones, C. 1986. "The Thesis of Constructionism". In *The Social Construction of Emotions*, R. Harre (ed.), 32–56. Oxford: Basil Blackwell.

Asad, T. 1993. "Remarks on the Anthropology of the Body". In *Religion and the Body*, S. Coakley (ed.), 42–51. Cambridge: Cambridge University Press.

Asprem, E. & K. Granholm (eds) 2013. *Contemporary Esotericism*. Sheffield: Equinox.

Aune, K., S. Sharma & G. Vincett (eds) 2008. *Women and Religion in the West: Challenging Secularization*. Aldershot: Ashgate.

Aupers, S. 2004. *In de ban van moderniteit: De sacralisering van het zelf en computertechnologie* [Under the Spell of Modernity: The Sacralization of Self and Computer Technology]. Amsterdam: Aksant.

271

Aupers, S. 2005. "We Are All Gods: New Age in the Netherlands 1960–2000". In *The Dutch and Their Gods*, E. Sengers (ed.), 181–201. Hilversum: Verloren.

Aupers, S. & D. Houtman 2003. "Oriental Religion in the Secular West: Globalization and Religious Diffusion". *Journal of National Development* 16: 67–86.

Aupers, S. & D. Houtman 2006. "Beyond the Spiritual Supermarket: The Social and Public Significance of New Age Spirituality". *Journal of Contemporary Religion* 21(2): 201–22.

Aupers, S. & D. Houtman 2008. "New Age. Post-christelijke religie in het geseculariseerde Westen". In *Handboek Religie in Nederland*, M. ter Borg, E. Borgman & M. Buitelaar (eds), 282–300. Zoetermeer: Meinema.

Aupers, S. & A. van Otterloo 2000. *New Age: een godsdiensthistorische en sociologische benadering*. Kampen: Kok.

Aupers, S., D. Houtman & I. Van der Tak 2003. "'Gewoon worden wie je bent': Over authenticiteit en anti-institutionalisme" ["Simply Becoming Who You Are": On Authenticity and Anti-Institutionalism]. *Sociologische Gids* 50: 203–23.

Baber, B. J. 1999. "Can't See the Forest for the Trees?" *Legal Assistant Today* 17: 84–5.

Bæck, U.-D. K. & G. Paulgaard 2012. *Rural Futures? Finding one's Place within Changing Labour Markets*. Stamsund: Orkana akademisk.

Baerveldt, C. 1996. "New Age-religiositeit als individueel constructieproces" [New Age-Religiosity as a Process of Individual Construction]. In *De kool en de geit in de nieuwe tijd: Wetenschappelijke reflecties op New Age* [The Fence, the Hare, and the Hounds in the New Age: Scientific Reflections on New Age], M. Moerland (ed.), 19–31. Utrecht: Jan van Arkel.

Barbalet, J. M. 1998. *Emotion, Social Theory, and Social Structure*. Cambridge: Cambridge University Press.

Barbalet, J. M. (ed.) 2002. *Emotions and Sociology*. Oxford: Blackwell Publishing.

Barcan, R. 2011. *Complementary and Alternative Medicine: Bodies, Therapies, Senses*. Oxford: Berg.

Barker, E. (ed.) 1982. *New Religious Movements: A Perspective for Understanding Society*. Lampeter: Edwin Mellen.

Barker, E. 1994. "Whatever Next?" In *Religions sans Frontières: Present and Future Trends of Migration, Culture and Communication*, R. Cipriani (ed.), 367–76. Rome: Presidenza del Consiglio dei Ministri.

Baron, J. 2008. *Thinking and Deciding*, 4th edn. Cambridge: Cambridge University Press.

Barrett, J. 1999. "Theological Correctness: Cognitive Constraint and the Study of Religion". *Method and Theory in the Study of Religion* 11(4): 325–39.

Bauman, Z. & L. Donsiks 2013. *Moral Blindness*. Cambridge: Polity.

Becker, H. S. 1966. *Outsiders: Studies in the Sociology of Deviance*. New York: Free Press.

Beckford, J. A. 2003. *Social Theory and Religion*. Cambridge: Cambridge University Press.

Beckford, J. A. & J. T. Richardson 2007. "Religion and Regulation". In *The Sage Handbook of the Sociology of Religion*, J. A. Beckford & N. J. Demerath III (eds), 396–418. London: Sage.

Bell, C. 1992. *Ritual Theory: Ritual Practice*. New York: Oxford University Press.

Bellah, R. N. 1967. "Religion in America". *Dædalus, Journal of the American Academy of Arts and Sciences* 96(1): 1–21.

Bendelow, G. 2009. *Health Emotion and the Body*. Cambridge: Polity Press.

Bender, C. 2007. "American Reincarnations: What the Many Lives of Past Lives Tell us about Contemporary Spiritual Practice". *Journal of the American Academy of Religion* 75(3), 589–614.

Bender, C. 2010. *The New Metaphysicals: Spirituality and the American Religious Imagination*. Chicago, IL: Chicago University Press.

Bender, C. 2012. "Practicing Religion." In *The Cambridge Companion to Religious Studies*, R. A. Orsi (ed.), 273–95. Cambridge: Cambridge University Press.

Berger, P. L. 1967. *The Sacred Canopy: Elements of a Sociological Theory of Religion*. Garden City, NY: Doubleday.

Berger, P. L. 1979. *The Heretical Imperative: Contemporary Possibilities of Religious Affirmation*. New York: Anchor.

Berger, P. L. 1999. "The Desecularization of the World: A Global Overview". In his (ed.) *The Desecularization of the World. Resurgent Religion and World Politics*, 1–18. Grand Rapids, MI: William B. Eerdmans.

Berger, P. L. & T. Luckmann 1966. *The Social Construction of Reality: A Treatise in the Sociology of Knowledge*. New York: Doubleday.

Berger, P. L. & T. Luckmann 1981. *The Social Construction of Reality: A Treatise of the Sociology of Knowledge*. Harmondsworth: Penguin.

Berghuijs, J., J. Pieper & C. Bakker 2013. "Being 'Spiritual' and Being 'Religious' in Europe: Diverging Life Orientations". *Journal of Contemporary Religion* 28(1): 15– 32.

Bergo, B. 2011. "Levinas' Project: An Interpretative Phenomenology of Sensibility and Inter-subjectivity". In *Continental Philosophy and Philosophy of Religion*, M. Joy (ed.), 61–88. Dordrecht: Springer.

Berman, M. A. 1999. "New Ideas, Big Ideas, Fake Ideas". *Across the Board* 36: 28–32.

Bernstein, M. 1956. *The Search for Bridey Murphy*. London: Hutchinson.

Besecke, K. 2005. "Seeing Invisible Religion: Religion as a Societal Conversation about Trans-cendent Meaning". *Sociological Theory* 23(2): 179–96.

Beyer, P. 2006. *Religions in Global Society*. London: Routledge.

Bloch, E., M. Keppens & R. Hegde (eds) 2010. *Rethinking Religion in India: The Colonial Construction of Hinduism*. London: Routledge.

Bloom, W. (ed.) 1991. *New Age: An Anthology of Essential Writings*. London: Rider.

Bloom, W. 1993. "Practical Spiritual Practice". *One Earth* 12: 18–21.

Bloom, W. (ed.) 2000. *The Holistic Revolution: The Essential New Age Reader*. London: Allen Lane.

Bochinger, C. 1994. *"New Age" und modern Religion: religionswissenschaftliche Analysen*. Gütersloh: Kaiser.

Boice, J. 1990. *At One With All Life: A Personal Journey in Gaian Communities*. Forres: Findhorn Press.

Borowik, I. & T. Doktór 2001. *Pluralizm religijny i moralny w Polsce*. Kraków: Nomos.

Botvar, P. K. 1993. *Religion uten kirke: Ikke-institusjonell religiøsitet i Norge, Storbritannia og Tyskland*. Oslo: Diakonhjemmets høgskolesenter.

Botvar, P. K. 2006. "The 'Spiritual Revolution' in Norway. Why New Age Spirituality will not oust Christianity". Paper presented at the Eighteenth Nordic Conference in Sociology of Religion, University of Aarhus.

Botvar, P. K. 2009. "Skjebnetro, selvutvikling og samfunnsengasjement: Den politiske betydningen av ulike former for religiøsitet blant norske velgere". Doctoral dissertation, Universitetet i Oslo.

Botvar, P. K. & J.-O. Henriksen 2010. "Mot en alternativreligiøs revolusjon". In *Religion i dagens Norge: Mellom sekularisering og sakralisering*, P. K. Botvar & U. Schmidt (eds), 60–80. Oslo: Universitetsforlaget.

Botvar, P. K. & U. Schmidt (eds) 2010. *Religion i dagens Norge: Mellom sekularisering og sakralisering*. Oslo: Universitetsforlaget.

Botvar, P. K. & S. S. Urstad (eds) 2012. *Tilstandsrapport for Den norske kirke*. Oslo: KIFO Stiftelsen Kirkeforskning.

Bovbjerg, K. M. 2001. *Følsomhedens etik: Tilpasning af personligheden i New Age og moderne management*. Højbjerg: Hovedland.

Bowker, G. & S. L. Star 1999. *Sorting Things Out: Classification and its Consequences*. Cambridge, MA: MIT Press.

Bowman, M. 1995. "The Noble Savage and the Global Village: Cultural Evolution in New Age and Neo-Pagan Thought". *Journal of Contemporary Religion* 10(2):139–49.

Bowman, M. 2000. "More of the Same? Christianity, Vernacular Religion and Alternative

Spirituality in Glastonbury". In *Beyond New Age*, M. Bowman & S. Sutcliffe (eds), 83–104. Edinburgh: Edinburgh University Press.

Bowman, M. & Ü. Valk 2012. *Vernacular Religion in Everyday Life: Expressions of Belief.* Sheffield: Equinox.

Braham, J. 1999. "The Spiritual Side". *Industry Week* 248: 48–56.

Braidotti, R. 2008. "In Spite of the Times: The Postsecular Turn in Feminism". *Theory, Culture and Society* 25: 1–24.

Braude, A. 1989. *Radical Spirits: Spiritualism and Women's Rights in Nineteenth-Century America.* Boston, MA: Beacon Press.

Bruce, S. 1998. "Good Intentions and Bad Sociology: New Age Authenticity and Social Roles". *Journal of Contemporary Religion* 13: 23–36.

Bruce, S. 2002. *God is Dead: Secularization in the West.* Oxford: Blackwell.

Bruinessen, M. van & J. D. Howell (eds) 2007. *Sufism and the "Modern" in Islam.* London: I. B. Tauris.

Brynn, G. & B. Brunvoll 2011. *Eirik Myrhaug. Sjaman for livet.* Oslo: Nova Forlag.

Burke, P. 2009. *Cultural Hybridity.* Cambridge: Polity Press.

Burkert, W. 1996. *Creation of the Sacred: Tracks of Biology in Early Religions.* Cambridge, MA: Harvard University Press.

Campbell, B. F. 1980. *Ancient Wisdom Revived.* Berkeley, CA: University of California Press.

Campbell, C. 1972. "The Cult, the Cultic Milieu and Secularization". In *A Sociological Yearbook of Religion in Britain* 5, M. Hill (ed.), 119–36. London: SCM Press.

Campbell, C. 1987. *The Romantic Ethic and the Spirit of Modern Consumerism.* Oxford: Basil Blackwell.

Campbell, C. 2007. *The Easternization of The West.* Boulder, CO: Paradigm Publishers.

Campbell, H. 2012. "Understanding the Relationship between Religion Online and Offline in a Networked Society". *Journal of the American Academy of Religion* 80(1): 64–93.

Campbell, K. K. 2005. "Agency: Promiscuous and Protean". *Communication and Critical/Cultural Studies* 2(1): 1–19.

Campion, N. 2012. *Astrology and Popular Religion in the Modern West: Prophecy, Cosmology and the New Age Movement.* Farnham: Ashgate.

Carrette, J. & R. King 2005. *Selling Spirituality: The Silent Takeover of Religion.* London: Routledge.

Carroll, B. 1997. *Spiritualism in Antebellum America.* Bloomington, IN: Indiana University Press.

Carroll, J. B. (ed.) 1956. *Language, Thought, and Reality.* Boston, MA: MIT Press.

Casanova, J. 2009. *Europas Angst vor der Religion.* Berlin: Berlin University Press.

CBOS [Public Opinion Research Center] 2009. "Wiara i religijność Polaków dwadzieścia lat po rozpoczęciu przemian ustrojowych", www.cbos.pl/spiskom.pol/2009/k_034_09.pdf.

Chen, S.-C. 2007. "Spiritual but not Religious, Transformational but not Salvational: A Sociological Examination of New Age Spiritualities in Taiwan". *Taiwan Journal of Religious Studies* 6(1): 57–112 (in Chinese).

Chen, S.-C. 2008. *Contemporary New Age Transformation in Taiwan: A Sociological Study of a New Religious Movement.* New York: Edwin Mellen Press.

Chidester, D. 1996. *Savage Systems: Colonialism and Comparative Religion in Southern Africa.* Charlottesville, VA: University of Virginia Press.

Chopra, D. 1993. *Creating Affluence: Wealth Consciousness in the Field of All Possibilities.* San Rafael, CA: New World Library.

Christensen, C. 2005. "Urfolk på det nyreligiøse markedet – en analyse av Alternativt Nettverk". Master's Thesis in the Study of Religion, University of Tromsø.

Christensen, C. 2007. "Urfolksspiritualitet på det nyreligiøse markedet: En analyse av tidsskriftet Visjon/Alternativt Nettverk". *Din: Tidsskrift for religion og kultur* 2007(1): 63–78.

Christensen, C. 2010. "Religion i Veiviseren: En analyse av samisk religiøs revitalisering". *Din: Tidsskrift for religion og kultur* 2010(1–2): 6–33.

Christensen, C. 2012. "Reclaiming the Past: On the History/Making Significance of the Sami Film The Kautokeino Rebellion". *Acta Borealia* 29(1): 56–76.

Christensen, C. & S. E. Kraft 2011. "Religion i Kautokeino-opprøret: En analyse av samisk urfolksspiritualitet". *Nytt Norsk Tidsskrift* 1–2: 18–27.

Christiano, J. 2007. "Assessing Modernities: From 'Pre-' to "Post-' to 'Ultra'". In *The Sage Handbook of the Sociology of Religion*, J. A. Beckford & N. J. Demerath III (eds), 39–56. London: Sage.

Chryssides, G. 2007. "Defining the New Age". In *Handbook of New Age*, D. Kemp & J. Lewis (eds), 5–24. Leiden: Brill.

Clarke, J. F. 1888. *Ten Great Religions: An Essay in Comparative Theology*. Boston, MA: James R. Osgood & Company.

Coats, C. 2011. "Spiritual Tourism – Promise and Problems: The Case of Sedona Arizona". In *Media, Spiritualties and Social Change*, E. M. Hoover & M. Emerich (eds), 117–26. New York: Continuum.

Cogswell, D. 1996. "Niche for the New Age". *Travel Agent* (21 October).

Collins, R. 2005. *Interaction Ritual Chains*. Princeton, NJ: Princeton University Press.

Comaroff, J. L. 2010. "Reflections on the Rise of Legal Theology: Law and Religion in the Twenty-First Century". In *Contemporary Religiosities: Emergent Socialities and the Post-Nation-State*, B. Kapferer, K. Telle & A. Eriksen (eds), 193–216. New York: Berghahn Books.

Connell, J. & C. Gibson 2004. "World Music: Deterritorialising Place and Identity". *Progress in Human Geography* 28(3): 342–61.

Corrywright, D. 2003. *Theoretical and Empirical Investigations into New Age Spiritualities*. Bern: Peter Lang.

Cousins, E. 1996. "Preface to the Series". In *Spirituality and the Secular Quest*, P. H. van Ness (ed.), xi–xii. New York: Crossroad.

Cox, H. 2001. *Fire From Heaven: The Rise of Pentecostal Spirituality and the Reshaping of Religion in the 21st Century*. Cambridge, MA: Da Capo Press.

Cox, J. 2007. *From Primitive to Indigenous: The Academic Study of Indigenous Religions*. London: Ashgate.

Crocker, D. 1977. "My Brother the Parrot". In *The Social Use of Metaphor: Essays on the Anthropology of Rhetoric*, J. D. Sapir & J. C. Crocker (eds), 164–92. Philadelphia, PA: University of Pennsylvania Press.

Crockett, A. & D. Voas 2006. "Generations of Decline: Religious Change in 20th-Century Britain". *Journal for the Scientific Study of Religion* 45(4): 567–84.

Csordas, T. 2004. "Asymptote of the Ineffable: Embodiment, Alterity, and the Theory of Religion". *Current Anthropology* 45(2): 163–85.

Czachowski, H. 2003. *Cuda, wizjonerzy i pielgrzymi: studium religijności mirakularnej końca XX wieku w Polsce*. Warsaw: Oficyna Naukowa.

Davie, G. 1994. *Religion in Britain since 1945: Believing without Belonging*. Oxford: Blackwell.

Davie, G. 2007. "Vicarious Religion: A Methodological Challenge". In *Everyday Religion: Observing Modern Religious Lives*, N. T. Ammerman (ed.), 21–35. Oxford: Oxford University Press.

Dawkins, R. 2006. *Unweaving the Rainbow: Science, Delusion and the Appetite for Wonder*. London: Penguin.

Day, A. 2012. "Nominal Christian Adherence: Ethnic, Natal, Aspirational". *Implicit Religion* 15(4): 439–56.

de Assis, C. F. 2000. *Ñeë Ryru Avañeë – Palavras dos Guarani*. Sao Paulo: Projeto Karumbe.

de Castro, E. V. 1992. *From the Enemy's Point of View: Humanity and Divinity in an Amazonian Society*. Chicago, IL: University of Chicago Press.

275

de Hart, J. 2011. *Zwevende gelovigen: Oude religie en nieuwe spiritualiteit*. Amsterdam: Bakker.

Deleuze, G. 2005. *Francis Bacon: The Logic of Sensation*. Minnesota, MN: University of Minnesota Press.

Douglas, M. 1966. *Purity and Danger: An Analysis of the Concepts of Pollution and Taboo*. London: Routledge & Kegan Paul.

Dowling, L. H. 1907. *The Aquarian Gospel of Jesus the Christ*. Los Angeles, CA: L. N. Fowler.

Drivenes, E. A. & E. Niemi 2000. "Også av denne verden? Etnisitet, geografi og læstadianisme mellom tradisjon og modernitet". In *Vekkelse og vitenskap*, Ø. Norderval & S. Nesset (eds), 156–86. Tromsø: Ravnetrykk 23.

Drury, N. 2004. *The New Age: The History of a Movement*. London: Thames & Hudson.

DuBois, T. 2000. "Folklore, Boundaries and Audience in The Pathfinder". In *Sami Folkloristics*, J. Pentikäinen (ed.), 255–74. Turku: NIF.

Dunning, D., J. A. Meyerowitz & A. D. Holzberg 1989. "Ambiguity and Self-evaluation: The Role of Idiosyncratic Trait Definitions in Self-serving Assessments of Ability". *Journal of Personality and Social Psychology* 57: 1082–90.

Durkheim, É. [1899] 1975. "Concerning the Definition of Religious Phenomena". In *Durkheim on Religion: A Selection of Readings with Bibliographies*, W. S. F. Pickering (ed.), 74–99. London: Routledge.

Durkheim, É. [1912] 1971. *The Elementary Forms of the Religious Life*, J. W. Swain (trans.). London: George Allen & Unwin.

Durkheim, É. [1912] 2008. *The Elementary Forms of the Religious Life*, C. Cosman (trans.), abridged with introduction and notes by M. S. Cladis. Oxford: Oxford University Press.

Durkheim, É. & M. Mauss [1903] 1963. *Primitive Classification*. Chicago, IL: University of Chicago Press.

Endsjø, D. Ø. & L. I. Lied 2011. *Det folk vil ha: Religion og populærkultur*. Oslo: Universitetsforlaget.

Engedal, L. G. & A. T. Sveinall (eds) 2000. *Troen er løs: Bidrag til belysning av forholdet mellom folkereligiøsitet, nyreligiøsitet og kristen tro*. Trondheim: Tapir Akademisk Forlag.

Engelsviken, T., R. Olsen & N. R. Thelle (eds) 2011. *Nye guder for hvermann? Femti år med alternativ spiritualitet*. Trondheim: Tapir Akademisk Forlag.

Eriksen, A. 1999. *Historie, Minne og Myte*. Oslo: Pax Forlag AS.

Eriksson, J. 1988. *Samisk shamanism*. Stockholm: Vattumannen.

Eurobarometer 2005. *Special Eurobarometer 225 Social Values, Science and Technology*. European Commission. www.ec.europa.eu/public_opinion/archives/ebs/ebs_225_report_en.pdf.

Evans-Pritchard, E. E. 1937. *Witchcraft, Oracles and Magic among the Azande*. Oxford: Clarendon Press.

Evans-Pritchard, E. E. 1965. *Theories of Primitive Religion*. Oxford: Clarendon Press.

Fabian, S. M. 1992. *Space-Time of the Bororo*. Gainesville, FL: University Press of Florida.

Fazel, S. 1994. "Is the the Bahá'í Faith a World Religion?" *Journal of Bahá'í Studies* 6(1): 1–16.

Ferguson, N. 2008. *The Ascent of Money: A Financial History of the World*. London: Penguin.

Fitzgerald, T. 1990. "Hinduism and the World Rreligion Fallacy". *Religion* 20(1): 101–18.

Fitzgerald, T. 2000. *The Ideology of Religious Studies*. Oxford: Oxford University Press.

Fitzgerald, T. 2007. *Discourse on Civility and Barbarity: A Critical History of Religions and Related Categories*. Oxford: Oxford University Press.

Flere, S. & A. Kirbiš 2009. "New Age, Religiosity, and Traditionalism: A Cross-Cultural Comparison". *Journal for the Scientific Study of Religions* 48(1): 161–9.

Fonneland, T. 2007. "Med fokus på det nære og lokale. Tromsø – ein samisk urfolksby?" *Din: Tidsskrift for religion og kultur* 2007(1): 79–88.

Fonneland, T. 2010. *Samisk nysjamanisme: i dialog med (for)tid og stad*. Doctoral thesis, University of Bergen.

Fonneland, T. 2012a. "Spiritual Entrepreneurship in a Northern Landscape: Tourism, Spirituality and Economics". *Temenos: Nordic Journal of Comparative Religion* 48(2): 155–78.

Fonneland, T. 2012b. "'De syv kaffekok': spirituelt entreprenørskap i et samisk landskap". *Tidsskrift for kulturforskning* 11(2): 27–44.

Fonneland, T. Forthcoming. "Isogaisa: Samisk sjamanisme i festivaldrakt". *Aura*.

French, S. 2011. "Partial Structures and the Logic of Azande". *Principia* 15(1): 77–105.

Friedman, J. 1999. "Indigenous Struggle and the Discreet Charm of the Bourgeoisie". *Journal of World-Systems Research* 2: 391–411.

Frisk, L. 1993. *Nya religiösa rörelser i Sverige: Relation till samhället/världen, anslutning och engagemang*. Åbo: Åbo Akademi.

Frisk, L. 1997. "Vad är New Age? Centrala begrepp och historiska rötter". *Svensk religionshistorisk årsskrift* 6: 87–97.

Frisk, L. 2005. "Is 'New Age' a Construction?" Paper presented at the 2005 CESNUR conference in Palermo, Sicily. www.cesnur.org/2005/pa_frisk.htm (accessed August 2013).

Frisk, L. 2007. "Quantitative Studies of New Age: A Summary and Discussion". In *Handbook of New Age*, D. Kemp & J. Lewis (eds), 103–21. Leiden: Brill.

Frisk, L. & P. Åkerbäck 2013. *Den mediterande dalahästen: Religion på nya arenor i samtidens Sverige*. Stockholm: Dialogos.

Fuller, R. C. 2001. *Spiritual but not Religious: Understanding Unchurched America*. New York: Oxford University Press.

Furseth, I. 2006. *From Quest for Truth to Being Oneself: Religious Changes in Life Stories*. Frankfurt am Main: Peter Lang.

Gadamer, H.-G. [1975] 1989. *Truth and Method*, 2nd rev. edn. New York: Crossroad.

Gallup 2008. "Belief in God Far Lower in Western US". Gallup poll, 28 July. www.gallup.com/poll/109108/belief-god-far-lower-western-us.aspx.

Gaski, H. 2004. "Indigenous Interdisciplinary Internationalism: The Modern Sami Experience with Emphasis on Literature". In *Circumpolar Ethnicity and Identity*, T. Irimoto & T. Yamada (eds), 371–87. Osaka: National Museum of Ethnology.

Gaup, A. 2005. *The Shamanic Zone*. Oslo: Three Bear Company.

Gawain, S. 1992. *Kreativ Visualisering*. Oslo: Soldag forlag (Originally published as *Creative Visualization*, Berkeley, CA: Whatever Publishing, 1978).

Geaves, R. 1998. "The Borders Between Religions: A Challenge to the World Religions Approach to Religious Education". *British Journal of Religious Education* 21(1): 20–31.

Geaves, R. 2005. "The Dangers of Essentialism: South Asian Communities in Britain and the 'World Religions' Approach to the Study of Religions". *Contemporary South Asia* 14(1): 75–90.

Geertz, A. 2004. "Can We Move Beyond Primitivism? On Recovering the Indigenes of Indigenous Religions in the Academic Study of Religion". In *Beyond Primitivism: Indigenous Religious Traditions and Modernity*, J. K. Olupona (ed.), 37–70. New York: Routledge.

Geertz, C. 1973. *The Interpretation of Cultures: Selected Essays*. New York: Basic Books.

Giddens, A. 1991. *Modernity and Self-Identity: Self and Society in the Late Modern Age*. London: Sage.

Gilhus, I. S. 2008. "*Orbis terrarum Romanorum est*: Globalization Processes in the Roman Empire". In *New Religions and Globalization*, A. W. Geertz & M. Warburg (eds), assisted by D. R. Christensen, 131–44. Aarhus: Aarhus University Press.

Gilhus, I. S. 2012a. "Angels in Norway: Religious Border-Crossers and Border-Markers". In *Vernacular Religion in Everyday Life: Expressions of Belief*, M. Bowman & Ü. Valk (eds), 230–45. Sheffield: Equinox.

Gilhus, I. S. 2012b. "Post-secular Religion and the Therapeutic Turn: Three Norwegian Examples". In *Post-secular Religious Practices*, Scripta Instituti Donneriani Aboensis 24, T. Ahlbäck & B. Dahla (eds), 62–75. Åbo: Donner Institute for Research in Religious and Cultural History.

Gilhus, I. & L. Mikaelsson 2000. "Multireligiøse aktører og kulturens refortrylling". *Sosiologi i dag* 30: 3–22.

Gilhus, I. S. & L. Mikaelsson 2001. *Nytt blikk på religion*. Oslo: Pax.

Gilhus, I. S. & L. Mikaelsson 2005. *Kulturens refortrylling: Nyreligiøsitet i moderne samfunn*, 2nd edn. Oslo: Universitetsforlaget.

Godwin, J. 1994. *The Theosophical Enlightenment*. Albany, NY: SUNY Press.

Goodman, P. 1988. *Towards A Christian Republic: Antimasonry and the Great Transition in New England, 1826–1836*. New York: Oxford University Press.

Goudsblom, J. 1985. "Levensbeschouwing en sociologie" [Ideology and Sociology]. *Amsterdams Sociologisch Tijdschrift* 12: 3–21.

Graham, S. 2001. "Parkinson's Patients Feel the Placebo Effect". *Scientific American* (10 August). www.scientificamerican.com/article.cfm?id=parkinsons-patients-feel.

Graham, S. 2004. "Scientists See How Placebo Effect Eases Pain". *Scientific American* (20): 453–72, www.scientificamerican.com/article.cfm?id=scientists-see-how-placeb.

Grant, D., K. O'Neil & L. Stephens 2004. "Spirituality in the Workplace: New Empirical Directions in the Study of the Sacred". *Sociology of Religion* 65: 265–83.

Grębecka, Z. 2006. *Słowo magiczne poddane technologii*. Kraków: Nomos.

Greer, J. M. 1998. *Inside a Magical Lodge: Group Ritual in the Western Tradition*. St Paul, MN: Llewellyn Publications.

Gregg, M. & G. Seigworth (eds) 2010. *The Affect Theory Reader*. Durham, NC: Duke University Press.

Gruber, H. 1910. "Masonry (Freemasonry)". *The Catholic Encyclopedia*, www.newadvent.org/cathen/09771a.htm (accessed 20 August 2012).

Hall, D. 2007. *New Age w Polsce: lokalny wymiar globalnego zjawiska*. Warsaw: Wydawnictwa Akademickie i Profesjonalne.

Hall, D. 2012. "Questioning Secularization? Church and Religion in Poland". In *The Social Significance of Religion in the Enlarged Europe*, D. Pollack, O. Müller & G. Pickel (eds), 121–42. Aldershot: Ashgate.

Hamilton, M. B. 2000. "An Analysis of the Festival for Mind-Body-Spirit, London". In *Beyond New Age: Exploring Alternative Spirituality*, S. Sutcliffe & M. Bowman (eds), 188–200. Edinburgh: Edinburgh University Press.

Hamilton, M. B. 2012. "The Concepts of Implicit and Non-Institutional Religion: Theoretical Implications". *Implicit Religion* 15(4): 523–33.

Hammer, O. 2001. *Claiming Knowledge: Strategies of Epistemology from Theosophy to the New Age*. Leiden: Brill.

Hammer, O. 2004a. "Contradictions of the New Age". In *The Encyclopedic Sourcebook of New Age Religions*, J. Lewis (ed.), 415–19. Buffalo, NY: Prometheus.

Hammer, O. 2004b. "Esotericism in New Religious Movements". In *The Handbook of New Religious Movements*, J. Lewis (ed.), 445–65. Oxford: Oxford University Press.

Hammer, O. 2006. "New Age". In *Brill Dictionary of Religion*, K. von Stuckrad (ed.), 1313–15. Leiden: Brill.

Hammer, O. 2010. "I Did It My Way? Individual Choice and Social Conformity in New Age Religion". In *Religions of Modernity: Relocating the Sacred to the Self and the Digital*, S. Aupers & D. Houtman (eds), 49–68. Leiden: Brill.

Hammer, O. & J. Sørensen Forthcoming. "Legitimacy/Legitimization". In *Vocabulary for the Study of Religion*, R. Segal & K. von Stuckrad (eds). Leiden: Brill.

Hanegraaff, W. J. 1996. *New Age Religion and Western Culture: Esotericism in the Mirror of Secular Thought*. Leiden: Brill.

Hanegraaff, W. 1999. "Defining Religion in Spite of History". In *The Pragmatics of Defining Religion: Contexts, Concepts and Contests*, J. G. Platvoet & A. L. Molendijk (eds), 337–78. Leiden: Brill.

Hanegraaff, W. J. 2001. "Prospects for the Globalization of New Age: Spiritual Imperialism versus Cultural Diversity". In *New Age Religion and Globalization*, M. Rothstein (ed.), 15–30. Aarhus: Aarhus University Press.

Hanegraaff, W. J. 2009. "New Age Religion". In *Religions in the Modern World*, L. Woodhead, H. Kawanami & C. Partridge (eds), 2nd edn. New York: Routledge.

Hanegraaff, W. 2012. *Esotericism and the Academy: Rejected Knowledge in Western Culture*. Cambridge: Cambridge University Press.

Harner, M. 1980. *The Way of the Shaman: A Guide to Power and Healing*. San Francisco, CA: Harper & Row.

Harre, R. (ed.) 1986. *The Social Construction of Emotions*. Oxford: Basil Blackwell.

Harris, S. 2005. *The End of Faith*. New York: W. W. Norton.

Harvey, G. (ed.) 2000. *Indigenous Religions: A Companion*. London: Cassell.

Hay, L. L. 1993. *Du kan helbrede ditt liv*. Oslo: Hilt & Hansteen (originally published in English as *You Can Heal Your Life*, Santa Monica, CA: Hay House, 1984).

Hayes, J. 1999. "Business Gurus Divine Spiritual Answers to Labor Issues". *Nation's Restaurant News* 33: 66.

Heath, J. & A. Potter 2004. *Nation of Rebels: Why Counterculture Became Consumer Culture*. London: HarperCollins.

Heelas, P. 1988. "Western Europe: Self-Religions". In *The Study of Religion, Traditional and New Religions*, P. Clarke & S. Sutherland (eds), 167–73. London: Routledge.

Heelas, P. 1992. "The Sacralization of the Self and New Age Capitalism". In *Social Change in Contemporary Britain*, N. Abercrombie & A. Warde (eds), 139–66. Cambridge: Polity Press.

Heelas, P. 1993. "The New Age in Cultural Context: The Premodern, the Modern and the Postmodern". *Religion* 23(2): 103–16.

Heelas, P. 1996. *The New Age Movement: The Celebration of the Self and the Sacralization of Modernity*. Oxford: Blackwell.

Heelas, P. 1999. "Prosperity and the New Age Movement". In *New Religious Movements: Challenge and Response*, B. Wilson & J. Cresswell (eds), 51–77. London: Routledge.

Heelas, P. 2006. "Challenging Secularization Theory: The Growth of 'New Age' Spiritualities of Life". *The Hedgehog Review: Critical Reflections on Contemporary Culture* 8(1–2): 46–58.

Heelas, P. 2008. *Spiritualities of Life: New Age Romanticism and Consumptive Capitalism*. Oxford: Blackwell.

Heelas, P. 2012a. "Theorizing the Sacred: The Role of the Implicit in Yearning 'Away'". *Implicit Religion* 15(4): 477–521.

Heelas, P. 2012b. "On Some Major Issues". In his (ed.) *Spirituality in the Modern World: Within Religious Traditions and Beyond*, vol. 1, 38–68. London: Routledge.

Heelas, P. 2012c. "On Some Significant Themes". In his (ed.) *Spirituality in the Modern World: Within Religious Tradition and Beyond*, vol. 1, 69–92. London: Routledge.

Heelas, P. Forthcoming a. "The Sacred, the Secular, and the Possibility of a 'Secular Age'". In *Contemporary Sociology*, M. Holborn (ed.). Cambridge: Polity.

Heelas, P. Forthcoming b. "Transpersonal Pakistan". *International Journal of Transpersonal Sociology*.

Heelas, P. & D. Houtman 2009. "RAMP Findings and Making Sense of the 'God Within Each Person rather than Out There'". *Journal of Contemporary Religion* 24(1): 83–98.

Heelas, P. & L. Woodhead 2001. "Homeless Minds Today?" In *Peter Berger and the Study of Religion*, L. Woodhead (ed., with P. Heelas & D. Martin), 43–72. London: Routledge.

Heelas, P. & L. Woodhead (assisted by B. Seel, B. Szerszynski & K. Tusting) 2005. *The Spiritual Revolution: Why Religion is Giving Way to Spirituality*. Oxford: Blackwell.

Heller-Roazen, D. 2009. *The Inner Touch: Archaeology of a Sensation*. Cambridge, MA: MIT Press.

Hemka, A. & J. Olędzki 1990. "Wrażliwość mirakularna". *Polska Sztuka Ludowa* 1: 8–14.

Hense, E., P. Nissen & F. Jespers (eds) Forthcoming. *Present-day Spiritualities: Contrasts and Overlaps*. Leiden: Brill.

Hill, A. 2011. *Paranormal Media: Audiences, Spirits and Magic in Popular Culture*. London: Routledge.

Hjarvard, S. 2008a. "The Mediatization of Society: A Theory of the Media as Agents of Social and Cultural Change". *Nordicom Review* 29(2): 105–34.

Hjarvard, S. 2008b. "The Mediatization of Religion: A Theory of the Media as Agents of Religious Change". *Northern Lights* 6: 9–26.

Hjarvard, S. 2011. "The Mediatisation of Religion: Theorising Religion, Media and Social Change". *Culture and Religion* 12(2): 119–35.

Hochschild, A. R. 1979. "Emotion Work, Feeling Rules, and Social Structure". *American Journal of Sociology* 85(3): 551–75.

Hochschild, A. R. 1983. *The Managed Heart*. Berkeley, CA: University of California Press.

Hochschild, A. R. 1998. "The Sociology of Emotion as a Way of Seeing". In *Emotion in Social Life*, G. Bendelow & S. J. Williams (eds), 3–15. New York: Routledge.

Hochschild, A. R. 2008. "One Thing I Know: Feeling Around the World". *Contexts* 7(2): 80.

Høeg, I. M. 2010. "Religiøs tradering: Kristen tradisjon og tradisjonsoverføring". In *Religion i dagens Norge: Mellom sekularisering og sakralisering*, P. K. Botvar & U. Schmidt (eds), 181–95. Oslo: Universitetsforlaget.

Horie, N. 2003. "Construction of Religion as Culture". Paper presented at American Academy of Religion, Atlanta, GA, 22 November 2003, www.academia.edu/attachments/26612719/download_file.

Horie, N. 2007. "Nihon no Supirichuariti Gensetu no Jōkyō" [The Situation Regarding Discourses on Spirituality in Japan]. In *Supirichuariti no Shinrigaku* [Psychology of Spirituality], Nihon Toransupasonaru Shinrigaku. Seishin'igakukai [Japanese Association for Transpersonal Psychology/Psychiatry] (ed.). Osaka: Seseragi Shuppan [in Japanese].

Horie, N. 2012. "Spirituality and the Spiritual in Japan: Translation and Transformation". *Journal of Alternative Spiritualities and New Age Studies* 5(2009–11), www.open.ac.uk/Arts/jasanas (accessed November 2012).

Houtman, D. & S. Aupers 2007. "The Spiritual Turn and the Decline of Tradition: The Spread of Post-Christian Spirituality in 14 Western Countries, 1981–2000". *Journal for the Scientific Study of Religion* 46(3): 305–20.

Houtman, D. & S. Aupers 2010. "Religions of Modernity: Relocating the Sacred to the Self and the Digital". In *Religions of Modernity: Relocating the Sacred to the Self and the Digital*, S. Aupers & D. Houtman (eds), 1–29. Leiden: Brill.

Houtman, D., S. Aupers & P. Heelas 2009. "A Rejoinder to Flere and Kirbiš, Christian Religiosity and New Age Spirituality: A Cross-Cultural Comparison". *Journal for the Scientific Study of Religion* 48(1): 169–79.

Houtman, D., S. Aupers & W. de Koster 2011. *Paradoxes of Individualization: Social Control and Social Conflict in Contemporary Modernity*. Aldershot: Ashgate.

Hunt, S. J. 2003. *Alternative Religion: A Sociological Introduction*. Aldershot: Ashgate.

Huxley, A. 1954. *The Doors of Perception*. New York: Harper.

Huxley, J. 1941. *Religion Without Revelation*. London: Watts & Co.

Idowu, E. B. 1973. *African Traditional Religion: A Definition*. London: SCM.

Illouz, E. 2008. *Saving the Modern Soul: Therapy, Emotions and the Culture of Self-help*. Berkeley, CA: University of California Press.

Inglehart, R. & C. Welzel 2005. *Modernization, Cultural Change, and Democracy: The Human Development Sequence*. Cambridge: Cambridge University Press.

Inoue, H. 2003. *Haka to Kazoku no Henyō* [Transformation of Graves and Families]. Tokyo: Iwanami Shoten (in Japanese).

Introvigne, M. 2001. "After the New Age: Is There a Next Age?" In *New Age and Globalization*, M. Rothstein (ed.), 58–69. Aarhus: Aarhus University Press.

Isomae, J. 2003. *Kindai Nihon no Shūkyō Gensetsu to sono Keifu* [Modern Japanese Discourses on Religion and their Genealogy: Religion, State and Shinto]. Tokyo: Iwanami Shoten (in Japanese).

Ivakhiv, A. 2001. *Claiming Sacred Ground: Pilgrims and Politics at Glastonbury and Sedona*. Bloomington, IN: Indiana University Press.

Iwersen, J. 1999. "Phenomenology, Sociology and History of the New Age: Review Article". *Numen* 46(2): 211–18.

James, H. & C. Ericker 2008. "Critical Thinking and Conceptual Enquiry: A Report on the Pilot of the International Baccalaureate World Religions Course". *Discourse: Learning and Teaching in Philosophical and Religious Studies* 8(1): 91–7.

James, W. [1902] 1974. *The Varieties of Religious Experience*. London: Collins.

Janzen, G. 1998. *Becoming Divine: Towards a Feminist Philosophy of Religion*. Manchester: Manchester University Press.

Jespers, F. (ed.) 2009a. *Nieuwe religiositeit in Nederland: Gevalstudies en beschouwingen over alternatieve religieuze activiteiten*. Budel: Damon.

Jespers, F. 2009b. "Holistische spiritualiteit achter Astro TV en Chinese geneeswijzen". In his (ed.) *Nieuwe religiositeit*, 185–212. Budel: Damon.

Jespers, F. 2010. "The Paranormal Market in the Netherlands: New Age and Folk Religion". *Fieldwork in Religion* 5(1): 58–77.

Jespers, F. Forthcoming. "Explorations in the Border Region of Religious and Secular Spiritualities". In *Present-day Spiritualities*, E. Hense, P. Nissen & F. Jespers (eds). Leiden: Brill.

Johnson, K. P. 1998. *Edgar Cayce in Context*. Albany, NY: SUNY Press.

Jonker, J. 2012. "Exploring the 'Mystical Experiences' of a New Spirituality: A Case Study of Reiki". *Studies in Spirituality* 22: 293–310.

Josephson, J. A. 2012. *The Invention of Religion in Japan*. Chicago, IL: University of Chicago Press.

Joy, M. 2011. "Encountering Otherness". In her (ed.) *Continental Philosophy and Philosophy of Religion*, 221–46. Dortrecht: Springer.

Kalvig, A. 2009. "TV Norge og kanal fem – den nye tids bodbringarar". *Din: Tidsskrift for religion og kultur* 2009(4): 45–63.

Kalvig, A. 2012. "Seanser og minnet om de døde". *Kirke og Kultur* 117(2): 128–43.

Kemp, D. 2001. "Christaquarianism: A New Socio-Religious Movement of Postmodern Society?" *Implicit Religion* 4(1): 27–40.

Kemp, D. 2003. *The Christaquarians? A Sociology of Christians in the New Age*. London: Kempress Ltd.

Kemp D. 2004. *The New Age: A Guide*. Edinburgh: Edinburgh University Press.

Kemp, D. 2007. "Christians and New Age". In *Handbook of New Age*, D. Kemp & J. R. Lewis (eds), 453–72. Leiden: Brill.

Kemp, D. & J. R. Lewis (eds) 2007. *Handbook of New Age*. Leiden: Brill.

Kemper, T. 1978. *A Social Interactional Theory of Emotions*. New York: Wiley.

Klin-Oron, A. 2011. "Beyond the Self: Local and Personal Meanings of Channeling in Israel". Unpublished Dissertation, Hebrew University, Jerusalem.

Klippenstein, J. 2005. "Imagine No Religion: On Defining 'New Age'". *Studies in Religion* 34(3–4): 391–403.

Knoblauch, H. 2008. "Spirituality and Popular Religion in Europe". *Social Compass* 55(2): 140–53.

Knoblauch, H. 2009. *Populäre Religion: Auf dem Weg in eine spirituelle Gesellschaft*. Frankfurt: Campus.

Knoblauch, H. 2010. "Popular Spirituality". *Anthropological Journal of European Cultures* 19(1): 24–39.

Kraft, S. E. 2007. "Natur, spiritualitet og tradisjon: Om akademisk romantisering og feilslåtte primitivismeoppgjør". *Din: Tidsskrift for religion og kultur* 2007(1): 53–62.

Kraft, S. E. 2008. "Märthas engler: En analyse av den norske mediedebatten". *Nytt Norsk Tidsskrift* 25: 123–34.

Kraft, S. E. 2009a. "Sami Indigenous Spirituality: Religion and Nation Building in Norwegian Sápmi". *Temenos. Nordic Journal of Comparative Religion* 45(2): 179–206.

Kraft, S. E. 2009b. "Kristendom, sjamanisme og urfolksspiritualitet i norsk Sápmi". *Chaos* 51: 29–52.

Kraft, S. E. 2010a. "Kjenner du varmen? Om Kolloens snåsamann". *Nytt norsk tidsskrift* 3: 243–53.

Kraft, S. E. 2010b. "The Making of a Sacred Mountain: Meanings of 'Nature' and 'Sacredness' in Sápmi and Northern Norway". *Religion. An International Journal* 40(1): 53–61.

Kraft, S. E. 2011. *Hva er nyreligiøsitet*. Oslo: Universitetsforlaget.

Kripal, J. J. 2007. *Esalen: America and the Religion of No Religion*. Chicago, IL: University of Chicago Press.

Kripal, J. J. 2010. *Authors of the Impossible: The Paranormal and the Sacred*. Chicago, IL: University of Chicago Press.

Kristiansen, R. 2005. *Samisk religion og læstadianisme*. Oslo: Fagbokforlaget.

Kronjee, G. & M. Lampert 2006. "Leefstijlen en zingeving". In *Geloven in het publieke domein*, W. van de Donk, A. P. Jonkers, G. J. Kronjee & R. J. J. M. Plum (eds), 176–80. Amsterdam: Amsterdam University Press.

Kruger, J. & D. Dunning 1999. "Unskilled and Unaware of It: How Difficulties in Recognizing One's Own Incompetence Lead to Inflated Self-Assessments". *Journal of Personality and Social Psychology* 77(6): 1121–34.

Kubiak, A. E. 2005. *Jednak New Age*. Warsaw: Jacek Santorski & Co.

Kuhling, C. 2011. "New Age Re-enchantment in Post-Celtic Tiger Ireland". In *Ireland's New Religious Movements*, O. Cosgrove, L. Cox, C. Kuhling & P. Mulholland (eds), 201–19. Newcastle-Upon-Tyne: Cambridge Scholars Publishing.

Kupari, H. 2011. "'Remembering God' Through Religious Habits: The Daily Religious Practices of Evacuee Karelian Orthodox Women". *Temenos* 47(2): 197–222.

Kurtz, E. 1991. *Not-God: A History of Alcoholics Anonymous*. Center City, MN: Hazelden.

Langley, N. 1968. *Edgar Cayce on Reincarnation*. New York: Hawthorne Books.

Lash, J. 1990. *The Seeker's Handbook: The Complete Guide to Spiritual Pathfinding*. New York: Harmony Books.

Latour, B. 1993. *We Have Never Been Modern*. Cambridge, MA: Harvard University Press.

Lau, K. J. 2000. *New Age Capitalism: Making Money East of Eden*. Philadelphia, PA: University of Pennsylvania Press.

Lemming, L. M. 2007. "Sociological Explorations: What is Religious Agency". *The Sociological Quarterly* 48: 73–92.

Lester, R. J. 2005. *Jesus in our Womb: Embodying Modernity in a Mexican Convent*. Berkeley, CA: University of California Press.

Levi-Strauss, C. [1969] 1983. *The Raw and the Cooked*. Chicago, IL: University of Chicago Press.

Lewis, J. & J. G. Melton (eds) 1992. *Perspectives on the New Age*. Albany, NY: SUNY Press.

Löfgren, O. & R. Willim 2005. "Introduction: The Mandrake Mode". In *Magic, Culture and the New Economy*, O. Löfgren & R. Willim (eds), 1–18. Oxford: Berg.

Lofland, J. & R. Stark 1965. "Becoming a World-Saver: A Theory of Conversion to a Deviant Perspective". *American Sociological Review* 30: 862–75.

Long, C. M. 2001. *Spiritual Merchants. Religion, Magic and Commerce*. Knoxville, TN: University of Tennessee Press.

Lord, C. G., L. Ross & M. R. Lepper 1979. "Biased Assimilation and Attitude Polarization: The Effects of Prior Theories on Subsequently Considered Evidence". *Journal of Personality and Social Psychology* 37: 2098–109.

Luckmann, T. 1967. *The Invisible Religion: The Problem of Religion in Modern Society*. New York: Macmillan.

Luckmann, T. 1990. "Shrinking Transcendence, Expanding Religion?" *Sociological Analysis* 50(2): 127–38.

Luckmann, T. 1996. "The Privatisation of Religion and Morality". In *Detraditionalisation: Critical Reflections on Authority and Identity*, P. Heelas, S. Lash & P. Morris (eds), 72–86. Oxford: Blackwell.

Luhrmann, T. M. 1989. *Persuasions of the Witch's Craft: Ritual Magic and Witchcraft in Contemporary England*. Cambridge, MA: Harvard University Press.

Luhrmann, T. M. 2012. *When God Talks Back: Understanding the American Evangelical Relationship with God*. New York: Knopf.

Lundby, K. 2010. "Medier som resssurs for religion". In *Religion i dagens Norge. Mellom sekularisering og sakralisering*, P. K. Botvar & U. Schmidt (eds), 111–31. Oslo: Universitetsforlaget.

Lund-Olsen, T. & P. Repstad (eds) 2003. *Forankring eller frikopling: Kulturperspektiver på religiøst liv i dag*. Kristiansand: Høyskoleforlaget – Norwegian Academic Press.

Lupton, D. 1998. *The Emotional Self*. London: Sage.

Lynch, G. 2012. *The Sacred in the Modern World: A Cultural Sociological Approach*. Oxford: Oxford University Press.

Lyon, D. 2000. *Jesus in Disneyland: Religion in Postmodern Times*. Oxford: Polity Press.

Lyon, M. L. & J. M. Barbalet 1994. "Society's Body: Emotion and the 'Somatization' of Social Theory". In *Embodiment and Experience*, T. Csordas (ed.), 48–66. Cambridge: Cambridge University Press.

MacCormac, S. 1999. "Ethnography in South America". In *The Cambridge History of the Native People of the Americas vol. III, part 1: South America*, F. Salamon & S. B. Schwartz (eds), 96–186. Cambridge: Cambridge University Press.

MacKian, S. 2012. *Everyday Spirituality*. London: Palgrave Macmillan.

MacLaine, S. 1984. *Out on a Limb*. New York: Bantham Books.

Macpherson, J. 2008. *Women and Reiki: Energetic/Holistic Healing in Practice*. London: Equinox.

MacWilliams, M. *et al.* 2005. "Religion/s between Covers: Dilemmas of the World Religions Textbook". *Religious Studies Review* 31(1–2): 1–36.

Madsen, O. J. 2010. *Den terapeutisk kultur*. Oslo: Universitetsforlaget.

Mahmood, S. 2005. *Politics of Piety: The Islamic Revival and the Feminist Subject*. Princeton, NJ: Princeton University Press.

Manchin, R. 2004. "Religion in Europe: Trust Not Filling the Pews", www.gallup.com/poll/13117/religion-europe-trust-filling-pews.aspx.

Markham, I. S. (ed.) 1996. *A World Religions Reader*. Malden, MA: Blackwell.

Märtha, L. & E. Samnøy 2009. *Møt din skytsengel: En innføring i å møte din unike kraft*. Oslo: Cappelen Damm.

Märtha, L. & E. Nordeng 2012. *Englenes hemmeligheter: Deres natur, språk og hvordan du åpner opp for dem*. Oslo: Cappelen Damm.

Martin, C. 2009. "On the Origin of the 'Private Sphere': A Discourse Analysis of Religion and Politics from Luther to Locke". *Temenos* 45(2): 143–78.

Martin, J. L. 2011. *The Explanation of Social Action*. New York: Oxford University Press.

Masuzawa, T. 2005. *The Invention of World Religions or, How European Universalism was Preserved in the Language of Pluralism*. Chicago, IL: University of Chicago Press.

Mathisen, S. R. 2010. "Indigenous Spirituality in the Touristic Borderzone". *Temenos: Nordic Journal of Comparative Religion* 46(1): 53–72.

Matsumura, K. 2007. "Religious Research". In *Encyclopedia of Shinto*, Kokugakuin University (ed.). http://eos.kokugakuin.ac.jp/modules/xwords/entry.php?entryID=1240.

Mauss, M. [1935] 1979. "Techniques of the Body". In his *Sociology and Psychology: Essays*, 95–123. London: Routledge & Kegan Paul.

Mayberg, H. S., J. A. Silva, S. K. Brannan, J. L. Tekell, R. K. Mahurin, S. McGinnis & P. A. Jerabek 2002. "The Functional Neuroanatomy of the Placebo Effect". *American Journal of Psychiatry* 159: 728–37.

Mazet, E. 1995. "Freemasonry and Esotericism". In *Modern Esoteric Spirituality*, A. Faivre & J. Needleman (eds), 248–76. New York: Crossroads.

McCleary, R. M. (ed.) 2011. *The Oxford Handbook of the Economics of Religion*. Oxford: Oxford University Press.

McCutcheon, R. 1997. *Manufacturing Religion: the Discourse on Sui Generis Religion and the Politics of Nostalgia*. New York: Oxford University Press.

McGuire, M. 2002. *Religion: The Social Context*. Belmont, CA: Wadsworth.

McGuire, M. 2008. *Lived Religion: Faith and Practice in Everyday Life*. Oxford: Oxford University Press.

McLoughlin, W. G. 1978. *Revivals, Awakenings, and Reform: An Essay on Religion and Social Change in America 1607–1977*. Chicago, IL: Chicago University Press.

Meester, M. 2008. *Nieuwe Spiritualiteit*. Kampen: Ten Have.

Mellor, P. & C. Shilling 1997. *Re-forming the Body: Religion, Community and Modernity*. London: Sage.

Melton, J. G. 1988. "A History of the New Age Movement". In *Not Necessarily the New Age*, R. Basil (ed.), 35–53. Buffalo, NY: Prometheus Books.

Melton, J. G. 1995. "Whither the New Age?" In *America's Alternative Religions*, T. Miller (ed.), 199–209. Albany, NY: SUNY Press.

Melton, J. G. 2007. "Beyond Millenialism: the New Age Transformed". In *Handbook of New Age*, D. Kemp & J. Lewis (eds), 77–97. Leiden: Brill.

Melton, J. G., J. Clark & A. A. Kelly 1991. *New Age Almanac*. New York: Visible Ink.

Meyer, B. & P. Geschiere (eds) 1999. *Globalization and Identity: Dialectics of Flow and Closure*. Oxford: Blackwell.

Mikaelsson, L. 2001. "Homo Accumulans and the Spiritualization of Money". In *New Age Religion and Globalization*, M. Rothstein (ed.), 94–112. Aarhus: Aarhus University Press.

Mikaelsson, L. 2004. "Den holistiske energikroppen". In *Kampen om kroppen. Kulturanalytiske blikk på kropp, helse, kjønn og seksualitet*, J. Børtnes, S. E. Kraft & L. Mikaelsson (eds), 365–96. Kristiansand: Høyskoleforlaget – Norwegian Academic Press.

Mikaelsson, L. 2008. "Regnbuens skjulte farer: trusselen fra New Age". In *Kjetterne og kirken. Fra antikken til i dag*, T. Hägg (ed.), 223–40. Oslo: Scandinavian Academic Press (published in German as *Kirche und Ketzer, Wege und Abwege des Christentums*, Cologne: Böhlau Verlag, 2010).

Mikaelsson, L. 2011. "Salg av spiritualitet". In *Nye guder for hvermann? Femti år med alternativ spiritualitet*, T. Engelsviken, R. Olsen & N. R. Thelle (eds), 71–86. Trondheim: Tapir Akademisk Forlag.

Minde, H. 2008. "Constructing 'Laestadianism': A Case for Sami Survival?" *Acta Borealia: A Nordic Journal of Circumpolar Societies* 15(1): 5–25.

Mitroff, I. I. & E. A. Denton 1999a. *A Spiritual Audit of Corporate America: A Hard Look at Spirituality, Religion, and Values in the Workplace*. San Francisco, CA: Jossey-Bass.

Mitroff, I. I. & E. A. Denton 1999b. "A Study of Spirituality in the Workplace". *Sloan Management Review* 40: 83–92.

Moltzan, A. 2001. *A Course in Light: A Spiritual Path for Enlightenment*, rev edn. Dallas, TX: AZ Reality Publishers.

Morgan, D. 2007. "Studying Religion and Popular Culture: Prospects, Presuppositions, Procedures". In *Between Sacred and Profane. Researching Religion and Popular Culture*, G. Lynch (ed.), 21–33. London: I. B. Tauris.

Morris, P. 2010. "Religious Studies in New Zealand: A Wrong Direction?" In *Religion and Retributive Logic: Essays in Honours of Professor Garry W. Trompf*, C. Cusack & C. Hartney (eds), 323–44. Leiden: Brill.

Morton, S. 2002. *Gayatri Chakravorty Spivak*. London: Routledge.

Mulholland, P. 2011. "Marian Apparitions, the New Age and the FÁS Prophet". In *Ireland's New Religious Movements*, O. L. Cosgrove, C. Cox, C. Kuhling & P. Mulholland (eds), 176–98. Newcastle-Upon-Tyne: Cambridge Scholars Publishing.

Muller, O. 2009. "Religiosity in Central and Eastern Europe". In *Church and Religion in Contemporary Europe*, G. Pickel & O. Muller (eds), 65–88. Wiesbaden: VS Verlag.

Muller, O. 2011. "Secularization, Individualization, or (Re)vitalization? The State and the Development of Churchliness and Religiosity in Post-Communist Central and Northern Europe". *Religion and Society in Central and Eastern Europe* 4(1): 21–37.

Mullins, M. R. 1992. "Japan's New Age and Neo-New Religions: Sociological Interpretations". In *Perspectives on the New Age*, J. R. Lewis & J. G. Melton (eds), 232–46. Albany, NY: SUNY Press.

Nadesan, M. H. 1999. "The Discourses of Corporate Spiritualism and Evangelical Capitalism". *Management Communication Quarterly* 13: 3–42.

Naisbitt, J. & P. Aburdene 1990. *Mega-Trends 2000*. London: Pan Books.

Neal, C. 1999. "A Conscious Change in the Workplace". *Journal for Quality and Participation* 22: 27–30.

Needleman, J. 1972. *The New Religions*. London: Allen Lane.

Nergård, J. I. 2006. *Den levende erfaring: en studie i samisk kunnskapstradisjon*. Oslo: Cappelen Akademisk forlag.

Nisbett, R. & L. Ross 1980. *Human Inference: Strategies and Shortcomings of Social Judgment*. Englewood Cliffs, NJ: Prentice-Hall.

Norman, A. 2011. *Spiritual Tourism: Travel and Religious Practice in Western Society*. New York: Continuum.

Nynäs, P., M. Lassander & T. Utriainen (eds) 2012. *Post-Secular Society*. New Brunswick, NJ: Transaction Publishers.

Obeyesekere, G. 2002. *Imagining Karma: Ethical Transformation in Amerindian, Buddhist, and Greek Rebirth*. Berkeley, CA: University of California Press.

O'Dell, T. 2005. *Spas: The Cultural Economy of Hospitality, Magic and the Senses*. Lund: Nordic Academic Press.

Okamoto, R. 2012. "Basho no Saihyōsyō: Shūkyō-Tourism-Ron kara Mita Power Spot" [Re-presentation of Sacred Place: The Powerspot Phenomena in Japanese Shrines]. *Tetsugaku Shisō Ronshū* [Studies in Philosophy] 37: 69–85 (in Japanese).

Olcott, H. 1891. "Constitution and Rules of the Theosophical Society". *The Theosophist* 12(4): 65–72, cited in wiki/Theosophical Society (accessed 18 August 2012).

Olson, C. 2008. "Trends and Competition within the World Religions Academic Marketplace". *Religious Studies Review* 34(4): 255–60.

Oppenheim, J. 1985. *The Other World: Spiritualism and Psychic Research in England, 1850–1914*. Cambridge: Cambridge University Press.

Orsi, R. 2005. *Between Heaven and Earth: The Religious Worlds People Make and the Scholars who Study them*. Princeton, NJ: Princeton University Press.

Owen, S. 2008. *The Appropriation of Native American Spirituality*. New York: Continuum.

Owen, S. 2011. "The World Religions Paradigm: Time for a Change". *Journal of the Arts and Humanities in Higher Education* 10(3): 253–68.

Pace, E. 1912. "Spiritism". *The Catholic Encyclopedia*, vol. 14, www.newadvent.org/cathen/14221a.htm (accessed 20 August 2012).

Palmisano, S. 2010. "Spirituality and Catholicism: The Italian Experience". *Journal of Contemporary Religion* 25(2): 221–41.

Paloutzian, R. F. & C. L. Park 2005. *Handbook of the Psychology of Religion and Spirituality*. London: Guilford Press.

Pals, D. 2006. *Eight Theories of Religion*. New York: Oxford University Press.

Parrinder, E. G. 1954. *African Traditional Religion*. London: Hutchinson's University Library.

Partridge, C. 2004–5. *The Re-enchantment of the West*, vols 1 and 2. London: T. & T. Clark International.

Partridge, C. 2007. "Truth, Authority and Epistemological Individualism in New Age Thought". In *Handbook of New Age*, D. Kemp & J. R. Lewis (eds), 231–54. Leiden: Brill.

Pearson, J. 2002. *Belief Beyond Boundaries: Wicca, Celtic Spirituality and the New Age*. Aldershot: Ashgate (in association with Open University).

Peterson, P. n.d. "Dolphin Children: Angels of Earth", http://paulapeterson.com/Dolphin_Children.html (accessed July 2013).

Pierard, R. V. & R. D. Linder 1988. *Civil Religion and the American Presidency*. Grand Rapids, MI: Zondervan.

Pike, S. M. 2004. *New Age and Neopagan Religions in America*. New York: Columbia University.

Pine, J. B. & J. H. Gilmore 1999. *The Experience Economy*. Boston, MA: Harvard Business School Press.

Piwowarski, W. 1984. "Blaski i cienie polskiej religijności: z ks. prof. dr. Władysławem Piwowarskiem rozmawia Józef Wołkowski". In *Oblicza katolicyzmu w Polsce*, J. Wołkowski (ed.). Warsaw: Instytut Wydawniczy PAX.

Popp-Baier, U. 2010. "From Religion to Spirituality – Megatrend in Contemporary Society or Methodological Artefact? A Contribution to the Secularization Debate from Psychology of Religion?" *Journal of Religion in Europe* 3(1): 34–67.

Posacki, A., M. Cholewa, R. Pindel & A. Zwoliński 1997. *Reiki: deszcz niebiańskiej energii?* Kraków: Stowarzyszenie Ewangelizacji przez Media "List".

Possamai, A. 2003. "Alternative Spiritualities and the Cultural Logic of Late Capitalism". *Culture and Religion* 4: 31–45.

Possamai, A. 2005. *In Search of New Age Spiritualities*. Aldershot: Ashgate.

Possamai, A. 2007. "Producing and Consuming New Age Spirituality: The Cultic Milieu and the Network Paradigm". In *Handbook of New Age*, D. Kemp & J. R. Lewis (eds), 151–65. Leiden: Brill.

Prince, R. & D. Riches 2001. *The New Age in Glastonbury: The Construction of Religious Movements*. Oxford: Berghahn Books.

Prins, H. 2002. "Visual Media and the Primitivist Perplex: Colonial Fantasies, Indigenous Imagination, and Advocacy in North America". In *Media Worlds: Anthropology on New Terrain*, F. D. Ginsburg, L. Abulughod & B. Larkin (eds), 58–74. Ewing, NJ: University of California Press.

Prothero, S. 1996. *The White Buddhist: The Asian Odyssey of Henry Steel Olcott*. Bloomington, IN: Indiana University Press.

Pylak, B. 2003. *Poznawać w świetle wiary: z emerytowanym metropolitą ordynariuszem lubelskim rozmawiają Irena Burchacka, Stefan Budzyński*. Warsaw: Oficyna Wydawniczo-Poligraficzna "Adam".

Redden, G. 2002. "The New Agents: Personal Transfiguration and Radical Privatization in New Age Self-help?" *Journal of Consumer Culture* 2(1): 33–52.

Redden, G. 2005. "The New Age Market: Toward a Market Model". *Journal of Contemporary Religion* 20(2): 231–46.

Redden, G. 2011. "Religion, Cultural Studies and New Age Sacralization of Everyday Life". *European Journal of Cultural Studies* 14(6): 649–63.

Redfield, J. 1993. *The Celestine Prophecy: An Adventure*. New York: Warner Books.

Redfield, R. 1956. *Peasant Society and Culture: An Anthropological Approach to Civilization*. Chicago, IL: University of Chicago Press.

Ridgeon, L. 2003. *Major World Religions: From their Origins to the Present*. London: RoutledgeCurzon.

Riesebrodt, M. 2010. *The Promise of Salvation: A Theory of Religion*. Chicago, IL: University of Chicago Press.

Riis, O. & L. Woodhead 2010. *A Sociology of Religious Emotion*. Oxford: Oxford University Press.

Roberts, K. A. & D. Yamane 2012. *Religion in Sociological Perspective*, 5th edn. London: Sage.

Roberts, R. 1994. "Power and Empowerment: New Age Managers and the Dialectics of Modernity/Postmodernity?" *Religion Today* 9: 3–13.

Robertson, R. 1992. *Globalization: Social Theory and Global Culture*. London: Sage Publications.

Roman, S. 1986a. *Living with Joy: Keys to Personal Power and Spiritual Transformation*. Tiburon: H. J. Kramer.

Roman, S. 1986b. *Personal Power through Awareness*. Tiburon: H. J. Kramer.

Roman, S. 2001. *Living a Soul Life, Part II of the Transforming with Divine Will Tape Series*. Medford: LuminEssence Productions.

Roman, S. & D. Packer 1988. *Creating Money: Keys to Abundance*. Tiburon, CA: H. J. Kramer.

Rønnevig, G. 2009–11. "Norwegian New Age: Alternativt Nettverk and Holistisk Forbund". *Journal of Alternative Spiritualities and New Age Studies* 5, www.open.ac.uk/Arts/jasanas.

Roof, W. C. 1999. *Spiritual Marketplace: Baby Boomers and the Remaking of American Religion*. Princeton, NJ: Princeton University Press.

Rose, S. 1996. "Transforming the World: An Examination of the Roles Played by Spirituality and Healing in the New Age Movement". PhD thesis, Lancaster University.

Rose, S. 1998. "An Examination of the New Age Movement: Who is Involved and What Constitutes its Spirituality". *Journal of Contemporary Religion* 13(1): 5–22.

Rosenberg, M. 1990. "Reflexivity and Emotions". *Social Psychology Quarterly* 53(1): 3–12.

Rosenberg, M. 1991. "Self Process and Emotional Experiences". In *The Self-Society Dynamic: Cognition, Emotion and Action*, P. L. Callero & J. A. Howard (eds), 123–42. Cambridge: Cambridge University Press.

Ross, A. 1991. *Strange Weather: Culture, Science, and Technology in the Age of Limits*. London: Verso.

Rossbach, S. 1983. *Feng Shui*. London: Hutchinson.

Roszak, T. 1975. *Unfinished Animal*. New York: Harper & Row.

Rothstein, M. (ed.) 2001. *New Age Religion and Globalization*. Aarhus: Aarhus University Press.

Rothstein, M. 2010. "Det problematiske emic-sprog". Seminar in Solstrand, Norway.

Ruah-Midbar, M. & A. Klin-Oron 2010. "Jew Age: Jewish Praxis in Israeli New Age Discourse". *Journal of Alternative Spiritualities and New Age Studies* 5, www.asanas.org.uk/files/005Ruah-Midbar&Oron.pdf (accessed August 2013).

Rüpke, J. 2010. "Hellenistic and Roman Empires and Euro-Mediterranean Religion". *Journal of Religion in Europe* 3: 197–214.

Rüpke, J. 2012. "Lived Ancient Religion: Questioning 'Cults' and 'Polis Religion'". Presentation of a new research programme, University of Erfurt, www.uni-erfurt.de/fileadmin/public-docs/Max-Weber-Kolleg/6-pdfs/projekte/2012-Ruepke_Lived_anc_rel.pdf (accessed August 2013).

Russell, B. 1975. *The Autobiography of Bertrand Russell*. London: Unwin.

Salamon, K. L. G. 2001. "Going Global from the Inside Out". In *New Age Religion and Globalization*, M. Rothstein (ed.), 150–71. Aarhus: Aarhus University Press.

Saler, B. 2000. *Conceptualising Religion: Immanent Anthrolopogists, Transcendent Natives, and Unbounded Categories*. New York: Berghahn.

Saler, B. 2009. *Understanding Religion: Selected Essays*. Berlin: Walter de Gruyter.

Salomonsen, J. 2002. *Enchanted Feminism: The Reclaiming Witches of San Francisco*. London: Routledge.

Sanday, P. R. 1986. *Divine Hunger. Cannibalism as a Cultural System*. New York: Cambridge University Press.

Satin, M. 1978. *New Age Politics: Healing Self and Society*. West Vancouver, BC: Whitecap Books.

Satter, B. 1999. *Each Mind a Kingdom: American Women, Sexual Purity, and the New Thought Movement, 1875–1920*. Berkeley, CA: University of California Press.

Scheff, T. 1990. *Microsociology: Discourse, Emotion, and Social Structure*. Chicago, IL: University of Chicago Press.

Scott, F. D. 1988. *Sweden. The Nation's History*. Carbondale, IL: South Illinois University.

Seaford, R. 2004. *Money and the Early Greek Mind*. Cambridge: Cambridge University Press.

Sebald, H. 1984. "New-Age Romanticism: The Quest for an Alternative Lifestyle as a Force of Social Change". *Humboldt Journal of Social Relations* 11(2): 106–27.

Segal, R. A. 1999. *Theorizing about Myth*. Boston, MA: University of Massachusetts Press.

Selberg, T. 2008. ""Vår" kulturarv – politisk myte eller realitet?" *Kirke og Kultur* 113(1): 21–30.

Selberg, T. 2011. *Folkelig religiøsitet. Et kulturvitenskapelig perspektiv*. Oslo: Scandinavian Academic Press.

Sharpe, E. [1975] 1986. *Comparative Religion: A History*. London: Duckworth.

Shermer, M. 1997. "The Myth of the Beautiful People. Why The Grass is Always Greener in the Other Century". *Skeptic Magazine* 5(1): 72–9.

Shilling, C. & P. A. Mellor 2007. "Cultures of Embodied Experience: Technology, Religion and Body Pedagogics". *The Sociological Review* 55(3): 531–49.

Shils, E. 1967. "The Sanctity of Life". *Encounter* (January): 42–53.

Shimazono, S. 1999. "'New Age Movement' or 'New Spirituality Movements and Culture'?" *Social Compass* 46(2): 121–33.

Shimazono, S. 2004. *From Salvation to Spirituality: Popular Religious Movements in Modern Japan*. Melbourne: Pacific Press.

Shimazono, S. 2007. *Spirituality no kōryū: Shin-reisei bunka to sono shūhen* [The Rise of Spirituality: New Spirituality Culture and its Surroundings]. Tokyo: Iwanami Shoten (in Japanese).

Shimazono, S. 2012. "From Salvation to Spirituality: The Contemporary Transformation of Religions Viewed from East Asia". *Religious Studies in Japan* 1: 3–23.

Shimazono, S. & Y. Tsuruoka 2003. "*Shūkyō" Saikō* [Rethinking "Religion"]. Tokyo: Pelican-sha (in Japanese).

Simmel, G. 1997. *Essays on Religion*. New Haven, CT: Yale University Press.

Slone, D. J. 2004. *Theological Incorrectness: Why Religious People Believe What They Shouldn't*. New York: Oxford University Press.

Smart, N. 1992. *The World's Religions*. Cambridge: Cambridge University Press.

Smith, E. 2010. "And They Lived Happily Together? On the Relationship Between Confessionalism, Establishment and Secularism under the Constitution of Norway". In *Law and Religion in the 21st Century – Nordic Perspectives*, L. Christoffersen, K. Å. Modéer & S. Andersen (eds), 123–43. Copenhagen: Djøf Publishing.

Smith, J. Z. 1972. "I Am a Parrot (Red)". *History of Religions* 11(4): 391–413.

Smith, J. Z. 1982. *Imagining Religion*. Chicago, IL: University of Chicago Press.

Smith, J. Z. (ed.) 1995. *HarperCollins Dictionary of Religion*. London: HarperCollins.

Smith, J. Z. 1996. "A Matter of Class: Taxonomies of Religion". *Harvard Theological Review* 89(4): 387–403.

Smith, J. Z. 1998. "Religion, Religions, Religious". In *Critical Terms for Religious Studies*, M. Taylor (ed.), 269–84. Chicago, IL: University of Chicago Press.

Smith, J. Z. 2000. "Classification". In *Guide to the Study of Religion*, W. Braun & R. McCutcheon (eds), 35–44. London: Continuum.

Smith, J. Z. 2003. "Here, There, and Anywhere". In *Prayer, Magic, and the Stars in the Ancient and Late Antique World*, S. Noegel, J. Walker & B. Wheeler (eds), 21–36. Pennsylvania, PA: Pennsylvania State University Press.

Smith, J. Z. 2004. "A Matter of Class: Taxonomies of Religion". In his *Relating Religion*, 160–78. Chicago, IL: University of Chicago Press.

Smith, W. C. [1962] 1991. *The Meaning and End of Religion*. Minneapolis, MN: Fortress Press.

Spangler, D. 1996a. *Everyday Miracles: The Inner Art of Manifestation*. New York: Bantam Books.

Spangler, D. 1996b. *Pilgrim in Aquarius*. Forres: Findhorn Press.

Spangler D. & W. I. Thompson 1991. *Reimagination of the World: A Critique of the New Age, Science, and Popular Culture*. Santa Fe, NM: Bear & Company.

Spanos, N. 1996. *Multiple Identities and False Memories: A Sociocognitive Perspective*. Washington, DC: American Psychological Association.

Spivak, G. C. 1987. "Subaltern Studies: Deconstructing Historiography". In her *In Other Worlds: Essays in Cultural Politics*. New York: Routledge.

Stark, R. 1984. "The Rise of a New World Faith". *Review of Religious Research* 26(1): 18–27.

Stark, R. 1999. "Secularization RIP". *Sociology of Religion* 60: 249–73.

Stark, R. & W. S. Bainbridge 1985. *The Future of Religion: Secularization, Revival and Cult Formation*. Berkeley, CA: University of California Press.

Stark, R. & W. S. Bainbridge 1996. *A Theory of Religion*. New Brunswick, NJ: Rutgers University Press.

Stausberg, M. (ed.) 2009. *Contemporary Theories of Religion: A Critical Companion*. London: Routledge.

Stavrum, H. 2009. "Alternative helsearbeidere – alternative kulturelle entreprenører?" In *Kulturelt entreprenørskap*, P. Mangset & S. Røyseng (eds), 191–216. Bergen: Fagbokforlaget.

Stets, J. E. & J. H. Turner 2007. *Handbook of the Sociology of Emotions*. New York: Springer.

Stevenson, I. 1974. *Twenty Cases Suggestive of Reincarnation*, 2nd edn. Charlottesville, VA: University of Virginia Press.

Steyn, C. 1994. *Worldviews in Transition: An Investigation into the New Age Movement in South Africa*. Pretoria: University of South Africa Press.

Stone, C. J. 1996. *Fierce Dancing: Adventures in the Underground*. London: Faber & Faber.

Storm, R. 1991. *In Search of Heaven on Earth*. London: Bloomsbury.

Strenski, I. 2006. *Thinking About Religion: An Historical Introduction to Theories of Religion*. Oxford: Blackwell.

Stringer, M. D. 2008a. *Contemporary Western Ethnography and the Definition of Religion*. London: Continuum.

Stringer, M. D. 2008b. "Chatting with Gran at her Grave: Ethnography and the Definition of Religion". In *God at Ground Level*, P. Cruchley-Jones (ed.), 23–40. Frankfurt-am-Main: Peter Lang.

Stuckrad, K. von 2010. "Reflections on the Limits of Reflection: An Invitation to Discursive Study of Religion". *Method and Theory in the Study of Religion* 22(2–3): 156–69.

Sugrue, T. 1973. *There is a River: The Story of Edgar Cayce*, revised edn. Virginia Beach, VA: A. R. E. Press.

Sutcliffe, S. 2003a. *Children of the New Age: A History of Spiritual Practices*. London: Routledge.

Sutcliffe, S. 2003b. "Category Formation and the History of 'New Age'". *Culture and Religion* 4(1): 5–29.

Sutcliffe, S. 2004. "The Dynamics of Alternative Spirituality: Seekers, Networks, and 'New Age'". In *The Oxford Handbook of New Religious Movements*, J. R. Lewis (ed.), 466–90. New York: Oxford University Press.

Sutcliffe, S. 2006. "Rethinking 'New Age' as a Popular Religious *Habitus*: A Review Essay on The Spiritual Revolution". *Method and Theory in the Study of Religion* 18(3): 294–314.

Sutcliffe, S. 2007. "The Origins of "New Age" Religion Between the Two World Wars". In *Handbook of New Age*, D. Kemp & J. Lewis (eds), 51–75. Leiden: Brill.

Sutcliffe, S. 2011. "Review Article: Seekership as Social Institution in Alternative Religion". *International Journal for the Study of New Religions* 2(2): 281–8.

Sutcliffe, S. & M. Bowman (eds) 2000. *Beyond New Age: Exploring Alternative Spirituality*. Edinburgh: Edinburgh University Press.

Swets, J. A. & R. A. Bjork 1990. "Enhancing Human Performance: An Evaluation of 'New Age' Techniques Considered by the US Army". *Psychological Science* 1: 85–96.

Talarico, J. M. & D. C. Rubin 2003. "Confidence, Not Consistency, Characterizes Flashbulb Memories". *Psychological Science* 14(5): 455–61.

Tattersall, T. 1996. *Journey: An Adventure of Love and Healing.* Forres: Findhorn Press.

Taves, A. 1999. *Fits, Trances, and Visions: Experiencing Religion and Explaining Experience from Wesley to James.* Princeton, NJ: Princeton University Press.

Taves, A. 2009. *Religious Experience Reconsidered: A Building Block Approach to the Study of Religion and Other Special Things.* Princeton, NJ: Princeton University Press.

Taves, A. 2012. "Special Things as Building Blocks of Religions". In *The Cambridge Companion to Religious Studies*, R. A. Orsi (ed.), 58–83. Cambridge: Cambridge University Press.

Taylor, C. 2007. *A Secular Age.* Cambridge, MA: Belknap Press.

ter Haar, G. 2000. "World Religions and Community Religions: Where Does Africa Fit In?" Occasional paper, Centre of African Studies, University of Copenhagen.

Thamm, R. A. 2007. "The Classification of Emotions". In *Handbook of the Sociology of Emotions*, J. E. Stets & J. H. Turner (eds), 11–37. New York: Springer.

Thrower, J. 1999. *Religion: the Classical Theories.* Edinburgh: Edinburgh University Press.

Tiele, C. P. 1884. "Religions". *Encyclopædia Britannica*, 9th edn, W. Robertson Smith (ed.). Edinburgh: A. & C. Black.

Tipton, S. M. 1992. *Getting Saved from the Sixties.* Berkeley, CA: University of California Press.

Tokarska-Bakir, J. 2000. *Obraz osobliwy: hermeneutyczna lektura źródeł etnograficznych.* Kraków: Universitas.

Tomka, M. 2010. "Religiosity in Central and Eastern Europe. Facts and Interpretations". *Religion and Society in Central and Eastern Europe* 3(1): 1–15.

Traynor, J. B. 1999. "Total Life Planning: A New Frontier in Work-Life Benefits". *Employee Benefit Journal* 24: 29–32.

Trevelyan, G. 1977. *A Vision of the Aquarian Age.* London: Coventure.

Troeltsch, E. 1981. *The Social Teaching of the Christian Churches*, vols 1 and 2. Chicago, IL: University of Chicago Press.

Trompf, G. 2012. "History and the End of Time in New Religions". In *The Cambridge Companion to New Religions*, O. Hammer & M. Rothstein (eds), 63–79. Cambridge: Cambridge University Press.

Turner, J. 1999. "Spirituality in the Workplace." *CA Magazine* 132: 41–2.

Turner, J. H. & J. E. Stets 2005. *The Sociology of Emotions.* New York: Cambridge University Press.

Tweed, T. A. 2006. *Crossing and Dwelling: A Theory of Religion.* Cambridge, MA: Harvard University Press.

Urban, H. 2011. *The Church of Scientology: A History of a New Religion.* Princeton, NJ: Princeton University Press.

Urubshurow, V. K. 2008. *Introducing World Religions.* London: Routledge.

Utriainen, T. 1999–2000. "Bodies and Others Making Religion: Phenomenology of the Body and the Study of Religion". *Temenos* 35–6: 249–70.

Utriainen. T. 2011. "The Post-secular Condition and Enchanted Bodies". In *Religion and the Body*, T. Ahlbäck & B. Dahla (eds), 417–32. Åbo: Donner Institute for Research in Religious and Cultural History.

Utriainen, T. Forthcoming. "Healing Enchantment: How Does Angel Healing Work?" In *Religion, Healing, Psychiatry*, H. Basu & R. Littlewood (eds).

Utriainen, T., T. Hovi & M. Broo 2012. "Combining Choice and Destiny: Identity and Agency Within Post-secular Wellbeing Practices". In *Post-Secular Society*, P. Nynäs, M. Lassander & T. Utriainen (eds), 187–216. New Brunswick, NJ: Transaction Publishers.

Van den Bosch, L. P. 2002. *Friedrich Max Müller: A Life Devoted to Humanities.* Boston, MA: Brill.

Van Hoog, S. (ed.) 2001. *Klikgids 2002: Wegwijzer voor de natuurgerichte gezondheidszorg en bewustwording* [Click Directory 2002: Guide for Nature-Oriented Medicine and Consciousness-Raising]. Deventer: Buro Klik.

van Lommel, P. 2010. *Consciousness Beyond Life: The Science of the Near-Death Experience.* New York: HarperCollins (originally published in Dutch as *Eindeloos bewustzijn een wetenschappelijke visie op de bijna-dood ervaring,* Amsterdam: Ten Have, 2007).

Vásquez, M. A. 2011. *More Than Belief: A Materialist Theory of Religion.* Oxford: Oxford University Press.

Velde, P. van der (2009). "De dharma in de westerse praktijk: twee voorbeelden". In *Nieuwe religiositeit in Nederland,* F. Jespers (ed.), 97–128. Budel: Damon.

Vincett, G. & L. Woodhead 2009. "Spirituality". In *Religions in the Modern World,* 2nd edn, L. Woodhead, H. Kawanami & C. Partridge (eds), 330–37. London: Routledge.

Vincett, G., S. Sharma & K. Aune 2008. "Introduction: Women, Religion and Secularization: One Size Does not Fit All". In *Women and Religion in the West: Challenging Secularization,* K. Aune, S. Sharma & G. Vincett (eds), 1–19. Aldershot: Ashgate.

Virtue, D. 2002. *Messages From Your Angels Cards (Large Card Decks).* Carlsbad, CA: California Hay House.

Voas, D. 2009. "The Rise and Fall of Fuzzy Fidelity in Europe". *European Sociological Review* 25(2): 155–68.

Voas, D. & S. Doebler 2011. "Secularization in Europe: Religious Change Between and Within Birth Cohorts". *Religion and Society in Central and Eastern Europe* 4(1): 39– 62.

Vogel, V. J. 1986. *Indian Names in Michigan.* Ann Arbor, MI: University of Michigan Press.

von den Steinen, K. 1894. *Unter den Naturvolkern Zentral-Brasiliens.* Berlin: D. Reimer (Hoefer & Vohsen).

Wallerstein, I. 2003. *Historical Capitalism with Capitalist Civilization.* London: Verso.

Weber, M. 1920. *Gesammelte Aufsätze zur Religionssoziologie,* vol. 1. Tübingen: Mohr.

Weber, M. 1922. *The Sociology of Religion.* Boston, MA: Beacon.

Weber, M. 1970. "The Social Psychology of the World Religions". In *From Max Weber: Essays in Sociology,* H. H. Gerth & C. Wright Mills (eds and trans.), 267–301. London: Routledge.

Weber, M. 1995. *Den protestantiske etikk og kapitalismens ånd.* Oslo: Pax Forlag (translation of *Die Protestantische Ethik und der Geist des Kapitalismus,* Gesammelte Aufsätze zur Religionsoziologie, 1920).

Weerd, P. van de 2011. "Voor even niet anders: Een gevalstudie naar de spirituele praktijk binnen Stichting Mannenwerk". Master's thesis, Faculty of Religious Studies, Radboud University Nijmegen.

Weil, A. 1995. *Spontaneous Healing: How to Discover and Enhance Your Body's Natural Ability to Maintain and Heal Itself.* London: Little, Brown.

Weiss, B. L. 1988. *Many Lives, Many Masters.* New York: Simon & Schuster.

Welch, C. 2004. "Appropriating the Didjeridu and the Sweat Lodge: New Age Baddies and Indigenous Victims?" In *The Encyclopedic Source Book of the New Age,* J. Lewis (ed.), 349–75. New York: Prometheus Press.

Welch, C. 2007. "Complicating Spiritual Appropriation: North American Indian Agency in Western Alternative Spiritual Practice". *Journal of New Age and Alternative Spiritualities* 3: 97–117.

Welch, J. 1998. "Creed is Good". *People Management* 4(25): 28–33.

Whitehead, N. & M. Harbsmeier (eds) 2008. *Hans Staden's True History: An Account of Cannibal Captivity in Brazil.* London: Duke University Press.

Whitehouse, H. 2000. *Arguments and Icons: Divergent Modes of Religiosity.* Oxford: Oxford University Press.

Whitehouse, H. 2004a. *Modes of Religiosity: A Cognitive Theory of Religious Transmission.* Walnut Creek, CA: AltaMira.

Whitehouse, H. 2004b. "Toward a Comparative Anthropology of Religion". In H. Whitehouse

& J. Laidlaw (eds), *Ritual and Memory: Toward a Comparative Anthropology of Religion*. Walnut Creek, CA: AltaMira.

Whitehouse, H. & J. Laidlaw (eds) 2004. *Ritual and Memory: Toward a Comparative Anthropology of Religion*. Walnut Creek, CA: AltaMira.

Wilde, S. 1998. *The Money Bible: Including The Ten Laws of Abundance*. London: Rider.

Wilson, B. 1976. *Contemporary Transformations of Religion*. Oxford: Oxford University Press.

Winter, A. 1998. *Mesmerized: Powers of Mind in Victorian Britain*. Chicago, IL: University of Chicago Press.

Wiseman, R. 2009. *59 Seconds: Think a Little, Change a Lot*. New York: Random House.

Witham, L. 2010. *The Marketplace of the Gods: How Economics Explains Religion*. Oxford: Oxford University Press.

Wojcik, D. 1997. *The End of the World as We Know It: Faith, Fatalism, and Apocalypse in America*. New York: New York University Press.

Wood, M. 2007. *Possession, Power, and the New Age: Ambiguities of Authority in Neoliberal Societies*. Aldershot: Ashgate.

Wood, M. 2009. "The Nonformative Elements of Religious Life: Questioning the 'Sociology of Spirituality' Paradigm". *Social Compass* 56(2): 237–48.

Wood, M. 2010. "W(h)ither New Age Studies? The Uses of Ethnography in a Contested Field of Scholarship". *Religion and Society: Advances in Research* 1(1): 76–88.

Woodhead, L. 2010. "Real Religion and Fuzzy Spirituality? Taking Sides in the Sociology of Religion". In *Religions of Modernity: Relocating the Sacred to the Self and the Digital*, S. Aupers & D. Houtman (eds), 31–48. Leiden: Brill.

Wuthnow, R. 1994. *Sharing the Journey: Support Groups and America's New Quest for Community*. New York: Free Press.

Yamaori, T., K. Sasaki, N. Miyata & Y. Ikegami (eds) 1998. *Nihon Minzoku Shukyo Jiten* 日本民俗宗教辞典 [Dictionary of Japanese Folk Religion]. Tokyo: Tokyodo Shuppan (in Japanese).

Yomiuri Shinbun 2008. "Nenkan Renzoku Chōsa: Nihonjin (6) Shūkyōkan" [Annual Survey: Japanese (6) Views on Religion]". *Yomiuri Shinbun* (29 May).

York, M. 1995. *The Emerging Network: A Sociology of the New Age and Neo-Pagan Movements*. Lanham, MD: Rowman & Littlefield.

York, M. 2003. *Pagan Theology: Paganism as a World Religion*. New York: New York University Press.

York, M. 2009. *The A to Z of New Age Movements*. Lanham, MD: Scarecrow Press.

Young, K. 1992. "World Religions: A Category in the Making?" In *Religion in History: The Word, the Idea, the Reality/La Religion dans l'histoire: le mot, l'idée, la réalité*, M. Despland & G. Vallée (eds), 111–30. Waterloo, ON: Wilfred Laurier University Press.

Zaidman, N. 2003. "Commercialization of Religious Objects: A Comparison Between Traditional and New Age Religions". *Social Compass* 50: 345–60.

Zavou, M. "Gate of Angels", www.angels.gr/default.asp?V_LANG_ID=5 (accesed 23 April 2013).

Zieliński, A. 2004. *Na straży prawdziwej wiary: zjawiska cudowne w polskim katolicyzmie ludowym*. Kraków: Nomos.

Zowczak, M. 2008. "Między tradycją a komercją". *Znak* 634: 31–44.

Zuckerman, P. 2008. *Society without God*. New York: New York University Press.

Zuckerman, P. 2012. "Contrasting Irreligious Orientations: Atheism and Secularity in the USA and Scandinavia". *Approaching Religion* 2(1): 8–20.

INDEX